LEGALLY COMBATING ATROCITIES ON SCHEDULED CASTES & SCHEDULED TRIBES

By the Same Author

Law of Prevention of Atrocities on the Scheduled Castes and Scheduled Tribes

---

About the Author

Dr. T.R. Naval, born at Kankarkuie, Shaharanpur, U.P. on 23rd July, 1956. Completed his primary education in his village and middle education in village Nelhera Gujjar and graduated in Arts and Laws from Meerut University at Saharanpur. Migrated to Delhi to acquire higher education. Joined Master of Laws in Delhi University and awarded degree of Master of Laws in 1986. Took keen interest in laws concerning the Scheduled Castes and Scheduled Tribes. Joined service in Lok Sabha Secretariat as Legislative Committee Assistant and served Joint and Select Committees. Joined Delhi Judicial Service in 1985 and acted as Sub-Judge Ist Class, Metropolitan Magistrate and Additional Sessions Judge in Delhi and presently serving as Presiding Officer Labour Court in Delhi Higher Judicial Service. Wrote dissertation for Master of Laws on "Reservation of seats in Educational Institutions for socially and Educationally Backward Classes, Scheduled Castes and Scheduled Tribes—Indian Profile". Wrote a book on "*Law of Prevention of Atrocities on the Scheduled Castes and the Scheduled Tribes*". Awarded degree of Doctor of Philosophy by Delhi University in 2000 on approval of thesis on "A Study of the Impact of the Scheduled Castes and the Scheduled Tribes (Prevention of Atrocities) Act : With a special reference to the Problem of Atrocities on the Scheduled Castes and Judicial Response in Northern India". This book, in fact, is that thesis.

LEGALLY COMBATING ATROCITIES ON SCHEDULED CASTES AND SCHEDULED TRIBES

(This is a thesis on, "A Study of the Impact of the Scheduled Castes and the Scheduled Tribes (Prevention of Atrocities) Act : With a special reference to the problem of atrocities on the Scheduled Castes and Judicial response in northern India" and that has been approved by the University of Delhi for the award of the Ph.D. degree in Law)

By

DR. T. R. NAVAL

LL.M. & Ph.D. (Delhi)
Additional District & Sessions Judge
Delhi

CONCEPT PUBLISHING COMPANY, NEW DELHI-110059

ISBN : 81-7022-994-4

First Published 2004

Published and Printed by
Ashok Kumar Mittal
Concept Publishing Company
A/15-16, Commercial Block, Mohan Garden,
New Delhi-110059 (India)

Phones : 25351460, 25351794
Fax : 091-11-25357103
Email : publishing@conceptpub.com

DEDICATED
TO
Bharat Ratna Baba Saheb Bhim Rao Ambedkar
M.A., Ph.D. (Columbia), D.Sc. (London), LL.D, (Columbia),
D. Litt. (Osmania), Bar-at-law (london)
and
My Teachers
and
My father Late Shri Hari Singh Naval
(1918-2002)

K. G. Balakrishnan
Judge
Supreme Court of India

3, Janpath
New Delhi 110 001
Tel. : 23012393

Foreword

The problem of caste system and its pernicious effects on the society have been a subject matter of study by many social anthropologists. The caste system is an intrinsic feature of Indian culture. Human history may be viewed as a record of victory of different castes, tribes and races. Originally, the caste system and the social arrangement were devised to serve the purpose of maintaining the domination of the victorious and subordination of the vanquished. The victorious groups, to serve their common purpose created a social arrangement of pursuing division of labour with the system of command and obedience. Later, this system degenerated into an exploitative relationship of domination and subordination. Dominant sections wanted to protect their vested interests and this was achieved either by glorifying suitable ideology to legitimise their position in society or by brute force where the first weapon did not prove effective. It is not simply the poverty or lack of opportunity, but the caste system which touches upon the basic right to have self-respect in the society and the opportunity to live a decent life. The problem of caste and untouchability is so serious that it is not something that can be wished away. 'Apartheid' is nowhere near the social evil of casteism practised in India.

Modern law and ethics lay an emphasis on equal enjoyment of certain elementary rights, including the right of self-advancement. That is how the idea of social justice comes to the forefront. A rational model of social justice would always pay special regard to human dignity as such and not to the chosen few who have managed to amass riches mostly by unfair or foul means. Its purpose is not to dilute excellence, but to enrich it by developing potentialities of all human beings. Agnes Heller in her book *'Beyond Justice'* opined : "Persons are like atoms. They all pursue their interests. They are endowed with a greater or lesser degree of talent. Some of these talents are won in the 'natural lottery'; others could be considered as meritorious. The more talent one has, the greater the chances of high income, success and the like. This is unfair. The state must perform the task of redistribution, preferably with the consent of all." The learned author further observed that "socially disadvantaged persons do not argue for equality of income but equality of life chances."

More than fifty years have passed after the Constitution banned untouchability. Still we know that there are innumerable caste atrocities taking place in this country. The Scheduled Castes and Scheduled Tribes (Prevention of Atrocities) Act was passed with the object of instilling confidence and self-esteem in the downtrodden sections of the society. If there is self-esteem, one can say that he can stand on his feet. Although the Act did not achieve its object or purpose, still it had some benevolent effect on the society, ironically, though a sizeable percentage of our population still suffers the worst indignities and live without any human rights simply because of an accident of birth. The Act was intended at least to bring to book those who are responsible for committing worst form of social crimes.

It is alleged by some critics that this Act is being misused by some people to obtain personal gains. This criticism is based on the fact that the majority of the crimes registered under the provisions of the Act do not end in conviction of the accused. But this by itself is no reason to support the criticism that the Act is being misused by some people. The culprits do not get punished because of inherent defects in our criminal justice delivery system. Generally, the victims of atrocities are socially disadvantaged persons. They are easily won over by the dominant classes, who perpetrate such crimes. Therefore, in most of the cases, the accused is able to go scot-free either by winning over the witnesses or by settlement through coercive means. But that is not a flaw of the law, and these types of failure of justice could be corrected by innovative measures. For example, the cases registered under the Act could be investigated by special teams consisting of officers who have got some sensitivity and dedication to the social cause for which these laws are made. The victims can be given proper legal aid to pursue their grievances.

The learned author Dr. T.R. Naval, in this book, has dealt with all these aspects of the Act. The in-depth study done by the author brings out the various aspects regarding the practice of untouchability and the problems surrounding the social evil. The learned author has also made certain suggestions to overcome the inadequacies of the Act. The book is illuminating and deals with the subject comprehensively. The author deserves to be complemented for his efforts aimed at achieving the objectives set out in the relevant Act.

(K.G. Balakrishnan)
(8-9-2003)

PREFACE

This book infact is my thesis on *"A Study of the Impact of The Scheduled Castes and the Scheduled Tribes (Prevention of Atrocities) Act : With A Special Reference to the Problem of Atrocities on the Scheduled Castes and Judicial Response in Northern India"* and that has been approved by the University of Delhi, Delhi for the award of the Ph.D. degree in Law.

My objective, while writing this thesis, has been to explore the history of practice of untouchability and commission of atrocities on the Scheduled Castes; trace out and determine the causes and factors responsible for its origin and continuance of atrocities on the Scheduled Castes by analyzing the available records on the subject right from the ancient time till present day; to explicate the provisions of the Act; and to examine all the available material, in the form of decided cases, reports and journals; to assess the responses of the legal system functionaries towards the law enacted for prevention of atrocities to remove the factors responsible for commission of atrocities; besides, to search out all the aspects of atrocities by empirical research.

The entire work has been divided into two parts. First part is purely doctrinal in its nature. It covers two chapters. Second part is empirical. It consists of six chapters. Since this work is mainly empirical so, it also contains 77 Tables and 145 Graphs.

The Introduction deals with the origin of caste disabilities and the problem of atrocities on the Scheduled Castes. The history of the caste disabilities and atrocities, its development and changing forms from ancient period till present day. How caste system developed and gave rise to caste prejudice and caste hatred? How castes were formed? The attitude of the rulers towards this problems and how the governments after independence have tried to prevent the atrocities and remove the caste disabilities through various enactments?

The first chapter deals with the concept of atrocity. Its various aspects such as personal, physical, economic, educational and social, besides its grave aspect. What are the causes of the atrocities? Who are Scheduled Castes? What is the position of a SC who embraces either Buddhism or converts to Arya Samaj or Mahanubhav Panth or Sikhism or Christianity? What is the effect of his re-conversion to Hinduism? What is the position of a member of SC who solemnizes his marriage with non SC & ST person? What is the importance, meaning and effect of the phrase 'in relation to that state' on the Scheduled Castes as incorporated in Art. 341 of the Constitution of India?

The second chapter covers law as an instrument for combating atrocities. What are various models of crime control and legal measures to combat this evil? It also contains salient features of the Act, *i.e.*, creation of new type of offences, commission of offences only by specified person, protection against various kind of atrocities, creation of special reports, appointments of special public prosecutors, externment of potential offenders, punishment for neglect of duties and compensation to the victims or their legal heirs, *etc.*

The third chapter gives introduction to the empirical research. The issues that are focused are: The hypothesis chosen for test, the methodology adopted, the tools for data collection, the mode of collection and analysing the data and the presentation of the results in theoretical, graphical and tabular forms.

The fourth chapter deals with the analysis of data regarding awareness of incidents of atrocities on the SCs and its impact on the development of our country; causes of atrocities, *i.e.*, caste system, endogamy, caste hatred, untouchability, religion, cultural backwardness, illiteracy, poverty, economic dependence or backwardness, ignorance of law, self-assertion by the Scheduled Castes and lack of political will.

The fifth chapter deals with the analysis of data regarding awareness of provisions of the Act, its enforcement, Rules, applicability of provisions of the Act only on Non SC & ST, prohibitions of anticipatory bail and benefit of probation, special courts, special public prosecutors, SCs & STs protection cells, nodal and special officers, punishment to public servants for neglect of duties, filing of complaint to court and lodging of F.I.R. It also deals with position of illiterates amongst the SCs & STs on above aspects.

The sixth chapter deals with implementation realities of provisions of the Act on the aspects of attachment of properties of offenders, forfeiture of properties of convicts, services of senior advocate to the victim, taking of preventive action, grant of and cancellation of arm licence, attitudes of investigating officers, special public prosecutors, other concerned officials, working of SCs & STs protection cells, coordination amongst nodal officer, district magistrate and superintendent of police.

The seventh chapter deals with reasons for failure of the Act. These includes, non-coverage of all possible forms of atrocities; facing atrocities but not reporting to police; failure of police to lodge F.I.R. and supplying copy thereof to the victims; procedural drawbacks, lack of infrastructure with investigating agencies; special courts; non-availability of time with police officials; special courts; cumbersome procedure; low rate of convictions; and inadequacy of fora.

The eighth chapter deals with analysis of the data regarding suggestions for prevention of atrocities, widening the definition of atrocities to cover asking of questions relating to caste, employment of children, blockade of service career, economic exploitation, practice of untouchability and indignities, humiliations and harassment Besides, utility of refresher courses, publicity of the provisions of the Act, simplification of procedure, establishment of exclusive special courts and rehabilitation of victims. Legal aid for prevention of atrocities is also dealt with. It also contains analysis of data regarding creation of Centralised Special Enforcement Agency, removal of untouchability, inter-caste marriages, expunction of anti SCs & STs literature for prevention of atrocities.

The research ends with a set of conclusions and suggestions. To complete the thesis, list of abbreviations and table of cases have been given in the beginning whereas bibliography and annexures are appended in the end.

T. R. NAVAL

Since large number of persons, in one way or other, has contributed in completion of this work, so it is not feasible to quote their names. I express my profound appreciation to all those and all my teachers who have taught me to do selfless work for others, guided and encouraged me to complete this work. So, I dedicate this work to them.

I am also thankful to the library staff of Campus Law Centre, Indian Law Institute and Ministry of Law, Justice and Company Affairs, for their assistance.

Mr. Ramabadran, in feeding and analyzing of data as well as preparation of tables and graphs on computer and Mr. Bhuwan Chand Sati, in typing this thesis on computer and in preparation of graphs on computer have performed essential task, cheerfully and efficiently. They are entitled for thanks.

Although care has been taken to avoid mistakes in the work, yet mistakes are bound to take place in work like this. So, whatever errors remain are mine.

Delhi

25th December, 2001 **T. R. NAVAL**

ACKNOWLEDGMENTS

I wanted to do something for those who have contributed a lot for development of our nation but were never given their due share. Rather, they have been maltreated, humiliated, degraded, despite their giving all they have in the service of the society. Even after working throughout the day, not only by male adult but also females and children, they are hardly in a position to make two ends meet. They are forced to live in slums, where often they find shelter in *Jhuggis* and makeshifts of mud, grass, tattered cloths or *Tirpal.* They are going without education, medical care and other cultural attributes.

This book is a result of guidance and motivation of Prof. B.B. Pande. Prof. of Law, University of Delhi. He enlightened me and in series of successive meetings, he gave moulding shape to this work. I admit that I could not have produced this work but it could be possible only due to his fruitful guidance. I owe debt of gratitude to him.

I gratefully acknowledge a profound debt to High Court of Delhi for granting not only permission to peruse this research study but also granted me adequate earned leave to complete this work. I am beholden to it.

Shri Babu Lal, Additional District & Sessions Judge, Delhi, has cheerfully gone through the entire manuscript of this book. I am thankful to him. I am also thankful to Shri V.K. Sukhija, who has gone through the first proof of this work.

I must say that in completion of this work a lot of sacrifices of my wife Mrs. Sudesh Naval are hidden. I appreciate her patience as well as contribution for providing congenial working environment at home. I also appreciate co-operation of my daughter Miss Shalini, sons Aakash and Abhishek Naval.

CONTENTS

CHAPTER–4

CHAPTER – 5

LIST OF ABBREVIATIONS

In this book in citing cases, references to the States and the Union have been abbreviated as follows :

All.	Allahabad	Mad.	Madras
A.P.	Andhra Pradesh	M.P.	Madhya Pradesh
Bom.	Bombay	Mys.	Mysore
Cal.	Calcutta	Nag.	Nagpur
Cut.	Cuttack	Pat.	Patna
Guj.	Gujarat	P&H	Punjab & Haryana
Gau.	Guwahati	Punj.	Punjab
J&K	Jammu and Kashmir	Raj.	Rajasthan
Kar.	Karnataka	W.B.	West Bengal
Ker.	Kerala	S.Ct.	Supreme Court (U.S.A.)
Lah.	Lahore	U.S.	United States

The full title of Acts, Codes, *etc.*, have been cited in an abbreviated form as follows :

The Code	The Code of Criminal Procedure, 1973
I.P.C.	The Indian Penal Code, 1860
P.C.R. Act	The Protection of Civil Rights Act, 1955
The Act	The Scheduled Castes and the Scheduled Tribes (Prevention of Atrocities) Act, 1989 (No. 33 of 1989)
The Rules	The Scheduled Castes and the Scheduled Tribes (Prevention of Atrocities) Rules, 1995

U.O. Act	The Untouchability (Offences) Act, 1955

Name of the appellate courts have been abbreviated as follows :

H.C.	High Court
P.C.	Privy Council
S.C.	Supreme Court

Name of the journals have been abbreviated as follows :

A.D.	Apex Decisions
A.I.R.	All India Reporter
All. CRI.	Allahabad Criminal
All. CRI. R.	Allahabad Criminal Reports
All. L.J	Allahabad Law Journal
A.L.T. (CRI.)	Allahabad Law Times (Criminal)
Andhra L.J.	Andhra Law Journal
Ann. Serv. AM.L.	Annual Survey of American Law
All. W.R. (HC)	Allahabad Weekly Reports (High Court)
Bom. H.C.R.	Bombay High Court Reports
Bom. L.R.	Bombay Law Reports
Bom. L.R.	Bombay Law Review
C.P.L.R.	Central Provinces Law Report
Cut.L.T.	Cuttack Law Times
C.W.N.	Calcutta Weekly Notes
CRI.L.J.	Criminal Law Journal
Ele.L.R.	Election Law Review
Del.L. Rev.	Delhi Law Review
I.A.	Indian Appeal
I.A.C.	Indian Appeal Cases
I.C.	Indian Cases
I.C.J.	Indian Cases Journal

I.I.P.A.	Indian Institute of Public Administration
I.L.R.	Indian Law Reports
Jab.L.J.	Jabalpur Law Journal
J.T.	Judgment Today
Ker.L.J.	Kerala Law Journal
Ker.L.R.	Kerala Law Reports
Ker.L.T.	Kerala Law Times
Mad.L.J.	Madras Law Journal
Mad.L.W.	Madras Law Weekly
Mah.L.J.	Maharashtra Law Journal
M.L.J. (Cri.)	Madras Law Journal (Criminal)
M.P.C.	Madhya Pradesh Cases
M.P.L.J.	Madhya Pradesh Law Journal
M.P.W.N.	Madhya Pradesh Weekly Notes
P.L.R.	Punjab Law Reporter
Raj. L.W.	Rajasthan Law Weekly
RCSCST	Report of Commissioner for Scheduled Castes & Scheduled Tribes
S.C.A.	Supreme Court Appeals
S.C.C.	Supreme Court Cases
S.C.R.	Supreme Court Reports
S.C.J.	Supreme Court Judgments
S.C.W.R.	Supreme Court Weekly Reports
W.R.	Weekly Reports

Names of the Official Reports have been abbreviated as follows :

First Annual Report	Annual Report on The Scheduled Castes and the Scheduled Tribes (Prevention of Atrocities) Act, 1989 for the Year 1990 (First Report) Govt. of India, Ministry of Welfare, New Delhi.
Second Annual Report	Annual Report on the Scheduled Castes

	and the Scheduled Tribes (Prevention of Atrocities) Act, 1989 for the Year 1991 and 1992 (Second Report) Govt. of India, Ministry of Social Justice and Empowerment, New Delhi.
First Report of N.C.S.C. & S.T.	Report of The National Commission for Scheduled Castes and Scheduled Tribes, First Report, 12 March, 1992 to 31 March, 1993.
Fifth Report of C.F.S.C. & S.T.	Report of The Commission for Scheduled Castes and Scheduled Tribes, (April 1982—March 1983), Fifth Report.
Sixth Report of C.F.S.C. & S.T.	Report of The Commission for Scheduled Castes and Scheduled Tribes, (April 1983—March 1984), Sixth Report.
Seventh Report of C.F.S.C. & S.T.	Report of The Commission for Scheduled Castes and Scheduled Tribes, (April 1984—March 1985), Seventh Report.
Eighth Report of C.F.S.C. & S.T.	Report of The Commission for Scheduled Castes and Scheduled Tribes, (April 1985—March 1986), Eighth Report.
Twenty-Eighth Report of C.F.S.C. & ST.	Report of The Commission for Scheduled Castes and Scheduled Tribes, Twenty-Eighth Report (1986-87).
Twenty-Ninth Report of C.F.S.C. & S.T.	Report of The Commission for Scheduled Castes and Scheduled Tribes—Twenty Ninth Report (1987-89).
Thirtieth Report of C.F.S.C. & S.T.	Report of The Commission for Scheduled Castes and Scheduled Tribes, Thirtieth Report (1989-91).
Action Taken Memo	Action Taken Memorandum on The Recommendations Made in The First Report of the National Commission for Scheduled Castes & Scheduled Tribes, Ministry of Social Justice & Empowerment, Govt. of India.

Twenty-Third Report	Committee on The Welfare of Scheduled Castes and Scheduled Tribes (Tenth Lok Sabha), Twenty-Third Report, Lok Sabha Secretariat, New Delhi.
Forty-Sixth Report	Committee on The Welfare of Scheduled Castes and Scheduled Tribes (1994-95), (Tenth Lok Sabha) Forty-Sixth Report, Ministry of Welfare and Ministry of Home Affairs. Action Taken by Government on the recommendations of the Committee on the Welfare of Scheduled Castes and Scheduled Tribes contained in their Twenty-Third Report (Tenth Lok Sabha)— Atrocities on Scheduled Castes and Scheduled Tribes and pattern of Social Crimes towards them. April 1995.

Signals used in the book have been abbreviated as follows :

Signal	Significance
Accord	Law of different jurisdictions are introduced by the word "accord" where the law is exactly same.
But See	Cited authority strongly suggests a contrary proposition.
Cf.	Cited authority is different from that in text.
Et seq.	Et Sequences (& those that follow).
Ibid.	*Ibidem* (in the same place).
Id.	*Idem* (the same). "Id." is used whenever a citation is to the same authority as that in immediately preceding citation within the same footnote.
Infra citations,	Means below; "Infra" is referred to those cited fully in succeeding footnotes.
Loc. Cit.	*Loco citato* (in the place cited).
Op. Cit.	*Opere citato* (in the work cited), in preceding footnotes.

See	Cited authority constitutes basic source material supporting an opinion or conclusion.
See also	Cited authority develops a question analogous to discussion in the text.
Supra	Means above or on the upper side. Whenever an authority has been fully cited in preceding footnotes, the "supra" is used.

MISCELLANEOUS ABBREVIATIONS

In Re. In the matter of

Words used in the book have been abbreviated as follows :

Art.	Article
Arts.	Articles
D.A.	Dearness Allowance
D.L.V. & M.C.	District Level Vigilance & Monitoring Committee
D.M.	District Magistrate
D.Ms.	District Magistrates
D.U.L.S.	Different Units of Legal System
Ext.	Extraordinary
F.B.	Full Bench
F.C.I.	Food Corporation of India
Gaz.	Gazette
I.A.S.	Indian Administrative Service
L.M. & O.M.	Law Makers and Opinion Makers
M.A.	Maintenance Allowance
M.Ps.	Members of Parliament
N.O.C.	Notes of Cases
N.G.Os.	Non-Governmental Organizations
p	Page
P.C.S.	Provincial Civil Service

P.S.O.	Police Station Officer
Pt.	Part
Sec.	Section
S.C.	Scheduled Caste
SCs.	Scheduled Castes
S.L.V. & M.C.	State Level Vigilance & Monitoring Committee
S.R.O.	Statutory Rules and Orders
S.P.	Superintendent of Police
S.Ps.	Superintendents of Police
Ss.	Sections
S.T.	Scheduled Tribe
S.Ts.	Scheduled Tribes
T.A.	Transport Allowance
UND.	Undecided
U/S	Under Section

TABLE OF CASES

A

B

C

D

E

G

P

Q

R

S

T

V

W

INTRODUCTION

I. THE ORIGIN OF CASTE DISABILITIES AND THE PROBLEM OF ATROCITY ON THE SCHEDULED CASTES

All human beings are born free and equal in dignity and rights. They are endowed with reason and conscience and should act towards one another in spirit of brotherhood.[1] Everyone is entitled to all the rights and freedoms without distinction of any kind, such as race, colour, sex, language, religion, political or other opinion, national or social origin, property, birth or other status.[2] Everyone has right to life, liberty and security of person.[3] No one can be subjected to torture or to cruel, inhuman or degrading treatment or punishment.[4] No one shall be held in slavery or servitude.[5] Everyone has the right to own property alone as well as in association with others. No one shall be arbitrarily deprived of his property.[6] Everyone has the right of equal access to public service in his country.[7] Everyone who works has the right to just and favourable remuneration ensuring for himself and his family an existence worthy of human dignity, and supplemented, if necessary, by other means of social protection.[8] Everyone has the right to education.[9] Everyone has the right to participate in the cultural life of the community, to enjoy the arts and to share in scientific advancement and its benefits.[10]

As against these cherished declarations which are considered necessary for all-round development of a person, one-sixth population[11] of our country had been deprived of these essential facilities, requirements and opportunities, due to the caste based prejudices.[12] Denial thereof has resulted in caste disabilities.

After tracing various disabilities from various *Smirities* and *Dharma Sutras*,[13] which had been imposed on the untouchables and *Shudras*, Dr. Ambedkar had summarised these disabilities as under:

(1) That the *Shudra* had to take the last place in the social order.

(2) That the *Shudra* was impure and therefore no sacred act should be done within his sight and within his hearing.

(3) That the *Shudra* is not to be respected in the same way as the other classes.

(4) That the life of a *Shudra* is of no value and anybody may kill him without having to pay compensation and if at all, of small value as compared with that of the *Brahmina, Kshatriya* and *Vaishya.*

(5) That the *Shudra* must not acquire knowledge and it is a sin and a crime to give him education.

(6) That a *Shudra* must not acquire property. A *Brahmin* can take his property at his pleasure.

(7) That a *Shudra* cannot hold office under the State.

(8) That the duty and salvation of the *Shudra* lies in his serving the higher classes.

(9) That the higher classes must not inter-marry with the *Shudra.* They can however keep a *Shudra* woman as a concubine. But if the *Shudra* touches a woman of the higher class he will be liable to dire punishment.

(10) That the *Shudra* is born in servility and must be kept in servility forever.[14]

These disabilities have no parallel anywhere in the world.[15] These disabilities on the basis of caste prejudices had resulted into untouchability and atrocities on the Scheduled Castes. Scheduled Caste is a social categorization that represents the lowest rung of the caste ladder, as well as a legal categorization that relates to the constitutionally ordained mechanism for identifying certain caste groups for the purpose of various constitutional entitlements (hereinafter referred to as SC).

II. PREJUDICE ON THE BASIS OF RACE, NATIONALITY, RELIGION, GENDER, AGE AND CASTE : A BANE OF ALL HUMAN SOCIETIES

The prejudice[16] on the basis of race, nationality, religion, gender, age and caste is a bane of all human societies. If a person or class of persons are differentiated on the basis of race, nationality, religion, gender, age and caste, he, she or they will not be able to live like a human being. It will have an adverse impact on his educational, social, religious, cultural and political as well as physical advancement. The discrimination or prejudice on any one or more of the above grounds will lead to subjugation of one person by another which will result into curtailment of all his freedoms, liberties and basic necessities which will hamper all-round development of concerned human beings, besides, forcing him to lead a life of servitude without any honour and dignity.

III. CASTE PREJUDICE—A DOMINANT KIND OF PREJUDICE IN INDIA

The literal meaning of caste, according to the Chambers Dictionary[17] is, "a social class amongst Hindus in India; an exclusive or hereditary social class; a type of individual in some polymorphic social insects."

Definition of Caste

Dr. Ketkar defines caste as "a social group having two characteristics : (i) Membership is confined to those who are born of members and includes all persons so born; (ii) the members are forbidden by an inexorable social law to marry outside the group."[18]

Mr. Nesfield defines caste as "a class of the community which disowns any connection with any other class and can neither intermarry nor eat nor drink with any but persons of their own community".[19]

Dr. Ambedkar defines caste as "an artificial chopping of the population into fixed and definite units, each one prevented from fusing into another through the custom of endogamy. Thus the conclusion is inevitable that Endogamy is the only characteristic that is peculiar to caste".[20]

Prejudice may be based on various reasons. But in India prejudice is dominantly based on caste basis. Caste has destroyed the sense of public charity and it has made public opinion impossible. A Hindu's identity is his caste. His responsibility is only to his caste. His loyalty is restricted only to his caste. Virtue has become caste-ridden and morality has become caste-bound. There is no sympathy to the deserving. There is no appreciation of virtue but only when the man is a fellow caste-man.[21]

Caste prejudice is so dominant in India that can be judged from few instances. A SC youth was thrashed as he dared to chew betal in presence of so called upper caste-men.[22] The SC students are not allowed to take their meal on the table which is used by upper caste student in the mess of a hostel situated in the capital of India.[23] SCs are not allowed to draw water from the top of the well, where the fresh water is pumping out in a clear stream.[24] In single state of Bihar in 28 major massacres, which had been committed since the year 1977, 487 SCs were killed.[25] Instances of caste clashes are numerous and reflect the deep-seated prejudices still dwelling in the hearts of the upper castes against SCs. Whenever Dalits[26] have organised themselves, there has been a backlash from the feudal lords, resulting in mass killings of SCs, gang-rapes and burning of their *basties*, *i.e.*, residences.[27] One can deduce from these examples as to how acute caste prejudice is in India even in present days.

IV. GENESIS OF CASTE

It is believed that castes had their birth in ancient India, but one does not know exact origin of caste system. Some believe that caste were deliberately created to establish patterns of domination, while others feel that originally the caste system was created as a division of labour and all the perversities crept into it much later. The other assumption is that caste system happened as a result of the movement of the ancient Indian civilization.[28]

The history of genesis of caste can be traced since the age of *Rig Vedic* period. The factor which contributed most to the creation of social divisions was the conquest of the indigenous inhabitants by the *Aryans*. The *dasas* and the *dasyus*, who were conquered by the *Aryans*, were treated as slaves and *shudra*. Gradually the tribal society was divided into three groups—warriors, priests and the people. The fourth division called the *shudras* appeared towards the end of the *Rig Vedic* period.[29]

Purusha Sukta, a hymn in *Rigveda*, says that the *Brahmin* came from the mouth, the *Kshatriya* from the arms, the *Vaisya* from the thigh and *Shudra* from the feet of the Supreme *Purusha*.[30] Accordingly, the society was divided into four *varnas*—*Brahmins*, *Kshatriyas*, *Vaisyas* and *Shudras*. Each *varna* was assigned well-defined functions. The *Brahmins,* first in the hierarchy, were given the functions of priests and teachers, *Kshatriyas* ranked second in the *varna* hierarchy and were given the job of governance. The *Vaisyas* were engaged in agriculture, cattle-rearing and trade. The *Shudras* were meant for serving the three higher *varnas.*[31] The constitution of society prescribed by the *Purusha Sukta* is known as *Chaturvarnya.*

According to Dr. Ambedkar the *Shudras* were one of the *Aryan* communities of the Solar race. There was a time when the *Aryan* society recognized only three *varnas,* namely, *Brahmins, Kshatriyas* and *Vaishyas.* The *Shudra* did not form a separate *varna.* They ranked as part of the *Kshatriya varna* in the *Indo Aryan* Society.[32]

The caste system in its early stage was quite elastic. Gradually these four castes were multiplied into various castes and sub-castes as the social fabric expanded with the absorption of different religious faiths.

V. WIDE RANGE OF SOCIAL CONSEQUENCES OF CASTE PREJUDICE

Caste prejudice has resulted in wide range of social consequences. The first outcome of it is endogamy. The result is that caste prejudices created hindrance in inter-caste dining. The endogamy has made the caste system very rigid as no member of one caste could marry a member out of his caste. This and restrained of inter-caste dining has helped in perpetuation of caste system. Both these have given birth to various social and caste disabilities. For example, denial of twice-born ceremony *i.e., Upanayana* and ban on temple entry has resulted into religious backwardness of SCs. Denial of education to SCs led to illiteracy that made them ignorant and consequently they became educationally backward. Ex-communication and social boycott promoted the practice of untouchability which resulted into social backwardness. Caste hatred and scarcity of water made them ugly, unseeable and unapproachable that resulted into cultural backward-ness. Denial of property made them poor and economic dependent on others resulted into economic backwardness. Combination of religious, educational, social, cultural and economic backwardness made them vulnerable for commission of atrocities on them. How it could be culminated, is being analysed hereinbelow?

VI. FORMATION OF CASTES TO CASTE DISABILITY

In the later *Vedic* period, the division of society into four *varnas* became rigid. During this period, those three *varnas* deprived the *Shudra* from the sacred thread ceremony, called *Upanayana.* The *Dharmasutras* laid down the duties of each of the four *varnas*, and the civil and criminal law came to be based on the *varna* division. The higher the *varna* the purer it was, and the higher was the order of moral conduct expected by civil and criminal law. All kinds of disabilities were imposed on the *shudras.* They were deprived of religious and legal rights and were relegated to the lowest position in society. Crimes committed by them against the *Brahmins* and others were punished severely. On the other hand the crime committed against the *Shudras* were punished lightly. The members of higher *varnas* shunned the company of the *Shudras,* avoided the food touched by them and refused to enter into marriage relations with them.[33]

Dr. Ambedkar was of the view that in continuous feud between the *Shudra* kings and the *Brahmins,* the *Brahmins* were subjected to many tyrannies and indignities, as a result of which *Brahmins* refused to invest the *Shudras* with the sacred thread which sank them below the rank of *Vaishyas* and they became socially degraded.[34]

The writers of all *Dharmashastras* start with the presumption that all the *Varnas—Brahmina, Kshatriya, Vaishya* and *Shudra* are arranged in descending order and that the last is the downmost.[35] *Shudra* and women are marked out in the *Dharmashastras* for indignities of every conceivable kind. They are dealt with more harshly than others. Their disabilities are grave and onerous, and they are debarred from most of the ordinary grace of life. It was for the *nivavasita Shudras*—the *Chandals* and the *Shuapachas*—that the worst indignities were reserved.[36] Even as a sympathetic reader of the *Dharmashastras* as P.V. Kane was obliged to concede that a life of *Shudra* was not worth much.[37] Manu observed that the dwellings of the *Chandalas* and *Shuapachas* shall be outside the village...their dress are the garments of dead...their food...given to them...in broken dish.[38] He also affirmed that while the *tapas* (arduous duty) of the *Brahmin* is *Janana,* of the *Kshatriya* is affording protection to others, of the *Vaishya* is *varta,* i.e., agriculture, trade and cattle raising, that of the *Shudra* is *sevanam,* i.e., service.[39]

The *Manusmrity* affirms that *Shudras* are created by God for serving (*dasya*) the *Brahmins.*[40] *Parashar Smriti* contained that the only look of a *Chandala* pollutes a caste Hindu (*Brahmin*) which can only be purified after having a look (*Darshan*) of the Sun.[41] Gautam stresses that if any *Shudra* hears any *Veda Mantra,* the molten glass or lead should be poured in his ears, and if he recites any verse or words of the *Veda,* his tongue should be cut down and if he remembers the *Veda Mantras,* his body should be cut into pieces by an axe.[42]

Thus the authors of *Dharmashastras* made all efforts to describe the most suppressed status of *Shudra* and for centuries it continues to be so in reality. This position remained unchanged in the Ages of *Jainism* and *Buddhism,* except that they could be admitted to new religious order, but their general position continued to be low.[43] During Gupta age, their position slightly changed and they were allowed to listen to the epics and the *Puranas* and were permitted to worship new god Krishna.[44]

VII. PSYCHOLOGICAL SLAVERY

The SCs had also been victims of psychological slavery,[45] in formation of caste system and practice of untouchability. The propensity to imitate is a deep-seated one in the human mind. The conditions of imitation are (i) that the source of imitation must enjoy prestige in the group and (ii) that there must be "numerous and daily relations" among members of a group.[46] These conditions were present in India. The *Brahmins* were considered as semi-gods and their prestige was unquestionable. As the endogamy had originated from the *Brahmin* caste so it was whole-heartedly imitated by all the non-*Brahmin* sub-divisions or classes, who in their turn became endogamous castes. Any innovation that seriously antagonises the ethical, religious and social code of the caste was not likely to be tolerated by the caste and the recalcitrant members of a caste were in danger of being thrown out of the caste and left to their own fate without having the alternate of being admitted into or absorbed by other castes. A noble way of thinking will create a new caste for the old ones will not tolerate it. The penalty was ex-communication and the result was the new caste. This was the process of caste formation in India.[47]

The denial of *Upanayana* to the *Shudra* had introduced a new factor in the *Indo-Aryan* society. It made the *Shudra* look up to the higher classes as their superiors and enabled the three higher classes to look down upon the *Shudra* as their inferiors.[48] This had helped in perpetuation of practice of untouchability on the SCs.

Untouchability is an indirect form of slavery and in fact it is worst than slavery. Slavery was not obligatory but untouchability was obligatory. Once a slave always a slave was not the fate of the slave. In untouchability there is no escape. Once an untouchable always an untouchable. In slavery there was room for education, virtue, happiness, culture or wealth. In untouchability there is none. In slavery, the duty to maintain the slave in life and body falls upon the master. Untouchability carries no security as to livelihood. Thus untouchability has all the disadvantages of a free social order and slavery has all the advantages of unfree social order.[49]

VIII. ILLITERACY AND LACK OF SKILL DEVELOPMENT

Education plays an important role in the overall development of human beings. It infuses awakening and social consciousness; helps in removing quagmire of ignorance; kindles the lamps of new hopes and aspirations in the human mind; promotes social mobility; enhances their ability to think about their betterment; raises their level of consciousness against exploitation; and provides the chance of placement in Government and Semi-Government services. In nutshell, education is instrumental in reshaping the quality of human beings.

Unfortunately, due to inhibition of caste prejudice and practice of untouchability, the SCs were not allowed to get even glimpse of education in the pre-independence period.[50]

In the matter of the spread of knowledge two conditions are prerequisites. There must be formal education. There must be literacy. Without formal education, it is not possible to transmit all the resources and achievements of a complex society. Without formal education the accumulated thought and experience relating to a subject cannot be made accessible to the young and which they will never get if they were left to pick up their training in informal association with others. Without formal education, he will not get new perceptions. His horizon will not be widened and he will remain an ignorant slave of his routine work.[51] The conception of formal education in Hinduism was of a very limited character. Formal education was confined only to the study of the *Vedas.* The rules framed by Manu provided that the *Brahmins* alone have the right to teach the *Vedas.* But in case of *Shudra,* he has not only not to study the *Vedas* but also he should not be allowed to hear or read.[52] The successors of Manu made the disability of the *Shudra* in the matter of the study of the *Veda* into an offence involving dire penalties.[53]

The ancient world may be said to have been guilty for failing to take the responsibility for the education of the masses. But never has any society been guilty of closing to the generality of its people the study of the books of its religion. Never has society been guilty of prohibiting the mass of its people from acquiring knowledge. Never has society made any attempt to declare that any attempt made by the common man to acquire knowledge shall be punishable as a crime. Manu is the only divine law giver who has denied the common man the right to knowledge. This had resulted that reading and writing had become the right of the high class few and illiteracy had become the destiny of the low class many.[54]

In the year 1881-82, only 0.87% of the population of aboriginal and Hili Tribes and low caste Hindu had primary education. Percentage of population having secondary and collegiate education of low caste Hindu was zero.[55] In the year 1931, the rate of literacy of the SCs was as low as 1.9% as against 9.5% for all communities. The rate of literacy of SCs for the census year 1941 and 1951 is not available. According to census of the year 1961, it increased to 17.25% and in the census year of 1971 and 1981 it has risen to 22.90% and 31.12%.[56] The rate of literacy of SC women for the census years, 1931, 1961, 1971 and 1981 was 0.20, 3.29, 6.44 and 10.93% respectively.[57]

In view of such a poor incidence of education in the pre-independence period, it would be assumed that these communities have significantly acquired education during the post-independence period even though their pace of achievement has been slower than that of the general population.[58]

For the same reason, there was lack of skill development amongst the population of SCs. Each class managed to transmit to its members the ways of doing things it was traditionally engaged in doing. The artisan class or the craftsman who sprung out the *Shudra* class also taught the arts and crafts to their children. This education was domestic and practical. It had only increased the skill to do a particular thing. It did not lead to new perceptions. It did not widen horizon, with the result that the practical education taught him only an isolated and uniform way of acting so that in the changing environment the skill turned out to be gross ineptitude.[59]

IX. FROM CASTE DISABILITIES TO COMMISSION OF ATROCITIES

The social system by and large worked well from the age of the Buddha to Gupta times. But around the third century A.D. the old social formation was afflicted with a deep crisis. The *Puranas* of Kali age of the Third and Fourth century A.D., described the *Varna-Samkara, i.e.,* intermixture of *varnas* or social order, which implies that the *Vaisyas* and *Shudras* (peasants, artisans and labourers) either refused to perform producing functions assigned to them or else the *vaisya* peasants declined to pay taxes and the *Shudras* refused to make their labour available. They did not observe the *varna* boundaries relating to marriage and other type of social intercourse. The epics of that age and Manu emphasized the importance of *danda* or coercive measures. He laid down that the *Vaishyas* and *Shudras* should not be allowed to deviate from their duties. The king appears as upholder and restorer of the *varna* system.[60] Those who departed from their functions and were found guilty of offences were subjected to secular punishments as well as the performance of rituals and penances, all differing according to the *Varnas.*[61]

Thus the authors of *Dharmashastras* made all efforts to describe the most suppressed status of *Shudra* and for centuries it continued to be so in reality. This resulted into perpetuation of socio-economic injustices by the so-called higher castes on the lower castes who have been systematically denied equal chance in the opportunities and facilities of the larger society. This also resulted into social and economic inequalities among humans. Inevitably, it gave rise to gradation and put a premium on snobbery. The caste system tended to develop into group snobbery as upper castes started looking down upon lower castes. Thus there came into being social hierarchy and stratification resulting in perpetration of atrocities by the so-called higher castes on the lower castes.[62]

X. GENESIS OF CASTE SYSTEM

Initially and upto the age of *Rigveda* the division of society was based on occupation. Even members of a family used to profess different occupations.[63] Individuals and groups could rise in the *varna* scale, and they could also fall. Sometimes, it was found difficult to classify new castes in the *varna* scale. An instance of this is the *Kayastha* caste, which begins to be mentioned more prominently from the beginning of medieval India, *i.e.*, 800-1200 A.D. It seems that originally people from different castes, including *Brahmins* and *Shudras,* who worked in the royal establishments, were called *Kayastha.*[64] In course of time, they emerged as a distinct caste. Hinduism was expanding rapidly during this period. Not only it absorbed large numbers of Buddhists and Jains within its fold, but many indigenous tribes and foreigners were also Hinduized. These new section formed new castes and sub-castes, and often continued their own customs, rituals of marriage ceremonies and even their own tribal gods and goddesses. The society and religion became more and more complex. The *varna* system enjoyed the sanction of both State and the religion.[65] In course of time, despite initial protest by *Kshatriyas,*[66] *varnas* or social classes and *jaties* or caste came to be regarded hereditary in the eyes of both law and religion.[67]

XI. SUPPORT TO CASTE SYSTEM

In the ages of later *Vedic* period, *Jainism* and *Buddhism, i.e.,* later part of ancient India and beginning of medieval India, there has been constant support of religion and rulers to the caste system. In the 18th century, the people were already divided by religion, region, tribe, language and caste. Caste was the central feature of the social life amongst Hindus. Apart from the four *varnas,* Hindus were divided into numerous castes which differed in their nature from place to place. The caste system rigidly divided people and permanently fixed their place in the social scale. The higher caste, headed by the *Brahmins,* monopolised all social prestige and privileges. Caste rules were extremely rigid. Inter-caste marriages and inter-dining among members of different castes were forbidden. In some cases persons belonging to higher castes could not take food touched by person of lower caste. Castes often determined the choice of profession, though exceptions did occur. Caste regulations were strictly enforced by caste councils, *Panchayats* and caste chiefs, through fines, penances (*Prayaschita*) and expulsion from the caste.[68]

XII. MOVEMENTS AGAINST CASTE DISABILITIES AND ATROCITIES

Inheritance of caste birth and teachings of various Hindu epics including *Bhagavadgita* so strongly ingrained in the mind of various classes to carry out their respective functions, that they never thought deviating from their functions. Conversely, they worked hard in the firm belief that they would deserve a better life in the next world or birth. This belief had lessened the intensity and frequency of tensions and conflicts between haves and have nots. What was done by slaves and other producing section in Greece and Rome under the threat of Whip was done by the *Vaisyas* and *Shudras* out of conviction formed through *brahmanical* indoctrination.[69]

In the medieval Indian period, particularly during the *Bhakti* period, saints, like Kabir, Nanak, Ravidas, *etc*., had criticised the existing social order and emphasised the broadest human sentiments and preached a religion of love which would unite all castes and creeds. Despite their efforts, they could not be able to make an effective breach in the caste system. However, they softened its rigour and built a platform for unity.[70]

XIII. FROM SUPPORT TO NOTIONAL WITHDRAWAL

There has been support of law and religion to the caste system upto the period till Britishers established their rule in India. British introduced the modern concept of the rule of law. This meant that their administration was to be carried out, at least in theory, in obedience to laws, which clearly defined the rights, privileges and obligation of the subjects and not according to the caprice or personal discretion of the ruler.[71] The Indian legal system under the British was based on the concept of equality before law. This meant that in the eyes of law, all men were equal. The same law applied to all persons irrespective of their caste, religion or class, in contravention of the pre-British Judicial system where distinctions were made between the so-called high born and low-born. For the same crime, lighter punishment was awarded to a *Brahmin* than to a non-*Brahmin.* Similarly, in practice *zamindars* and nobles were not judged as harshly as commoner. In fact, very often they could not be brought to justice at all for their actions. Now the humble could also move the machinery of justice.[72] But in practice, there emerged another type of legal inequality. Justice became quite expensive, as court fees had to be paid, lawyers engaged and the expenses of witnesses met. Courts were often situated in distant towns. Law suits dragged on for years. The complicated laws were beyond the grasp of the illiterate and ignorant peasants. Invariably, the rich could turn and twist the laws and courts to operate in their own favour. The mere threat to take a poor person through the long process of justice from the lower court to the highest court of appeal and thus to face him with complete ruin often sufficed to bring him to heel.[73] Besides, practices of untouchability obtained indirect support from the law. As *shastric* and customary law was supplanted, the use of caste as a criterion in the application of general criminal, civil and commercial law was restricted, and eventually discarded. In the application of Hindu law to family and ceremonial matters, *varna* and caste distinctions remained relevant in some areas, but these legal categories did not spread to other fields. The abolition of slavery at the middle of the nineteenth century extended elementary rights to many untouchables. These lowest orders then enjoyed equality in the eyes of the law and had access to it, at least formally. In practice legal institutions often adapted themselves to prevailing patterns of disability. While the general features of the legal system were not articulated for a system of graded inequality, the overall British policy towards caste was a policy of non-interference.[74]

XIV. SUPPORT BY THE COURTS FOR IMPOSITION OF DISABILITIES

Caste groups did enjoy active support of the courts in upholding their claims for precedence and exclusiveness. Courts granted injunctions to restrain members of particular castes from entering temples – even those that were publicly supported and dedicated to the entire Hindu community.[75] Damages were awarded for purificatory ceremonies necessitated by the pollution caused by the presence of lower castes, such pollution was actionable as a trespass on the person of the higher caste worshippers.[76] It was a criminal offence for a member of an excluded caste knowingly to pollute a temple by his presence.[77] These rights to exclusiveness were vindicated by the courts not only where the interlopers were "untouchables", but also against such "touchables", as *Palshe Brahmins* and *Lingayats,* whose presence in the particular temple was polluting.[78]

In *Anandrav Bhikaji Phadke* Vs. *Shankar Daji Charya*[79], the Bombay Court upheld the right of *Chitpavan Brahmins* to exclude *Palshe Brahmins* from worshipping at a temple, on the ground that such an exclusive right is one which the courts must guard, as otherwise all high-caste Hindus would hold their sanctuaries and perform their worship, only so far as those of the lower castes chose to allow them.

In *Sankaralinga Nadan and others* Vs. *Raja Rajeswara Dora and others*[80] the Privy Council upheld the exclusion of *Shanars* from a temple, and granted damages for its purification under a careful scrutiny of their social standing. The Court concluded that the presence of *Shanars* was repugnant to the religious principles of the Hindu worship of *Shiva* as well as to the sentiments and customs of the caste Hindu worshippers.[81]

Untouchable *Mahars* who entered the enclosure of a village idol were convicted on the ground that "where custom.....ordains that an untouchable, whose very touch is in the opinion of devout Hindus causes pollution, should not enter the enclosure surrounding the shrine of any Hindu god, ..." such entry is a defilement in violation of Section 295 of the Penal Code.[82] In the year 1945, *Nair* users of a public temple were granted damages for pollution for the purificatory ceremonies necessitated by *Ezhavas* bathing in tanks.[83]

The attitude of the courts regarding secular public facilities such as schools, wells and roads was, however, different. The courts declared that no right could be maintained to exclude other castes or sects from the use of streets and roads.[84] The situation was more complicated in regard to the use of water sources. For a low-caste person to take water from a public well was held not to be the offence of corrupting or fouling a well under Section 277 of the Indian Penal Code. It was held that the "defiling" or "corrupting" in the statute referred to "some act which physically defiles or fouls the water".[85] The Lahore court held that other users had no right to prevent *Chamars* from drawing water from a public well.[86] However, other courts conceded that a right to exclude might be upheld if a custom of exclusive use by higher castes could be proved. However, such customs were difficult to prove.[87]

XV. INDIRECT SUPPORT BY THE COURTS FOR NOT REMOVING CASTE DISABILITIES

The courts were reluctant to interpret the law so as to provide remedies against imposition of caste disabilities by self-help of the members of higher castes. Where *Sonars,* excluded from social intercourse and from use of the village well by other Hindus, brought criminal charges against leading villagers, the court found that the villagers' conduct amounted to neither a nuisance nor an insult with intent to provoke breach of peace.[88] Where members of the *Nilgiri Mahratta* caste assembled and resolved that others were members of an inferior caste, it was held not to amount to criminal defamation.[89] Where *Reddis* asserted their superiority over *Balijas* and resolved to have no social intercourse with them and that village servants should not serve them, the *Balijas* brought charges of criminal defamation. The Madras High Court held that this conduct was not criminal defamation.[90] "The evidence discloses only the combination of one caste against another.....and however inconsiderate and oppressive such a combination may be it is not penal unless it is for one of the purposes specified in Section 141, Indian Penal Code."[91]

XVI. STRUGGLE AGAINST CASTE SYSTEM

The caste system was attacked by the Social Reform Movement. It was realised that not only caste system humiliate the human beings but also it causes social disintegration. The *Brahmo Samaj,* the *Prarthana Samaj,* the *Arya Samaj,* the *Ramakrishna Mission,* the *Theosophists*, the *Social Conference*, and nearly all the great reformers of the 19th century, attacked it. Even though many of them defended the system of four *varnas,* they were critical of the caste (*jati*) system. In particular they condemned the inhuman practice of untouchability. They also realised that national unity and national progress in political, social and economic fields could not be achieved so long as millions were deprived of their right to live with dignity and honour.[92]

Gandhiji also did a considerable job for abolition of untouchability. He even founded the *All India Harijan Sangh* in the year 1932 for this purpose.[93] Dr. B.R. Ambedkar, who belonged to one of the Scheduled Castes, devoted his entire life to fight against caste tyranny. He organised the All India Depressed Classes Federation for the purpose. Several other scheduled caste leaders founded the All India Depressed Classes Association. In South India, the non-*Brahmins* organised during the 1920s the self-respect movement to fight the disabilities which *Brahmins* had imposed upon them. Numerous *satyagraha* movements were organised all over India by the depressed castes against the ban on their entry into temples and other such restrictions.[94]

XVII. FROM SUPPORT TO ABOLITION OF CASTE SYSTEM

At the turn of the 19th century, the "depressed classes" became an important focus of concern among reformers. It was only after 1909 that fears of diminished Hindu majorities and proposals for special legislative representation for "untouchables" propelled "untouchability" from the realm of philanthropy into the political arena. In 1917 the Indian National Congress reversed its long-standing policy to exclude "social reform" from its programme to pass a hesitant anti-disabilities resolution.[95]

Between 1932 and 1936 a number of temple-entry and anti-disabilities bills were introduced in the Central Legislative Assembly and in the Madras and Bombay Legislatures.

In 1938 the Madras Legislature passed the first comprehensive and penal Act[96] to remove social disabilities, making it an offence to discriminate against untouchables not only in regard to publicly supported facilities such as roads, wells and transportation but also in regard to "any other secular institution" to which the general public was admitted, including restaurants, hotels, shops, *etc.* The Act also barred judicial enforcement of any customary right or disability based on membership in such a group. Violation was made a cognizable offence, with a small fine for the first offence, larger fines and upto six months' imprisonment for subsequent offences.[97]

Between the end of the Second World War and the enactment of the Constitution, with power passing entirely into Indian hands, Acts removing civil disabilities of untouchables were passed in most of the provinces and in many of the larger princely States.[98] With some variation in detail, these statutes followed the general lines of the Madras Removal of Civil Disabilities Act. Enforcement of disabilities against untouchables,[99] variously described as *Harijans,* scheduled castes, excluded classes, backward classes or depressed classes, was outlawed in regard to public facilities like wells and roads and places of public accommodation like shops, restaurants and hotels. Violations were made criminal offences, in most cases cognizable.[100] Judicial enforcement of customs upholding such disabilities was barred.

During the same period, the provincial legislatures were active in the temple-entry field. The pre-war temple entry legislation had been only permissive. It protected trustees and excluded groups from legal penalties if the former chose to ignore the customary practices of exclusion. But trustees were under no obligation to do so and excluded groups had no enforceable right to enter temples.[101]

Madras again took the lead in enacting a comprehensive temple-entry Act,[102] making it a criminal offence for any person to prevent any Hindu from entering or worshipping at any temple to the same extent as Hindus generally.[103] Similar Acts, varying slightly in detail, were passed in most of the provinces and a number of the larger princely States.[104] The Acts withdrew any judicial enforcement, either civil or criminal, of customary rights of exclusion and gave untouchables[105] an enforceable right of entry in temples.[106]

XVIII. POSITION OF CASTE DISABILITIES AND ATROCITIES AT THE DAWN OF INDEPENDENCE

The British Government of India neglected *Shudras* and untouchables and never thought seriously of taking any constructive and concrete measures for their socio-economic and educational development. What were the conditions of these persons in India before independence may be inferred from one of speeches of Dr. B.R. Ambedkar. He described the traditional status of untouchables and caste disabilities in the following words :

> (T)he doors of education were closed for the untouchables. They were not allowed to bear arms. They could not earn enough money or acquire wealth in any manner. Even in the matters of words, they were not allowed free choice. They could not use decent culture, language but instead they were required to use crude language in order to help identification. They had to live outside the villages and far away from the towns in caves, on the trees or huts or tents made of tattered clothes. They could not own animals other than pigs, dogs and donkeys. They were not allowed to eat wholesome food, not to wear decent clothes. In certain reigns they were not allowed to put on loin cloth which went below the knee cap. They could enter the village only during day time and had to return to their huts before sunset. They were branded as untouchables, unseeables and unapproachable.[107]

Thus, the caste into which a man was born determined large areas of his life. It determined whom he would marry and with whom he would dine. It largely determined his profession as well as his social loyalties. The untouchables suffered from numerous and severe disabilities and restrictions. Their touch were considered impure and was a source of pollution. Even their shadow was to be avoided. His dress, food, place of residence were carefully regulated. He could not draw water from wells and tanks used by the higher caste. He could do so only from wells and tanks specially reserved for them. If there existed no such well or tank, he had to drink dirty water from ponds and irrigation canals. He could not enter the Hindu temples or study the *Shastras.* Public services such as police and army were closed to him. He was forced to take up menial and other such jobs which were considered un-cleaned for example, scavenging, shoe making, removing dead bodies, skinning dead animals, tanning hides and skins. He was denied ownership of land.[108]

The commission and continuation of caste disabilities since the period of later *Vedic* period, *i.e.* for a period of more than 3000 years had created inequalities in political, social, economical, educational, religious, cultural and all other conceivable spheres of human activities amongst the inhabitants of our country. It is evident from the speech of Dr. B.R. Ambedkar which is as follows :

> "...We must begin by acknowledging first that there is complete absence of two things in Indian society. One of these is equality. On the social plane, we have in India a society based on privilege of graded inequality which means elevation of some and degradation for others. On the economic plane we have a society in which there are some who have immense wealth as against the many who are living in abject poverty. On the 26th January, 1950, we are going to enter into a life of contradictions. In politics, we will have equality. In politics we will be recognizing the principle of one man and one vote and one vote one value. In our social and economic structure, continue to deny the principle of one man and one value.[109]

Sir Edwin Markham, described their conditions as under :

> Bowed by the weight of centuries he leans,
> Upon his hoe and gazes on the ground,
> The emptiness of ages in his face,
> And on his back the burden of the world,
> Who made him dead to rapture and despair,

A thing that grieves not and that never hopes,
Stolid and stunned, a brother to the ox?
Who loosened and let down this brutal jaw?
Whose was the hand that slanted back this brow?
Whose breath blew out the light within this brain?

* * *

Through this dread shape humanity betrayed,
Plundered, profaned and disinherited,
Cries protest to the Judges of the World,
A protest that is also prophecy.[110]

Thus in nutshell, it can be concluded that at the dawn of the independence, social disabilities were at its peak and *Shudras* and untouchables were suffering from all kinds of disabilities.

XIX. ABOLITION OF CASTE DISABILITIES THROUGH THE CONSTITUTION OF INDIA

To make the fundamental rights of equality really meaningful to the *Shudras* and untouchables of Indian society, the founding fathers of Indian Constitution enumerated several provisions in the Constitution of India so that caste disabilities can be removed and they could be brought to the main stream of Indian society.

The preamble of the Constitution of India contemplates the basic constitutional goals for the nation.[111] These goals are sought to be achieved by a two-fold means embodied in Parts III and IV of the Constitution.[112] While Fundamental Rights (Part III) embodies and guarantees certain individual freedoms, directive principles of State Policy (Part IV) lays down important non-justifiable positive directives and commands the State to implement these directions,[113] so that the constitutional goals enshrined in the Preamble are realised.[114] In consonance with the above constitutional scheme, the preambular promise of equality of status and of opportunity has been concretised and clothed with flesh and blood by the provisions of Articles 14 to 17, 19, 21, 23, 25 and 29, read with Articles 37 to 39, 39A, 41 to 45 and 46.

Article 14[115] guarantees the principles of equality in general terms. This is exemplified and particularised in Articles 15 and 16. It has been rightly held that Article 14 is the genus of the guarantee of equality of which Articles 15 and 16 are the species.[116] Article 14, which has to be interpreted in the light of Articles 38 and 46, seems to enjoin the State to ensure substantive or factual equality.[117] Accordingly, this provision confers on the State a wide latitude to provide for protective discriminatory measures with minimum of judicial interference. The permissible judicial scrutiny under Article 14 is confined to the ascertainment of the reasonableness of the impugned legislative classification on the anvil of the well established two-fold test :

(1) Classification must be founded on an intelligible differentia which distinguishes persons or things that are grouped together from the others left out of the groups ; and

(2) the differentia must have a rational relation to the object sought to be achieved by the statute in question.[118]

Article 15(2) provides that :

(2) No citizen shall, on grounds only of religion, race, caste, sex, place of birth or any of them, be subject to any disability, liability, restriction or condition with regard to–

(a) access to shops, public restaurants, hotels and places of public entertainment, or

(b) the use of wells, tanks, bathing *ghats*, roads and places of public resort maintained wholly or partly out of State funds or dedicated to the use of the general public.[119]

Article 16(1) ensures to all citizens equality of opportunity in matters relating to employment in State services.[120] Article 16(2) further provides that :

(2) No citizen shall, on grounds only of religion, race, caste, sex, descent, place of birth, residence or any of them, be ineligible for, or discriminated against in respect of, any employment of office under the State.[121]

Article 17 forbids the practice of untouchability. It runs as under :

17. Abolition of Untouchability

> "Untouchability" is abolished and its practice in any form is forbidden. The enforcement of any disability arising out of "Untouchability" shall be an offence punishable in accordance with law.[122]

Article 19 provides certain freedoms.[123] Article 21 provides protection of life and personal liberty.[124] Article 23 prohibits trafficking in human beings and forced labour.[125] Article 25 provides right of freedom of religion.[126] Article 29(2) forbids persons in charge of "any educational institution..... receiving aid out of State funds" to deny admission to an applicant "on grounds only of religion, race, caste, language or any of them".[127]

Article 17, not only forbids the practice of "untouchability" but declares that "enforcement of disabilities arising out of 'Untouchability' shall be an offence punishable in accordance with law."[128] Article 35 provides that "Parliament shall have, and the Legislature of a State shall not have, power to make laws.... prescribing punishment for those acts which are declared to be offences under this part" (*i.e.* the Fundamental Rights section of the Constitution). Parliament is specifically directed to "make laws prescribing punishment" for acts declared offences in Part III "as soon as may be after the commencement of this Constitution." Until Parliament discharged this duty, existing laws prescribing punishment for such acts were continued in force, "until altered or repealed or amended by Parliament." Thus existing State, *i.e.*, provincial law was continued in force, but was frozen in its then existing form, beyond the power of the State legislatures to modify or repeal.[129]

XX. REMOVAL OF CASTE DISABILITIES THROUGH THE UNTOUCHABILITY (OFFENCES) ACT, 1955

In exercise of the power enumerated in part second of Art. 17 and Art. 35(a)(ii) of the Constitution of India the Untouchability

(Offences) Act, 1955 was enacted, for giving effect to epoch-making declaration of abolition of Untouchability and practice of Untouchability in any form. The enforcement of any disability arising out of untouchability shall be an offence punishable under various sections of U.O. Act. It was also provided that whosoever will take any part in the ex-communication of, or imposition of any social disability on any person who refuses to practise untouchability or does any act to defeat the objects of U.O. Act, will also be guilty of the offence, in addition to the normal penalty for an offence. It was provided that the Court may also cancel or suspend any licence in respect of profession, trade, calling or employment, when an offence is committed under this law within the course of any such profession, trade calling or employment.[130] The imposition of disabilities is made a crime punishable by fine upto Rs. 500/-, imprisonment for upto six months, cancellation or suspension of licences and/or public grant.[131]

XXI. PROTECTION OF CIVIL RIGHTS THROUGH THE PROTECTION OF CIVIL RIGHTS ACT

Although untouchability was abolished by Art. 17 of the Constitution and in pursuance of the provisions of Art. 35 of the Constitution, the U.O. Act, 1955 was passed by Parliament to make the practice of untouchability as a cognizable offence, yet during the working of the Act, it was noticed that there were some lacunae in the provisions and that these loopholes needed to be plugged. In April 1965, the Government of India appointed the Committee on Untouchability, Educational and Economic Development of the Scheduled Castes under the Chairmanship of Shri L. Elavaperumal to examine, *inter alia* the problem of untouchability *vis-a-vis* the working of the Untouchability (Offences) Act, 1955 and to make recommendations to the Government for amendments to the Act. The Committee submitted its report in January, 1969 in which it made certain recommendations with a view to plug the loopholes and to make the penal provisions more stringent. To give effect to some of the recommendations made by the said Committee, the U.O. Act was amended in 1976 as "Protection of Civil Rights Act".[132]

The provisions of the Protection of Civil Rights Act and the

Constitution of India seek to serve three-fold purposes : (i) outlawed the disabilities to which *Dalits* are subjected to : (ii) these are made an offence under the Act ; and (iii) provided rights to enforce these as civil rights. Untouchability is the root cause and consequently any religious, social, customary or moral grounds to enforce untouchability no longer subsists nor valid after January 26, 1950. Enforcement of any disability is a crime against human rights and the Constitution entails the wrong-doer with punishment. All customs, usages and practices directly or indirectly recognising or encouraging the practice of untouchability in any form is void, being opposed to public policy. Even a contract, convenant or any private transaction tending to recognise, encourage or effectuate untouchability in any form is, therefore, *void ab initio.*[133]

After 42 years of the Constitution coming into force, the first case to reach the Supreme Court was *State of Karnataka* Vs. *Appa Balu Ingale and others.*[134]

It seems fair to say that the U.O. Act has not fared well in the High Courts, in contrast with the earlier State legislation, which generally received favourable interpretations from these courts. This unfavourable reception by the High Courts seems to involve three problem areas : the requirement that the forbidden act be committed "on grounds of untouchability"; uncertainty about coverage of private property ; and limitation of rights to those enjoyed by members of the same religious denomination.[135]

The Supreme Court played a significant role in interpreting the provisions of the U.O. Act/the P.C.R. Act. It was held by the Supreme Court that the Protection of Civil Rights Act is not a penal law simplicitor but bears behind it, monstrous untouchability relentlessly practised for centuries dehumanising the Scheduled Castes, Constitution's animation to have it eradicated and to assimilate one- fifth of nation's population in the main stream of national life.[136]

XXII. PREVENTION OF ATROCITIES THROUGH THE SCHEDULED CASTE AND THE SCHEDULED TRIBES (PREVENTION OF ATROCITIES) ACT, 1989

Despite various measures to improve the socio-economic conditions of the Scheduled Castes and the Scheduled Tribes, they remain vulnerable. They are denied number of civil rights. They are subjected to various offences, indignities, humiliations and harassment. They have, in several brutal incidents, been deprived of their life and property. Serious crimes are committed against them for various historical, social and economic reasons.[137] The social indignities emanating from the practice of untouchability and acute economic disparity arising out of landlessness, bondage, *etc.*, leads the SCs to succumb to atrocities by dominant castes who start retaliatory pressures to dilute and weaken the force of compensatory measures.[138] The increasing incidents of atrocities on SCs are the direct outcome of agrarian tensions, ineffective implementation of the PCR Act, the Minimum Wages Act, rural indebtedness, practice of bonded labour and half hearted implementation of various developmental measures like allotment of surplus ceiling land to SCs.[139]

Because of the awareness created amongst the Scheduled Castes and the Scheduled Tribes through spread of education, *etc.*, they are trying to assert their rights and this is not being taken very kindly by others. When they assert their rights and resist practices of untouchability against them or demand statutory minimum wages or refuse to do any bonded or forced labour, the vested interests try to cow them down and terrorise them. When the Scheduled Castes and the Scheduled Tribes try to preserve their self-respect or honour of their woman, they become irritants for the dominant and the mighty. Occupation and cultivation of even the Government allotted land to the Scheduled Castes and Scheduled Tribes is resented and more often these people become victims of attacks by the vested interests. Of late, there has been an increase in the disturbing trend of commission of certain atrocities like making the Scheduled Castes persons to eat inedible substances, like human excreta; attacking and mass killings of helpless Scheduled Castes and Scheduled Tribes and rape of their women.[140]

Under the circumstances, the existing laws like the Protection of Civil Rights Act, 1955 and the normal provisions of the Indian Penal Code have been found inadequate to check these crimes. A special legislation to check and deter crimes against them committed by non-Scheduled Castes and non-Scheduled Tribes has, therefore, become necessary.[141]

Consequently, the Scheduled Castes and the Scheduled Tribes (Prevention of Atrocities) Act, 1989 for short the Act was passed which came into force on 30 January, 1990.[142]

XXIII. EMERGING NEW FORMS OF ATROCITIES

The past and present has been full of innumerable instances of atrocities, indignities and practices of untouchabilities.[143] In spite of passing and coming into force of the Act and Rules[144] framed thereunder for prevention of atrocities, the atrocities are still being committed on the *Shudras* and Untouchables now recognised and enlisted as SCs and Scheduled Tribes and inhuman and barbaric treatment is met out to them by their own country men.[145] Sometimes their minor daughters and women are raped and children are butchered like animals.[146] Their marriage processions are attacked and bridegroom and members of marriage party are mercilessly beaten. Their social, cultural and religious processions are welcome by stones, brickbats and rotten eggs.[147] Their homes are burnt at whim, destroying their meagre source of livelihood. The barbaric massacre of *Chunder*, a village of *Penali* division of *Guntoor* district of Andhra Pradesh in which 28 Scheduled Caste persons were massacred,[148] a *Belchi, Arrah* and *Pipra* carnages of Bihar and *Kilven Mani* of Tamil Nadu in which large number of Scheduled Castes were massacred, are some examples of this.[149] It is disgusting that the protector of law, who are entrusted with the duty to save and safeguard Scheduled Castes, committed atrocities on them. In *Morena* Jail of MP, two Scheduled Caste persons were victimised with the connivance of jail staff. They were beaten mercilessly and unnatural offence and sodomy was committed with them. They were made to lick penis of co-prisoners.[150] A legislator committed rape of Scheduled Caste woman in Bihar.[151] A police officer raped a daughter of Scheduled Caste man in his presence and he died with shame committing suicide as he could not bear this inhuman act.[152]

On March 23, on the eve of *Holi,* 10 landless *Musahars* were killed, allegedly by the *Ranvir Sena,* a private army of upper-caste landlords, in *Hawaspur Musharitola* village in Patna District.[153] Three *Harijans* were massacred on 28th March by armed raiders at *Akopur* village under *Arwal* block of Jehanabad district, 95 Km

South-west of Patna. The victims had dared to protest the rape of a *Harijan* girl by an upper caste youth of the same area on that day.[154] At least 10 *Dalits* were gunned down and several injured in armed attack in two villages in Gaya District.[155] Four *Dalits* working at brick kiln were beheaded in *Indraruk* village in rural Kanpur, allegedly by the members of the upper caste.[156] Six *Dalit* wood-cutters were killed in the night of January 6, 1997, in *Hastinapur* forest by a *Gujjar* gang which is allegedly having close links with the forest mafias operating in the area since long.[157]

The magnitude of the problem is that even the educationally, economically and politically advanced persons belonging to Scheduled Castes, holding the high political or executive or police post could not be liberated from this social evil of untouchability and atrocities. Their social position, status and prestige are still deemed low. A District Magistrate of Gopal Ganj district of Bihar, a Scheduled Caste, member of Indian Administrative Service, was stoned to death by a mob.[158]

These incidents create tense atmosphere in the society. Sometimes it resulted into caste and class war. For example, after few days of incidence of six *Dalits* killing in Meerut,[159] six *Gujjars* were killed in the *Hastinapur* area of Meerut District.[160] *Hastinapur* town came to a standstill as markets remained close and shops downed their shutters in protest against the killings. Acrimonious scenes were witnessed. Roads were blocked and windows of a few cars were smashed.[161] At *Narayanpur* village of *Jehanabad* district of Bihar some SCs were massacred in the second week of February, 1999.[162] In retaliation victimisation, 35 upper caste men, *i.e.* non SC & ST, were killed at *Senari* village of same district.[163] These incidents are like a drop in ocean reminding us about the gravity of the problem.

Unless this problem is tackled and solved cautiously, effectively and expeditiously, the various persons living in our society cannot live in peace and harmony. The problem of commission of atrocities and practice of untouchability and its after effects have not only disintegrated the Indian society but also nation as a whole.[164]

Therefore, this problem is required to be tackled and solved cautiously, effectively and expeditiously so that commission of atrocities and practice of untouchability may be abolished, eradicated, prevented and minimised and our nation can be saved from disintegration, disharmonies, disparities and inhuman and heinous crimes.

"Unity in Diversity" is one of the basic characteristics of India. Commission and continuation of atrocities on the Scheduled Castes, due to hatred based on caste prejudice and practice of untouchability, *etc.*, is one of the major challenges to this characteristics. So a workable solution for the problem of atrocities based on caste prejudice or hate may be devised.

This will promote the theme "Live and Let Live" which in result would enable the weak and strong; rich and poor; backward and forward ; servant and master; and Scheduled Caste and non-Scheduled Caste persons to live in peace and co-exist together with mutual love and respect.

Notes and References

1. *See,* The Universal Declaration of Human Rights, Adopted and Proclaimed by the General Assembly of the United Nations on December 10, 1948. A.1.
2. *Ibid.* A.2.
3. *Ibid.* A.3.
4. *Ibid.* A.5.
5. *Ibid.* A.6.
6. *Ibid.* A.7.
7. *Ibid.* A.21(2).
8. *Ibid.* A.23(2).
9. *Ibid.* A.26(1).
10. *Supra,* note 1, A.27(1).
11. *See, INDIA,* 1999 : A reference Annual Research Reference and Training Division, Ministry of Information and Broadcasting, Government of India at 13. The population of SCs is 16.8% as per 1991 Census.
12. This situation is still persisting. *See,* News item, Caste clashes in medical hostel. *Indian Express,* 24.2.1999. (It was also reported that in the mess there was one table for SCs & STs students and they were not allowed to sit anywhere in the mess in the hostel of Guru Tegh Bahadur Medical College at Shahdara, a part of capital Delhi.)
13. *See,* The *Kathaka Samhita* (xxxi. 2 & xi.10) ; *The Maitrayani Samhita* (vii.1.1.6 & iv.13; i.8.3) ; *The Panchavimsa Brahmana* (vi.1.11.) ; *The Satapatha Brahmana* (xiv.1.31.) ; The *Aitareya Brahmana* (vii.29.4) ; The *Apastamba Dharma Sutra,* 4, 5 & 6, *Prasna* 1. *Patala* 5, *Khanda* 16, *Sutras* 21 & 22, *Prasna* 1, *Patala* 2, *Khanda* 5, *Sutras* 16 & 17, *Prasna* II, *Patala* 2, *Khanda* 4, *Sutra* 19 & 20, *Prasna* II, *Patala* 10,

Khanda 27, *Sutras* 8 & 9 ; The *Vasistha Dharma Sutra*, Chapter II, Verses 1-4, Chapter IV, Verse 3, Chapter XIV, Verses 1-4, Chapter XVIII, Verses 11-15, Chapter VI, Verses 26-29 & 24 ; The *Manu Smriti,* Chapter I, Verses 31, 87-91, Chapter IV, Verses 61, 78-81, 99, Chapter III, Verses 110-112, 156 & 178, Chapter X Verse 129, Chapter XII, *Sutras* 2 & 3, Chapter V, Verse 92, Chapter II, Verses 135-137, 154-156, Chapter VIII, Verses 20-22, 267, 268 & 374, *Prasna* II, *Patala* 10, *Khanda* 26, *Sutras* 14-16; *Vishnu Smriti,* Chapter XIX, *Sutras* 1-4, Chapter V, *Sutra* 115, Chapter V, *Sutras* 19-25, Chapter XXVII, *Sutras* 9 ; *Gautama Dharma Sutra,* Chapter XII, *Sutras* 1, 7, 8-13, Chapter XX, *Sutras* 4-6, Chapter X, *Sutras* 50 & 56-59 ; *Brihaspati Dharma Shastra,* Chapter XX, Verses 7-11, Chapter XII, Verse 12, *Narada Smriti,* Chapter XV, Verses 2-27.

14. *See,* Dr. Ambedkar, B.R., Who were the Shudras? How they came to be the Fourth Varna in the Indo-Aryan Society? in *Dr. BABA SAHEB AMBEDKAR : WRITINGS AND SPEECHES,* Education Department, Govt. of Maharashtra, (1990), Vol. 7 at 55 & 56.
15. *Supra,* note 14 at 57, *See,* also, Jiloha, R.C., *The Native Indian : In Search of Identity.* Bluemoon Books, 1995 at 1.
16. Prejudice is the holding of pejorative attitudes based on strongly held views about the appropriate capacities or limits of individuals or the group of which they are members. Discrimination is the behaviour which may result. Not all discrimination flows from prejudice. It may flow from stereotyping, by which we arbitrarily attribute those characteristics to the group of which he or she is a member, or discrimination may flow from indifference or neglect. Thus it can be said that where there is a prejudice there is discrimination. *See,* Rosalie Silberman Abella, "Equality, Human Rights, Women and the Justice System," *McGILL LAW JOURNAL,* Vol. 39, No. 3 at 494.
17. Allied Chambers (India) Limited, New Delhi, 1996 at 265.
18. *See,* Dr. Ambedkar, B.R., Castes in India : Their Mechanism, Genesis and Development, in *DR. BABASAHEB AMBEDKAR : WRITINGS AND SPEECHES,* Education Department, Govt. of Maharashtra, (1979), Vol. 1 at 7.
19. *Ibid.* Dr. Ambedkar criticised definition of these writers on the ground that these include too much or too little; none is complete or correct by itself and all have missed the central point in mechanism of the caste system. Their mistake lies in trying to define caste as an isolated unit by itself and not as a group within and with definite relations to, the system of caste as a whole.
20. *Supra,* note 18 at 7.
21. *See,* Dr. Ambedkar, B.R., Annihilation of Caste, in *DR. BABASAHEB AMBEDKAR : WRITINGS AND SPEECHES*, Education Department, Govt. of Maharashtra, (1979), Vol. 1 at 56 & 57.
22. News Item, "Dalit youth thrashed for chewing Pann", *The Hindustan Times,* 4.11.1998 at p. 8, Column 5 (This incident occurred at Duni Bus Stand in Tonk District of Rajasthan).
23. *Supra,* note 12.
24. Ghose, Sanjay, "Animal & Untouchable Not Allowed", *Indian Express* 12.8.1990, Magazine p. 2, Column 1.
25. News Item, "Ranvir Sena Strikes Again : 11 Shot Dead", *The Hindustan Times,* 12.2.1999, p.1, Column 6.
26. Dalit is another term used for SCs.

27. Pathak, Bindeshwar, "The Plight of Dalits", *The Hindustan Times*, 29.10.1998, at p. 11, Editorial.
28. It is believed that it had entrenched in Indian society by about AD 200. *See* Oliver Mendelsohn and Marika Vicziany, "Untouchables" in *The Rights of Subordinated Peoples* edited by Oliver Mendelsohn and Upendra Baxi, Delhi Oxford University Press, 1996 at 70. *See also,* Satish Chandra, A.V., "The Annihilation of Caste : The unfinished task of Dr. Ambedkar", *Ambedkar and Social Justice,* Publication Division, Ministry of Information and Broadcasting, Govt. of India, 1992, Vol. 1 at 85.
29. *See, Ancient India,* N.C.E.R.T., 1983 at 49 ; *See also,* Jiloha, R.C., *The Native Indian : In Search of Identity.* Bluemoon Books, 1995 at 14.
30. *Supra,* note 14 at 22 ; *See,* also Goyal, B.R. *Educating Harijans,* viii (1981) at 1.
31. *Supra,* note 29 at 60.
32. *Supra,* note 14 at 11 & 204.
33. *Supra,* note 29 at 84; *See also, Supra,* note 14 at 55 & 56.
34. *Supra,* note 14 at 11 & 204.
35. Tiwari, Chitra, *Shudra in Manu,* 18 (1963).
36. *Supra,* notes 13 & 14.
37. Kane, P.V., *History of Dharmashastras,* 163 (1974), Vol. II, Part I.
38. *Law of Manu,* VIII, X ; 51-2 ; *See also,* Dr. Ambedkar, B.R., The Untouchables : Who Were They and Why They Become Untouchable? In *DR. BABASAHEB AMBEDKAR : WRITINGS AND SPEECHES,* Education Department, Govt. of Maharashtra, (1990), Vol. 7 at 271.
39. *Ibid.* XI, 235.
40. *Supra,* note 38 VIII at 413.
41. *Parashar Smriti,* Ch. VI, V : 24 quoted by Surender Kumar in Hindu Dharam and Shudra, *Sarita* (Ed. 640) 26, (December 2, 1981).
42. *Ibid.* at 24, *Gautam Sutra* (2:3:3); *See also* Har Dutt, *Mutakshar Virati*; *See also Brihaspati Smriti,* Chapter XII, Verse 12.
43. *Supra,* note 29 at 84 ; *See also, Supra,* note 37.
44. *Ibid.* at 142.
45. A slave is one who is owned by another and deprived of most or all rights and freedoms. The slave is dependent on the whim of the owner, who may generally force him to any service and, at least in principle, may usually even dispose of his life. *See, The New Encyclopaedia Britannica,* William Benton Publisher, 1943-1973 at 853.
46. *Supra,* note 18 at 18.
47. *Ibid.* at 18 & 19.
48. *Supra note* 14 at 171.
49. *See,* Dr. Ambedkar, B.R., Unpublished Writings Untouchables or the Children of India's Ghetto and other Essays on Untouchables and Untouchability: Social Political-Religious, in *DR. BABASAHEB AMBEDKAR : WRITINGS AND SPEECHES,* Education Department, Govt. of Maharashtra, (1989) Vol. 5, at 15-18.
50. *See Supra,* notes 13, 14 & 42 ; *See also Infra,* note 51.
51. *See,* Dr. Ambedkar, B.R., Philosophy of Hinduism, in *DR. BABASAHEB AMBEDKAR : WRITINGS AND SPEECHES,* Education Department, Govt. of Maharashtra, (1987) Vol. 3 at 41.
52. *Ibid.* at 43.

53. *Supra,* note 51 at 43; *See* also *Supra*, note 42.
54. *Id.*
55. *See,* Dr. Ambedkar, B.R., The Untouchables and the Pax Britannica, *in DR. BABASAHEB AMBEDKAR : WRITINGS AND SPEECHES,* Education Department, Govt. of Maharashtra, (1993) Vol. 12 at 102 & 103.
56. *See,* (i) 14h Report of the Committee on the Welfare of Scheduled Castes and Scheduled Tribes (Fourth Lok Sabha), 4, 91, 92 (1970).
    (ii) Mitra, Ashok, *India's Population : Aspect of Quality and Control,* Vol. I, 1978 at 400, 404 and 408.
    (iii) Chaudhari, Buddhadeb (Ed.), *Tribal Development in India,* 395 (1981).
    (iv) Census of India, 1981, Series I at XXVI.
    (v) Goyal, B.R., *Educating Harijans,* 98 (1981).
57. *Supra,* note 56.
58. *Ibid.* (v) at 98.
59. *Supra,* note 51 at 42.
60. *Supra,* note 29 at 176.
61. *Ibid.* at 178.
62. Singh, Dr. Parmanand, *Equality, Reservation and Discrimination in India,* 109 (1982).
    The terms 'high caste' or 'low caste' are used in the sense of purity and pollution but partly in their historical context and partly in connection with the present overall economic and educational condition of the members of the group. The high or upper caste are those which enjoyed dominance over economic resources in the recent past before independence, and today the majority of its members are relatively well off, enjoy dominance (not necessarily political offices) and are better educated than the members of the other social groups. The condition of 'lower caste' is the opposite of this.
    See also, Shah, Ghanshyam, "Caste, Class and Reservation", *Economic and Political Weekly,* 132 (January 19, 1985).
63. *Supra,* note 29, at 49.
64. *Medieval India,* NCERT, 1983, at 26.
65. *Supra,* note 29, at 178.
66. *Ibid.* at 60.
67. *Ibid.* at 178.
68. *Modern India,* N.C.E.R.T., 1983 at 39.
69. *Supra,* note 29, at 178.
70. *Supra,* note 64, at 114.
71. *Supra,* note 69, at 112.
72. *Ibid.* at 113.
73. *Supra,* note 69, at 113.
74. *See,* Galanter, Marc, Untouchability And The Law at II-11 ; *Economic and Political Weekly,* Annual Number, January, 1969 at 131; *See also, Supra note,* 29 at 70.
75. *Supra,* note 74; *See also* Murphy, Arthur W. And Others, *Law and Poverty, Cases and Materials,* 1973 at 54; *See also, Infra,* Notes 78 at 323 and 80 at 177.
76. *Ibid.* at 186 ; *Cf. S.K. Wodeyar* Vs. *Ganapati,* AIR, 1935 Bom. 371.
77. *Atmaram* Vs. *King Emperor,* AIR 1924 Nagpur 121.

78. *Anandrav Bhikaji Pakdke* Vs. *Shankar Daji Charya,* ILR 7 (Bom.) (1883) 323 ; *S.K. Wodeyar* Vs. *Ganapati,* AIR 1935 Bom., 371.
79. ILR 7 (Bom.) (1883) 323.
80. 35 IAC 176 (1908).
81. *Supra,* note 80 at 186.
82. *Supra,* note 35 at 55 & 56 ; *Atmaram* Vs. *King Emperor,* AIR 1924 Nagpur 121.
83. *Chathunni* Vs. *Appukuttan,* AIR 1945 Mad., 323.
84. Eg. *Sadogapacharior* Vs. *Rama Rao,* ILR 26 Mad. 376. Local restrictions on the use of thorough fares had sometimes elicited official support.
85. *Queen Empress* Vs. *Bhagi Kom Nathuba,* 2 Bom. L.R. 1078 (1900) (Magistrate had convicted a Vanjari woman of corrupting water in a public cistern and causing the water less fit for drinking purpose under S. 61 of the District Police Act when she had contravened the repeated directions and objections of higher castes not to touch it). *Empress* Vs. *Pandia Mahar,* 3 CPLR 92 (1890).
86. *Kazan Chand* Vs. *Emperor,* AIR 1926 Lah. 683.
87. *Ibid.*
88. *Ramditta* Vs. *Kirpa Singh,* 1883, Punjab Record (Crimes) 3. The Sonars here were members of the Shumree sect (followers of a *pir* named Shums–Tabrez) and had peculiar customs like burying dead. The court suggested that if they had a right to use the well, they should seek a remedy by civil suit rather than a criminal prosecution.
89. *Solar Mannaji Raw* Vs. C. *Herojee Row,* 1 Weir, 614 Mad. HC 1887. The magistrate had found infirmities in the caste proceedings, but the high court reversed the conviction on the ground that the matter was within exclusive cognisance of caste assemblies and the court was debarred from going into the merits.
90. 1 Weir 575 Mad. HC, 1885.
91. S. 141 of the Indian Penal Court makes unlawful assemblies for such object as intimidating public servants, resisting of law, committing mischief or trespass and by means of criminal force to take another's property or compel any person to do what is not bound to do or to omit to do what he is legally entitled to do.
92. *Supra,* note 68 at 232.
93. *See,* Dr. Ambedkar, B.R., "What Congress and Gandhi have done to the Untouchables" and "Mr. Gandhi and the Emancipation of the Untouchables," in *DR. BABASAHEB AMBEDKAR : WRITINGS AND SPEECHES,* Vol. 9, Education Department, Government of Maharashtra, 1990, Vol. 9 at 250.
94. *Ibid.* at 333.
95. *See, Supra* note 93 at 1. The resolution was : "This Congress urges upon the people of India the necessity, justice and righteousness of removing all disabilities imposed by custom upon the Depressed classes, the disabilities being of a most vexatious and oppressive character, subjecting those classes to considerable hardship and inconvenience"; *See also Supra* note 74 at II–18.
96. *Supra,* note 74 at II-18.
97. *See, infra,* note 98(7) Section 6.
98. *See,*
    1. The Bihar Harijan (Removal of Civil Disabilities) Act, 1948 (Bihar Act XIX of 1949).

2. The Bombay Harijan (Removal of Social Disabilities) Act, 1946 (Bombay Act X of 1947).
3. The Bombay Harijan Temple Entry Act, 1947 (Bombay Act XXXV of 1947).
4. The Central Provinces and Berar Scheduled Castes (Removal of Civil Disabilities) Act, 1947 (Central Provinces and Berar Act XXIV of 1947).
5. The Central Provinces and Berar Temple Entry Authorisation Act, 1947 (Central Provinces and Berar Act XLI of 1947).
6. The East Punjab (Removal of Religious and Social Disabilities) Act, 1948 (East Punjab Act XVI of 1948).
7. The Madras Removal of Civil Disabilities Act, 1938 (Madras Act XXI of 1938).
8. The Orissa Removal of Civil Disabilities Act, 1946 (Orissa Act XI of 1946).
9. The Orissa Temple Entry Authorisation Act, 1948 (Orissa Act XI of 1948).
10. The United Provinces Removal of Social Disabilities Act, 1947 (U.P. Act XIV of 1947).
11. The West Bengal Hindu Social Disabilities Removal Act, 1948 (West Bengal Act XXXVII of 1948).
12. The Hyderabad Harijan Temple Entry Regulation 1358F (No. LV of 1358 Fasli).
13. The Hyderabad Harijan (Removal of Social Disabilities) Regulation, 1358F (No. LVI of 1358 Fasli).
14. The Madhya Bharat Harijan Ayogta Nivaran Vidhan, Samvat 2005 (Madhya Bharat Act No. 15 of 1949).
15. The Removal of Civil Disabilities Act, 1943 (Mysore Act XLII of 1943).
16. The Mysore Temple Entry Authorisation Act, 1948 (Mysore Act XIV of 1948).
17. The Saurashtra Harijan (Removal of Social Disabilities) Ordinance (No. XL of 1948).
18. The Travancore-Cochin Removal of Social Disabilities Act, 1125K (Travancore Cochin Act VIII of 1125).
19. The Travancore-Cochin Temple Entry (Removal of Disabilities) Act, 1950 (Travancore-Cochin Act XXVII of 1950).
20. The Coorg Scheduled Castes (Removal of Civil and Social Disabilities) Act, 1949 (Coorg Act I of 1949).
21. The Coorg Temple Entry Authorisation Act, 1949 (Coorg Act II of 1949).

99. Some of these Acts conferred rights explicitly on untouchable. *See, e.g.*, U.P. Removal of Social and Religious Disabilities Act (XIV of 1947) but others were more broadly worded to confer rights on non-touchable groups as well. *e.g.*, Travancore-Cochin Removal of Social Disabilities Act (VIII of 1125, 1950) outlawed discriminations of any person on grounds of belonging to a particular caste or religion, Ss. 3, 4 & 6.

100. The Orissa and U.P. Acts were the only ones in note 98 as one under which offences are non-cognizable.

101. *Supra*, note 34 at II-18 & 136.

102. Madras Temple Entry Authorisation Act, 1947 (V of 1947) and Amending Act of 1949 (XIII of 1949).
103. For an example of efficacious use of this Act of local militants as leverage to effect temple entry, *See,* Aiyappan, *Social Revolution in a Kerala Village : A Study in Culture Change,* Asia Publishing House, Bombay, 1965 at 144.
104. *Supra,* note 98 at Sl. No. 3, 5 & 9.
105. Like the Social Disabilities Acts (*See Supra note 98)* some of these temple entry Acts concerned only rights of 'untouchable' making it an offence.
106. Except for the United Provinces and Coorg Act, all created cognisable offences.
107. Om Prakash, *Untouchables,* 1-2 (1970). *See* also Kirpal Vinay, "Higher Education for the Scheduled Castes and Scheduled Tribes", *Economic and Political Weekly,* 13 (4-5) 28th January and 4th February, 1978 at 165.
108. *Supra,* Note 68 at 231 ; *See* also *The Framing of India's Constitution,* 1967, Select Documents, Vol. II at 105. The Appendix – I of the Sub-committee on Fundamental Rights has revealed as to how miserable life of SCs people was in the year 1947.
109. Dr. Ambedkar's Address to the C.A., 25th November (1949) (C.A. Speech, Vol. 2 at 184-187).
110. Justice Krishna Iyer, V.R., *Social Justice to Dalits and Soshits, Ambedkar and Social Justice,* Vol. I, at 35.
111. The Preamble, *Constitution of India,* reads :
    WE, THE PEOPLE OF INDIA, having solemnly resolved to constitute India into a SOVEREIGN SOCIALIST SECULAR DEMOCRATIC REPUBLIC and to secure to all its citizens ; JUSTICE, social, economic and political ; LIBERTY of thought expression, belief, faith and worship; EQUALITY of status and of opportunity and to promote among them all FRATERNITY assuring the dignity of the individual and the unity and integrity of the nation.
112. Errabbi, B., "Protective Discrimination : Constitutional Perspectives and Judicial Perception", 10 & 11, *Del. L. Rev.* 67 (1981-82).
113. Art. 37, *Constitution of India* expressly states :
    The provisions contained in this Part shall not be enforceable by any court, but the principles therein laid down are nevertheless fundamental in the governance of the country and it shall be duty of the State to apply these principles in making laws.
114. *Supra,* note 112 at 67.
115. Art. 14, *Constitution of India* provides :
    The State shall not deny to any person equality before the law or the equal protection of the laws within the territory of India.
116. *State of Kerala* Vs. *N.M. Thomas,* A.I.R. 1976 S.C. 490 at 497, 519, 521 and 546 (per Ray, C.J., Methew, Beg and Fazl Ali, JJ., respectively).
117. *P.C.I.J.* Series A/B 64 of 1935, *See* also, Methew, J., *Supra* Note 116, at 69 and *K.C. Vasanth Kumar* Vs. *State of Karnataka* A.I.R. 1985 S.C. 1495 at 1502.
118. *See State of W.B.* Vs. *Anwar Ali Sarkar,* A.I.R. 1952 S.C. 75; *Ramkrishna Dalmia* Vs. *S.R. Tandolkar,* A.I.R. 1958 S.C. 478 ; *R.K. Garg* Vs. *Union of India,* A.I.R. 1981 S.C. 2138 and *A.B.S.K. Sangh (Rly.)* Vs. *Union of India,* A.I.R. 1981 S.C. 298.
119. *The Constitution of India.*

120. *Ibid.*
121. *Ibid.*
122. *Ibid.*
123. Article 19, *Constitution of India* states :
    19. (1) Protection of certain rights regarding freedom of speech, etc. :
    (i) All citizens shall have the right :
    (a) to freedom of speech and expression ;
    (b) to assemble peaceably and without arms ;
    (c) to form associations or unions ;
    (d) to move freely throughout the territory of India ;
    (e) to reside and settle in any part of the territory of India ; and
    (f) to practice any profession, or to carry on any occupation, trade or business.
124. Article 21, *Constitution of India* runs as under :
    21. *Protection of life and personal liberty :* No person shall be deprived of his life of personal liberty except according to procedure established by law.
125. Article 23(1) *Constitution of India* provides :
    23. *Prohibition of traffic in human beings and forced labour:—*
    (1) Traffic in human beings and *begar* and other similar forms of forced labour are prohibited and any contravention of this provision shall be an offence punishable in accordance with law.
126. *See,* Article 25, *Ibid.*
127. *See,* Article 29, *Ibid.*
128. *See Infra* Note 164 at 665. Sh. V.I. Muniswamy Pillai stated that "... a sixth of the population of the whole of India will welcome the introduction and the adoption of a section to root out the very practice of untouchability in this country. *** under the device of caste distinction a certain section of people have been brought under the rope of untouchability, who have been suffering for ages under the tyranny of the so-called caste Hindus and all those people who style themselves as landlords and zamindars *** not allowed the ordinary rudimentary facilities required for a human being".
129. *Supra,* note 74 at II-21.
130. *See,* Statement of Objects and Reasons of Untouchability (Offences) Act, 1955 ; *See* also *State of Karnataka* Vs. *Appa Balu Ingale and Others,* AIR 1993 SC 1126 at 1129-30.
131. *See,* Ss. 4 to 7 and 8 to 10 of Untouchability (Offences) Act, 1955.
132. *See,* S.O.R. – Gazette of India 13-4-1972, Pt. II, S. 2. Ext., p. 294.
133. AIR 1993 SC 1126 at 1129-30.
134. *Ibid.*
135. *Supra,* note 74 at II-28 ; *Economic and Political Weekly,* 1969 at 144.
136. *Supra,* note 133 at 1129.
137. Statement of Objects and Reasons of the Scheduled Castes and the Scheduled Tribes (Prevention of Atrocities) Act, 1989.
138. *See,* Baxi, Upendra, *Law And Poverty : Critical Essays,* 1988 at 162.
139. *See,* RCSCST 2 (1978-79). *See,* also RCSCST IInd Report, 313-20 (1980-81).
140. *Supra,* note 137.
141. *Ibid.*
142. Act no. 33 of 1989.

143. The Reports of the Commission for Scheduled Castes and Scheduled Tribes, Eighth Report, 1985-86 at 44-48, Seventh Report, 1984-85 at 28, 29, 30, 32, 34 ; Sixth Report, 1983-84, at 92 and 93, Fifth Report, 1982-83 at 111 and 112 ; *See* also *Infra,* note 161.
144. *See,* Gazette of India (Ext.) Part-II Section 3(i), Dated 31.3.1995 at 24.
145. *See,* Kamle, N.D., *Atrocities on Scheduled Caste* (1981).
146. News Item, "Shame", *The Hindustan Times,* August 21, 1994 Sunday at 5.
147. Tapas, Om Prakash, "Dalit Dulhe Ke Ghori Chadne per Hamla", *Nav Bharat Times,* June 9, 1990 at 1, C-2. *See* also *Infra* note 161.
148. Parliamentary Forum of Scheduled Castes and Scheduled Tribes, *Socio-Economic & Political Status of the SCs and STs* (1992) at 47.
149. *Ibid. at* 48.
150. Singh, Narender Kumar, "Sabak Sikhane Ka Vashi Tarika, *India Today,* August 15, 1994 at 56.
151. Ahmed, Farj N., "Mahangi Pari Mardangi", *India Today,* December *15,* 1994 at 88.
152. Sethi, Lokpal, "Raped in Custody, father kills self", *The Hindustan Times,* December 20, 1994 at 1, C-2.
153. Chaudhuri, Kalyan, "A Massacre in Bihar", Landlordism and Caste oppression" *Frontline,* May 2, 1997 at 46.
154. News Item, "3 Dalits massacred in Bihar", *The Hindustan Times,* March 30, 1997 at 24, C-4.
155. News Item, "Ten Dalits done to death in Gaya", *The Hindustan Times,* December 25, 1991 at 1, C-1.
156. News Item, "Four Dalits beheaded in Kanpur", *The Hindustan Times,* March 10, 1993, at 24, C-1.
157. News Item, "Six Dalits killed in Meerut District", *The Hindustan Times,* January 7, 1997, at 1, C-1.
158. Ravi, Atul Krishna, "Political Mileage Out of Murder", *The Hindustan Times,* December 11, 1994 at 13, C-3.
159 *Supra,* note 157.
160. News Item, "Gang War intensifies ; six gunned down near Meerut", *The Hindustan Times,* January 18, 1997 at 1, C-3.
161. News Item, "Hastinapur comes to a standstill", *The Hindustan Times,* January 19, 1997, at 5, C-4.
162. See, *The Hindustan Times*, dated February 13, 1999.
163. *Ibid.* dated March 20, 1999.
164. *See,* Constituent Assembly Debates, Book No. 2, Vol. No. VII, 29th Nov., 1948 at 666. Dr. Manomohan Dass stated, "The custom of untouchability has not only thrown missions of the Indian population into the dark abyss of gloom and despair, shame and disgrace, but it has also eaten into the very vitality of our nation." *See,* also Oliver Mandelsohn & Upendra Baxi, *The Rights of Subordinated Peoples,* Oxford University Press, 1996 at 1. They are of the view that the State would incur steeply rising damage to its own interests if it continued to deny such people their rights as ordinary human beings.

PART-I

DOCTRINAL

CHAPTER 1

ATROCITIES AND THE SCHEDULED CASTES

1.1 General

This part of the book will focus on the origin of caste disabilities and history of caste system and problem of atrocities. What is atrocity and in what manner, it had been committed and being committed? What are various aspects of atrocities? It will be explored whether caste system, untouchability, endogamy, caste hatred, religion, illiteracy, poverty, economic backwardness, cultural backwardness, lack of political will, awakening of scheduled castes and resultant demands of their rights and ignorance of law, were or were not the reasons for commission of atrocities? What are the kinds of atrocities? This part will also focus on the issue whether law can play an important role or can law be an instrument for combating the atrocities? What are the salient features of the Scheduled Castes and Scheduled Tribes (Prevention of Atrocities) Act? What is the framework, machinery for controlling, preventing atrocities and to provide rehabilitative relief to the victims?

This part of the book will also evaluate the decisions of various High Courts and Supreme Court in order to see the attitude of Courts towards tackling of this social evil.

A. ATROCITY

1.2 Meaning of Atrocity

In common parlance, the term "Atrocity" denotes an act of extreme heinous cruelty. The term "Atrocity" has not been defined in law. Even the Act has not defined this term.[1] In the absence of any legal definition, its meaning has been derived from the various instruments issued by Government of India from time to time. The States have tended to apply their own interpretations about the term "Atrocity". Ministry of Home Affairs, has clarified this term as "any offence under the Indian Penal Code committed against members of the Scheduled Castes by any non-Scheduled Caste person. Similarly, all offences under the IPC committed by non-Scheduled Tribe against the member of Scheduled Tribe are atrocities. Caste consideration as a motive is not necessary to make such an offence in case of atrocity."[2]

Ministry of Home Affairs has again clarified the term "Atrocity" as, "Crimes which have ingredients of infliction of suffering in one form or the other should be included for reporting." This is based on the assumption that "where the victims of crime are members of Scheduled Castes and the offenders do not belong to Scheduled Castes, caste consideration are really the root cause of the crime, even though caste consciousness may not be the vivid and immediate motive for the crime."[3]

In the first report of the Commission, Atrocity mainly denoted grave offences like murder, rape, arson, and violence resulting in grievous hurt.[4] It appears that behind the selection of these four particular serious offences as atrocity, *mens rea* regarding caste was an important factor. Otherwise, there appears to be no explanation as to why serious offences like dacoity have not been specifically mentioned, whereas all cases of grievous hurt (including the breaking of a tooth which affects a poor person much less than loss of property and the like) were considered to be atrocities. It would have been better if all such cases in which SCs & STs were victims and the offenders non-SCs or non-STs and which were treated as specially reported cases were generally enumerated under the heading "atrocity".[5]

Thus, there has been controversy on the definition of "atrocity". If we were to say that the more serious offence should be classified as "atrocities" we would still be left with problems of defining the notion of "serious" offences. Apart from murder and grievous offences, one would have to fall back upon the measure of punishment provided by the Code in defining what constitute "serious" offences. But this measure can hardly be relied upon : this is so, because the prescribed punishments depend on the nature of the criminal act and not upon the impact of such act on the historically situated victim groups as a whole.[6]

A Jurist examined, whether violation of the Civil Right Protection Act should be considered "atrocity". He opined that the level of punishments is very low but the CRA deals with a specifically disadvantaged group for whom Constitution shows some special solicitude. To include CRA offences in the concept of "atrocities" would be able to accept the impact of the crime upon specific social groups as a criterion for selection of other offences, under the general penal law of the land, whether in that concept this may not be an easy decision to take? This procedure might be problematic. Also, if the CRA is vigorously enforced this would enhance, from year to year, the incidence of "atrocities".[7]

A recent study by the Bureau of Police Research and Development, Union Ministry of Home Affairs, calls for a "meaningful" definition of the term, which is in "conformity with the realities of the situation". What is meant by this is strikingly borne out by the comment that "in order to constitute atrocity, there must be an element of cruelty, brutality or wickedness in the commission of a particular offence, or it should have the background of having been committed with a view to teach a lesson to the *Harijans*".[8]

This is a sensible suggestion but it does not help us overcome the problem of definition of "atrocities" and its possible scope. The expressions "cruelty, brutality and wickedness" are much open to subjective interpretation, influenced no doubt by levels of sensitivity of the group which has to enforce the law and of the wider community.[9]

1.3 Personal Aspect of Atrocity

On commission of atrocity, the victim suffers not only of bodily and mental pain but also imminent feeling of insecurity, which is not present in the victim of any other crime. He thinks himself a very pitiable person. Even after recovery of bodily hurt, he continues to suffer mental pain during rest of his life. Sense of insecurity impede him to leave his place of residence, village. He tries to locate any other secure habitable place, which he rarely finds. This everlasting process goes on, which result into deterioration of physical, mental, educational, social, economical and psychological status of victim of atrocity.

In case atrocity is committed in the absence of others, he tries to conceal it rather than to lodge a First Information Report in the Police Station, thinking that by doing so he will save his reputation. He thinks that if incident of atrocity is known by the public, particularly, his relatives and castemen, his reputation will be lowered in their eyes.

During the process of victimisation, the role of the victim is learned through the interaction with the offender or with people in the social vicinity of the victim. The victim is pushed or "socialised" into his/her victim role and with time he/she grows accustomed to becoming a victim. The person concerned learns to define him/herself as a victim. And rather often it is the inappropriate reactive process following instances of primary victimisation, the so-called secondary victimisation, which leads to a lasting internalisation of the role of the victim. Such inappropriate reactions of authorities in the field of formal social control as well as of people in the victim's social vicinity may victimise the primary victim again. Once more he/she is made object. At the end of this process of degradation and stigmatisation, the victim adopts a victimal conception of him/herself.[10]

In explaining the process of learning the role of the victim, reference may also be taken to the theory of learned helplessness. According to this theory, human beings learn from experience that their action may have negative consequences upon which they cannot exert an influence; for if somebody realises again and again that negative consequences cannot be averted, even by determined action, he/she will become passive. Such a person will then not even try to take promising counteraction against an impending disaster or danger. Persons of that sort tend to give up their resistance. They internalise their impression that even purposeful action will be of no use whatsoever.[11]

1.4 Physical Aspect of Atrocity

In atrocities, where the victim suffers physical injuries on his body, he undergoes bodily pain according to the nature of injuries. Acuteness and period of bodily pain varies according to grievousness of hurt caused on the body. In many cases of atrocity, even limbs of person are amputated which makes the victim infirm. His physical strength is deteriorated resulting into unfit or less fit in his profession and occupation.

1.5 Economic Aspect of Atrocity

Commission of atrocity also affects the economic position of victim. In some kind of atrocities, such as destruction and damage of properties, *etc.*, victim suffers direct financial losses. In some other kind of atrocities such as bodily injuries, he has to spend lot of money on his treatment. Besides, he loses his earnings during the period of his illness. In addition to this, his wealth is wasted in litigation. Thus, his wealth is minimised which shatters his economic position and he becomes poorer.

1.6 Educational Aspect of Atrocity

Commission of atrocity also affects adversely, the educational progress not only of victim but also of his family members. In case the victim is acquiring education himself then commission of atrocities on him, hampers his education directly by bodily pain, infirmity and financial loss. If his family member are acquiring education, then their education suffers adversely, because inability of the victim to help them due to his bodily injuries, bodily and mental pain, infirmity, loss of mental peace, earnings and financial damages, he suffered in the commission of atrocity.

1.7 Social Aspect of Atrocity

Not only the victim of atrocity but also society at large, particularly, the persons who are castemen of victim do suffer both by mental pain and sense of insecurity. The status and reputation of the victim is lowered in the society. His castemen also feel insulted and humiliated. Their reputation also goes down in the society. This. generates caste feelings, which disintegrate the society and divide them on caste lines.

According to the social structural victimisation theory, the social structure and distribution of power within a given society are to be seen as responsible for the extent of victimisation as well as for its patterns and reasons. The social structure constitutes the framework and the basis of all interactions between victims and offenders, which take place within the society in question and which prove to be failures. If minorities are being pushed away or marginalized in society, their people tend to be victims of social structural and cultural victimisation, which results from customs, tradition, religion and ideology.[12]

Examples of social structural victimisation are the so-called hate crimes, which depict the symbolic status of the crime victim. The victim belongs to a social out-group the members of which symbolise what the respective in-group, to which the offenders belong, do not want to be criminal offences in this context serve the feeling of solidarity and identity within the in-group and, equally, strengthen the in-group's self-esteem.[13]

According to the victimisation model, fear of crime originates from first and second hand experience with criminal victimisation.[14] Personal conversations with victims of violent acts are said to be the reason for the spread of fear of crime. Some expert, however, contest that victimisation leads to a greater fear of crime, since it can just as well produce a better understanding .of crime and thus reduce fear of crime.[15] At any rate, the victims' mental traumas which are caused by acts of violence and sexual offences have a psychic quality that is significantly different from those of the abstract anxiety of criminality and of the concrete, emotional fear of crime of people who have never been victimized.[16]

1.8 Grave Aspect of Atrocity

Police is the protector of law and it is one of the duties of the police to save the SCs from commission of atrocities upon them by others. But if police, instead of saving them from atrocities, commit atrocities on them, then the position of atrocity becomes grave.

A three-month old infant of *dalit* stonemason staying in a makeshift shelter with other like families was allegedly tramped to death by six policemen of the *Uchahar* police station in Rae Bareli.

They also severely beat up a number of stonemasons at local Railway Station during a search operation to apprehend the kidnappers of a child. The SHO in a fit of rage trampled the infant underfoot. The child began bleeding from the mouth, nose and ear. The other policemen followed the SHO and turned the rage at child who died on the spot.[17]

Mangolpuri police on charge of stabbing a head constable picked up a *Harijan* youth. He died in the police lock-up. His mother alleged that the policemen killed him, when she could not fulfil their money demand. The autopsy report found 29 external injuries on his body which, barring two, were inflicted during custody.[18]

In *Morena* Jail of Madhya Pradesh, two SC persons were victimised with the connivance of Jail staff. They were beaten mercilessly and unnatural offence and sodomy was committed with them. They were made to lick penis of co-prisoners.[19]

A police officer raped a daughter of SC man in his presence and he died with shame committing suicide, as he could not bear this inhuman act.[20]

A co-probationer humiliated a young IPS probationer by calling him a '*chamar*'. He lost his job as he was discharged from service.[21]

Police in Mumbai shot dead 11 and injured 27 SC persons in police firing.[22]

It is said that Police has become a tool in the hands of unscrupulous, self-seeking politicians.[23]

SHO of a local Delhi Police Station and the former councillor of the area allegedly called a SC doctor a '*Chamar*'. Instead of taking action against councillor, the SHO berated him and repeatedly called the doctor an 'untouchable'.[24]

Police also commit atrocities on the SCs by implicating them in false criminal cases.[25] These instances show that police sometimes by their acts of commission and sometimes by implicating SCs in false criminal cases commit atrocities on them.

It is disgusting that the protectors of law, who are entrusted with the duty to save and safeguard SCs commit atrocities on them.

B. CAUSES OF ATROCITIES

1.9 Caste System, Endogamy and Caste Hatred

One of the main factors for commission of atrocity is caste, and caste system.[26] Dr. B.R. Ambedkar was of the view that "caste has ruined the Hindus * * * the reorganisation of the Hindu society on the basis of *chaturvarna* is impossible because the *Varna Vyavastha* is like a leaky pot or like a man running at the nose. It is incapable of sustaining itself by its own virtue and has an inherent tendency to degenerate into a caste system unless there is a legal sanction behind it which can be enforced against everyone trespassing his *Varna*".[27] The massacre by the *Ranvir Sena* on another group of *Dalits*, near *Haibaspur* village within a few kilometres from Patna, along with the murder of four others in adjoining *Bhojpur* and *Garhwa* Districts, is a painful reminder of the grim reality that today Bihar is in the grip of a virtual class war.[28] Numerous government and non-government reports have from time to time indicated that the weaker sections of our people still suffer from untouchability and other forms of social discrimination based on the caste system.[29]

As discussed in previous chapter, caste gives us endogamy, *i.e.*, a system of marriage within caste and system of no inter-dining. These two factors make the caste system rigid which help in perpetuation of caste system. Ultimately, various types of caste disabilities, namely no twice born ceremony, *i.e. Upanayana,* no temple entry, no education, ex-communication, social boycott, caste hatred, no right over water and property, originated from the caste system. Outcaste group, *i.e.*, *Sudras* and Untouchables have suffered from these caste disabilities. Disability of no twice born ceremony, *i.e., Upanayana* combined with no right of temple entry had and is resulted into religious backwardness of *Sudras* and Untouchables, now known as SCs and STs. Disability of providing no education coupled with any right of temple entry has resulted into illiteracy of these persons. Consequently, they became ignorant and educationally backward. A disability of ex-communication, social boycott caste hatred and no right over water has resulted into practices of untouchability. Consequently, social backwardness and cultural backwardness flow from it. Disability of no right of property has resulted into poverty which made these persons economically dependent upon other and ultimately this resulted into economic backwardness.

If all these are combined into one, then we will find that these persons became religiously, educationally, socially, culturally and economically backward. Atrocity is the product/outcome of all these backwardness. If atrocity is combined with lack of political will and demand of statutory right by SCs, then it results into aggravated form of atrocities on the SCs by others. Diagram No. 1 depicts the co-relation between the caste and atrocity on SCs.

As shown in the Diagram No. 1, caste has originated caste system, endogamy and caste hatred. Caste is not just a social institution. Caste is not merely a political form nor is it a religious phenomenon only. Caste is basically an economic structure. It is basically the economic plinth and spine of social edifice. Caste system though primarily an economic structure of Hindu Society, yet it is definitely a religious organ. It has social characteristics as well as in-built political directives. Indeed, the caste system is some sort of, we may say, a four in one, a religious, political, social and economic structure. Yet, caste is distinctly and primarily an economic structure.[30]

The caste system prevents common activity and by preventing it, it has prevented the Hindus from becoming a society with unified life and a consciousness of its own being.[31]

As discussed in the previous chapter, caste system, endogamy and caste hatred is product of the caste. These have divided and disintegrated the Indian society. People of higher castes started looking down upon the people of lower castes resulting into caste vindictiveness and caste hatred encouraging the people of one caste to commit atrocity on the people of other caste. It was found one of the motive even for committing murders.[32] Various committees on the welfare of scheduled castes and scheduled tribes, were of the view that caste system, and caste hatred were the main reasons for commission of atrocities on SCs.[33]

1.10 Causes of Atrocities : Untouchability

Practice of untouchability has its root in caste system. Although

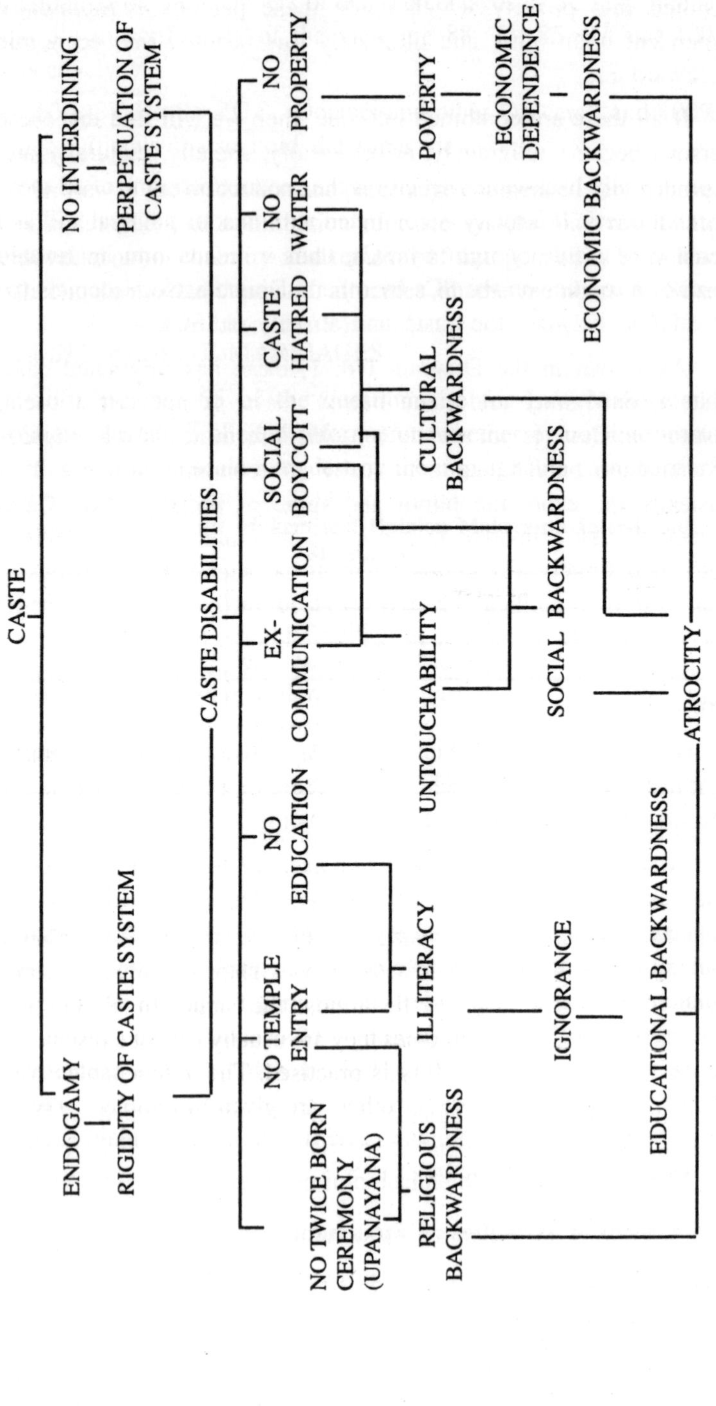
CASTE
ENDOGAMY
NO INTERDINING
RIGIDITY OF CASTE SYSTEM
PERPETUATION OF CASTE SYSTEM
CASTE DISABILITIES
NO TWICE BORN CEREMONY (UPANAYANA)
NO TEMPLE ENTRY
NO EDUCATION
EX-COMMUNICATION
SOCIAL BOYCOTT
CASTE HATRED
NO WATER
NO PROPERTY
RELIGIOUS BACKWARDNESS
ILLITERACY
UNTOUCHABILITY
CULTURAL BACKWARDNESS
POVERTY
IGNORANCE
SOCIAL BACKWARDNESS
ECONOMIC DEPENDENCE
EDUCATIONAL BACKWARDNESS
ATROCITY
ECONOMIC BACKWARDNESS

DIAGRAM NO. 1

untouchability stands abolished by article 17 of the Constitution of India and its practice in any form is forbidden, yet this obnoxious practice is still prevalent in nearly all parts of the country in its overt or covert form.[34] The practice of untouchability pushed the SCs down to the lowest ladder in the caste hierarchy.[35] "The system of untouchability is a gold mine to the Hindus. In it the 240 millions of Hindus have 60 millions of Untouchables to serve as their retinue to enable the Hindus to maintain pomp and ceremony and to cultivate a feeling of pride and dignity befitting a master class, which cannot be fostered and sustained unless there is beneath it a servile class to look down upon. In it, the 240 millions of Hindus have 60 millions of untouchables to be used as forced labourer ***. In it, 240 millions of Hindus have 60 millions of untouchables to do the dirty work of scavengers and sweepers which the Hindu is debarred by his religion to do and which must be done by non-Hindus who could be no others than untouchables. In it, the 240 millions of Hindus have 60 millions of Untouchables who can be used as shock-absorbers in slumps a dead-weights in booms, for in slumps it is the Untouchable who is fired first and the Hindu is fired last and in booms the Hindu is employed first and the Untouchable is employed last.[36] Untouchability is not only a religious system but also an "economic system which is worse than slavery,"[37] which gave rise to graded inequalities among the people. In every matter lower castes segregated from the higher ones. The Untouchables and other so called impure classes who formed the nethermost layers of the caste ridden Hindu society were further debarred from various rights which were essential for the advancement of a man.[38]

In rural India, the *Dalits* are still treated as untouchables. They continue to live separately from the village. Their relationship with the caste Hindus remains to be almost the same. In all public functions, festivals and ceremonies they are usually kept at a distance. Even in tea stalls untouchability is practised. The untouchables are given tea in mud cups, whereas others are given in tumblers. They are made to sit in corner, away from those of other castes. Furthermore, the converted *Harijan Christians* also suffer many humiliations just as their ex-counterpart. Even the *Neo-Buddhists* (converted *Harijan Buddhists)* also could not experience much desired change in this regard.[39] They have retained their identity as a subordinated people within Indian society and their condition is for in severe than merely being bottom of an inevitable hierarchy.[40]

1.11 Causes of Atrocities : Illiteracy

Due to inhibition of caste, prejudice and untouchability and other kinds of social disabilities, which have already been discussed herein before, the SCs were not allowed to get even glimpse of education in the pre-independence period. This has resulted into educational inequality and educational backwardness of the Scheduled Caste. Till recently most of the parents of Scheduled Caste and Scheduled Tribe boys and girls had no interest in sending them to school. In rural areas it is true with girls as the parents have to work on the farms of landlords, and the girls have to look after the domestic matters.[41]

In the year 1931 the rate of literacy of Scheduled Castes was as low as 1.9 per cent. It rose to 0.7 per cent in the year 1951, 14.67 in the year 1971, 21.38 per cent in the year 1981.[42] The SCs are still far behind the general population in educational accomplishments.[43]

The denial of education to the Scheduled Castes has resulted into illiteracy. Due to illiteracy, ignorance crippled into them and they became educationally backward and dependent on others which made them vulnerable to the atrocities. Mahatama Jotirao Phooley, nicely narrated corelation of illiteracy and atrocities in following lines:

For want of education, their intellect deteriorated ;
For want of intellect, their morality decayed ;
For want of morality, their progress stopped ;
All their sorrows sprang from illiteracy.[44]

1.12 Causes of Atrocities : Poverty, Economic Dependence or Backwardness

Most of the SCs are poor. The SCs and STs constitute the bulk of the poorest sections of the population.[45] Majority of them are without land or other productive assets. The poverty of SCs arises predominantly from their positions in the productive process. Their main occupation is agriculture on a seasonal basis. So, most of them are dependent, in some way or other, on agriculture.[46] The incidence of poverty is higher in rural than urban areas. Vast numbers of them live in bonded conditions, which varied only marginally from the status of slavery. They are unfree in the sense that they lacked the right as well as the practical power to leave the family for whom they worked and to whom they were perpetually indebted.[47] Minimum wages are not paid to them. So, tension and bitterness is created on account of non-payment or underpayment of minimum wages prescribed by the State Government. This tension and bitterness leads to commission of atrocities on the SCs.[48]

A local Member of Legislative Assembly engaged a SC woman. She was working under the condition of bondage. She asked her employer to pay a little more wages. She was mercilessly beaten up and thrown out with severe injuries.[49] There are innumerable like instances in our country.

The SCs agricultural workers are occupationally vulnerable to exploitation.[50] Mainly because of their low economic status, members of SCs are often subjected to atrocities.[51]

It is, therefore, believed that poverty, economic dependence or backwardness of SCs is other main reasons for commission of atrocities on them.

1.13 Causes of Atrocities : Self-Assertion by the Scheduled Castes

Awakening of the SCs about their rights and protection is another main reason for commission of atrocities on them. This awakening, to some extent, taught SCs to live with human dignity. The two crucial elements for a life with dignity are personal liberty and adequate means of livelihood.[52] The honour and dignity of a person is dependent on his work, his right over means of productions and his right to manage the system.[53] The SCs started claiming their legal rights. This resulted into land disputes, demand of minimum wages, freedom from bondage of bonded labour and demand of political rights, *etc.* This developed animosity between dominant class and SCs and ultimately resulted into commission of atrocities on SCs.[54] Unresolved land disputes relating to allotment of government land or distributions of surplus land to the landless SCs, tension and bitterness created on account of non-payment or under payment of minimum wages prescribed by State governments and resentment against manifestation of awareness amongst the SCs about their rights and privileges as enshrined in the Constitution and various legislative and executive measures are considered main reasons for commission of atrocities on SCs.[55] Resisting forced and bonded labour was also considered as one of the reasons of commission of atrocities on SCs.[56]

1.14 Causes of Atrocities : Ignorance of Law and Lack of Political Will

Majorities of persons of SCs are illiterates and consequently ignorant about present law enacted for their welfare. Like is the position of persons who usually commit atrocities on SCs. They are also ignorant about the provisions of the Act. Their ignorance further leads to commission of atrocities on SCs. Due to ignorance the victims of atrocities in most cases do not lodge police report. Sometimes, they feel that no useful purpose would be served in reporting of case to the police as offenders are generally acquitted due to low rate of conviction for so many reasons.

Lack of political will is also considered as one of the reasons for commission of atrocities on SCs. The commissioners, commissions and National Commissions for SCs & STs have made several recommendations to prevent atrocities on SCs, but most of the recommendations were never acted upon.[57] Although the Act was enacted in the year 1989 and was notified on 30th January, 1990 yet the Rules were made and notified only in the year 1995. This delay is considered, as lack of political will to enforce the Act vigorously. Sec. 21(4) casts a duty on the Central Government to place on the table of each House of Parliament, every year, a report on the measures taken by itself and by the State governments in pursuance of provisions of this section. The Central Government has not placed any separate report as prescribed under the section. Only annual common reports by concerned Ministry of the Government were laid on the Parliament.[58]

C. SCHEDULED CASTE

1.15 Legal Connotation of the Term 'Scheduled Caste'

The term 'scheduled caste' is defined in clause (db) of Sec. 2 of the Protection of Civil Rights Act, 1955.

The extract of the Clause is as under:

"2. *Definitions* : In this Act, unless the context otherwise requires,—

***

(db) "Scheduled Castes" has the meaning assigned to it in Clause (24) of Article 366 of the Constitution;

***."

Clause (e) of Sec. 2 of the Scheduled Castes and the Scheduled Tribes (Prevention of Atrocities) Act, 1989 also defines the term 'Scheduled Caste' alike. The extract of the clause is as under:

"2. *Definition.*—(1) In this Act, unless the context otherwise requires.

***

(c) "Scheduled Castes and Scheduled Tribes" shall have the meanings assigned to them respectively under Clause (24) and Clause (25) of Article 366 of the Constitution;

*** "

Clause (24) of Article 366 of the Constitution of India defines the term Scheduled Caste as under :

"*Scheduled Castes*" means such castes, races or tribes or parts of or groups within such castes, races or tribes as are deemed under article 341 to be Scheduled Castes for the purposes of the Constitution."

The text of article 341 of the Constitution of India is as under :

"341. *Scheduled Castes.*—(1) The President may with respect to any State or Union Territory, and where it is a State (***) after consultation with the Governor (* * *) thereof, by public notification, specify the castes, races or tribes or parts of or groups within castes, races or tribes which shall for the purposes of this Constitution be deemed to be Scheduled Castes in relation to that State or Union Territory, as the case may be.

(2) Parliament may by law include in or exclude from the list of Scheduled Castes specified in a notification issued under Clause (1) any caste, race or tribe or part of or group within any caste, race or tribe, but save as aforesaid a notification issued under the said clause shall not be varied by any subsequent notification."

1.16 Notification of Presidential Order

Language used in Art. 341 is self-explanatory to the effect that castes, races or tribes or groups within castes, races or tribes notified according to the Presidential Order in accordance with the provisions in Art. 341(1) can only be regarded as SCs and caste not finding place in the list notified as per the Presidential Order cannot be regarded as a SC. Any modification in that list by addition and deletion can only be made by following the provisions of law in Art. 341(2).[59]

This raises a question, What is Caste ? A 'caste', as pointed out by the Madras High Court in *Cooppoosami Chetty* Vs. *Duraisami Chetty.*[60] "is a voluntary association of persons for certain purposes. It is a well defined yet fluctuating group of persons governed by their own rules and regulations for certain internal purposes". How castes are formed depends not only on community of religion, but also on community of functions.[61] A change in the occupation sometimes creates a new caste. A common occupation sometimes combines members of different castes into a distinct body that become a new caste. Migration of masses to another place sometimes gives birth to a new caste.[62]

It is thus clear that Scheduled Castes are no independent caste in the Hindu fold but it is an mosaic of castes, races, groups, tribes, communities or parts thereof found on investigation to be the lowest and need of massive State aid and notified as such by President.[63]

Therefore, in order to determine, whether or not a particular caste is a Scheduled Caste within the meaning of Article 341, one has to look at the public notification issued by the President in that behalf.[64]

One Shri Bhaiya Lal, *Dohar* by caste had contested election held in February, 1962 from a reserved seat of Bersaia constituency in the district of Sehore in Madhya Pradesh and he was declared elected. But his election was challenged on the ground that *Dohar* caste was not sub-caste of *Chamar* and he was not a Scheduled Caste in the public notification issued by President under Art. 341 of the Constitution of India. Agreeing with this contention, Election Tribunal declared his election invalid. High Court also upheld this.

He went in appeal before Supreme Court. The Supreme Court upheld decisions of election Tribunal and High Court and also held that the President can specify castes, races or tribes or parts thereof in relation not only to the entire State, but in relation to part of the State where he is satisfied that the examination of the social and educational backwardness of the race, caste or tribe justifies such specification.[65]

1.17 Restrictions on Subsequent Notification

Clause (2) of Art. 341 of the Constitution of India clearly provides that the caste, race or tribe cannot be altered by subsequent notification of the President, except the law made by Parliament in this regard. Thus, only the Parliament by law can include or exclude from the initial list of Scheduled Castes specified in a notification[66] issued by the President under clause (1) of Article 341 of the Constitution of India.

Whether or not a caste, race or tribe can be changed by subsequent notification came for adjudication before Madhya Pradesh High Court in case of *Naunihal Singh* Vs. *Kishori Lal.*[67] In the Constitution (Scheduled Caste) Order, *1950 Chamar,* throughout the State of Madhya Pradesh was notified as a Scheduled Caste. That Order was modified by the Scheduled Castes and Scheduled Tribes List (Modification) Order, 1956, issued under Sec. 41 of the States Reorganisation Act, *1956. Chamar* was mentioned in the modification Order as Scheduled Caste in the district of Hoshangabad in M.P. On 1.11.56, *Narsimhapur,* was constituted into a separate district. Prior to that date, it formed a tahsil in the Hoshangabad district. The respondent, who was a *Chamar* and resided at *Narsimhapur,* contested the election held after reorganisation for the reserved seat in a double member constituency and was elected. His election was challenged on the ground that since Hoshangabad district did not, on that date, include in the territory comprised the district of *Narsimhapur,* the respondent could not be deemed to be a member of the Scheduled Caste.[68]

The High Court of Madhya Pradesh held that under Art. 341 (2) of the Constitution of India, without any law made by Parliament, the original Scheduled Castes Order, 1950, specifying *Chamar* as a Scheduled Caste in the entire area of Madhya Pradesh, could not be varied by any subsequent notification. No such law except the States Reorganisation Act, had been made by Parliament.

It was further held that the power under Sec. 41 of the States Reorganisation Act, extended only to make such modification in the original Scheduled Castes Order, as was compatible with the territorial changes and formation of new States. That Power, therefore, did not authorise the President to exclude any person from the category of a Scheduled Caste, who enjoyed that status under the original Scheduled Castes Order. Accordingly, the respondent who was a member of a Scheduled Caste under that Order, could not be deprived of his status by the subsequent notification.[69]

Thus the position of law is very clear that the castes, races or tribes or groups within the castes, races or tribes which have been notified as per the Presidential Order made under Art. 341(1) has to be accepted on its face value and the courts or any other authority, except the President of India and the Parliament, has no jurisdiction to add or delete from that list.[70]

In case of *Narayan Sahoo* Vs. *State,*[71] a question which has been raised before Orissa High Court for decision is as to whether a caste not notified as Scheduled Caste in the Presidential Order and Notification under Art. 341 of the Constitution can be regarded as Scheduled Caste being described in that manner in District Gazetteer. The court discussed various cases[72] and held that with the above settled position of law and on making a reflection of facts, it appears that in the Notification made under the Presidential Order, *i.e.*, the Constitution (Scheduled Castes) Order, 1950 (as amended from State of Orissa). *'Katia'* appears as a Scheduled Caste *vide* Serial No. 44 in that list. *'Khatia'* caste is not there in that list. Hence, if at all *'Khatia'* caste has been defined as a Scheduled Caste in the Puri District Gazetteer, that being not a part or parcel of the Presidential Order made under Art. 341, such description, if any, in that Gazetteer does not qualify *'Khatia'* as a Scheduled Caste under Arts. 341 and 366 of the Constitution.[73]

In exercise of the power conferred by Clause (1) of Art. 341 of the Constitution of India, the President made order in this respect, which was notified and called as the Constitution (Scheduled Castes) Order, 1950, which was amended from time to time. Its Clause (3) contemplates that a person who professes a religion other than the Hindu or the Sikh or the Buddhist cannot be a member of a Scheduled Caste.[74]

In case of *N. W. Karwadi* Vs. *P.H. Shambharkar and another,*[75] it was held that the meaning of the phrase "professes a religion" in paragraph 3 of the Constitution (Scheduled Caste) Order, 1950 is "to enter publicly into a religious state." The word "professes" was used particularly for entering into any religious order. In order to attract the provisions of this paragraph, it has to be established that the person concerned has publicly entered a religion different from the Hindu or the Sikh religion. Mere declaration falling short of this, would not be sufficient.[76]

1.18 Importance, Meaning and Effect of the Phrase "In Relation to that State"

The Orissa High Court in case of *K. Appa Rao* Vs. *Director of Posts and Telegraphs, Orissa,*[77] the Punjab High Court in case of *V.B. Singh* Vs. *State of Punjab,*[78] and Bombay High Court in *M.S. Mahalhi* Vs. *Commissioner Nagpur Division,*[79] held that the phrase "in relation to that State" read with phrase "for the purpose of this Constitution in Arts. 341 and 342 of the Constitution, makes it clear that SCs and STs status is provincial in character and not all India. But the Gujarat High Court in case of *Gujarat Dalit and C.C. Rights Pratipadan Samithi* Vs. *Union of India*[80] held that phrase "in relation to that State" means in connection with or in regard to that State and not that a person belonging to SC and ST only in that State or area of the State in relation to which his caste has been specified as such but all over India.

The Supreme Court of India in cases of *Marrichandra* Vs. *Dean, S.G.S., Medical College,*[81] and *Action Committee on issue* of *Caste Certificates to Scheduled Castes and Scheduled Tribes in State of Maharashtra and another* Vs. *Union of India and others,*[82] has settled the divergent views propounded by Orissa, Punjab and Bombay High Courts on the one hand and Gujarat High Court on the other and held that the phrase "in relation to that State" means that status of the Scheduled Castes and Scheduled Tribes is provincial in character and not all India.

Thus, SCs and STs of one State cannot be regarded as such in other State of the Union for the purpose of constitutional entitlements except in the State where that caste is included in Scheduled Castes or Scheduled Tribes.

1.19 Conversion of Scheduled Caste

Sometimes, for various reasons members of SCs either convert them to another religion such as Christianity or Islam or start professing other religious sect, such as *Buddhism, Arya Samaj, Mahanubhava Panth.* This may affect their social and legal status. Let us see the effect of their conversion.

1.20 The Effect of Conversion to Buddhism

Whether or not a *Buddhist* after conversion can be treated as a member of Scheduled Caste, came for consideration before Bombay High Court in case *Ku. Mangala Parashram Kelkar and others* Vs. *State of Maharashtra.*[83] The brief facts of the case were that on 4th March, 1977 at about 7 P.M. at village *Bhalavali* in Ratnagiri district there was a palanquin procession. After its completion, several villagers including complainant gathered in front of the house of Parashram Kelkar. The fathers of some accused persons witness the play before the palanquin. Soon thereafter, Mangala and Nandu Kumar accused came out of the house and insulted the complainant and others of his community telling them that they had become Buddhists and stopped playing bands, had instead started dancing before and watering the palanquin and they should, therefore, leave. On 10th March, 1977 matter was reported to the Police who ultimately filed challan against accused. Accused were prosecuted under Sec. 7 of the PCR, Act and trial magistrate convicted the accused. In appeal, Sessions Judge held that provision of Sec. 7 of PCR, Act could not apply as the complainants were not members of Scheduled Caste but persons professing *Buddhism.* The High Court upheld this view and observed that *Buddhists* or any one, who is professing *Buddhism,* does not belong to Scheduled Caste within the meaning of the PCR, Act. Consequently, the provision of the Protection of Civil Rights Act, 1955 would not apply to one who is professing *Buddhism.*

1.21 The Position of Buddhists after Amendment

Consequent upon the inclusion of the term *"the Buddhist"* in paragraph 3 of the Constitution (Scheduled Castes) Order, 1950 by the Constitution (Scheduled Castes) Order (Amendment) Act, 1990[84] after the words "the Hindu and the Sikh" the conversion by a member of Scheduled Caste into Buddhism would not alter his status in respect of his caste. Thus, after coming into force of this Amendment Act, a person professing Buddhism can be a member of Scheduled Castes. Consequently, all those persons, who converted into *Buddhism* from any caste, recognised as Scheduled Caste will continue to be treated as a member of Scheduled Caste for the purpose of receiving and giving benefits or favoured treatment to them.[85]

1.22 The Effect of Conversion to Arya Samaj

It is a matter of common knowledge that *Arya Samaj* is not a religion like Christianity or Islam different from the Hindu religion. Therefore, if a member of Scheduled Caste adopts *Arya Samaj* belief, he will continue to be a member of Scheduled Caste.

The Mysore High Court in case of *Shyamsunder* Vs. *Shankara Deo*[86] decided this controversy. The question in that case before the court was whether Shankara Deo who was elected from the reserved seat had by becoming a member of Arya Samaj Organisation ceased to be a member of Scheduled Caste known as Samgar? The court observed:[87]

> "It is, therefore, plain that Arya Samaj unlike Christianity or Islam, is not a new religion entirely distinct from Hinduism and that the mere profession of Arya Samajism by a person does not make him cease to be a Hindu and cannot have the effect of excluding him from Hinduism although he was born in it. It is equally clear that such a person never becomes separated from the religious communion in which he was born."

The court further held that the evidence in the case was sufficient to come to the conclusion that by reason of Shankara Deo having become a member of the *Arya Samaj,* he did not cease to belong to the *Samgar* caste in which he was born.[88]

1.23 The Effect of Conversion to Mahanubhava Panth

As discussed above the conversion of Scheduled Caste into *Mahanubhava Panth* by professing the same will not change his caste. He will continue to be treated as member of Scheduled Caste for all practical purposes in respect to favoured treatment to him by special legislation.

A question, whether a SC on conversion of the tenets of the *Mahanubhava Panth,* has ceased to be a member of Scheduled Castes, has arisen before the Supreme Court in case of *Chatturbhuj Vithaldas* Vs. *Moreshwar Parashram?*[89] In this case the Supreme Court has considered the status of a person belonging to the *Mahar* caste, who had converted into *Mahanubhava Panth.* It was held that whatever the views of the founder of this seat may have been about caste, it was evident that there had been no right adherence to them among his followers in later years. The court, therefore, did not determine whether the *Mahanubhava* tenets encouraged repudiation of caste only as a desirable ideal or made it a fundamental of the faith, because it was evident that present day *Mahanubhava* was admitted to their fold, persons who elect to retain their fold or old caste customs. It was on this basis that the court held that it was easy for the old caste to regard the converts as one of themselves despite the conversion which for all practical purposes was only ideological and involved no change of status. Therefore, conversion to *Mahanubhava Panth* does not alter the status or caste of the Scheduled Caste.

1.24 The Effect of Conversion to Christianity

In case a member of the Scheduled Caste converts into any religion other than *Sikh or Buddhist,* he will cease to be a member of a Scheduled Caste. Therefore, if a member of Scheduled Caste converts into Christianity, the effect would be that he would cease to be a member of Scheduled Caste.

The Supreme Court had an occasion to consider and adjudicate this issue in case of *S. Rajagopal* Vs. *C.M. Arumugam and others*[90] The facts of the case were that S. Rajagopal and C.M. Arumugam and others filed nomination papers for election to the Legislative Assembly of the State of Mysore for the General Elections held in 1967 in respect of reserved seat of Kolar Gold fields. C.M.

Arumugam raised an objection against the nomination of S. Rajagopal on the ground that nomination was in respect of a seat reserved for a member of a Scheduled Caste and S. Rajagopal was not a member of Scheduled Caste as he had converted himself as a Christian some time in the year 1949.

The Returning Officer rejected the objection. Polling took place in February, 1967. S. Rajagopal was declared elected. C.M. Arumugam filed election petition challenging the validity of election of S. Rajagopal on the same ground. A question arose before High Court of Mysore and Supreme Court whether S. Rajagopal, on the date of election was an Indian Christian by conversion and not a member of the Scheduled Caste belonging to *Adi Dravida* Caste? It was pleaded by S. Rajagopal that he never became a convert to Christianity and that in any case even if it be held that he had once become a Christian in the year 1949, he was professing the Hindu religion at the relevant time in the year 1967.

The Supreme Court agreed with the finding of the High Court on the point that when appellant embraced Christianity in 1949, he lost the membership of the *Adi Dravida* Hindu caste. It was further observed :[91]

> "The Christian religion does not recognise any caste classifications. All Christians are treated as equals and there is no distinction between one Christian and another of the type that is recognised between members of different castes belonging to Hindu religion. In fact, caste system prevails only amongst Hindus or possibly in some religions closely allied to the Hindu religion like Sikhism. Christianity is prevalent not only in India, but almost all over the world and nowhere does Christianity recognise caste division. The tenets of Christianity militate against persons professing Christian faith being divided or discriminated on the basis of any such classification as the caste system. It must, therefore, be held that, when the appellant got converted to Christianity in 1949, he ceased to belong to be Adi Dravida Caste."

1.25 The Effect of Reconversion to Hinduism

In case a member of Scheduled Caste, who had converted to any other religion, reconverts to the Hinduism, then he again becomes the member of that caste of Scheduled Caste from which he had converted into other religion, if the member of that caste accepted him as a member. Like situation arose before the Supreme Court in case *C.M. Arumugam* Vs. *S. Rajagopal.*[92] The facts of the case were that C.M. Arumugam and S. Rajagopal filed their nominations for the General Election which took place in the year 1972, to the Mysore Legislative Assembly in respect of the reserved seat of Kolar Gold Fields Constituency. The nomination of S. Rajagopal was objected by C.M. Arumugam on the ground that he had converted himself to Christianity and he had ceased to be a member of *Adi Dravida* caste. S. Rajagopal pleaded that he never converted to Christianity and that in an event if it was held[93] that he had become a Christian, he had reconverted to Hinduism since long and he was accepted by the members of the *Adi Dravida* caste as belong to him and was, therefore, an *Adi Dravida* professing Hindu religion at the material date.

The Returning Officer upheld the objection and rejected the nomination of S. Rajagopal taking the view that on conversion to Christianity S. Rajagopal had ceased to be an *Adi Dravida* and, therefore, on reconversion, he could not claim the benefit of the Constitution (Scheduled Castes) Order, 1950. Consequently, S. Rajagopal could not contest the election and on having obtained the highest number of votes, C.M. Arumugam was declared elected.[94]

Aggrieved by this, S. Rajagopal filed election petition before the High Court of Mysore challenging the validity of election of C.M. Arumugam. The High Court of Mysore observed:[95]

> "It is settled law that reconversion to Hinduism does not require any formal ceremony or rituals or expiatory ceremonies, that a reconvert to Hinduism can revert to his original Hindu caste on acceptance by the members of that caste and that the quantum and degree of proof of acceptance depends on the facts and circumstances of each case, according to the established customs prevalent in a particular locality amongst the caste there."

The High Court held that the nomination of S. Rajagopal was improperly rejected and accordingly set aside the election.

The Supreme Court, while discussing various old cases,[96] on the point observed that these cases showed that on reconversion to Hinduism a person can once again become a member of the caste in which he was born and to which he belonged before conversion to another religion, if the members of that caste accepted him as a member. It was held that if a person who had embraced another religion could be reconverted to Hinduism, there is no rational principle why he should not be able to come back to his caste if the other members of the caste were prepared to re-admit him as a member.[97] The object and purpose of the Constitution (Scheduled Castes) Order, 1950 would be advanced rather than retarded by taking the view that "on reconversion to Hinduism, a person can once again become a member of the Scheduled Caste to which he belonged prior to his conversion and High Court, therefore, right in coming to the conclusion that at the material time S. Rajagopal belonged to the *Adi Dravida* so as to fall within the category of Scheduled Castes under Paragraph-2 of the Constitution (Scheduled Caste) Order, 1950."[98]

1.26 The Effect of Marriage with Non-Scheduled Caste and Non-Scheduled Tribe Person

The marriage of a SC person with non-SC person will not change his caste. The question, whether a lady marrying a SC, ST or OBC citizen, or one transplanted by adoption or any other voluntary act, *ipso facto*, becomes entitled to claim reservation under Article 15(4) or 16(4), as the case may be arose before the S.C. in case *Vasamma Paul* Vs. *Cochin University and others.*[99] The Apex Court observed that the advancement of socially and educationally backward class citizens cannot be defeated by including candidates by allowance or any other mode of joining the community and it would tantamount to making mockery of the constitutional exercise of identification of socially and educationally backward class of citizens. Therefore, it was held that "the persons who by birth belong to Scheduled Castes, Scheduled Tribes or Backward Classes alone are entitled to the benefit of Arts. 15(4) and 16(4) of the Constitution of India. By marriage, adoption or any other device, *viz.* by procuring false social status certificates, they are not eligible to avail of protective discrimination for appointment to an office or to a post under the State or admission in educational institution."[100]

In case of *Kaliya Perumal* Vs. *State*[101] it was argued on behalf of the petitioner before Madras High Court that complainant who was member of SC ceased to be a member of SC on her marriage with his relative who belong to *Yadhava* community and sought quashing of a FIR, registered against him U/s 3(l)(x) of the Act as the provisions of the Act cannot be invoked in her favour while discussing and relying on *Vasamma Paul* Vs. *Cochin University and others,*[102] the Court rejected the plea and held that:

> "such marriage does not create a conversion of the caste in the same way,*** Harijan lady who has suffered all wrong from her birth, the handicap, disadvantages and restrictions to which the members of SCs community were subjected to, married a member of the backward class community, she cannot be said to have acquired the backward class status by losing her birth right of reservation**."[103]

It is, therefore, concluded that status of Scheduled Castes and Scheduled Tribes can only be acquired by birth. Neither marriage nor adoption can confer or debar a member or SCs or STs for this status.

Notes and References

1. *See*, Statement of objects and reasons of the Scheduled Castes and the Scheduled Tribes (Prevention of Atrocities) Act, 1989 (No. 33 of 1989).
2. *See*, Fifth Report of C.F. S.C. & S.T. at 111.
3. *See*, Eighth Report of C.F. S.C. & S.T. at 35.
4. *See*, Sixth Report of C.F. S.C. & S.T. at 92.
5. *Id.*
6. *See*, Baxi, Upendra, UNTOUCHABILITY: CONSTITUTION, LAW AND PLAN, *Law and Poverty*, 1973 at 183.
7. *Supra*, note 6.
8. *Ibid.* at 183.
9. *Id.*
10. Schneider, Hans Joachim, The Present Situation of Victimology in the World, Especially in the United States and Germany, *Eurocriminology*, Vol. 10, 1996 at 21; *Indian Journal of Criminology*, Vol. 24 (1 & 2) January & July 1996 at 24.
11. *Supra*, note 10 at 25.
12. *Ibid.* at 26.
13. *Ibid.* at 26 and 27.
14. *See*, Skogan, W.G. / Maxfield, M.G. (1981) : Coping with Crime, Beverly Hills, London : Sage.

15. Fattah, E.A. (1993) : Research on Fear of Crime: Some Common conceptual and Measurement Problems. (In :) W. Bilsky/C. Pfeiffer/P. Wetzels (eds.), *Fear of Crime and Criminal Victimisation,* at 45-70, Stuttgart: Enke.
16. *Supra,* note 10 at 32.
17. News item, "Cops on Kidnappers trail trample kid to death", *The Hindustan Times,* May 2, 1997 at 1, C-1.
18. Banerjee, Nandini, G., "In custody of DEATH", *The Hindustan Times,* March 29, 1995, at 1.
19. Singh, Narender Kumar, "Sabak Sikhane Ka Vahsi Tarika", *India Today,* August 15, 1994 at 56.
20. Sethi, Lokpal, "Raped in Custody, father kills self", *The Hindustan Times,* December 20, 1994 at 1, C-1.
21. Bhatnagar, Ramesh, "SC denies leniency to IPS probationer", *The Times of India,* April 29, 1991 at 3, C-7.
22. News item, "Police open fire: 11 Killed", *The Hindustan Times,* July 12, 1997, at 1, C-1.
23. Singh, Prakash, "Police and the question of accountability", *The Hindustan Time,* February 5, 1996 at Editorial.
24. News items, "Untouchable takes SHO to High Court", *The Hindustan Times,* January 27, 1997.
25. *See,* Committee on the Welfare of Scheduled Castes and Scheduled Tribes (Tenth Lok Sabha) (1992-93) Twenty-Third Report at 13 ; See, also First Report of N.C. S.C. & S. T. at 104, 130 and 131 ; See, also *Infra,* note 42 at 234.
26. *See,* Crime in India 1994, National Crime Records Bureau, Ministry of Home Affairs, Government of India, New Delhi, at 270. See also Report of National Convention on Socio-Economic & Political Status of the SCs and STs in Contemporary India, Parliamentary Forum of SC & ST, 1992 at 23.
27. Ambedkar, B.R., *Annihilation of Caste,* Appendix-II : A reply to the Mahatma, Jalandhar, Bheempatrika, 1987 at 144.
28. Editorial, "Bihar's Class War", *The Times of India,* March 28, 1997.
29. Editorial "Raw deal for Dalits", *The Hindustan Times,* February 27, 1991.
30. *See,* Biswas, S.K., "Dr. Ambedkar, Science and Society", *AMBEDKAR AND SOCIAL JUSTICE,* Publication Division, Ministry of Information and Broadcasting, Govt. of India, Vol. I, at 121 & 122.
31. *Supra,* note 2, at 28 ; See, also Reddy, K. Venkata, "B.R. Ambedkar and Beyond", *AMBEDKAR AND SOCIAL JUSTICE,* Publication Division, Ministry of Information and Broadcasting, Govt. of India, Vol. II, at 37.
32. *Supra,* note 26 at 275.
33. *See* Thirty-First Report of Sixth Lok Sabha of Committee on the Welfare of Scheduled Castes and Scheduled Tribes (1978-79) at 11 ; *Infra,* note 35 at 19 ; and *Supra,* note 25 at 7.
34. *Supra,* note 25 at 17.
35. *See,* Committee on the Welfare of Scheduled Castes and Scheduled Tribes (Eighth Lok Sabha) Eleventh Report (1985-86) at 19.

36. *Infra,* note 37 at 23.
37. Baxi, Upendra, "Emancipation as Justice : Babasaheb Ambedkar's Legacy and Vision", *AMBEDKAR AND SOCIAL JUSTICE,* Publication Division, Ministry of Information and Broadcasting, Govt. of India, Vol. 1, at 23; See also, Inaugural oration : *Babasaheb Ambedkar Centenary Celebrations:* University of Madras, 5th December, 1991.
38. Makwana, Yogendra, "Dr. Baba Saheb Ambedkar—A Crusader", *AMBEDKAR AND SOCIAL JUSTICE,* Publication Division, Ministry of Information and Broadcasting, Govt. of India, Vol. I, at 44.
39. Reddy, Dr. B. Krishna, "Anthropological perspectives on the visions of Ambedkar for the Upliftment of Dalits", *AMBEDKAR AND SOCIAL JUSTICE,* Publication Division, Ministry of Information and Broadcasting, Govt. of India, Vol. I, at 73.
40. *See*, Oliver Mendelsohn and Marika Vicziany, "Untouchables" in *The Rights of Subordinated Peoples,* Edited by Oliver Mendelsohn & Upendra Baxi, Delhi Oxford University Press, 1996 at 115.
41. Vakil, A.K., Reservation Policy and Scheduled Castes in India (1985), at 131.
42. *See*, (i) 14th Report of the Committee on the Welfare of Scheduled Castes and Scheduled Tribes (Fourth Lok Sabha), 4, 91 and 92 (1970).
    (ii) Mitra, Ashok, India's Population : Aspect of Quality and Control, Vol. 1, 1978 at 400, 404 and 408.
    (iii) Chaudhari, Buddhadeb (Ed.), *Tribal Development in India,* 395 (1981).
    (iv) Census of India, 1981, Series I at XXVI.
    (v) Goyal, B.R., Educating Harijans, 98 (1981).
43. *Supra*, note 41 at 58.
44. Keer, D., *Mahatama Jotirao, Phooley, The Father of Our Social Revolution,* (1964) at 23.
45. *See*, First Report of N.C. S.C & S.T. at 44.
46. *See*, Twenty-Ninth Report of C.F. S.C. & S.T. at (viii); See, also *Supra*, note 4 at 79.
47. *Ibid* at 86 ; See, also *Supra*, note 2 at 112.
48. *See*, Twenty-Eighth Report of C.F. S.C. & S.T. at 228.
49. *Ibid.* at 234.
50. *See*, First Annual Report at 36.
51. *See*, *Supra* note 4 at 92; See, also *Infra*, note 56 at 24 and *Supra,* note 45 at 145.
52. *See*, *Supra,* note 46 at (iii).
53. *Ibid.* at (v).
54. *Supra,* note 50 at 36 & 37; See, also Second Annual Report at 38.
55. *Supra*, note 48 at 228.
56. *See*, Seventh Report of C.F. S.C. & S.T. at 24 ; See, also Supra, notes 45 at 103, 48 at 39 & 40, 4 at 94 & 95.
57. *See*, Action Taken Memo at 1 to 44 ; See, also *Supra*, notes 2 at 199,

3 at 89, 4 at 123, 45 at 134, 56 at 67, 50 at 35 and Second Annual Report at 38.

58. *See*, Annual Report of Government of India, Ministry of Welfare, New Delhi, 1996-97 ; and Annual Report of the Government of India, Ministry of Social Justice and Empowerment, New Delhi, 1998-99.
59. *Narayan Sahoo* Vs. *State,* 1999 (1) *Crimes* 605 at 607.
60. 1910 ILR 33 Mad. *6 ; 9* Mad. L.J. 714; See, also *Barte Subrayalu* Vs. *Robert Mariadasson* 1987 CR.L.J. 272 at 279 and *Infra,* note 92 at 945.
61. Risley, H. Sir, *People of India,* Quoted in *Infra,* note 92 at 945..
62. *Muthuswami* Vs. *Masilamoni* (1910) ILR 33 Mad. 342 *; See,* also *Infra,* note 92 at 945.
63. *State of Kerala* Vs. *N.M. Thomas,* A.I.R. 1976 S.C. 490 at 534 ; See, also Prasad, Anirudh, *Reservation Policy and Practice in India,* 1991 at 14.
64. *Bhaiya Lal* Vs. *Hari Kishan Singh* A.I.R. 1965 S.C. 1557 at 1559.
65. *Supra*, note 64 at 1560.
66. The Constitution (Scheduled Castes) Order, 1950.
67. A.I.R. 1961 M.P. 84.
68. *Supra*, note 67 at 86 & 87.
69. *Supra*, note 67 at 87.
70. *Supra*, note 59 at 607.
71. *Ibid.* at 605.
72. *Palghat Jilla Thandan Samudhaya Samrakshana Samiti and another* Vs. *State of Kerala and another,* (1994) 1 S. C. C. 359 ; *Neikham Surchandra Singh and others etc.* Vs. *The Representative of "Lios" Kakching, Manipur (a Scheduled Caste Uplift Body) and others,* 1996 (8) Supreme 229 ; *Rama Chandra Sahoo* Vs. *Collector, Mayurbhanj and others*, 82 (1996) C.L.T. 155 ; and *Nityananda Sharma and another* Vs. *State of Bihar*, A.I.R. 1996 SC 782.
73. *Supra*, note 59 at 608.
74. Added by the Constitution (Scheduled Caste) Order (Amendment) Act, 1990.
75. A.I.R. 1958 Bombay 296.
76. *Supra*, note 75 at 297.
77. A.I.R. 1969 Orissa, 220.
78. I.L.R. (1976) P & H 769.
79. A.I.R. 1989 Bom. 138.
80. A.I.R. 1989 Guj. 197.
81. (1990) 3 SCC 130.
82. J.T. 1994 (4) S.C. 423 ; See, also Aslam, Mohammad, "Scheduled Caste : Some Unresolved Problems" 32 *J.I.L.I.* (1990) 110 ; and Reddy, V. Reveendra, "MARRIAGE, CASTE AND RESERVATIONS", A note on *D. Neelima* Vs. *The Dean of P.G. Studies, A.P. Agriculture University, Hyderabad,* A.I.R. 1993 A.P. 229 : A.I.R. 1994, Journal 55.
83. A.I.R. 1979 Bombay 282.
84. This Act No. 15 of 1990 amended the following Acts:—
   (i) The Constitution (Scheduled Castes) Orders, 1950.
   (ii) The Constitution (Scheduled Castes) Union Territories Order, 1951.

(iii) The Constitution (Jammu and Kashmir) Scheduled Castes Order, 1956.

(iv) The Constitution (Dadra and Nagar Haveli) Scheduled Castes Order, 1962.

(v) The Constitution (Pondicherry) Scheduled Castes Order, 1964.

(vi) The Constitution (Sikkim) Scheduled Castes Order, 1978.

85. Consequently following rulings will be inapplicable on a member of Scheduled Caste:

(i) *Punjabrao* Vs. *D.P. Meshrani,* A.I.R. 1965 S.C. 1179.

(ii) *Ku. Mangla Parashram Kelkar and others* Vs. *State of Maharashtra,* A.I.R. 1979 Bombay 282 and the controversy arisen *in Ganpat* Vs. *Presiding Officer and others* A.I.R.1975 S.C. 420 would not arise in future.

86. A.I.R. 1960 Mysore 27.

87. *Ibid.* at 30.

88. *Ibid.* at 33.

89. 1954 S.C.R 817 ; See, also *Infra,* note 91 at 108.

90. A.I.R. 1967 S.C. 101.

91. *Supra*, note 90 at 107.

92. A.I.R. 1976 S.C. 939.

93. *Supra*, note 90.

94. *Supra*, note 92 at 942.

95. *Ibid.* at 943.

96. *Cooppoosami Chatty* Vs. *Duraisami Chetty* (1910) I.L.R. 33 Mad. 66; *Muthusami* Vs. *Masilamgri* (1910) I.L.R 33 Mad. 342 ; *C. Michael* Vs. *S. Venkateswaran,* I.L.R. (1953) Mad. 106 : A.I.R. 1952 Mad. 474 ; *Narasayya* Vs. *Jammana Jogi* (1967) 30 Ele. L.R. 199 (AP) ; K. *Narasimha Reddy* Vs. *G. Bhupathi* (1967) 31 Ele. L.R. 211 (AP) ; *Ganpat* Vs. *Returning Officer* (1975) S.C.C. 589 : A.I.R. 1975 S.C. 420*; Jasani V. Moreshwar* Vs. *Parashram* 1954 S.C.R. 817 : A.I.R. 1954 S.C. 236; *Administrator General of Madras* Vs. *Anandachari* (1886) I.L.R 9 Mad. 466 ; *Gurusami Nadar* Vs. *Irulappa Konar,* A.I.R. 1934 Mad. 630.

97. *Supra*, note 92 at 949.

98. *Ibid.* at 951.

99. A.I.R. 1996 S.C. 1011; 1996 (3) S.C.C. 545.

100. *Ibid.* at 1022.

101. 1998 CRI.L.J. 1467.

102. *Supra*, note 99.

103. *Supra*, note 101 at 1469.

CHAPTER 2

LAW FOR COMBATING ATROCITIES

A. LAW AS AN INSTRUMENT FOR COMBATING ATROCITIES

2.1 General

Law is a social science. It is an indispensable institution in a civilized society. It grows and develops with the society.[1]

Reason is the soul of law; when reason is dead, law is dead. Law can never be static. Social conditions keep on changing and laws have to keep pace with such changes, whether such changes are brought about by new laws or by suitable adaptations of existing laws.

In every society there is multiplicity of legal system. In modern India, it has been noted that values of Non-State Legal System differ drastically from those State Legal Systems. The constitutionally desired social order seek to foster through State Legal System the value of equality of man, whereas the North Indian Society operates on a reverse hypothesis: man are not born equal.[2] This is the root cause of some of our social problems including practices of untouchability and commission of atrocities on the SCs.

Ancient Hindu view of law was that 'law' is the command of God and not of any political superior (sovereign). The ruler is also bound to obey it and is under a duty to enforce it. Thus, law is part of *Dharma.* This being the view about law, we found moral and religious injunctions mingled up with legal precepts.[3]

Hindu Legal System is perhaps one of the most ancient legal systems of the world. According to *Hindu* view, law owes its existence to God. Law is given in *'Shruti'* (that which is heard-known as *Vedas*) and *'Smrities'*. The king is simply to execute that law and he himself is bound by it and if he goes against this law he should be disobeyed. *Puranas* are full of instances where the kings were dethroned and beheaded when they went against the established law.[4] This is the reason for perpetuation of practices of untouchability and commission of atrocities on the SCs.

In the introduction of this study, we have seen as to how various *Samhitas*, *Brahmanas*, *Dharmasutras*, *Smrities* and other Hindu religious literatures have imposed social disabilities on one section of our society which are now recognized as SCs? And how various Rulers and prevalent legal system was supporting and enforcing social disabilities on SCs?

In a democratic society, like ours, the problems are to be solved and progress is to be made through the instrument of law. The objectives, whether social, political or economical are to be achieved through it. The manifold problems and the big challenges that the country is facing, including the problem of practices of untouchability and commission of atrocities on the SCs, are to be solved and met through the agency of law. Law is, therefore, to be used as an instrument to bring social change.

Law reflects a struggle of competing interest groups, some of whom are more powerful than others.[5] According to Friedman, "What makes law, then, is not 'public opinion' in the abstract, but public opinion in the sense of exerted social force."[6]

It is the conflicts that create the dilemmas; and it is the conflicts toward which State intervention is directed. The contradictions create conflicts and dilemmas which people try to solve. In the resolution of conflicts and dilemmas, other contradictions are revealed and created, other conflicts are generated, and a multitude of dilemmas and struggles insured.[7]

The conflicts between untouchable communities and other Hindu communities significantly started in the second decade of twentieth century. Untouchable communities became conscious about their social action. They started temple entry *Satyagrahas*. Demand of temple entry began in 1917 in *Kerala* followed by *Vaikom Satyagraha* of 1924-25. Throughout the 1920s and in the early 1930s the issue of temple entry was bitterly fought for and led to considerable violence, even bloodshed, in case of Western India.[8] *Ambedkar* moment was in the forefront of the temple entry campaign.

The first resolution of this conflict by the State came in the form of Montagu-Chelmsford reforms in the year 1919. Provisions were made in Government of India Act, 1919 for the nomination of seven members of the depressed classes to the Legislative Council, the first recognition that the untouchables had an interest separate from that of other Hindus.[9] The British Government recognized them as Indian Minority. The Simon Commission, the two Round Table Conferences and the Poona Pact during the period 1929-1932 gave institutional success to untouchables. The Simon Commission declared that the election of untouchable candidate was needed to train them in politics.[10] In the Government of India Act, 1935, the untouchables were styled as Scheduled Caste and were given compensatory discrimination. The key Indian Politician continued to see untouchability as a marginal issue.[11] However, there were continued agitations of SCs for temple entry. This conflict was further solved by passing various enactments regarding removal of social disabilities and allowing temple entries[12] and subsequently the enactments for protection of Civil Rights and prevention of atrocities on the SCs and STs.

2.2. Various Models

On analysing the existing Indian statutes, we find the legislations based on the following models for crime control:

1. Constitutional Provisions
2. Mild Crime Model
3. Hard Crime model

(i) Constitutional Provisions

The founding fathers of Indian Constitution were aware about the plight of SCs and need for removal of caste disabilities and practices of untouchability,[13] so they incorporated several provisions in the Constitution.

The Constitution of India, by incorporating Art. 17 in it, has abolished untouchability and has forbidden its practice in any form. It has also declared that the enforcement of any disability arising out of untouchability shall be an offence punishable in accordance with law.[14]

The untouchables do not exist as a legal category since the Constitution of India purported to abolish the condition of untouchability and made its practice an offence. But this was a formal and instrumental declaration, not a sociological statement. The same Constitution recognized the persistence of the problem of the untouchables by laying the legal basis for a scheme of the compensatory action for the SCs.[15]

(ii) Mild Crime Model

The Protection of Civil Rights Act, 1955 is based on mild crime model for removing the practice of untouchability. This Act was enacted for giving effect to the provisions of Art. 17 of the Constitution of India. Initially it was named as "The Untouchability (Offences) Act, 1955" which was amended in the year 1976 as "The Protection of Civil Rights Act, 1976," as during working of this Act some lacunae were noticed in it. These loopholes were plugged. This Act remained a symbolic piece of legislation.

It seems fair to say that the U.O. Act has not fared well in the High Courts, in contrast with the earlier State legislation, which generally received favourable interpretations from these Courts. This unfavourable reception by the High Courts seems to involve three problem areas; the requirement that the forbidden act be committed "on grounds of untouchability"; uncertainty about coverage of private property; and limitation of rights to those enjoyed by members of the same religious denomination.[16]

The Supreme Court played a significant role in interpreting the provisions of U.O. Act/P.C.R. Act. It was held by the Supreme Court that the Protection of Civil Rights Act is not a penal law simplicitor but bears behind it, monstrous untouchability relentlessly practiced for centuries dehumanizing the Scheduled Castes,

Constitution's animation to have it eradicated and to assimilate one-fifth of nation's populations in the main stream of national life.[17]

(iii) Hard Crime Model

The Scheduled Castes and the Scheduled Tribes (Prevention of Atrocities) Act, 1989, is based on hard crime model for prevention of atrocities on the SCs. It was noticed that despite various measures to improve the socio-economic conditions of the Scheduled Castes and the Scheduled Tribes, they remained vulnerable. They are denied number of civil rights. They are subjected to various offences, indignities, humiliations and harassment. They have, in several brutal incidents, been deprived of their life and property. Serious crimes are committed against them for various historical, social and economical reasons.[18] The social indignities emanating from the practice of untouchability and acute economic disparity arising out of landlessness, bondage, *etc.*, led the SCs to succumb to atrocities by dominant castes who started retaliatory pressures to dilute and weaken the force of compensatory measures.[19] The increasing incidents of atrocities on SCs are the direct outcome of agrarian tensions, ineffective implementation of the PCR Act, Minimum Wages Act, rural indebtedness, practice of bonded labour and half-hearted implementation of various developmental measures like allotment of surplus ceiling land to SCs.[20]

The Act comes under the definition of Hard Crime Model because so many new features were incorporated in the Act. Certain behaviours, which were no offences up to the passing of the enactment, were made offences with severe punishments. Even the officials, who are entrusted to enforce the provisions of the Act, could be punished under the Act, if he is adjudged negligent in performing his duties. Provisions were also made for enhancement of punishment for some offences; denial of anticipatory bail and probation to convict; cancellation of arm licence of accused and externment of potential offenders, *etc.*

2.3 Legal Measures

The legal measures for prevention of atrocities on the SCs are mainly the provisions of the Act under study. The term "atrocity" has not been defined so far. It is considered necessary that not only the term atrocity should be defined but also stringent measures should be introduced to provide for higher punishment for committing such atrocities. It is also proposed to enjoin the States and the Union Territories to take specific preventive and punitive measures to protect the Scheduled Castes and the Scheduled Tribes from being victimised and where atrocities are committed, to provide adequate relief and assistance to rehabilitate them.[21]

The first case in which constitutional validity of the Act, was challenged is *Jai Singh and another* Vs. *Union of India and others.*[22] The Rajasthan High Court held the Act as valid and constitutional. But the Madhya Pradesh High Court did not agree with this view and contrarily held in *Dr. Ram Krishan Balothia* Vs. *Union of India and others*[23] that Sec.18 of the Act is violative of Arts. 14 and 21 of the Constitution as provisions of this section did not conform to the norms of justice and fair play besides, prescribing unfair and unreasonable procedure.[24]

In Appeal, the Supreme Court in case of *State of M.P. and another* Vs. *Ram Krishan Balothia*[25] overruled the above decision and held that the court was agreed with the view taken by Full Bench of Rajasthan High Court in *Jai Singh's case*[26] and held that looking to the historical background relating to practice of "untouchability and the social attitude which lead the commission of such offences against SCs and STs, there is justification for an apprehension that if benefit of anticipatory bail is made available to the persons who are alleged to have committed such offences, there is every likelihood of their misusing their liberty while on anticipatory bail to terrorise their victims and to prevent a proper investigation. It is in this context Sec. 18 has been incorporated in the Act and it cannot be considered in any manner as violative of Arts. 14 and 21 of the Constitution.[27]

In case of *Abdul Rasheed Siddiqui and another* Vs. *State of Madhya Pradesh and others,*[28] the validity of the Act was challenged but MP High Court disposed of the writ petition without going into the *vires* of the provisions of the Act.[29]

In case of *Raju Gounder and others* Vs. *Union of India and others,*[30] the validity of Sec. 18 of the Act was challenged on the ground that the provisions contained therein are violative of Arts.

14 and 21 of the Constitution. The Madhya Pradesh High Court observed that offences under the Act and the offences under the other penal laws of the country fall under different categories. As such, there is no comparison and they cannot be grouped in one class. That being so, there is no question of any unreasonable classification or that the Act is discriminatory. The question of violation of the right guaranteed under Art. 21 also have no substance. Art. 21 does not ensure or does not confer a right that a person who commits an offence or those accused of committing of certain offences, would not be liable to be dealt with in accordance with the valid provisions of the Act.[31]

These provisions of Sec. 18 of the Act were again challenged in *Phulla Dass* Vs. *State of Punjab and others.*[32] But Punjab and Haryana High Court relying on the findings of *State of MP* Vs. *Ram Krishna Balothia,*[33] case held that in view of clear and unambiguous findings of the Supreme Court, further discussion on the same becomes unnecessary.[34]

In case of *K.C. Ravindran Pillai* Vs. *Union of India and others,*[35] validity of Sec. 3 (x) of the Act was challenged. The Kerala High Court observed that the petitioner could not establish how and in what manner the provisions of the Act violate Arts. 14 and 21 of the Constitution of India. The Scheduled Caste and the Scheduled Tribe (Prevention of Atrocities) Act, 1989 was enacted to prevent the commission of offences of atrocities against the members of the Scheduled Castes and the Scheduled Tribes, to provide for special Courts for the trial of such offences and for the relief and rehabilitation of the victims of such offences and for matters connected therewith or incidental thereto. The Act was enacted in line with various constitutional provisions giving special privileges and rights to members of the Scheduled Castes and Scheduled Tribes. Art. 17 of the Constitution of India provides that untouchability is abolished and its practice in any form is forbidden. The enforcement of any disability arising out of untouchability shall be an offence punishable in accordance with law. Article 17 makes the practice of untouchability an offence read with Article 35(a)(ii) which confers upon the Parliament the exclusive power to make law prescribing punishment for those acts which are declared to be offences under Part III of the Constitution. Art. 17 is a significant provision particularly from the point of view of equality of law. It guarantees social justice and dignity of life which were denied to vast section of the society for centuries.[36] The Court held that there is no legal infirmity in Sec. 3(1)(x) of the Act and the Act is legal and valid.

In case of *Smt. Vasantha* Vs. *Sivanthi and others*,[37] Supreme Court observed that the Judges should adapt purposive interpretation of the dynamic concepts under the Constitution and the Act with its interpretative armoury to articulate the felt necessities of the time. Social legislation is not a document for fastidious dialects but means of ordering of the life of the people. To construe law one must enter into its spirit, its setting and history. Law should be capable to expand freedom of the people and the legal order can weigh with utmost equal care to provide the underpinning of the highly inequitable social order. Judicial review must be exercised with insight into social values to supplement the changing social needs. The existing social inequalities or imbalances are required to be removed and social order is required to be readjusted through rule of law.[38]

B. SALIENT FEATURES OF THE SCHEDULED CASTES AND SCHEDULED TRIBES (PREVENTION OF ATROCITIES) ACT, 1989

2.4 Creation of New Types of Offences

One of the salient features of the Act is that it has created new types of offences. It has thus expanded the horizons of criminal liability. The act(s) and omissions which were neither covered under Indian Penal Code nor Protection of Civil Rights Act, 1955 nor in any other special legislation were made offences by the Act, with the object to provide dozens of protections to the SCs and STs to save them from various crimes and atrocities committed on them on the basis of hate or bias, *etc.*, based primarily on caste.

These offences may be described as hate crime or bias crime because the offender intentionally selects the person against whom the crime is committed or selects the property, which is damaged or is otherwise effected by the crime on the basis of his caste.

2.5 Commission of Offences Only by Specified Persons

The other salient feature of the Act is that if the behaviour, act or omission, as mentioned in the Act, is committed by members of SCs and STs, it will not be an offence under the Act, but if the same behaviour, act, omission is caused by a person who is neither a member of SCs nor STs, it will be an offence under the Act. This is unique feature of the Act incomparable to any other existing statute.[39]

Section 3(1) of the Act makes this clear. The relevant extract thereof is as under:

> "3. *Punishment for offence of atrocities.*—(1) Whoever, not being a member of Scheduled Caste or Scheduled Tribe,—*** shall be punishable with imprisonment for a term which shall not be less than six months but which may extend to five years and with fine."

In case of *Panibushan Behera and others* Vs. *State of Orissa*,[40] the Orissa High Court held that in order to constitute an offence under the Act, one of the essential ingredient is that the offender must be a person other than member of SCs or STs and the victim should be a member of SC or ST.[41]

In case of *T. Taranath & Anr.* Vs. *State of A.P. & Ors.*[42] admittedly the petitioner belonged to Scheduled Tribe community and accused belonged to Scheduled Caste community. The Andhra Pradesh High Court held that the very opening words of Section 3 would show that the offence punishable u/s 3 of the Act can be attributed to only a person who does not belong to a member of the Scheduled Caste or Scheduled Tribe. The provisions of the Act are not attracted even if the alleged utterance is made as the one punishable u/s 3(1)(x) of the Act by a person who belonged to Scheduled Caste or Scheduled Tribe. The Court quashed the F.I.R so far as it related to Section 3(1)(x) of the Act and made it clear that the investigation against the accused for the offences punishable u/ss 341 and 323 I.P.C. would proceed.[43]

2.6 Protection from Various Kinds of Atrocities

The Act provides protections to the SCs & STs from various kinds of atrocities. These protections may, broadly, be divided into following categories:

1. Protection from social disabilities.
2. Protection from personal atrocities.
3. Protection from atrocities affecting properties.
4. Protection from malicious prosecution.
5. Protection from political disabilities.
6. Protection from economic exploitation.

2.6.1 Protection from Social Disabilities

The members of SCs and STs are provided protections from denial of access to certain places and to use customary passage and to get water from any spring, reservoir or any other source. These protections may be divided into two heads, namely:

(i) Protection from denial of access to certain places and use of customary passage.

(ii) Protection against fouling of water.

(i) Protection from Denial of Access to Certain Places and Use of Customary Passage

The members of SCs and STs were provided protection from denial of access to any place of public resort to which other members of public or any section thereof has a right of access to. They have also protection from denial of use of customary passage.

This protection was made available to the members of SCs and STs by clause (xiv) of section 3(1) of the Act.

The relevant extract thereof is as under:

"3. *Punishment for offences of atrocities.*—(1) Whoever, not being a member of a Scheduled Caste or a Scheduled Tribe,—

* * *

(xiv) denies a member of a Scheduled Caste or a Scheduled Tribe any customary right of passage to a place of public resort or obstructs such member so as to prevent him from using or having access to a place of public resort to which other members of public or any section thereof have a right to use or access to :

* * *

shall be punishable with imprisonment for a term, which shall not be less than six months but which may extend to five years and with fine.* * *"

The phrase "place o]f public resort" means that place to which the public are admitted, such as, parks, recreation ground, hospital.[44]

(ii) Protection against Fouling of Water

The members of SCs and STs have protection from denial to use the water of any spring, reservoir or any other source without any interception in any manner without getting it polluted, if they have been using water from such spring, reservoir or source. Whosoever corrupts or fouls that water is liable for punishment. Thus, impliedly members of SCs and STs have right to get foul-free water from any spring, reservoir or any other source, if they have been ordinarily getting the water from these sources.

This protection was made available to these persons by clause (xiii) of section 3(1) of the Act.

The relevant extract of the clause is as under:

"3. *Punishment for offences of atrocities.*—(1) Whoever, not being a member of a Scheduled Caste or a Scheduled Tribe,—

* * *

(xiii) corrupts or fouls the water of any spring, reservoir or any other source ordinarily used by members of the Scheduled Castes or the Scheduled Tribes so as to render it less fit for the purpose for which it is ordinarily used ;

* * *

shall be punishable with imprisonment for a term which shall not be less than six months but which may extend to five years and with fine.* * *"

2.6.2 Protection from Personal Atrocities

The members of SCs and STs have been provided some special protections to save them from different kinds of atrocities. These protections have effect of giving them an honourable life. No person can force them to eat or drink anything, which is inedible or obnoxious. They have right to wear the clothes they like. Their females have right to preserve their modesty. Forceful stripping or outraging the modesty or sexual exploitation is made offences.

For the sake of clarity and convenience, these protections may be divided into following two heads, namely:

1. Protection from atrocities affecting body.
2. Protection from atrocities affecting reputation.

1. Protection from Atrocities Affecting Body

The members of SCs & STs have been provided some protections to save them from different kinds of atrocities affecting their bodies. These protections can be sub-divided into following heads:

(i) Protection against forceful drinking or eating of inedible or obnoxious substance.

(ii) Protection against stripping.

(iii) Protection against outrage of modesty.

(iv) Protection against sexual exploitation.

(v) Protection against injury or annoyance.

(i) Protection against Forceful Drinking or Eating of Inedible or Obnoxious Substance

Every person whether belongs to the SC or ST or not has a right not to eat anything, which is inedible or obnoxious. As there has been repeated instances forcing the members of SC and ST to eat or drink those things that are not meant for the purpose of eating or drinking, therefore, such acts were made offences. No person can force members of these communities to eat or drink anything, which is not meant for drinking or eating.

This protection was conferred to the members of the SCs and STs by clause (i) of section 3(1) of the Act.

The relevant extract of the clause is as under:

"3. *Punishment for offences of atrocities.*—(1) Whoever, not being a member of a Scheduled Caste or a Scheduled Tribe,—

(i) forces a member of a Scheduled Caste or a Scheduled Tribe to drink or eat any inedible or obnoxious substance :

* * *

shall be punishable with imprisonment for a term which, shall not be less than six months but which may extend to five years and with fine. * * *"

(ii) Protection against Stripping

The members of SCs and STs were provided protections against any restriction on them to wear any clothe they like. The act of removing clothes from their bodies is made an offence.

This protection against stripping was made available to them by Clause (iii) of Section 3 of the Act.

The relevant extract of the clause is as under:

"3. *Punishment for offences of atrocities.*—(1) Whoever, not being a member of a Scheduled Caste or a Scheduled Tribe,—

* * *

(ii) forcibly removes clothes from the person of a member of a Scheduled Caste or a Scheduled Tribe or parades him naked or with painted face or body or commits any similar act which is derogatory to human dignity ;

* * *

shall be punishable with imprisonment for a term, which shall not be less than six months but which may extend to five years and with fine. * * *"

(iii) Protection against Outraging of Modesty

It is repeatedly reported in the Newspapers and Magazines, etc., that females belonging to the SCs and STs are teased or/and their modesty is outraged without any reason simply because they are poor and belongs to the caste which is either the SC or ST. Using of force or making assault on the women belonging to the SCs and STs with intention to dishonour or outrage their modesty was made an offence under Clause (xi) of Section 3 of the Act.

The relevant extract of the clause is as under:

"3. *Punishment for offences of atrocities.*—(1) Whoever, not being a member of a Scheduled Caste or a Scheduled Tribe,—

* * *

(xi) assaults or uses force to any woman belonging to a Scheduled Caste or a Scheduled Tribe with intent to dishonour or outrage her modesty ;

* * *

shall be punishable with imprisonment for a term, which shall not be less than six months but which may extend to five years and with fine. * * *"

In *Raju* Vs. *State of Madhya Pradesh,*[45] it was held that an act suggestive of sex to a woman amounts to outraging her modesty. In case of *State of Punjab* Vs. *Major Singh*[46] it was observed :

> "*** [T]he essence of a woman's modesty is her sex. The modesty of an adult female is writ large on her body. Young or old, intelligent or imbecile, awake or sleeping, the woman possesses modesty capable of being outraged.*** The reaction of the woman is very relevant, but its absence is not always decisive, as for example, when the accused with a corrupt mind stealthily touches the flesh of a sleeping woman. She may be an idiot, she may be under the spell of anaesthesia, she may be sleeping, she may be unable to appreciate the significance of the act, nevertheless, the offender is punishable under the section."

It was further observed that:

"*** In my judgement, when an act done to or in the presence of a woman is clearly suggestive of sex according to the common notions of making, that act must fall within the mischief of this section."[47]

(iv) Protection against Sexual Exploitation

The woman belonging to the SCs or STs has right to earn her livelihood without any exploitation. Nobody can exploit her sexually. If any person who is in a position to dominate the will of such woman exploit her sexually, then he is liable for punishment. This protection was given to them by clause (xii) of Section 3(1) of the Act.

The relevant extract of the clause is as under:

"3. *Punishment for offences of atrocities.*—(1) Whoever, not being a member of a Scheduled Caste or a Scheduled Tribe,—

* * *

(xii) being in a position to dominate the will of a woman belonging to a Scheduled Caste or a Scheduled Tribe and uses that position to exploit her sexually to which she would not have otherwise agreed ;

* * *

shall be punishable with imprisonment for a term, which shall not be less than six months but which may extend to five years and with fine. * * *"

In case of *Gujula Satyanarayana Reddy* Vs. *State of Andhra Pradesh,*[48] it was held by the Andhra Pradesh High Court that in order to attract section 3(1)(xii) of the Act the upper caste man should be in a position to dominate the will of a woman belonging to SCs or STs and he should use the position to exploit her sexually to which she would not have otherwise agreed. In this case, the complainant being a tribal woman was going for coolie work to the field of the accused who belonged to Reddy caste. He exploited her sexually. It was held that he was certainly in a position to dominate the will of the woman. He also used his position to exploit her sexually assuring that he would marry her. It was further held that all the requirements of the section were made out in the case.[49]

In case of *Thana Ram* Vs. *State of Rajasthan,*[50] appellant was convicted under section 376 IPC and section 3(1)(xi) of the Act as he was found guilty of committing rape of a minor girl aged 5 years belonging to Meghwal community of SC. The Rajasthan High Court upheld his conviction and also held that the non-examination of prosecutrix aged 5-6 years, who had not developed the faculty of understanding, was not fatal to the prosecution case.[51]

In case of *Panibhusan Behera and others* Vs. *State of Orissa,*[52] the Orissa High Court held that the ingredients of the offence are that (i) the offender must be a person who is not a member of SC or ST, (ii) he must be in a position to dominate the will of a woman belonging to a SC or a ST, (iii) the said position was used to exploit the woman sexually, to which she would not have otherwise agreed. In order to attract application of the provision, sexual exploitation must have taken place because of the offenders' position of dominance. The word 'otherwise' is significant and clearly points that the exploitation was with agreement of the helpless woman that she would not have agreed but for the offender's position of dominance. Use of the expression 'would not have otherwise agreed' is intended to convey that the agreement would not have been there, but for the position of dominance. It is not a free and voluntary consent. 'Exploit' means to make an illegitimate use of, to utilise for one's own ends, and treat selfishly as more workable material (person, *etc.*) to make capital out of. To have carnal knowledge of a woman by use of position of dominance is sexual exploitation if the victim would not have agreed to the act, but for the position. In the present case, the offenders are not shown to have dominated the will of the victim girl. Therefore, the conviction under section 3(1)(xii) of the Act are set aside.[53]

In case of *M.C. Prasannan* Vs. *State,*[54] the accused, a class teacher, used to commit sexual intercourse with the victim, a student with the assurance of marrying her. The matter was reported to the police several months after the commission of sexual intercourse and only after pregnancy was shown. The accused was prosecuted and convicted u/s 376 of IPC and section 3(1)(xii) of the Act. The Calcutta High Court, however, acquitted the accused by giving benefit of doubt, observing *inter alia* that victim willingly and with full consent had sexual intercourse with accused; it was not established that victim was minor ; there was no question of exploitation or dominating will of victim ; and FIR was lodged after more than 3 months by stranger to the case.[55]

(v) Protection against Injury or Annoyance

Every member of the SCs or STs has been protected from inflict of injury of causing annoyance by the members of other communities. Whosoever will violate this protection will be liable for punishment.

This protection was made available to every member of the SCs and STs *vide* clause (ii) of Section 3(1) of the Act.

The relevant extract of the clause is as under:

"3. *Punishment for offences of atrocities.*—(1) Whoever, not being a member of a Scheduled Caste or a Scheduled Tribe,—

* * *

(iii) acts with intent to cause injury, insult or annoyance to any member of a Scheduled Caste or a Scheduled Tribe by dumping excreta, waste matter, carcasses or any other obnoxious substance in his premises or neighbourhood ;

* * *

shall be punishable with imprisonment for a term, which shall not be less than six months but which may extend to five years and with fine. * * *"

2. Protection against Atrocities affecting Reputation

The members of the SCs and STs have been provided some protections to save their reputation from different kinds of atrocities. These protections can be sub-divided into following heads, namely:

(i) Protection against insult.

(ii) Protection against humiliation.

(i) Protection against Insult

The members of the SCs or STs have also been provided with

protection so that they may live with honour and maintain their dignity. Insulting them whether by dumping excreta, waste matter, carcasses, obnoxious substance in his premises or neighbourhood or by parading them naked or with painted face or painted body or by any other similar act that is derogatory to human dignity are made offences. For the sake of clarity and convenience, these protections may be divided into following heads, namely:

(a) Protection against insult by dumping obnoxious substance.

(b) Protection against insult by naked parading.

(c) Protection against insult by painting face.

(d) Protection against insult by painting body.

(e) Protection against insult by any other similar act which is derogatory to human dignity.

These protections were provided to the members of the SCs and STs by clauses (ii) and (iii) of Section 3(1) of the Act.

The relevant extracts of these clauses are as under:

"3. *Punishment for offences of atrocities.*—(1) Whoever, not being a member of a Scheduled Caste or a Scheduled Tribe,—

* * *

(ii) acts with intent to cause injury, insult or annoyance to any member of a Scheduled Caste or a Scheduled Tribe by dumping excreta, waste matter, carcasses or any other obnoxious substance in his premises or neighbourhood;

(iii) forcibly removes clothes from the person of a member of a Scheduled Caste or a Scheduled Tribe or parades him naked or with painted face or body or commits any similar act which is derogatory to human dignity ;

* * *

shall be punishable with imprisonment for a term, which shall not be less than six months but which may extend to five years and with fine. * * *"

In case of *E. Krishnan Nayanar* Vs. *Dr. M.A. Kuttappan,*

Member, Kerala Legislative Assembly and others[56] the Kerala High Court observed that two kinds of insults against the members of SCs or STs are punishable u/s 3, one as defined under clause (ii) and other as defined u/s (x) of the said section. A combined reading of the two sub-sections shows that under clause (ii) insult can be caused to a member of SC or ST by dumping excreta, waste matter, carcasses or any other obnoxious substance in his premises or neighbourhood and to cause such insult, the dumping of excreta, *etc.*, need not necessarily be done in the presence of the person insulted.[57]

(ii) Protection against Humiliation

It is a matter of common knowledge that members of the SCs and STs are also humiliated in one pretext or other. Therefore, they were provided protection against humiliation by clause (x) of Section 3(1) of the Act.

The relevant extract of the clause is as under:

"3. *Punishment for offences of atrocities.*—(1) Whoever, not being a member of a Scheduled Caste or a Scheduled Tribe,—

* * *

(x) intentionally insults or intimidates with intent to humiliate a member of a Scheduled Caste or a Scheduled Tribe in any place within public view ;

* * *

shall be punishable with imprisonment for a term, which shall not be less than six months but which may extend to five years and with fine. * * *"

In case of *Ravinder Kumar Mishra* Vs. *State of Madhya Pradesh,*[58] it was held that section 3(1)(x) is attracted only when the alleged insult or intimidation as caused with intent to humiliate a member belonging to the SC community with reference to his community. It is only such insult or intimidation that is attracted to section 3(1)(x). The words of abuse attributed to the petitioner-accused against the complainant in the case were only 'Idiot' and

'Nonsense' which have no reference to the community and from those words it cannot be inferred that the intention or intimidation were with reference to the community to which the complainant belonged.[59]

In case of *Haridas* Vs. *State of Maharashtra (through P.S.O. Police Station Deoli),*[60] the Bombay High Court held that in the matter of an offence under section 3(1)(x) ...where the prosecution rests on certain words uttered by the accused, what exactly those words were would be of paramount importance. Those words would suggest as to whether the accused intended to insult the said member of the SC or ST or as the case may be, intended to insult the modesty of such member? Words are not to be proved verbatim but the prosecution must bring home what was really uttered and whether what was uttered was with the idea to hurl insult in the name of Caste?[61]

In case of *Chandra Poojari* Vs. *State of Karnataka,*[62] the petitioner sought quashing of the charge-sheet and dismissal of the complaint under section 3(1)(x) of the Act on the ground that incident had not taken place in public view. While allowing the petition Karnataka High Court held that from the perusal of the complaint, it is clear that the incident had taken place in the chamber of the complainant who was working as a CTO. To attract the provisions of section 3(1)(x), it is necessary that it should be in a place where public could view the incident.[63]

In case of *E. Krishnan Nayanar* Vs. *Dr. M.A. Kuttappan, Member, Kerala Legislative Assembly and others*[64] the Kerala High Court observed that two kinds of insults against the members of a SC or ST are made punishable under clause 3, one as defined under clause (ii) and the other as defined under clause (x) of the said section. Under clause (x) insult can be caused to the person insulted only if he is present "in any place within public view" the words "within public view" are referable to the person insulted and not to the person who insulted him as the said expression is conspicuously absent in clause (ii) of section 3.[65] The Court held that if the person insulted was not present, then no offence under section 3(1) (x) of the Act is made out.[66]

In case of *Phulla Dass* Vs. *State of Punjab and another*[67] the facts of the case were that petitioner abused complainant and said, "*Bhian Choda Chamara* after taking the milk of cows now left the cows to wander in the village". The complainant and his relatives tried to prevail upon the petitioner not to do so but he entered their home and thereupon said "come out *Chamaro,* let me see you today". The petitioner gave a blow from the reverse side of the *gandasi* on the complainant and also threatened that the complainant would be eliminated. The complainant lodged FIR. Petitioner approached Punjab and Haryana High Court for anticipatory bail, which was rejected.[68]

In case of *K.C. Ravindran Pillai* Vs. *Union of India and others,*[69] petitioner in a writ of *certiorari* sought quashing of FIR of complainant. Complainant had lodged FIR on the allegations that petitioner had assaulted him who belonged to SCs community of Kallady by calling his caste name at a public place.[70] The Kerala High Court upholding the validity of Sec. 3(1)(x) of the Act dismissed his petition.[71]

In case of *Karansingh and others* Vs. *The State of Madhya Pradesh*[72] the petitioner sought quashing of FIR on charge u/s 3(1) (x) of the Act. It was alleged in FIR that on 27.06.91, complainant with four others were fishing in a tank in other village. At 11.00 O'clock, petitioner abused them and challenged them to come out, without knowing their identity. They also threatened them not to try to escape else they would kill them and also fired in the air. Then, complainant party told them that they were residents of *Gularziri* and had come for fishing. On this accused party exclaimed that these were *Biilalas (Bhilade).* They were caught and taken forcibly to the place of petitioner where they were tied with a rope and were assaulted. The Madhya Pradesh High Court held that in the circumstances of the case, only calling a person belonging to ST by the name of his tribe would not be sufficient to make out an offence u/s 3(1)(x) of the Act.[73] It was further held that incident having taken place at late hours at night and accused party was only present on spot and what transpired between them had not been alleged to have taken place within public view, it cannot be said that incident took place at place within public view and it cannot be said that all ingredients of offence u/s 3(1)(x) were made out.[74]

In case of *Kaliya Perumal* Vs. *State,*[75] the petitioner sought quashing of the FIR registered against him under section 3(1)(x) of the Act on the ground that the averments made in the FIR would not constitute an offence on mere calling of the caste name by itself would not amount to dishonouring the caste to which the complainant belongs. The Madras High Court held that the averments would definitely attract the relevant sections of the Act as the petitioner has abused the complainant in her caste name, in filthy language, thereby causing insult and intimidation to her.[76]

In case of *State of Gujarat* Vs. *Ansuyaben Vanilal Patel,*[77] complainant was the teacher and accused was the administrator. It was alleged that accused had asked the complainant as to where and how time-table was lost and thereafter the accused told the complainant, "This is not residential area of *harijans* that you are showing colour of that community". The complainant belonged to SC and by uttering aforesaid prohibited words, the accused committed an offence punishable u/s 3(1)(x) of the Act. The Court, however, acquitted the accused for the reasons that FIR was lodged 3 days after the commission of offence ; and testimony of the witnesses and complainant was found unreliable.[78]

2.6.3 Protection against Atrocities affecting Properties

The members of the SCs and STs were also provided protections against atrocities affecting their properties. They have been provided protection to retain and own their land and protect the same from any wrongful occupation or dispossession. They have also been provided protection to retain their residential premises from any mischief either by fire or other explosive substance. For the sake of convenience, these protections can be divided into three heads, namely:

1. Protection against atrocities affecting land.
2. Protection against atrocities affecting residential premises.
3. Protection against atrocities affecting existence of properties.

1. Protection against Atrocities affecting Land

There have been continuous instances of dispossession of the members of the SCs and STs from their properties and occupying their properties wrongfully. They have been provided some protections to save their land. These protections may be sub-divided into following two heads, namely:

(i) Protection against Wrongful Occupation of Land ; and
(ii) Protection against dispossession from land or premises or water.

(i) Protection against Wrongful Occupation of Land

The members of the SCs and STs have been provided protections to occupy or cultivate their land without any hindrance by any other person. Wrongful occupation or cultivation of their land is made an offence under clause (iv) of Section 3(1) of the Act.

The relevant extract of the clause is as under:

"3. *Punishment for offences of atrocities.*—(1) Whoever, not being a member of a Scheduled Caste or a Scheduled Tribe,—

* * *

(iv) wrongfully occupies or cultivates any land owned by, or allotted to, or notified by any competent authority to be allotted to, a member of a Scheduled Caste or a Scheduled Tribe or gets the land allotted to him transferred;

* * *

shall be punishable with imprisonment for a term, which shall not be less than six months but which may extend to five years and with fine. * * *"

(ii) Protection against Dispossession From Land Premises or Water

Every member of the SCs and STs has protections against any hindrance in his right to enjoy with his property or premises or the water in the way he likes to enjoy it. If any person dispossesses a member of the SCs or STs from his land or premises or if he interferes in the enjoyment of his rights then he will be liable for punishment. This protection against dispossession from their land or premises or water is made available to them by clause (v) of Section 3(1) of the Act.

The relevant extract of the clause is as under:

"3. *Punishment for offences of atrocities.*—(1) Whoever, not being a member of a Scheduled Caste or a Scheduled Tribe,—

* * *

(v) wrongfully dispossesses a member of a Scheduled Caste or a Scheduled Tribe from his land or premises or interferes with the enjoyment of his rights over any land or premises or water ;

* * *

shall be punishable with imprisonment for a term, which shall not be less than six months but which may extend to five years and with fine. * * *"

2. Protection against Atrocities affecting Residential Premises

There are instances where members of the SCs and STs were forced to leave their houses, village or other place of residence. In order to protect them from any such act from any person they have been provided protections. Forcing or causing a member of SC or ST to leave his house, village or any place of the residence is an offence punishable under clause (xv) of Section 3(1) of the Act.

The relevant extract of the clause is as under:

"3. *Punishment for offences of atrocities.*—(1) Whoever, not being a member of a Scheduled Caste or a Scheduled Tribe,—

* * *

(xv) forces or causes a member of a Scheduled Caste or a Scheduled Tribe to leave his house, village or other place of residence;

* * *

shall be punishable with imprisonment for a term, which shall not be less than six months but which may extend to five years and with fine.* * *"

3. Protection against Atrocities affecting Existence of Properties

The members of SCs and STs have been provided protections not only to possess land, residential premises and other properties but also they have been provided protection against atrocities by damaging or destroying their properties by mischief. These protections may be sub-divided into two heads, namely:

(i) Protection against atrocities causing damage to properties.

(ii) Protection against atrocities causing destruction to properties.

(i) Protection against Atrocities causing Damage to Properties

The members of SCs and STs have been provided protection against damage of their property by mischief either by fire or explosive substances. Whosoever will cause damage to their properties is liable for punishment. This protection has been provided by clause (iii) of Section 3(2) of the Act.

The relevant extract of the clause is as under:

"3. *Punishment for offences of atrocities.*—*** (2) Whoever, not being a member of a Scheduled Caste or a Scheduled Tribe, —

* * *

(iii) commits mischief by fire or any explosive substance intending to cause or knowing it to be likely that he will thereby cause damage to any property belonging to a member of Scheduled Caste or a Scheduled Tribe, shall be punishable with imprisonment for a term which shall not be less than six months but which may extend to seven years and with fine;* * *"

(ii) Protection against Atrocities Causing Destruction to Properties

The members of SCs and STs have also been provided protections to safeguard their properties from destruction. The destruction of their properties by mischief either by fire or explosive substance is made serious offence. This is provided by clause (iv) of Sec. 3(2) of the Act.

The relevant extract of the clause is as under:

"3. *Punishment for offences of atrocities.*—(2) Whoever, not being a member of a Scheduled Caste or a Scheduled Tribe,—

* * *

(iv) commits mischief by fire or any explosive substance intending to cause or knowing it to be likely that he will thereby cause destruction to any building which is ordinarily used as a place of worship or as a place for human dwelling or as a place for custody of the property by a member of a Scheduled Caste or a Scheduled Tribe, shall be punishable with imprisonment for life and with fine.* * *"

2.6.4 Protection against Atrocities by Litigation

The members of the SCs and STs have also been protected from atrocities by way of false, malicious or vexatious suit or other litigation.[79] This protection is made available to them by clause (viii) of Section 3(1) of the Act.

The relevant extract of the clause is as under:

"3. *Punishment for offences of atrocities.*—(1) Whoever, not being a member of a Scheduled Caste or a Scheduled Tribe,—

* * *

(viii) institute false, malicious or vexatious suit or criminal or other legal proceedings against a member of a Scheduled Caste or a Scheduled Tribe;

* * *

shall be punishable with imprisonment for a term, which shall not be less than six months but which may extend to five years and with fine. * * *"

In case of *Abdul Rasheed Siddique and another* Vs. *State of Madhya Pradesh and others,*[80] a question arose as to when can a case be reported under this section to the police? The court held that an offence can be registered only after the court dealing with suit or other proceedings which is alleged to be false, malicious or vexatious, is disposed of. Registration of cases during the pendency of such proceedings would amount to prejudging the issue, which the civil or criminal court in such proceedings may be called upon to decide. Whether an offence has been committed or not can be decided only after the suit or proceedings is over.[81]

Protection against Atrocities by Public Servant on False Information

Sometimes false information is given to the public servant with the intention that such public servant will use his lawful power to the injury or annoyance of a member of SC or ST. They have been provided protection against such type of atrocities. This protection is provided to them by clause (ix) of section 3(1) of the Act.

The relevant extract of the clause is as under:

"3. *Punishment for offences of atrocities.*—(1) Whoever, not being a member of a Scheduled Caste or a Scheduled Tribe,—

* * *

(ix) gives any false or frivolous information to any public servant and thereby causes such public servant to use his lawful power to the injury or annoyance of a member of a Scheduled Caste or a Scheduled Tribe ;

* * *

shall be punishable with imprisonment for a term, which shall not be less than six months but which may extend to five years and with fine. * * *"

Protection against Atrocities by Court on False Evidence

Atrocities on members of SCs and STs are also committed by giving false evidence against them with the purpose to get them convicted of an offence by the court. The Courts inflict sentences on the basis of false evidence on the innocent members of SCs or STs. The sentence may be capital or severe. The members of SCs and STs have also been protected from these types of atrocities. For the sake of convenience, these protections can be divided into two heads, namely:

(a) Protection from atrocities by court on false evidence when the intention was to get convicted of offence with capital punishment.

(b) Protection from atrocities by court on false evidence when the intention was to get convicted of offence with severe punishment.

Protection from Atrocities by Court on False Evidence when the Intention was to get Convicted of an Offence with Capital Punishment

The members of SCs and STs have also been provided protections to save them from punishment by the Courts on the basis of false evidence. Whosoever, will give or fabricate false evidence against any member of SCs or STs with the intention to get him convicted of an offence which is capital will be liable for punishment. This protection is made available to them by clause (i) of section 3(2) of the Act.

The relevant extract of the clause is as under:

"3. *Punishment for offences of atrocities.*—*** (2) Whoever, not being a member of a Scheduled Caste or a Scheduled Tribe,—

(i) gives or fabricates false evidence intending thereby to cause, or knowing it to be likely that he will thereby cause any member of a Scheduled Caste or a Scheduled Tribe to be convicted of an offence which is capital by the law for the time being in force shall be punished with imprisonment for life and with fine ; and if an innocent member of a Scheduled Caste or a Scheduled Tribe be convicted and executed in consequence of such false or fabricated evidence, the person who gives or fabricates such false evidence, shall be punished with death ; ***"

Protection from Atrocities by Court on False Evidence when the Intention was to get Convicted of an Offence with Severe Punishment

The members of SCs and STs have also been provided protections to save them from the atrocities by courts on false evidence in an offence having severe punishment. In order to prevent such atrocities, clause (ii) in section 3(2) of the Act has been incorporated for punishing those offenders who will give or fabricate false evidence against any member of SCs or STs.

The relevant extract of the clause is as under:

"3. *Punishment for offences of atrocities.*—*** (2) Whoever, not being a member of a Scheduled Caste or a Scheduled Tribe,—

* * *

(ii) gives or fabricates false evidence intending thereby to cause, or knowing it to be likely that he will thereby cause, any member of a Scheduled Caste or a Scheduled Tribe to be convicted of an offence which is not capital but punishable with imprisonment for a term of seven years or upwards, shall be punishable with imprisonment for a term which shall not be less than six months but which may extend to seven years or upwards and with fine ; ***"

Protection against Atrocities by Destruction of Evidence of Atrocities

It has been realised that after commission of atrocities on members of SCs or STs, the evidence of commission of atrocities is either destroyed or allowed to disappear with the result that offenders are not punished and further mental atrocities is caused on the members of SCs or STs, when offenders escape from the punishment. So, every member of SCs and STs has been protected from such type of atrocities. This protection is made available to them by clause (vi) of section 3(2) of the Act.

The relevant extract of the clause is as under:

"3. *Punishment for offences of atrocities.*— *** (2) Whoever, not being a member of a Scheduled Caste or a Scheduled Tribe, —

* * *

(vi) knowingly or having reason to believe that an offence has been committed under this Chapter, causes any evidence of the commission of that offence to disappear with the intention of screening the offender from legal punishment, or with that intention gives any information respecting the offence which he knows or believes to be false, shall be punishable with the punishment provided for that offence ; ***"

2.6.5 Protection against Political Disabilities

There have been repeated reports that members of SCs or STs are not allowed to cast their votes in elections and thereby atrocities are committed on them. If they assert their right of franchise as made available to them by the Constitution of India and the Representation of People Act they are beaten and their properties are damaged or destroyed. To save them from such type of atrocities, provisions have been made in the Act. This protection is made available to them by clause (vii) of section 3(1) of the Act.

The relevant extract of the clause is as under:

"3. *Punishment for offences of atrocities.*—(1) Whoever, not being a member of a Scheduled Caste or a Scheduled Tribe,—

* * *

(vii) forces or intimidates a member of a Scheduled Caste or a Scheduled Tribe not to vote or to vote a particular candidate or to vote in a manner other than that provided by law ;

* * *

shall be punishable with imprisonment for a term, which shall not be less than six months but which may extend to five years and with fine. * * *"

In case of *Hari Shankar and others* Vs. *State*[82] complainant had lodged a FIR against petitioner to the effect that petitioner, concededly a *Brahmin*, went to the *Mohalla* of the complainant, concededly a *Jatav*, and intimidated him that he should cast his vote to lotus symbol of Narottam Mishra, otherwise he will be killed. When complainant asserted his right of voluntarily casting of vote, he was abused and beaten. Petitioner prayed for grant of anticipatory bail. The Madhya Pradesh High Court dismissed his bail application.[83]

2.6.6 Protection from Economic Exploitation

The members of SCs and STs have also been afforded protections from economic exploitations. None of them can be compelled or enticed to do begging or other similar forms of forced or bonded labour.

This protection was made available to the members of SCs and STs by clause (vi) of section 3(1) of the Act.

The relevant extract thereof is as under:

"3. *Punishment for offences of atrocities.*—(1) Whoever, not being a member of a Scheduled Caste or a Scheduled Tribe,—

* * *

(vi) compels or entices a member of a Scheduled Caste or a Scheduled Tribe to do 'begar' or other similar forms of forced or bonded labour other than any compulsory service for public purpose imposed by Government;

* * *

shall be punishable with imprisonment for a term, which shall not be less than six months but which may extend to five years and with fine. * * *"

2.7 Creation of Special Courts

The other salient feature of the Act is that it provides establishment of special courts to try the offences under the Act. The object of establishing the Special Courts is to provide speedy trial.[84] It is for that purpose that the State Government with the concurrence of the Chief Justice of the High Court, is required, by notification in the Official Gazette, to specify for each district a Court of Sessions to be a Special Court to try the offences under the Act.[85] Specification of a Court of Sessions to be a Special Court to try the offences under the Act does not affect the status or the powers of such

Sessions Court which it enjoys and exercises by virtue of being a Court of Sessions constituted under Section 9 of the Code. In fact, the word 'specify' used in the language of Section 14 of Act presupposes the existence of a Court of Sessions. It does not take away the powers and jurisdiction of such Court of Sessions which it has under various provisions of code. The various provisions contained in the Code and those of the Act are to be so construed as may promote their smooth and harmonious functioning without causing any damage to each other. A Court of an Additional Sessions Judge, exercising the powers as such in a Sessions Division may be specified to be a Special Court for the purposes of Sec. 14 of the Act without in any manner adversely affecting its jurisdiction and powers as a Court of Sessions. Its specification as a Special Court for purpose of Sec. 15 of the Act would be in addition to and not in derogation of its powers and jurisdiction as a Judge/ Additional Sessions Judge. Such a construction of Sec. 14 of the Act advances and promotes the proper and harmonious functioning of various provisions contained in the two statutes is, therefore, quite proper.[86]

The Rajasthan High Court in *Hanuman Singh* Vs. *Union of India*[87] held that the jurisdiction of the Special Judge, who heard and disposed of petitioner's appeal against his conviction against the Act in the present case was not excluded by any provision of law or by any specific or general order made by the State Government/High Court. Since the Sessions Judge to whom the appeal was made by the petitioner was legally competent to make over such appeal for hearing and disposal to the Additional Sessions Judge functioning as such within the Sessions Division and who was also specified as a Special Judge for purpose of Sec. 14 of the Act, the transfer of petitioner's appeal by him to the Special Judge SC/ST cases, who was competent to hear and decide such appeal was not bad in law.[88]

In case of *Babaldas Beeharbhai* Vs. *State of Gujarat*,[89] complainant sought cancellation of bail on the ground that it was not granted by Special Court. The Gujarat High Court dismissed his application on two grounds. Firstly, although it is desirable that Special Court himself should try the case and decide the bail application of the accused who are charged with the offence under the Act yet only in exceptional and unavoidable circumstances, he should transfer that to the Additional or Assistant Judge. And secondly, that application for cancellation of bail was not filed by the State and court would not cancel bail on the application of complainant, *i.e.*, a private party.[90]

In case of *Pratap Chandra Barik* Vs. *State of Orissa*,[91] the accused, armed with a gun, came to the residence of the complainant and instructed his supporters to take away his household articles. They took away cash, furniture and paddy bags and demolished the house. On the basis of complaint, a FIR was lodged by the police. Chargesheet was filed. The magistrate took the cognisance u/s 27 of the Arms Act and Sec. 3 of the Act. The order was challenged on the ground that magistrate was not empowered to take cognisance and only Special Judge has power to do so. The High Court of Orissa set aside the order and held that only Special Judge duly empowered under the Act, can take cognisance. The Special Judge, was directed to proceed with the matter.[92]

2.8 Position of Juvenile Accused

In case of *In re : Sessions Judge, Kalpetta,*[93] a question which was referred to Kerala High Court was whether a juvenile who stands charged with offences punishable u/ss 450, 376 and 506(ii) of IPC and also u/s 3(1)(xii) of the Act, is to be tried by a Sessions Court or by the court established under the Juvenile Justice Act, 1996?[94] The court held that the Juvenile Justice Act is a special enactment which deals with juvenile offenders. The provisions of that Act cannot be nullified by the Juvenile Justice Act, which deals with an entirely different field. Therefore, the Act cannot override the provisions of the Act, which specifically deal with juvenile offenders. The juvenile is to be tried by a juvenile court.[95]

2.9 Appointment of Special Public Prosecutors

The other salient feature of the Act is that it provides appointment of Special Public Prosecutors to conduct trial of offences under the Act in the Special Court. Section 15 of the Act, which deals with appointment of Special Public Prosecutors, is reproduced hereunder:

> "15. *Special Public Prosecutor.*—For every Special Court, the State Government shall, by notification in the Official Gazette,

specify a Public Prosecutor or appoint an advocate who has been in practice as an advocate for not less than seven years, as a Special Public Prosecutor for the purpose of conducting cases in that Court."

2.10 Externment of Potential Offenders

The other salient feature of the Act is that it empowers Special Court to extern potential offenders from the Scheduled areas and Tribal areas. Sec. 10 of the Act deals with externment, which is as under:

> "10. *Removal of person likely to commit offence.*—(1) Where the Special Court is satisfied, upon a complaint or a police report that a person is likely to commit an offence under Chapter II of this Act in any area included in 'Scheduled Areas' or 'Tribal Area' as referred to in Article 244 of the Constitution, it may, by order in writing, direct such person to remove himself beyond the limits of such area, by such route and within such time as may be specified in the order, and not to return to that area from which he was directed to remove himself for such period, not exceeding two years, as may be specified in the order.
>
> (2) The Special Court shall, along with the order under sub-section (1), communicate to the person directed under this sub-section the grounds on which such order has been made.
>
> (3) The Special Court may revoke or modify the order made under sub-section (1), for the reasons to be recorded in writing, on the representation made by the person against whom such order has been made or by any other person on his behalf within thirty days from the date of the order."

Sec. 11 of the Act further provides procedure on failure of person to remove him from area and not to enter thereon after his removal. Sec. 12 of the Act provides taking measurements, *etc.* of persons against whom order u/s 10 is made. It also provides that resistance to or refusal to allow the tâking of measurement or photographs shall be deemed to be offence u/s 156 of the IPC. Sec. 13 lays down penalty for non-compliance of order u/s 10.

2.11 Attachment and Forfeiture of Property

The other salient feature of the Act is that it empowers the Special Court to attach movable or immovable or both properties belonging to any person accused of any offence u/ss. 3 to 6 of the Act. It also empowers the Special Court to forfeit movable or immovable or both properties of convict under any offence punishable u/ss. 3 to 6 of the Act, in addition to awarding any punishment. Sec. 7 deals with the powers of the Special Courts. It runs as under :

> "7. *Forfeiture of property of certain persons.*—(1) Where a person has been convicted of any offence punishable under this Chapter, the Special Court may, in addition to awarding any punishment, by order in writing, declare that any property, movable or immovable or both, belonging to the person, which has been used for the commission of that offence, shall stand forfeited to Government.
>
> (2) Where any person is accused of any offence under this Chapter, it shall be open to the Special Court trying him to pass an order that all or any of the properties, movable or immovable or both, belonging to him shall, during the period of such trial, be attached, and where such trial ends in conviction, the property so attached shall be liable to forfeiture to the extent it is required for the purpose of realisation of any fine imposed under this Chapter."

2.12 Cancellation of Arm Licence of Potential Accused and Grant of Arm Licences to SCs

The other salient feature of the Act is that it provides rules for cancellation of arms licence of potential accused of an offence under the Act and also provides rules for grant of arm licences to the SCs.

Rule 3(iii) and (v)[96] deal with these, which are as under :

"3. *Precautionary and preventive measures.*—(1) With a view to prevent atrocities on the Scheduled Castes and the Scheduled Tribes, the State Government shall,—***

(iii) if deem necessary, in the identified area cancel the arm licences of the persons, not being members of the Scheduled

Castes or the Scheduled Tribes, their near relations, servants or employees and family friends and get such arms deposited in the Government Armoury ;

* * *

(v) with a view to ensure the safety of the person and property, if deem necessary provide arms licences to the members of the Scheduled Castes and the Scheduled Tribes ;

* * *"

2.13 Denial of Anticipatory Bail

The other salient feature of the Act is that it prohibits grant of anticipatory bail to the accused of offences under the Act.

Sec. 18 of the Act puts this bar which is as under:

"18.*Section 438 of the Code not to apply to persons committing an offence under the Act.*—Nothing in Section 438 of the Code shall apply in relation to any case involving the arrest of any person on an accusation of having committed an offence under this Act."

In case of *Hari Shankar and others* Vs. *State,*[97] the petitioner against whom complainant has lodged a FIR u/s 3(1)(vii) of the Act approached the Madhya Pradesh High Court, Gwalior Bench for anticipatory bail. The Court held that Sec. 18 of the Act overrides Sec. 438 of the Code so application u/s 438 of the Code, is untenable in law.[98]

In case of *Punjak D. Suthar* Vs. *State of Gujarat,*[99] it was reiterated by the Gujarat High Court that if the Courts are to apply provisions of Sec. 18 of the Act quite mechanically and blindly merely guided by some general and popular prejudices, based on some words and tricky accusations in the complaint on mere assumptions without intelligently scrutinising and testing the probabilities, truthfulness, genuineness and otherwise dependability of the accusations in the complaint, *etc.*, then it would be simply unwittingly and credulously playing in the hands of some scheming unscrupulous complainant in denying the justice. Virtually, it would tantamount to abdicating and relegating its judicial duty, function of doing justice in such matters in favour and hands of such unscrupulous complainant by making him a Judge in his own cause. This is simply unthinkable and, therefore, impermissible. Whether the provisions of any particular Act and for that purpose the Rules made thereunder are applicable to the facts of a particular case or not, is always and unquestionably a matter which lies strictly and exclusively within the domain of "judicial consideration *** discretion and, therefore, neither mere allegation made in the complaint by itself nor bare denials by the accused can either automatically vest or divest the Court from discharging its ultimate judicial function *** duty to closely scrutinise and test the *prima facie* dependability of the allegations made in the complaint and reach its own decision."[100]

In case of *Jai Singh and another* Vs. *Union of India and others,*[101] Full Bench of Rajasthan High Court had considered the scope of Sec. 438 of the Code *vis-à-vis* the provisions of Sec. 18 of the Act. It was held that Sec. 438 was not applicable to the cases arising under the Act. The enactment was a special measure which incorporates the various forms of indignities, humiliations, harassment and exploitation to form the basis of atrocities when committed against the members of SCs and STs.[102] It was further held that the right to anticipatory bail did not flow form Art. 21 of the Constitution either expressly or impliedly. This right has been conferred by the Parliament. The Parliament by enacting another law or by amending the Code could take it away also.[103]

In contrast of these findings of F.B. of Rajasthan High Court, a D.B. of Madhya Pradesh in case of *Dr. Ram Krishna Balothia* Vs. *Union of India and others*[104] observed that Sec. 18 of the Act does not merely introduce restrictions regarding application of Sec. 438 of the Code. It renders totally inapplicable provisions of Sec. 438 of the Code with regard to all offences under the Act.[105] The object of the statute to ensure advancement of members of SCs and STs by protecting them from harassment, humiliation, disgrace, indignity, exploitation and the like by members of stronger sections of the society. Sec. 18 of the Act in its present form renders the procedure of the Act unfair and unreasonable and offends the very soul and spirit of the Art. 21 of the Constitution.[106] The Court held that Sec. 18 of the Act which does not conform to the norms of justice and fair play and prescribed a procedure which is impermissible under the Constitution and is liable to be struck down and struck down Sec. 18 of the Act, as violative of Arts. 14 and 21 of the Constitution.[107]

In appeal, the Supreme Court in case of *State of M.P. and another* Vs. *Ram Krishna Balotia and another*[108] overruled this decision. The main argument advanced before the SC was whether right to seek anticipatory bail is an essential ingredient of Art. 21 of the Constitution? The Court held that anticipatory bail cannot be granted as a matter of right. It is essentially a statutory right conferred long after coming into force of the Constitution. It cannot be considered as an essential ingredient of Art. 21 of the Constitution. And its, non-applications to certain special category of offences cannot be considered as violative of Art. 21.[109]

The Court observed that the offences which are enumerated u/s 3 of the Act are offences which, to say the least, denigrate members of SCs and STs in the eyes of society and prevent them from leading a life of dignity and self-respect. Such offences are committed to humiliate and subjugate members of SCs and STs with a view to keep them in a State of servitude. These offences constitute a separate class and cannot be compared with offences under the Penal Code.[110] The Court also held that Sec. 438 of Code is not available to persons committing offences u/s 3(1) of the Act.

In case of *Abdul Rasheed Siddiqui and another* Vs. *State of Madhya Pradesh and others,*[111] the Madhya Pradesh High Court observed that Sec. 18 of the Act has taken away the application of Sec. 438 of the Code to any case involving the arrest of any person of an accusation of having committed an offence under the Act.[112]

In case of *Raju Gounder and others* Vs. *The Union of India and others,*[113] it was observed by Madras High Court that even though several penal provisions are contained in the IPC and the Protection of Civil Rights Act, 1955, nevertheless the atrocities against the SC and ST persons did not subside and they became victims of attack by vested interests and there has been an increase in the disturbing trend of commission of certain atrocities like making the SC persons eat inedible substances like human excreta and attacks on and mass killings of helpless SCs and STs, rape of women belonging to the SCs and STs. Therefore, the Parliament considered it necessary to pass a special law, *viz.*, the Act and specify the offences and the punishments therefor. While doing so, it was also considered necessary that in order to have an effective enforcement of the provision of the Act and to ensure that such atrocities are not repeated, the provision of Sec. 438 of the Code of Criminal Procedure are not made available for the offenders under the Act. Therefore, the Parliament has enacted the provision as contained in Sec. 18 of the Act, to exclude the applicability of Sec. 438 of the Code of Criminal Procedure, in relation to any case involving arrest of any person on an accusation of having committed an offence under the Act.[114] It was held that these provisions are not violative of Arts. 14, 19 and 21 of the Constitution.[115] Resultantly, no anticipatory bail is available to the offenders of an offence under the Act.

In case of *Bapu Gouda and another* Vs. *State of Karnataka,*[116] the Karnataka High Court followed the above decision of the Supreme Court and held that as police have registered a case u/s 3 of the Act against the petitioner, therefore, provisions of Sec. 438 of Code are not applicable and petition for grant of anticipatory bail is not maintainable.[117]

In case of *Phulla Dass* Vs. *State of Punjab and another,*[118] the Punjab and Haryana High Court discussing the findings of *Jai Singh and another* Vs. *Union of India and others,*[119] *State of Madhya Pradesh* Vs. *Ramkrishna Balothia,*[120] and *Bapu Gouda and another* Vs. *State of Karnataka,*[121] concluded that indeed there is no controversy with the said proposition. But, when there is specific bar u/s 18 of the Act, such power as given under Art. 226 of the Constitution would only be used in exceptional cases. If the court comes to the conclusion that the process of law is being misused, the petition is totally *mala fide* and vexatious, on the basis of which FIR is recorded; the court would certainly exercise its inherent powers and even powers under Art. 226 of the Constitution. But, it would certainly not to be ever used to defeat specific provision, *i.e.* Sec. 18 of the Act.[122]

In case of *Ghirdhari Lal and others* Vs. *State of Rajasthan,*[123] the Rajasthan High Court discussed a case *Rakesh* Vs. *State of Rajasthan,*[124] and held that it is the duty of the court to see that the stringent provisions of Sec. 18 are not misused. The aforesaid object can be achieved only if judicial scrutiny is made permissible to find out whether an offence under the Act has been committed by a person or a group of persons before refusing him or them as the case may be benefit of pre-arrest bail. The court enlarged 2 accused on anticipatory bail and denied anticipatory bail to 5 accused.[125]

In case of *K. Mallesham* Vs. *State of A.P.,*[126] the Andhra Pradesh High Court held that the Court's jurisdiction to issue appropriate directions in exercise of its jurisdiction under Sec. 438 of the Code would in no way be excluded by mere mentioning the provisions of the Prevention of Atrocities Act in the FIR or in the complaint, as the case may be. The Court's jurisdiction in no way could be affected by what the Station House Officer does at the time of registration of the crime. The crucial question would be as to whether the contents of the complaint or the FIR would attract the provisions of the Prevention of Atrocities Act. Mere mention or non-mention of the provisions of the Prevention of Atrocities Act is of no consequence. In a given case, the contents of the allegations may attract the provisions of the Prevention of Atrocities Act, though there is no such mention of the provisions at the time of registration of the crime. Likewise, the allegations in the FIR or the complaint may not attract the provisions of the Prevention of Atrocities Act, at all, though a mention is made in the FIR of those provisions. What is required is a pragmatic assessment of the contents of the complaint in very given case. Even if there is a single averment attracting the provisions of the Prevention of Atrocities Act, it would be enough to exclude the operation of Sec. 438 of the Code. What is important is to have an assessment of the cumulative effect of the allegations made in the complaint or the FIR, as the case may be.

In case of *Suresh Kumar* Vs. *State of Madhya Pradesh,*[127] High Court of Madhya Pradesh while discussing the cases of *Kalyan Singh* Vs. *State of M.P.,*[128] *Bablu* Vs. *State of M.P.*[129] and *Ram Dayal & Ors.* Vs. *State of M.P,*[130] held that the bar created to grant anticipatory bail for accusation u/s 18 of the Act shall not apply when no *prima facie* material is available on the case diary to raise suspicion of commission of any offence under the Act against the accused. The Court enlarged the accused on anticipatory bail observing that it did not find material for *prima facie* suspecting the appellant of having committed offence under the Act.

The conclusion that emerges from above discussion is that anticipatory bail as provided u/s 438 of the Code is generally not available to the accused of an offence under the Act.

2.14 Denial of Probation to Convict

The other salient feature of the Act is that Sec. 19 of the Act put restrictions on the powers of the Special Court to grant probation to the convict of an offence under the Act. It runs as under:

> "19. *Section 360 of the Code or the Provisions of the Probation of Offenders Act not to apply to persons guilty of an offence under the Act.*—The provisions of section 360 of the Code and the provisions of the Probation of Offenders Act, 1958 (20 of 1958) shall not apply to any person above the age of eighteen years who is found guilty of having committed an offence under this Act."

In case of *Abdul Rasheed Siddiqui and other* Vs. *State of Madhya Pradesh and others,*[131] the court observed that Sec. 19 of the Act takes away the applicability of Sec. 360 of the Code and the provisions of the Probation of Offenders Act, 1958 to persons above the age of eighteen years who found guilty of having committed an offence under the Act. It was also emphasised that consequences of registration of a case under the Act are more severe than the consequences of registration of a case under IPC.[132]

2.15 Enhanced Punishment for some Offences

The other salient feature of the Act is that it provides enhanced punishment for those offences under IPC which are punishable with imprisonment for a term of ten years or more *vide* Sec. 3(2)(v) of the Act, which reads as under:

> "3. *Punishments for offences of atrocities.*—*** (2) Whoever, not being a member of Scheduled Caste or a Scheduled Tribe,—
>
> * * *

(v) commits any offence under the Indian Penal Code (45 of 1860) punishable with imprisonment for a term of ten years or more against a person or property on the ground that such person is a member of a Scheduled Caste or a Scheduled Tribe or such property belongs to such member, shall be punishable with imprisonment for life and with fine.* * *"

In case of *Lalubha Keshrisingh Garasia and, etc.* Vs. *State of Guj. and others,*[133] the Gujarat High Court held that in order to convict under this section, prosecution must establish two things, firstly, that offence under IPC has been committed on a member of SC or ST, and secondly, that said offence has been committed on the ground that victim is a member of SC or ST.[134] It was observed by the court that second ingredient was not established by prosecution and consequently court set aside conviction u/s 3(2)(v) of the Act.[135]

2.16 Enhanced Minimum Punishment for Public Servant

The Act also provides for more minimum punishment to the accused of offence of atrocities, if he is a public servant. Sec. 3(2)(vii) of the Act deals with this enhanced punishment. It runs as under:

"3. *Punishment for offences of atrocities.*—*** (2) Whoever, not being a member of a Scheduled Caste or a Scheduled Tribe,—

***

(vii) being a public servant, commits any offence under this section, shall be punishable with imprisonment for a term which shall not be less than one year but which may extend to the punishment provided for that offence."

2.17 Punishment for Neglect of Duties

The other salient feature of the Act is that it provides punishment for neglect of duties. If a public servant belonging to other than SC or ST, wilfully neglects his duties required to be performed by him under this Act, he shall be liable for punishment.

Section 4 deals with punishment for neglect of duties. It runs as under:

"4. *Punishment for neglect of duties.*—Whoever, being a public servant but not being a member of a Scheduled Caste or Scheduled Tribe, wilfully neglects his duties required to be performed by him under this Act, shall be punishable with imprisonment for a term which shall not be less than six months but which may extend to one year."

In case of *Ram Pal* Vs. *State of Rajasthan,*[136] a complaint under Sec. 3(1)(iv), (v) and (vi) of the Act was sent to the police for investigation under sub-section (3) of Sec. 156 of the Code. The case was registered by the police in exercise of the powers given by the Code. The investigation was conducted by the petitioner public servant u/s 157 and other provisions of the Code and the final report was submitted. It was held that the submission of final report was in discharge of his duties u/s 173 of the Code and it cannot be said to be an act in exercise of the duty prescribed by or under the Act. Consequently, even if any neglect of duty in the conduct of investigation is committed by the Investigating Officer while purporting to act in exercise of powers conferred by the Code, the provisions of Sec. 4 of the Act would not be attracted unless it can be established that the wilful neglect of duty was committed by the Investigating Officer in relation to duty prescribed under the Act.[137]

2.18 Compensation to the Victims or their Legal Heirs

The other salient feature of the Act is that it provides Rules for awarding compensation to the victims of atrocities or their legal heirs.

Rule 12(4), (5) and (6) of the Rules deals with the compensation, which are as under:

"12. *Measures to be taken by the District Administration.*—***

(4) The District Magistrate or the Sub-Divisional Magistrate or any other Executive Magistrate shall make arrangements for providing immediate relief in cash or in kind or both to the victims of atrocity, their family members and dependants according to the scale as in the Schedule annexed to these Rules (Annexure-I read with Annexure-II). Such

immediate relief shall also include food, water, clothing, shelter, medical aid, transport facilities and other essential items necessary for human beings.

(5) The relief provided to the victim of the atrocity or his/her dependant under sub-rule (4) in respect of death, or injury to, or damage to, property shall be in addition to any other rights to claim compensation in respect thereof under any other law for the time being in force.

(6) The relief and rehabilitation facilities mentioned in sub-rule (4) above shall be provided by the District Magistrate or the Sub-Divisional Magistrate or any other Executive Magistrate in accordance with the scales provided in the Schedule annexed to these Rules.

The amount of payment of compensation differs from case to case, *e.g.*, it is Rs. 20,000.00 for violation of right to vote. It is Rs. 25,000.00 for forced or bonded labour; false, malicious or vexatious legal proceedings; It is up to Rs. 25,000.00 for insult, intimidation and humiliation. It is Rs. 25,000.00 or more for victims of drinking or eating inedible or obnoxious substance; wrongful occupation or cultivation of land, *etc.*; false and frivolous information; causing injury, insult or annoyance; derogatory act; relating to land, premises and water. It is Rs. 50,000.00 to each victim of the offence of outraging the modesty of a woman, sexual exploitation of woman and the victims of offences under the Indian Penal Code punishable with imprisonment for a term of 10 years or more. It is up to Rs. 1,00,000.00 to the victims of fouling of water and denial of customary rights of passage. It is at least Rs. 1,00,000.00 or full compensation of the loss or harm sustained by victims of giving false evidence or 100% incapacitation of non-earning member of a family or murder/death of non-earning member of a family. It is at least Rs. 2,00,000.00 for 100% incapacitation of earning member of a family or murder/death of earning member of a family. 25% of the compensation amount is to be paid to the victims or legal heirs at the time of lodging of FIR in case of *begar* or forced or bonded labour; and remaining 75% is to be paid on conviction in the lower court. 25% is to be paid to the victims or their legal heirs at the time of filing of charge sheet in the court and remaining amount of 75% is to be paid at the time of conviction by lower court in case of atrocities by drink or eat inedible or obnoxious substance; causing injury, insult or annoyance; derogatory act; insult, intimidation and humiliation. 50% of the compensation amount is to be paid to the victim of 100% incapacitation of non-earning or earning member of a family on lodging FIR and 25% at chargesheet and 25% on conviction by the lower court. 75% of the compensation amount is to be paid to the legal heirs of the victim of death/murder at the time after post mortem and 25% on conviction in lower court. In addition to, relief amounts as narrated above, victim of murder, death, massacre, rape, mass rape and gang rape, permanent incapacitation and dacoity are also entitled to other relief. Widow or other dependants of deceased SC and ST are entitled to get Rs. 1,000.00 per month as pension. Or, one member of family of the deceased is entitled to get employment, or provision of agricultural land, and house, if necessary by outright purchase, is to be made by the Government for them. Besides, full cost of the education and maintenance of the children of the victims is to be provided by the Government. Children may be admitted to Ashram, School/ residential schools. Victims are also entitled to get utensils, rice, wheat, pulses, *etc.* for a period of three months. Brick/stone masonry house to be constructed or provided to the victims of the atrocities at Government cost where it has been burnt or destroyed.

Notes and References

1. Tripathi, Dr. B.N. Mani, An Introduction to Jurisprudence and Legal Theory, 1977 at 77.
2. Baxi, Upendra, Approaches to the Study of Law in Developing Societies, Symposium on the Theory in Sociology of Law (Tokyo, September, 1975) at 10.
3. *Supra,* note 1 at 79.
4. *Ibid.* at 85.
5. *See,* William J. Chambliss, "The Criminalization of Conduct" in *Law and Deviance,* Edited by H. Laurence Ross, Sage Publication, London, 1981 at 49.
6. *Ibid. See,* also Friedman, L., *Law and Society: An Introduction,* 1977 at 99.
7. *Supra,* note 5 at 57.
8. *See,* Oliver Mendalsohn and Marika Vicziany, "The Untouchables" in *The Rights of Subordinated People,* edited by Oliver Mendalsohn and Upendra Baxi, Oxford University Press, Delhi at 73.

9. *Supra,* note 8 at 74.
10. *Ibid.* at 75.
11. *Ibid. at 77.*
12. *See*, footnote 98 of Introduction for Details and the Protection of Civil Rights Act, 1955 and The Scheduled Castes and The Scheduled Tribes (Prevention of Atrocities) Act, 1989.
13. *See*, Rao, B. Shiva, *Framing of India's Constitution—A Study,* 1968 at 202 and 203.
14. *See*, Art. 17 of *the Constitution of India*, 1950.
15. *Supra,* note 8 at 65.
16. *See*, Galanter, Mark, UNTOUCHABILITY AND THE LAW, at II-11, *Economic and Political Weekly*, Annual Number, January, 1989 at 144; See, also Khosla, Dinesh, *Myth and Reality of the Protection of Civil Rights Law: A Case Study of Untouchability in Rural India*, Hindustan Publishing Corporation (India), Delhi 1987.
17. *See*, *State of Karnataka* Vs. *Appa Balu Ingale and Others,* AIR 1993 SC 1126 at 1129-30.
18. Statement of Objects and Reasons of the Scheduled Castes and the Scheduled Tribes (Prevention of Atrocities) Act, 1989.
19. *See*, Baxi Upendra, *Law and Poverty* : *Critical Essays,* 1988 at 162.
20. *See*, RCSCST 2 (1978-79). See, also RCSCST IInd Report, 313-20, (1980-81).
21 *Supra,* note 18; See, also *Infra,* note 25 at 1200 and *Infra*, note 30 at 3391 and 3392.
22. AIR 1993 Raj. 177 ; 1993 CRI.L.J. 2705.
23. AIR 1994 MP 143.
24. *Ibid.* at 150 and 151.
25. AIR 1995 SC 1198 ; 1995 CRI.L.J. 2076.
26. *Supra,* note 22.
27. *Supra,* note 25 at 1201.
28. AIR 1995 M.P. 138.
29. *Ibid.* at 140.
30. 1995 CRI.L.J. 3390.
31. *Supra,* note 30 at 3392.
32. 1998 CRI.L.J. 157.
33. *Supra,* note 25.
34. *Supra,* note 32 at 158.
35. 1997 CRI.L.J. 1231.
36. *Supra,* note 35 at 1232.
37. 1999(1) Crimes 499.
38. *Supra,* note 37 at 507.
39. *Cf.* The Hate Crimes Sentencing Enhancement Act of 1994.
40. 1995 CRI.L.J. 1561.
41. *Ibid.* at 1568 ; See, also *Narayan Sahoo* Vs. *State*, 1999(1) CRIMES 605 at 606.
42. 1999(1) CRIMES 188.
43. *Supra,* note 42 at 190.
44. *See*, *Dev Raj* Vs. *State* (1968) 34 Cut. L.T. 168.

45 1987 (2) CRIMES 270.
46. A.I.R. 1967 S.C. 63 at 68.
47. *Supra,* note 46 at 67.
48. 1997 CRI.L.J. 948.
49. *Ibid.*
50. 1996 CRI.L.J. 502.
51. *Ibid.* at 505.
52. 1995 CRI.L.J. 1561.
53. *Supra,* note 52 at 1586.
54. 1999 CRI.L.J. 998.
55. *Supra,* note 54 at 1001 and 1003.
56. 1997 CRI.L.J. 2036.
57. *Ibid.* at 2039.
58. 1995 CRI.L.J. 3060.
59. *Ibid.* at 3061.
60. 1997 CRI.L.J. 122.
61. *Ibid.* at 125.
62. 1998 CRI.L.J. 53.
63. *Ibid.* at 54.
64. *Supra,* note 56.
65. *Ibid.* at 2039.
66. *Ibid.* at 2040.
67. *Supra,* note 32.
68. *Ibid.* at 159.
69. *Supra,* note 35.
70. *Ibid.* at 1231.
71. *Ibid.* at 1232.
72. 1992 CRI.L.J. 3054.
73. *Ibid.* at 3055.
74. *Ibid.* at 3056.
75. 1998 CRI.L.J. 1467.
76. *Ibid.* at 1468.
77. 1999 CRI.L.J. 557.
78. *Ibid.* at 559.
79. *Supra,* note 28 at 140.
80. *Id.*
81. *Id.*
82. 1990 CRI.L.J. 1799.
83. *Ibid.* at 1800.
84. *See, Hanuman Singh* Vs. *Union of India,* 1997 CRI.L.J. 1054.
85. Section 14 of the Act.
86. *Supra,* note 84, at 1058 and 1059.
87 *Ibid.*
88. *Ibid.* at 1059.
89. 1993(2) CRIMES 403.
90. *Supra,* note 89 at 404 and 405.
91. 1999 CRI.L.J. 562.
92. *Ibid.* at 565.

93. 1995 CRI.L.J. 330.
94. *Ibid.* at 331.
95. *Ibid.* at 334.
96. *See*, the Scheduled Castes and the Scheduled Tribes (Prevention of Atrocities) Rules, 1995 in Ministry of Welfare, G.S.R. 316(E), New Delhi, the 31st March, 1995.
97. 1990 CRI.L.J. 1799.
98. *Ibid.* at 1800.
99. 1999 CRI.L.J. 324.
100. *Ibid.* at 328 and 329.
101. *Supra,* note 22.
102. *Ibid.* at 183.
103. *Ibid.* 101 at 184.
104. *Supra,* note 23.
105. *Ibid.* at 150.
106. *Id.*
107. *Ibid.* at 151.
108. *Supra,* note 25.
109. *Ibid.* at 1201.
110. *Ibid.* at 1202.
111. *Supra,* note 28 at 140.
112. *Id.*
113. *Supra,* note 30.
114. *Ibid.* at 3392.
115. *Ibid.* at 3394.
116. 1996 CRI.L.J. 1117.
117. *Ibid.* at 1118.
118. *Supra,* note 32.
119. *Supra,* note 22.
120. *Supra,* note 25.
121. *Supra,* note 116.
122. *Supra,* note 32 at 159.
123. 1996 CRI.L.J. 1613.
124. *Ibid.* at 1614.
125. *Id.*
126. 1999 CRI. L.J. 324.
127. 1999(1) CRIMES 636.
128. 1995 (II) M.P.W.N. 9.
129. 1996 (II) M.P.W.N. 9.
130. 1991 JLJ 468.
131. *Supra,* note 28.
132. *Ibid.* at 140.
133. 1997 CRI.L.J. 3839.
134. *Ibid.* at 3848 and 3849.
135. *Ibid.* at 3849.
136. 1998 CRI.L.J. 3261.
137 *Supra,* note 136 at 3265.

PART-II

NON-DOCTRINAL

CHAPTER 3

EMPIRICAL ANALYSIS OF THE SCs AND STs (PREVENTION OF ATROCITIES) ACT, 1989

3.1 Wide Range of Underlying Issues Focused

The present study is an effort to find out the impact of the Scheduled Castes and Scheduled Tribes (Prevention of Atrocities) Act, 1989 on SCs. The impact of any Act depends upon many factors. For example, awareness of the people in general about the problem; impact of the problem on the society at large and ultimately on nation; causes of giving rise to that problem; the provisions of the particular Act; the machineries provided therein in order to prevent the problem; adjudicate the cases; and rehabilitate the victims, and likewise. This study is an endeavour to find out as to how people of this country respond to the problem of atrocities on the Scheduled Caste? What are the probable grounds, in their view for commission of atrocities on the SCs? Whether they are aware about the provisions of the Act? Their awareness about the machineries, fora, special courts, *etc.*, which have been provided to prevent the offences of atrocities; adjudicate the cases of atrocities; and rehabilitate the victims of atrocities under the Act, are to be measured. It has further to be seen how they react to the problems and their solution?

Their attitude has to be measured towards handling of this problem, besides it has to be seen, what is the opinion of the public in general about the provisions of the Act? And what they suggest to overcome the drawbacks in the Act? And what are their suggestions to tackle this problem and to improve the Act?

This research project proceeds to evaluate the authenticity and viability of above-mentioned points, which give origin to following questions:

1. Whether people are aware about commission of atrocities on the members of SCs?
2. What is the concept of atrocity in their mind?
3. What are the grounds/factors, which are responsible for commission of atrocities on them?
4. Whether people are aware about the provisions of the Act?
5. Whether people are aware about the machineries, fora and special courts envisaged under the Act?
6. How the machineries, fora and special courts are working?
7. What is the opinion of the persons/officials running the said machineries, fora and special courts?
8. What do they suggest for improvement of the Act?

3.2 Specific Hypothesis to be Tested

In order to get the answer of questions discussed herein before the present study addresses itself to answer the following hypotheses :

(i) (a) There is a poor social awareness of the problem of atrocities amongst the Target Group.

(b) There is a lack of consensus about the causes of atrocities.

(c) There is little awareness about the new law and its implications.

(ii) (a) The infrastructure provided under the Act is inadequate.

(b) There is little will amongst the functionaries to enforce the law.

(iii) The appellate courts policy responses on the Act are in consonance with the philosophy of the Act.

3.3 Importance and Utility of Research

It is well known fact that law cannot grow in vacuum. It requires its roots to go deep into the wishes of the masses. If the law is enacted contrary to the wishes of the masses, then there is likelihood that the Act may not succeed to get desired result sought to be achieved by that particular Act. Although, Temple Entry Acts, made by various State Governments before independence for the purpose of removal of caste disabilities and Constitution of India also declared abolition of untouchability *vide* Art. 17 and in furtherance of that declaration, the Untouchability (Offences) Act, 1955 which was amended in the year 1976 as the Protection of the Civil Rights Act, 1976 and subsequently, the Act under study was enacted in the year 1989, yet it is opined by legal experts that these remained symbolic pieces of legislation as these were against the opinion of the masses. The importance of the Research Project lies under the fact that view of general public are being taken on the various aspects of the Act which was enacted to prevent the atrocities.

3.4 Operationalisation of Terms

In order to have exact and specific research, it is necessary to take correct meaning of words used specifically in the hypotheses.[1] In this context the definitions of awareness, impact, judicial response, machineries, and sufficiency are to be specifically taken.

Awareness : In this work the term 'awareness' means that SCs have the knowledge of or sensitive to the Act or its provisions that confer protections to and other benefits on the SCs.

Impact : In this work the term 'impact' means the effect of the Act to prevent or minimize the incidences of atrocities on SCs.

Judicial Response : In this work the term 'judicial response' means the trend of judicial decisions in interpreting various provisions of the Act.

Machineries : In this work the term 'machineries' means the Special Courts, Special Public Prosecutors, Investigating Officers, Nodal Officers, SCs & STs Protection Cells, State and District Level Vigilance and Monitoring Committees and the rehabilitative Agencies envisaged under the Act or the Rules framed thereunder.

Sufficiency : In this work the term 'sufficiency' means that the protections provided to SCs and the fora envisaged under the Act are sufficient or adequate to prevent the atrocities on SCs.

3.5 Methodology : Empirical Analysis of the Act

This study is mainly an empirical study to find out the impact of Scheduled Castes and Scheduled Tribes (Prevention of Atrocities) Act on the Scheduled Castes. So, socio-legal research method will be applied, to find out the impact of the said Act on the Scheduled Castes.

Research, according to Encyclopedia Britannica is an act of searching into a matter closely and carefully, inquiry directed to the discovery of truth and in particular the trained scientific investigation of the principles and facts of any subject, based on original and first hand study of authorities or experiment. Investigations of every kind which have been on original source of knowledge may be styled as research and it may be said that without research no authoritative work have been written, no scientific discoveries or inventions made, no theories of any value propounded.[2]

3.6 Statement of Problem

The atrocities on the members of Scheduled Castes are still being reported in daily Newspapers, Journals, Reports, Magazines, *etc.* The core of the problem before us is if the Scheduled Castes and the Scheduled Tribes (Prevention of Atrocities) Act, 1989 has been enforced since 30.01.1990, then what impact this Act has left on the people for whose benefit this enactment was passed by the Parliament?

3.7 Development of Questionnaire and Interview Schedule

In order to get the responses of the general public including the people of Target Group, *i.e.*, members of Scheduled Castes and Scheduled Tribes, officials responsible for administration of Criminal Justice and the persons entrusted with the tasks of law making and public opinion making, three sets of questionnaire were prepared. First set of questionnaire is for the Target Group. Second set of questionnaire is for the officials responsible for administration of criminal justice, for example, Police Personnel, Prosecutors, Lawyers, Doctors, Judges, Magistrates and other Agencies involved under the

Act. The third set of questionnaire is prepared for Law Makers and Opinion Makers, *e.g.*, Members of Parliament, Legislatures, Academicians, Media Persons, Social Activists and members of Non-Governmental Organizations, *etc.* The first set of questionnaire consists of fifty questions. Second and third set of questionnaire consists of seventy questions each. Questionnaires are prepared in simple language. Initially, there were more questions than narrated above. Some of the questions were dropped and modified after taking pilot study of the questionnaire by feeding them to few subjects.

While framing first set of questionnaire for Target Group, care has been taken to frame the questions in very simple language. The forms of questions are kept very short so that the persons of target groups may easily understand it. While framing the second and third set of questionnaire, care has been taken to frame such questions which may elicit the information desired to be sought through these questionnaires. In addition, questions regarding concept of atrocities, impact of atrocities on the SCs, society and nation have been incorporated in every set of questionnaire. Question Nos. 1 to 5 of questionnaire for the Target Group and question Nos. 1 to 3 for remaining two sets are on these points. Question Nos. 6 to 15 of the first set, question Nos. 4 to 13 of second set and Question Nos. 4 to 15 and 18 are regarding probable cause of atrocities. Question Nos. 16 to 36 of first questionnaire, Question Nos. 14 to 40 of the second questionnaire and Question Nos. 16 & 17 and 19 to 23 of the third questionnaire are questions eliciting information about the provisions of the Act. Question Nos. 37 to 40 of first set, Question Nos. 41 to 59 of second set and Questions Nos. 24 to 51 of third set seek to elicit information of respective subjects about the working of the Act provisions and opinion on the subject thereon. Question Nos. 41 to 50 of the first set seek to elicit information of the subjects regarding suffering of atrocities by the subject and what action is contemplated under the law and what action they have usually taken in the event of actual commission of atrocity. In the second set of questionnaire, Question Nos. 60 to 70 and in the third set of questionnaire, Question Nos. 52 to 70 elicit information about the suggestions, the respective subjects may give to prevent the commission of atrocities and to improve the provisions of the Act.

The separate answer-sheets were prepared to record the responses of the subjects keeping in view that it would be more useful and convenient to analyse the data, if the responses were recorded separately.

The questionnaires were originally developed in English and later on these were translated into Hindi. While translating, care was taken about its simplicity, intelligibility and directness. For this purpose, the Hindi and English version of the questionnaires were given to two language experts and subject experts for checking whether or not the questions in Hindi form are in conformity with English version. Final sets of questionnaires were developed after a pilot study. In order to test the validity of the Hindi version of questionnaire, same set of questionnaire was given to subjects twice, first in English and then in Hindi.

3.8 Sampling and Data Collection

In the light of the objectives of the study and the sample, the choice for a method of collecting data is taken to be questionnaire.

In order to test the hypotheses, views of large sections of society from Target Groups, officials of Different Units of Legal System and Opinion Makers and Law Makers were collected by feeding questionnaire to them. Sampling done was stratified random sampling. Although questionnaire method of data collection is more open to respondents bias, nevertheless, its advantages in the present context apparently outweigh its disadvantages. Questionnaire method is economical in terms of both time and money. It allows for a large coverage and for a comparatively unhibited flow of information.[3]

Keeping in view that this study is with a special reference to the problem of atrocity on the Scheduled Caste in Northern India, care has been taken to get responses of the subjects from entire Northern India, covering Jammu & Kashmir, Himachal Pradesh, Chandigarh, Punjab, Haryana, Uttar Pradesh, Delhi, Bihar, Madhya Pradesh, Rajasthan, West Bengal, *etc.*

The object was to get 200 responses of persons belonging to SCs & STs covering Illiterates, Matric Pass, Under Graduates, Graduates, Post Graduates, Businessmen, Service Personnel and other categories professing different occupations; 100 responses from

Advocates; 50 responses each from Public Prosecutors; I.A.S., P.C.S., Doctors and other Officers; Judges; Police Officials; and M.Ps., Academician, Legislators, Media Persons, Social Activists, *etc.*, on the first, second and third sets of questionnaire. So a large number of questionnaires in Hindi and English with answer sheets were distributed in the desired groups through personal contacts.

As very less number of answer sheets were received from the subject, therefore, it was thought appropriate to get responses of subjects through personal interview, directly, feeding the questionnaire to the subject, personally as well as, in groups wherever it was possible. In order to get the desired number of responses a long span of time was spent on the data collections. In fact, it extended for over a period of one year.

3.9 Questionnaire and Interview Schedule

In order to elicit empirically different kinds of information regarding the law and its implementation and in particular, information about the concept of atrocities; awareness of the people regarding commission of atrocities on the members of SCs; factors responsible for commission of atrocities; awareness of provisions of the Act; the machineries provided thereunder; awareness of public regarding financial help, security and rehabilitating aspects; besides, the probable suggestions for prevention of atrocities, the questions were developed. Separate questionnaire for the Target Groups, *i.e.*, SCs and STs, Different Units of Legal System and Law Makers and Opinion Makers were also developed. Separate answer-sheets were developed for convenient analysis of the answers given in the questionnaire and interview schedule. Answer to each question is categorised into three categories, namely "Yes", "No" and "Undecided". Those subjects who want to answer the questions in affirmative were requested to put the right (√) mark under the category "yes". Those subjects who want to answer the question in negative were requested to put the right (√) mark under the category "No". There may be subjects who neither want to give answer in affirmative nor in negative, they were requested to put their answer, *i.e.* right (√) mark under the category "Undecided".

Example

Q. Are you aware that atrocities still being committed on the members of the SCs?

Yes	No	Undecided

Questionnaire and interview schedule were developed in bilingual, *i.e.*, English and Hindi, keeping in view that a large number of population of Target Group is illiterate or not highly educated and further that the inhabitants of Northern India have their language as Hindi. Questionnaire were given to a large number of persons of different strata residing at different places so that responses of required number of respondents could be obtained. Although attempts and efforts were made to obtain responses from different persons residing at different places covering entire Northern India, yet subjects were chosen from public randomly.

The questionnaire in English was fed to those persons who know English and accordingly questionnaire in Hindi was fed to Hindi knowing persons.

3.10 Analysis of Data and Results

On receipt of 550 responses consisting of 200 from Target Groups, 100 from Advocates, 50 from Public Prosecutors, 50 from I.A.S., P.C.S., Doctors and other officers, 50 from Judges, 50 from Police Personnel and 50 from M.Ps., Legislators, Academicians, Media Persons, Social Activists, N.G.Os., *etc.*, the work of analysis of data was started in the following manner.

3.11 Sorting out Answer Sheets

The first step for analysis of data was to sort out the answer sheets received/obtained from the different subjects. The answer sheets of first questionnaire were clubbed together and thereafter these were serial numbered 1 to 200. Likewise, the answer sheets of second questionnaire meant for officials concerning Different Units of Legal Systems were clubbed together after separating them from the rest. The responses of Lawyers were serial numbered from 201 to 300. The answer sheets of Public Prosecutors were separated, and were given serial numbers as 301 to 350. In the same manner answer sheets of I.A.S., P.C.S., Doctors, and other Officers were separated and were given serial numbers as 351 to 400. Likewise answer sheets of Judges were given serial numbers from 401 to 450 and answer sheets of Police Personnel were given serial numbers from 451 to 500. Similarly, answers sheets of M.Ps., academicians, *etc.*, were separated and were given serial number from 501 to 550.

While sorting out the answer sheets, it was found that some of the answer sheets were not complete. Those answer sheets were not taken for analysis and kept separately, but to complete the required numbers, other subjects were interviewed.

3.12 Preparation of Tables

After sorting out the answer-sheets, some Tables were prepared on calculating the responses manually. As it was not feasible to calculate the responses manually in person, so assistance was taken from account experts to calculate the answers given in "Yes", "No" and "Undecided" on each question. As this work was very time consuming, troublesome and monotonous and errors were bound to take place in calculation, it was thought appropriate to take assistance of computer to calculate the responses of large number of subjects. Before seeking the assistance of computer experts, some tables of responses of I.A.S., P.C.S., Doctors and other officers of each group, *i.e.*, SCs, STs and others were prepared manually. These tables were converted into percentage table and on the basis of these percentage tables, responses of I.A.S., P.C.S., Doctors and other officers were demonstrated through graphical representation so that the computer expert may understand how to prepare the tables of responses? And ultimately, how to represent the views through graphs, so that the reader may understand the results of the research promptly, easily and without wasting much time.

Preparation of Tables with the Help of Computer

All the 550 answer-sheets duly clubbed and serial numbered as discussed above were handed over to computer expert. He prepared programme suitable to calculate the responses. Thereafter, answers of answer-sheets from 1 to 550 were fed in the computer. A draft copy was taken out of the table showing views of the I.A.S., P.C.S.,

Doctors and others. It was found that there was some difference between the tables prepared manually and the table obtained through computer. In order to reconcile the situation, all the 550 answer-sheets were compared with the table shown on the screen of the computer. It was found that while feeding, computer experts had committed some error. All these errors were rectified and again a table was taken out of responses of I.A.S., P.C.S., Doctors and other officers. This time both the tables tallied. It was concluded that computer had correct feeding of answer-sheets.

Obtaining Tables from Computer

On ascertaining the correct feeding of the responses separate master tables showing the result of the study, as follows, were taken out. Table Nos. 1 to 77 were prepared on the basis of these tables. These tables are not being included in this work in order to avoid repetition.

S. No.	*Table Showing Result of Responses*	*Number of Responses*
1	Total persons of the Target group	200
2	Post Graduates – Target group	57
3	Graduates – Target group	68
4	Under Graduates – Target group	25
5	Matric Pass - Target group	34
6	Illiterates – Target group	16
7	Service personnel – Target group	124
8	Businessmen - Target group	12
9	Other categories – Target group	68
10	Different Units of the Legal System	300
11	Different Units of the Legal System — SCs	112
12	Different Units of the Legal System — STs	7
13	Different Units of the Legal System — Others	181
14	Lawyers	100
15	Lawyers — SCs	34
16	Lawyers — Others	66
17	Public Prosecutors	50
18	Public Prosecutors – SCs	11
19	Public Prosecutors – Others	39
20	I.A.S. *etc.*	50
21	I.A.S. *etc.* - SCs	30
22	I.A.S. *etc.* - STs	5
23	I.A.S. *etc.* – Others	15
24	Judges	50
25	Judges – SCs	25
26	Judges – Others	25

27	Police Officials	50
28	Police Officials – SCs	12
29	Police Officials – STs	2
30	Police Officials – Others	36
31	Law Makers & Opinion Makers	50
32	Law Makers & Opinion Makers – SCs	35
33	Law Makers & Opinion Makers – STs	1
34	Law Makers & Opinion Makers – others	14

3.13 Creation of Graphs

After taking out the above mentioned tables, the answers shown in the table were converted into percentage by the computer expert on the basis of conversion percentage table supplied to him of responses of I.A.S., P.C.S., Doctors and other officers, keeping in mind that answers of each and every question has to be depicted through graphical representation. In order to avoid thickness of the Research Project, percentage table were not drawn from the computer and were only used for drawing the graphs showing the views of the subjects/respondents on the questionnaires. As many as 66 graphs, as follows and having nos. 1 to 66, were taken out with the help of computer showing the views of respondents, question-wise depicting the result of questions of similar nature.[4] On the basis of these primary tables and graphs as many as 79 graphs having nos. 67 to 145, which are being discussed at relevant places while discussing the result of the data, were prepared to give bird's eye view of the opinion of respondents.

S. No.	*Description of Graphs*	*Graph No.*
	Graph Showing awareness of Atrocities on SCs –	
1.	• Target Groups – Q. Nos. 1 to 5	1
2.	• MPs, Legislators, Media Persons, Social Activists and Members of N.G.Os., *etc.*, – Q. Nos. 1 to 3	2
3.	• Judicial Officers, Public Prosecutors, Lawyers, Police Officials, I.A.S., P.C.S., Doctors and Other Officers – Q. Nos. 1 to 3	3
4.	• Judicial Officers – Q. Nos. 1 to 3	4
5.	• Public Prosecutors – Q. Nos. 1 to 3	5

Graph No. 1 : Views of Target Group on Atrocities

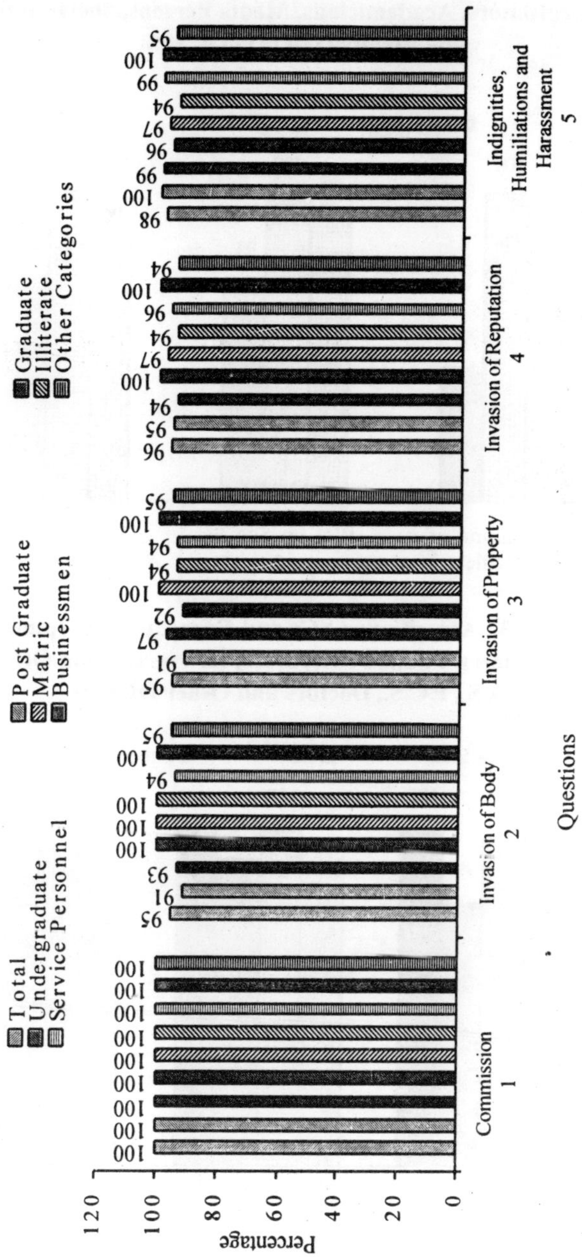

Graph No. 2 : Atrocities on SCs and Consequences Opinions of M.Ps., Legislators, Academicians, Media Persons, Social Activists and Members of N.G.Os. etc.

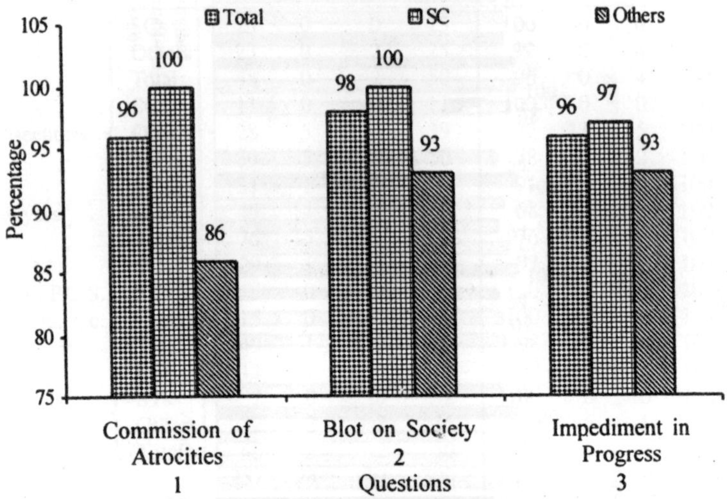

Graph No. 3 : Atrocities on SCs and Consequences Opinion of Judicial Officers, Public Prosecutors, Lawyers, Police Officials, I.A.S., P.C.S., Doctors and Other Officers

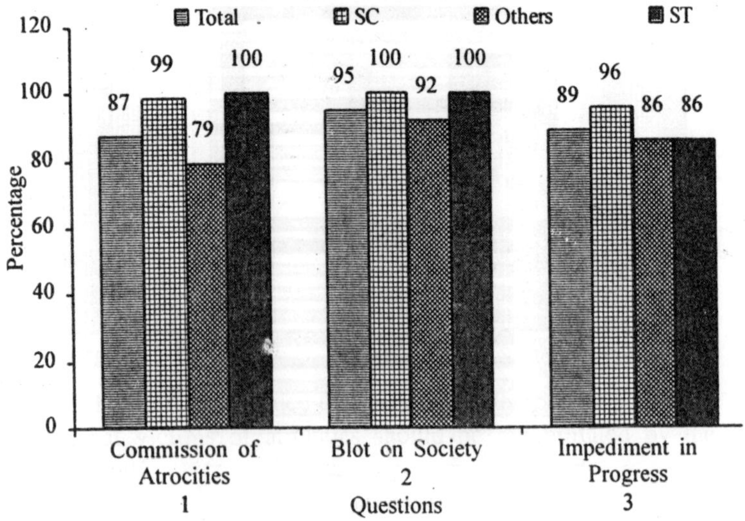

Graph No. 4 : Atrocities on SCs and Consequences Opinion of Judicial Officers

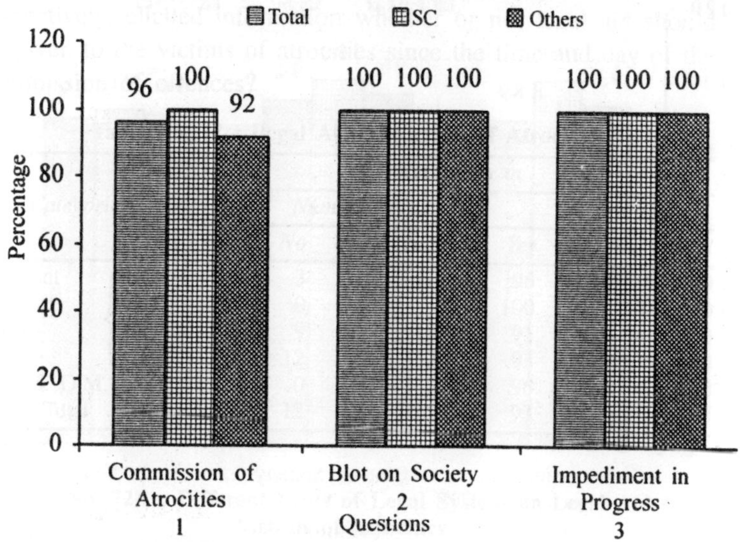

Graph No. 5 : Atrocities on SCs and Consequences Opinion of Public Prosecutors

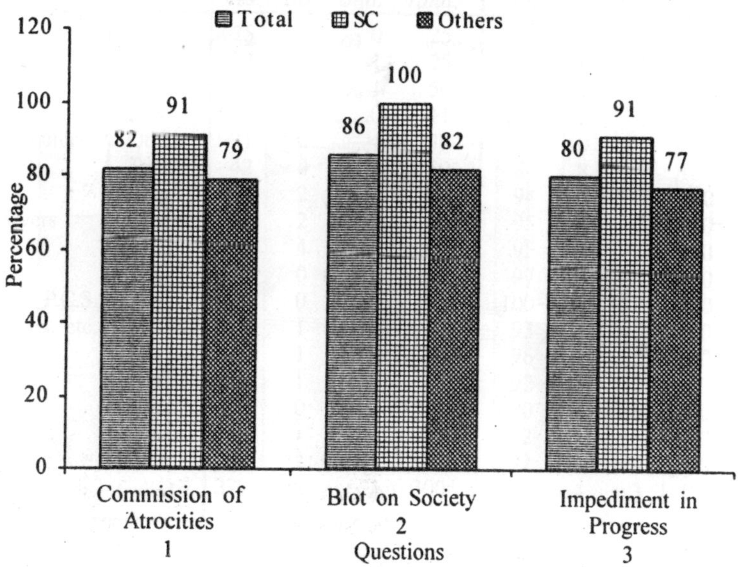

Graph No. 6 : Atrocities on SCs and Consequences Opinion of Lawyers

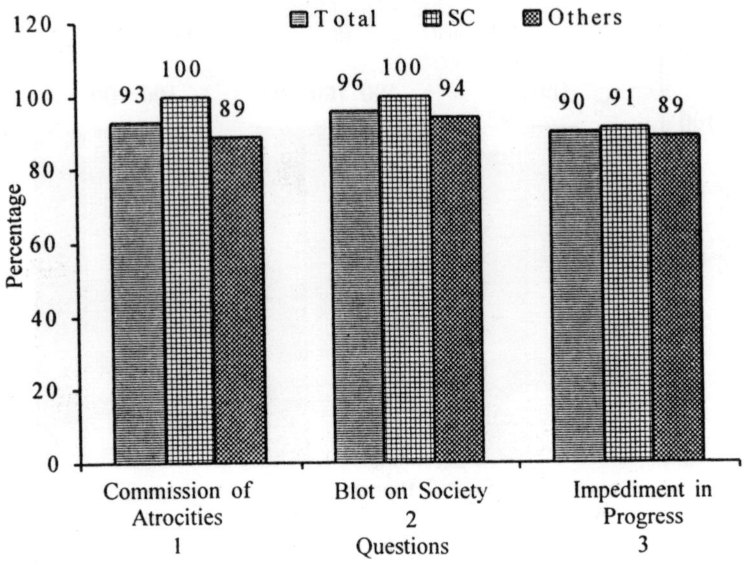

Graph No. 7 : Atrocities on SCs and Consequences Opinion of Police Officials

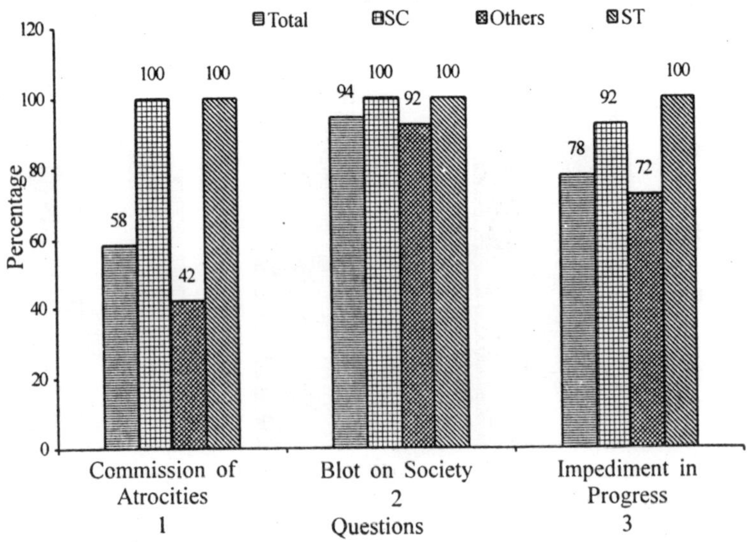

Graph No. 8 : Atrocities on SCs and Consequences Opinion of I.A.S., P.C.S., Doctors and Other Officers

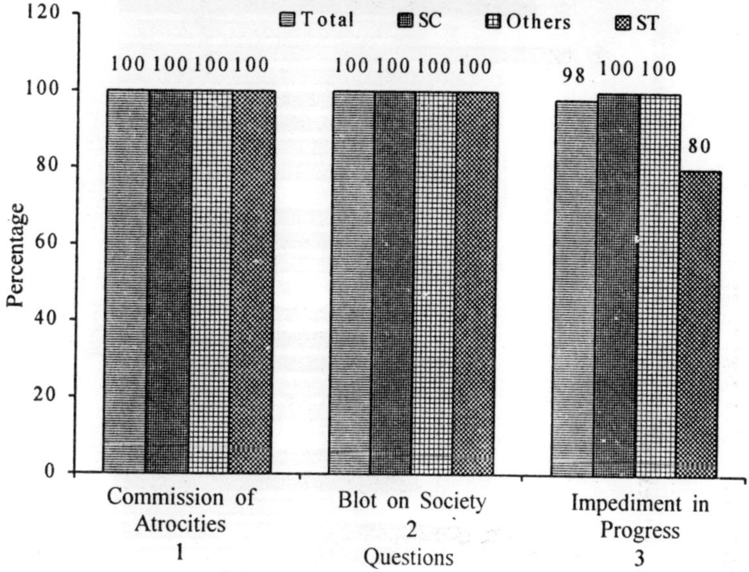

Graph No. 9 : Reasons for Commission of Atrocities on SCs according to Target Group

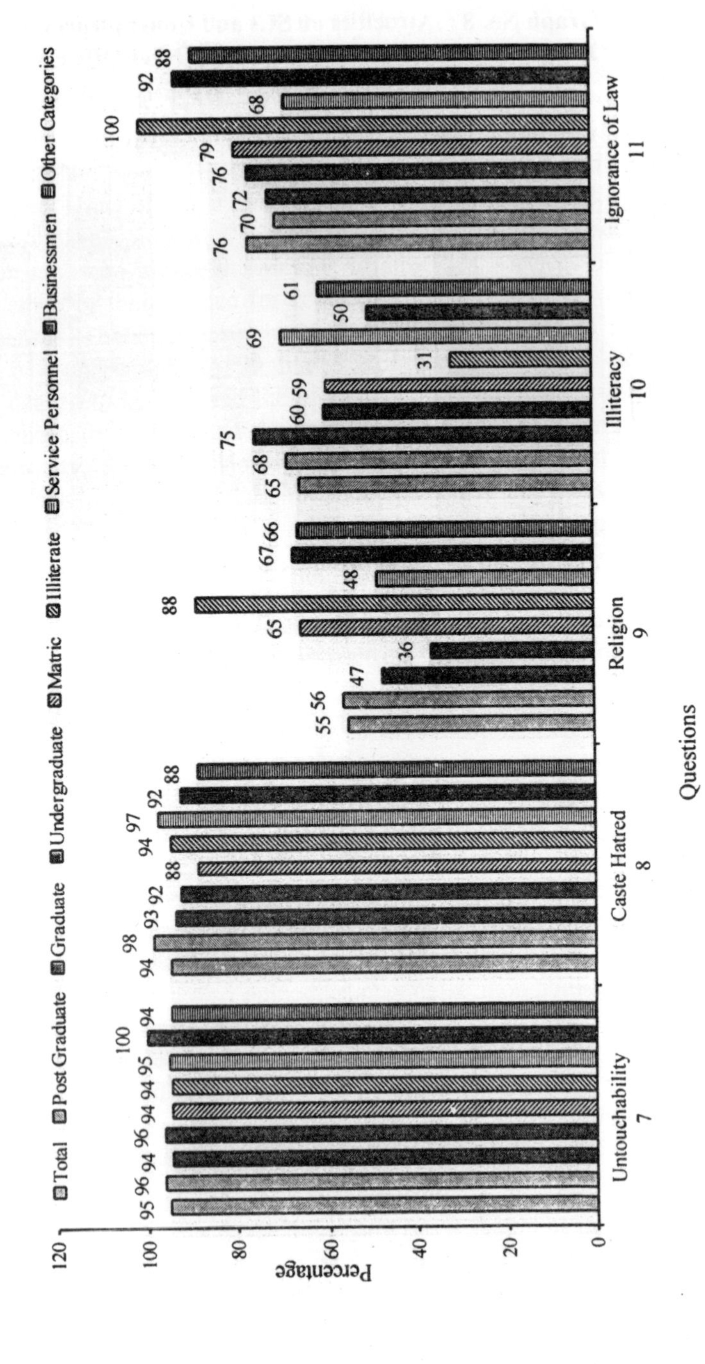

Graph No. 10 : Reasons for Commission of Atrocities on SCs according to Target Group

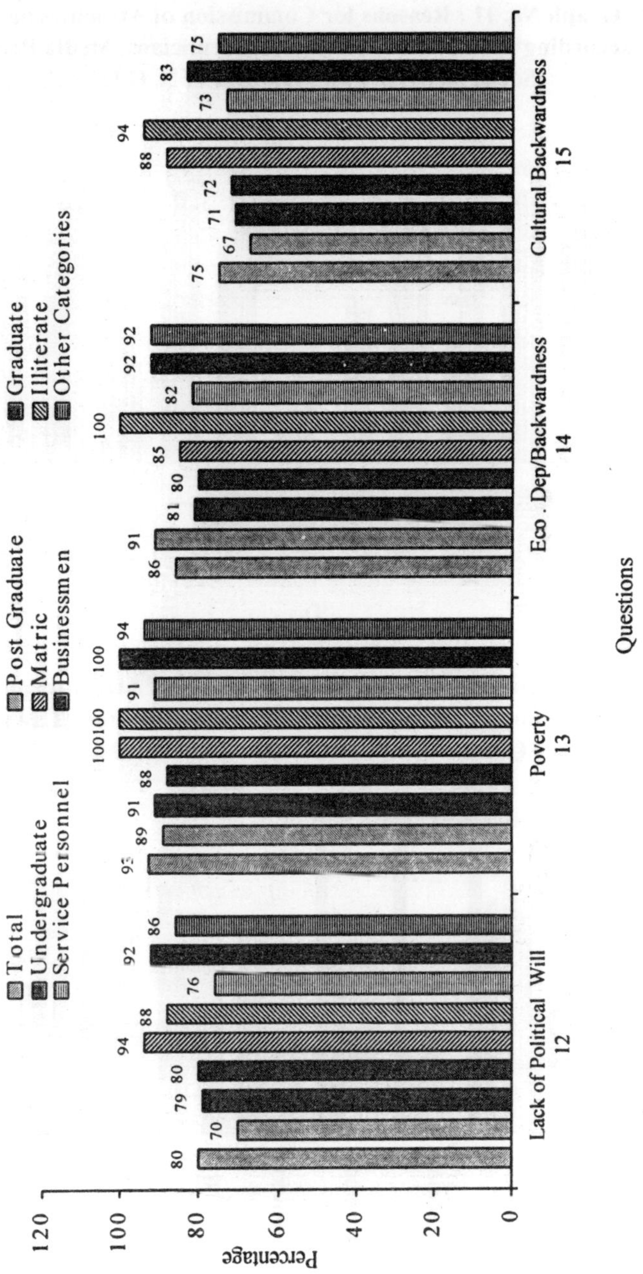

Graph No. 11 : Reasons for Commission of Atrocities on SCs according to M.Ps., Legislators, Academicians, Media Persons, Social Activists and Members of N. G.Os. etc.

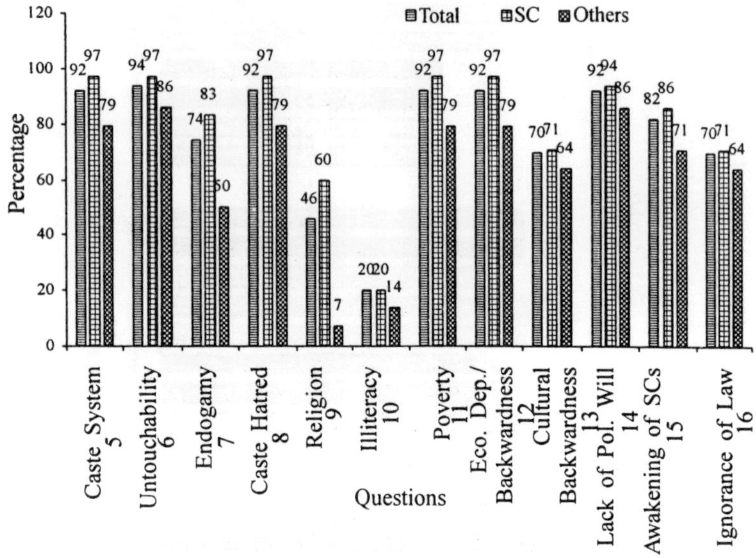

Graph No. 12 : Reasons for Commission of Atrocities on SCs according to Judicial Officers, Pubic Prosecutors, Lawyers, Police Officials, I.A.S., P.C.S., Doctors and Other Officers

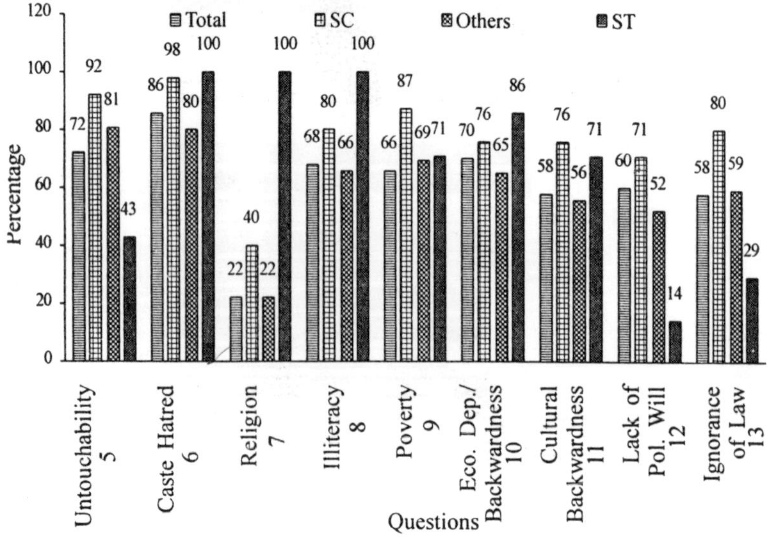

Graph No. 13 : Reasons for Commission of Atrocities on SCs according to Judicial Officers

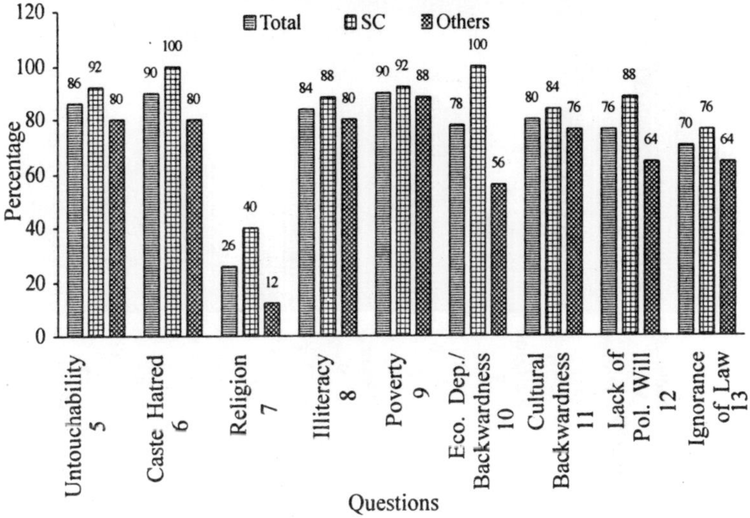

Graph No. 14 : Reasons for Commission of Atrocities on SCs according to Public Prosecutors

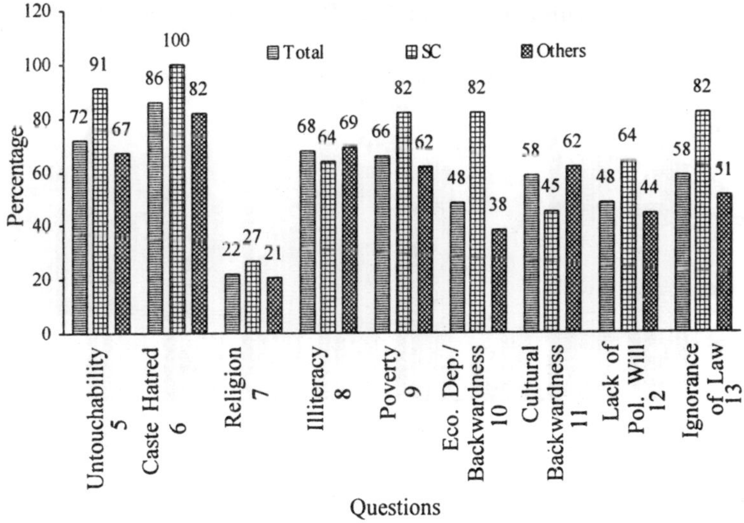

Graph No. 15 : Reasons for Commission of Atrocities on SCs according to Lawyers

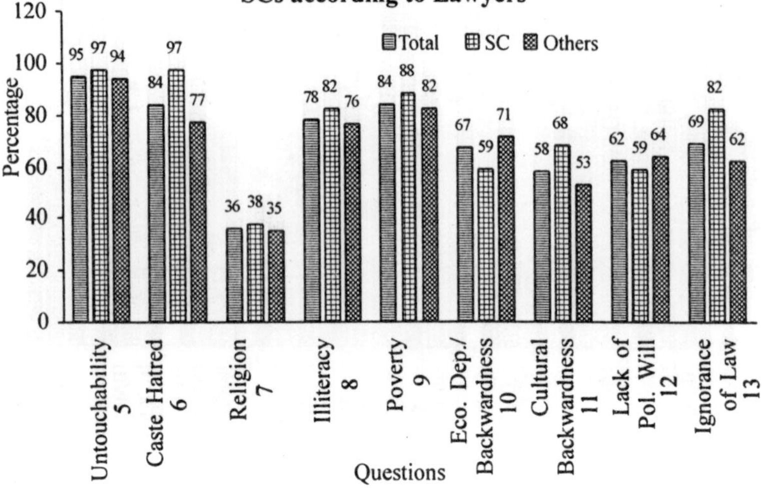

Graph No. 16 : Reasons for Commission of Atrocities on SCs according to I.A.S., P.C.S., Doctors and Other Officers

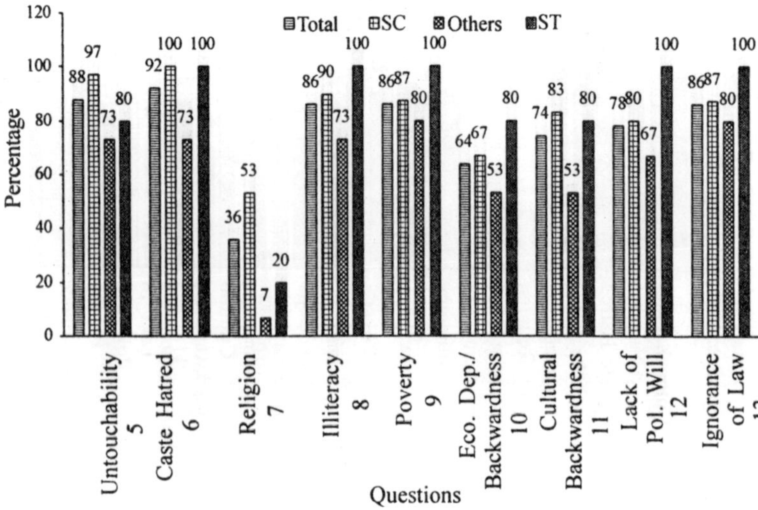

Graph No. 17 : Reasons for Commission of Atrocities on SCs according to Police Officials

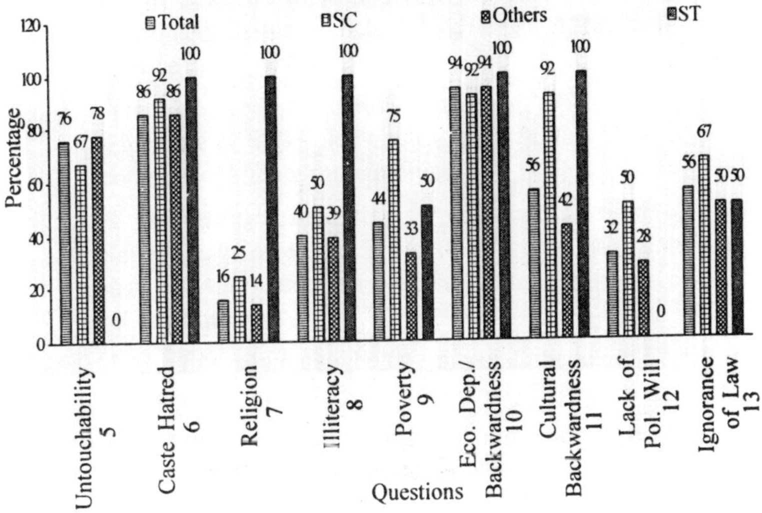

Graph No. 18 : Awareness of Provisions of the Act amongst Target Group

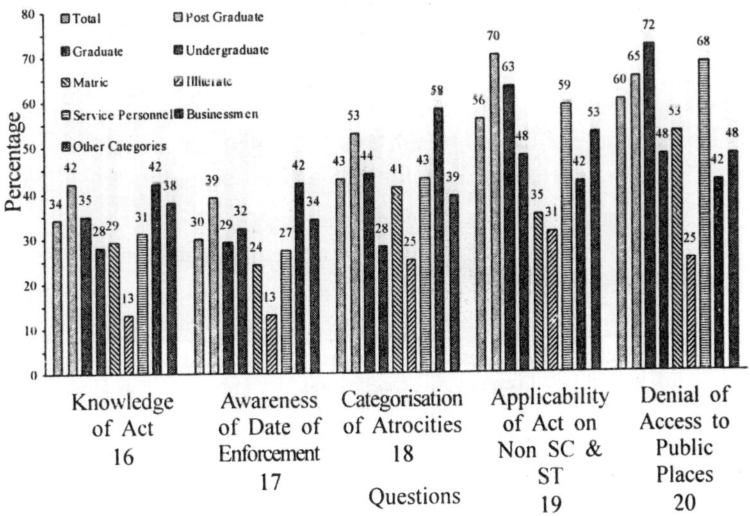

Graph No. 19 : Awareness of Provisions of the Act amongst Target Group

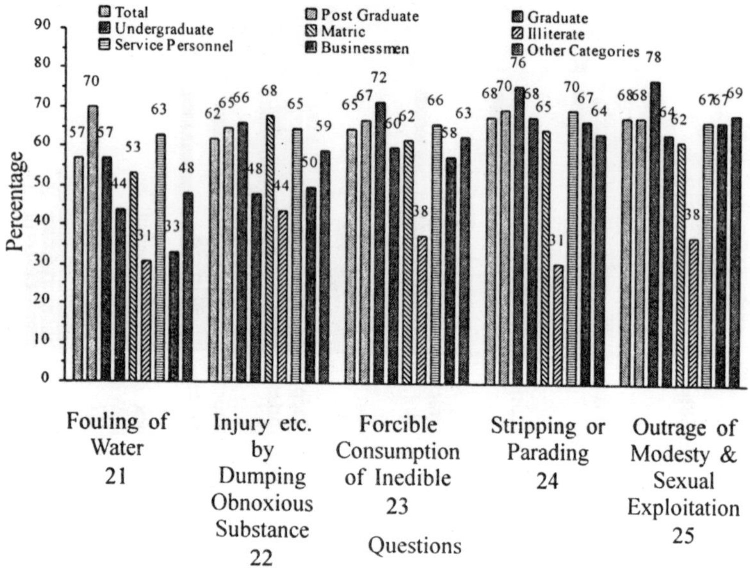

Graph No. 20 : Awareness of Provisions of the Act amongst Target Group

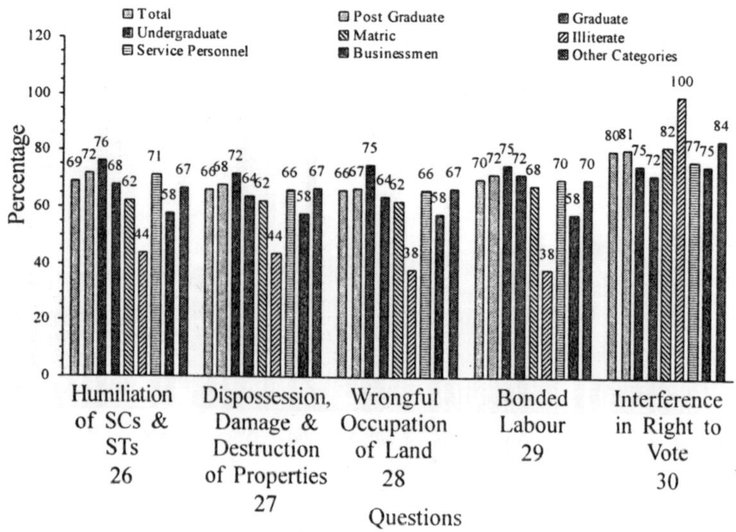

Graph No. 21 : Awareness of Provisions of the Act amongst Target Group

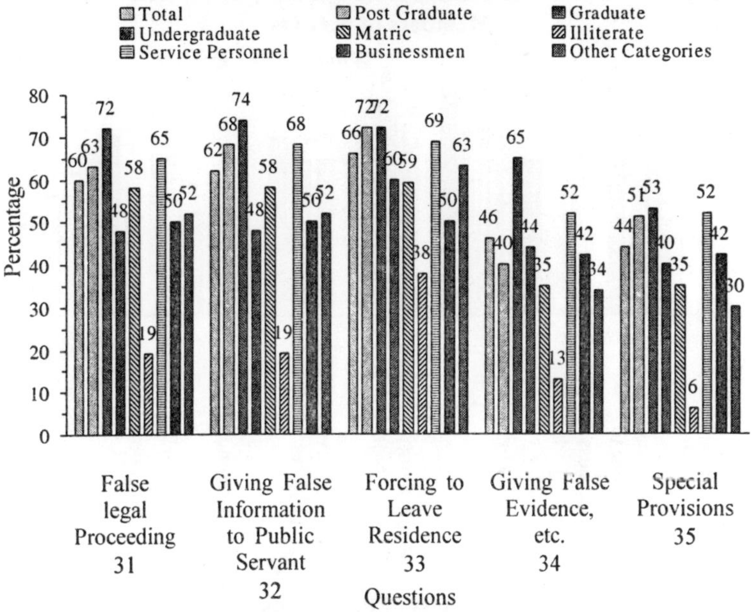

Graph No. 22 : Awareness of Provisions of the Act amongst Target Group

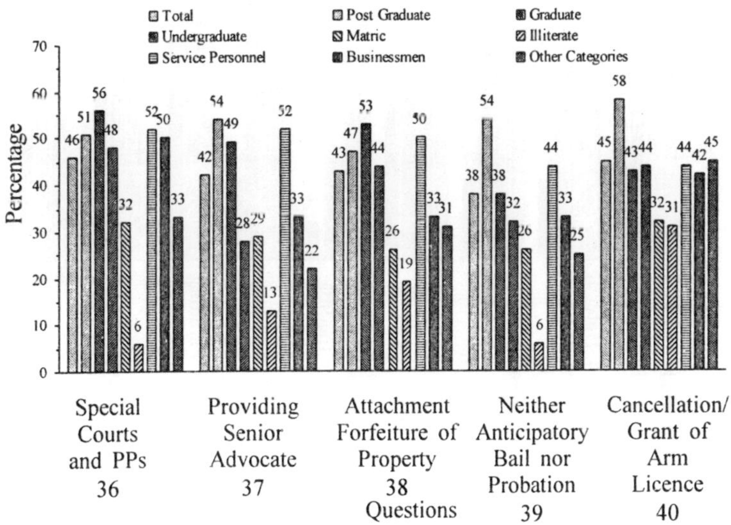

Graph No. 23 : Awareness of Provisions of the Act amongst M.Ps., Legislators, Academicians, Media Persons, Social Activists and Members of N.G.Os.

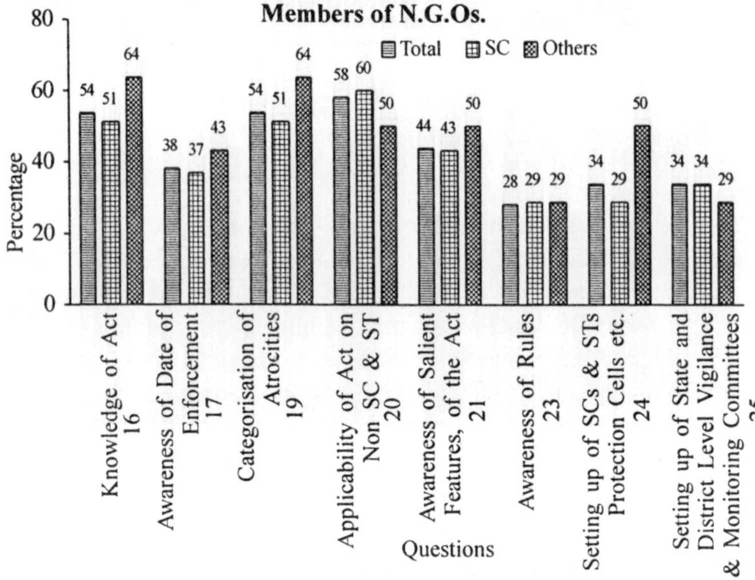

Graph No. 24 : Awareness of Provisions of the Act amongst Judicial Officers, Public Prosecutors, Lawyers, Police Officials, I.A.S., P.C.S., Doctors and Other Officers

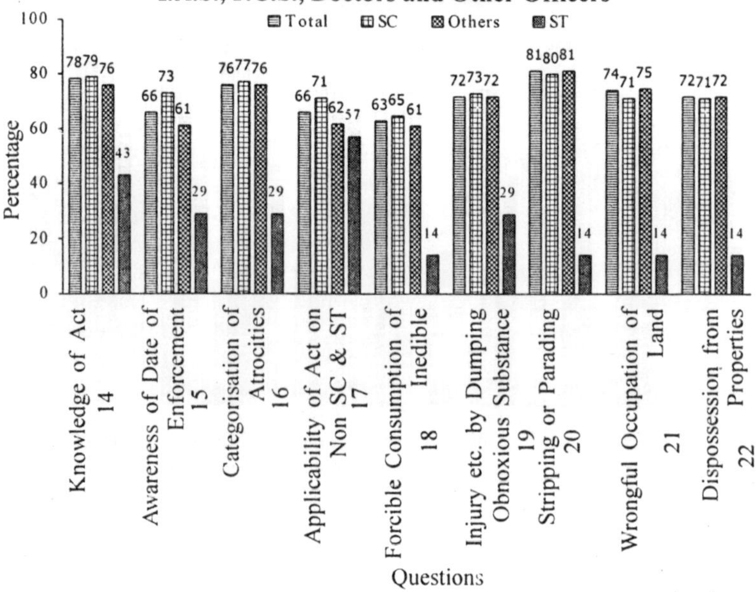

Graph No. 25 : Awareness of Provisions of the Act amongst Judicial Officers

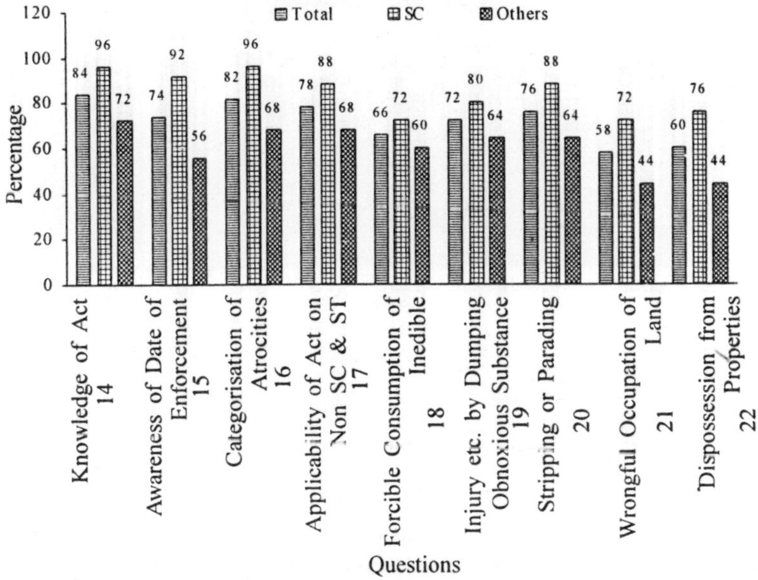

Graph No. 26 : Awareness of Provisions of the Act amongst Public Prosecutors

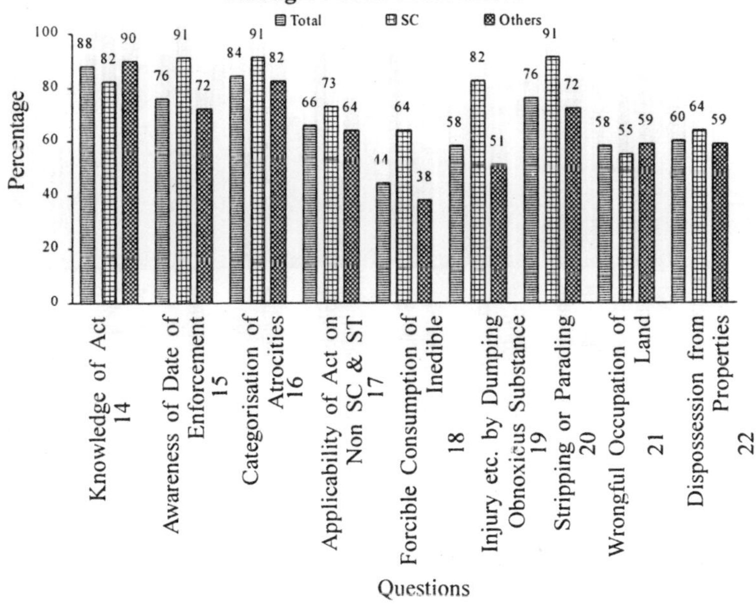

Graph No. 27 : Awareness of Provisions of the Act amongst Lawyers

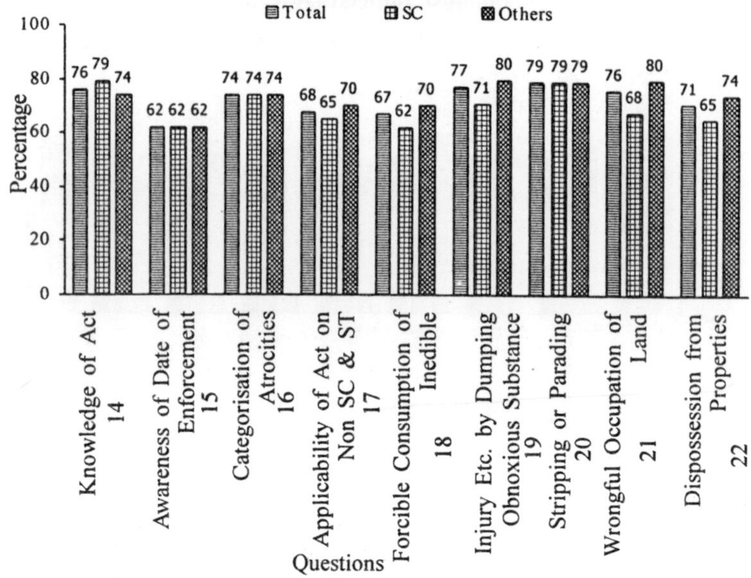

Graph No. 28 : Awareness of Provisions of the Act amongst I.A.S., P.C.S., Doctors and Other Officers

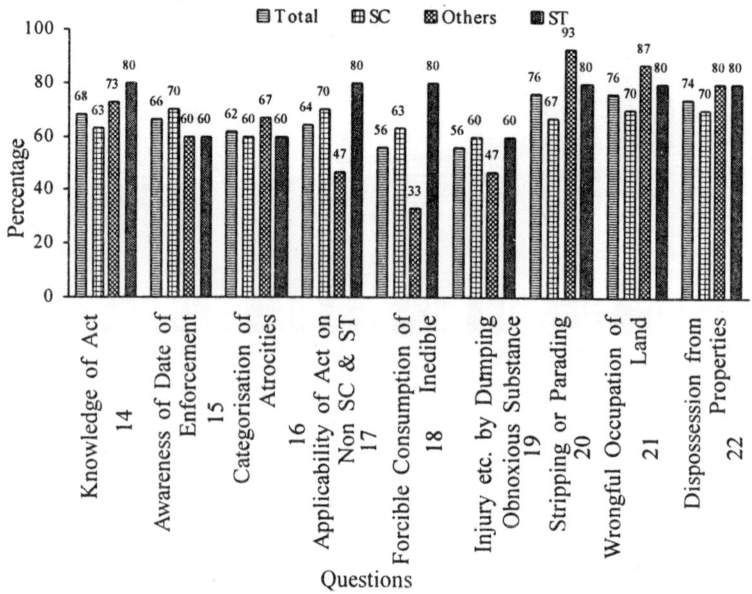

Graph No. 29 : Awareness of Provisions of the Act amongst Police Officials

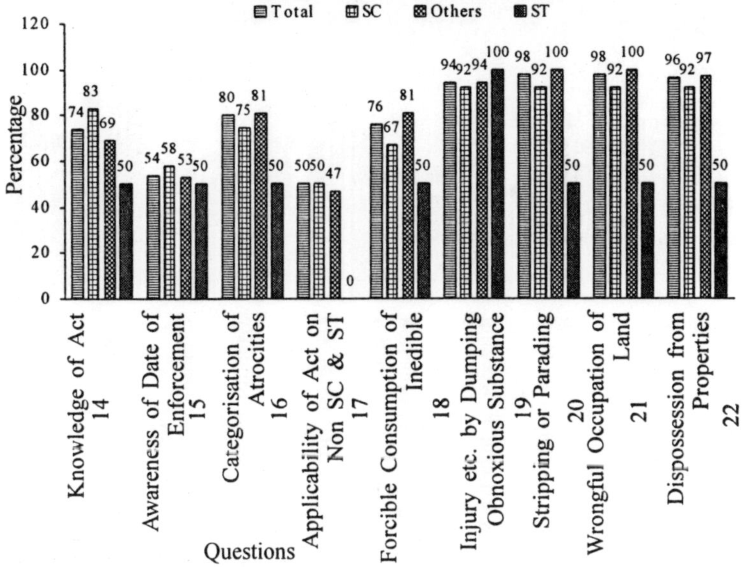

Graph No. 30 : Awareness of Provisions of the Act Amongst Judicial Officers, Public Prosecutors, Lawyers, Police Officials, I.A.S., P.C.S., Doctors and Other Officers

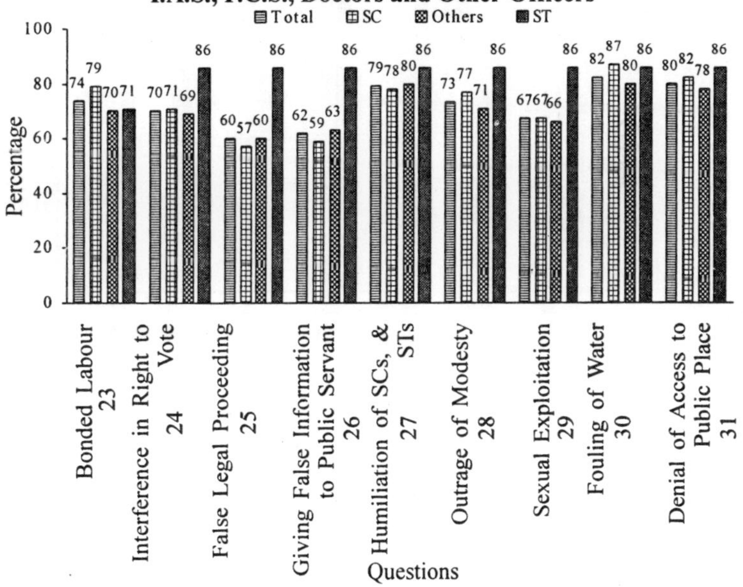

Graph No. 31 : Awareness of Provisions of the Act amongst Judicial Officers

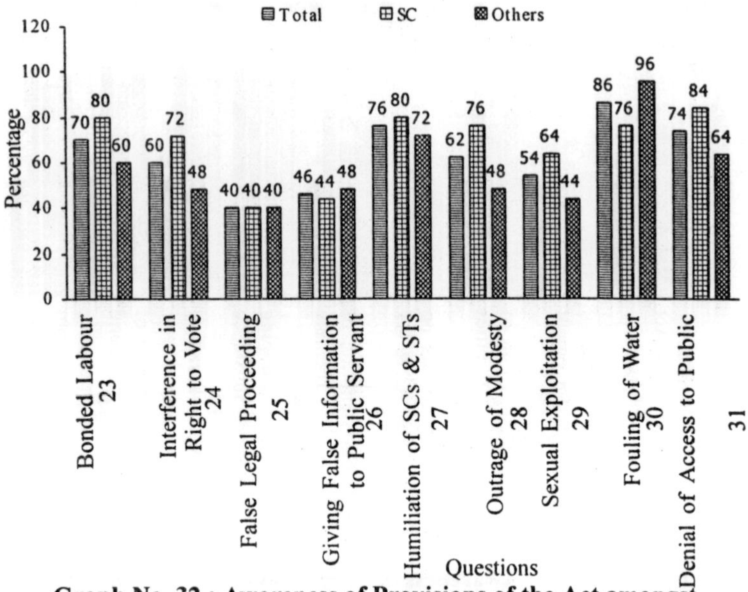

Graph No. 32 : Awareness of Provisions of the Act amongst Public Prosecutors

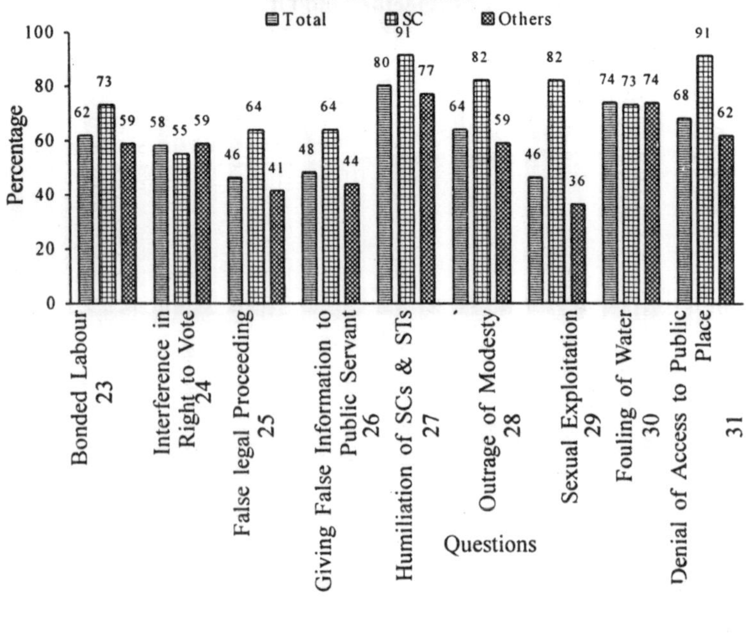

Graph No. 33 : Awareness of Provisions of the Act amongst Lawyers

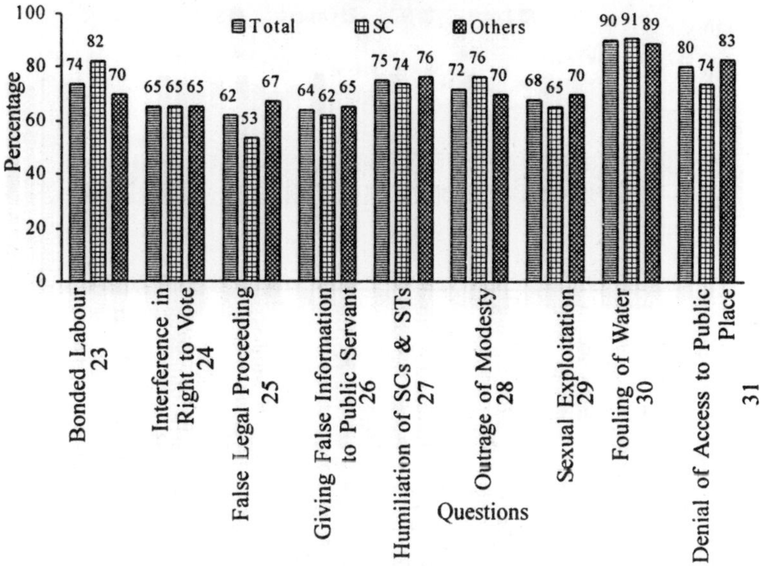

Graph No. 34 : Awareness of Provisions of the Act amongst I.A.S., P.C.S., Doctors and Other Officers

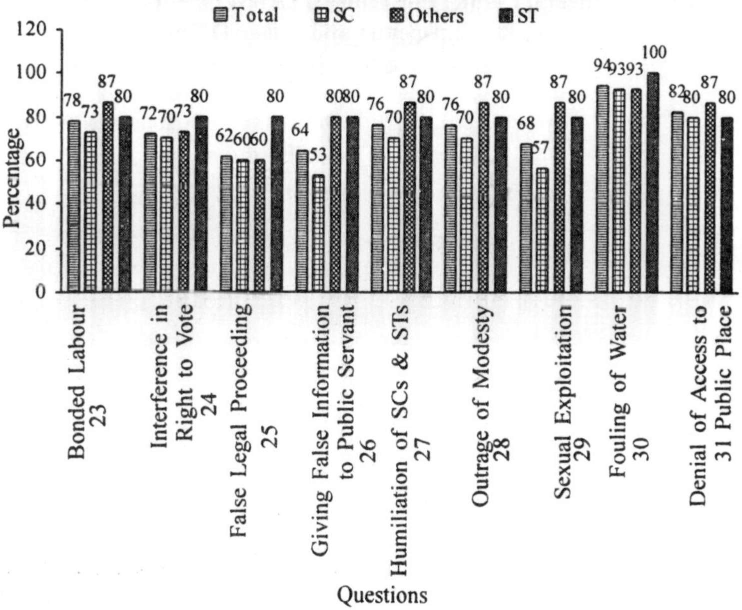

Graph No. 35 : Awareness of Provisions of the Act amongst Police Officials

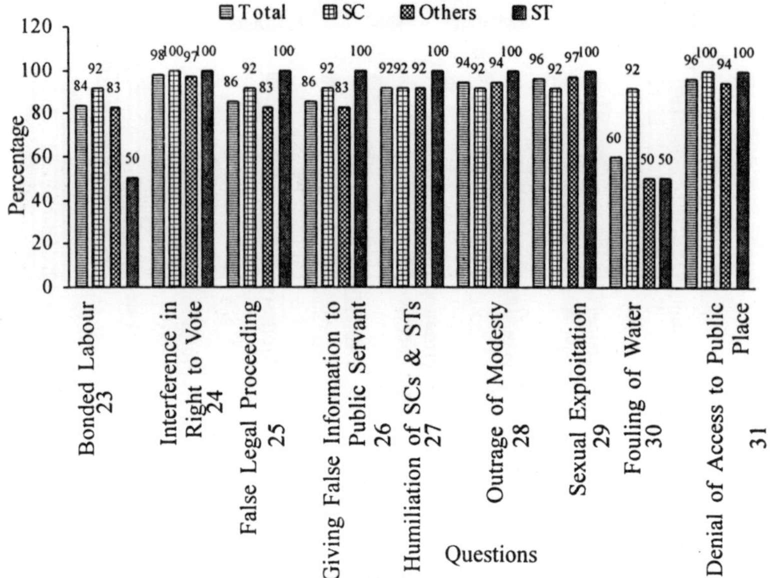

Graph No. 36 : Awareness of Provisions of the Act amongst Judicial Officers, Public, Prosecutors, Lawyers, Police Officials, I.A.S., P.C.S., Doctors and Other Officers

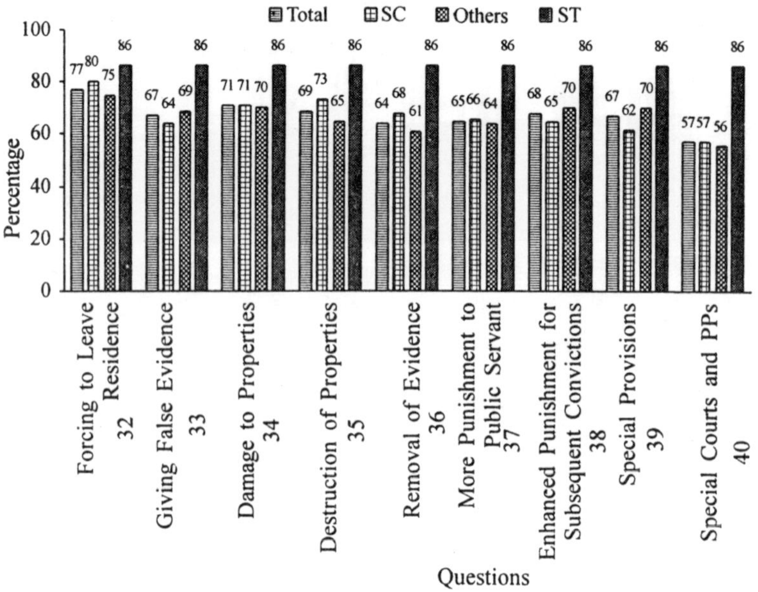

Graph No. 37 : Awareness of Provisions of the Act amongst Judicial Officers

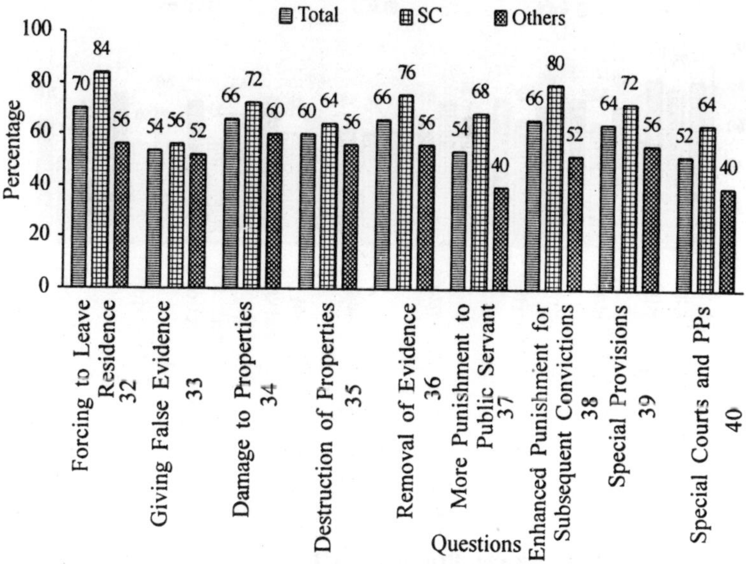

Graph No. 38 : Awareness of Provisions of the Act amongst Public Prosecutors

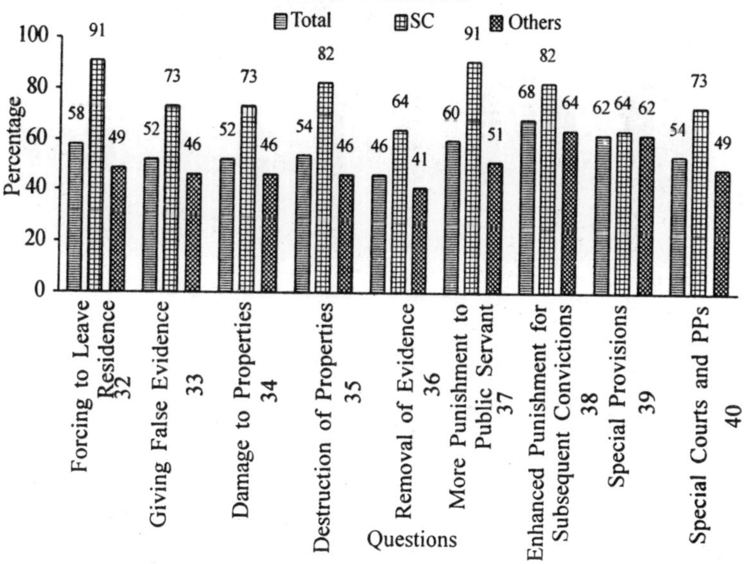

Graph No. 39 : Awareness of Provisions of the Act amongst Lawyers

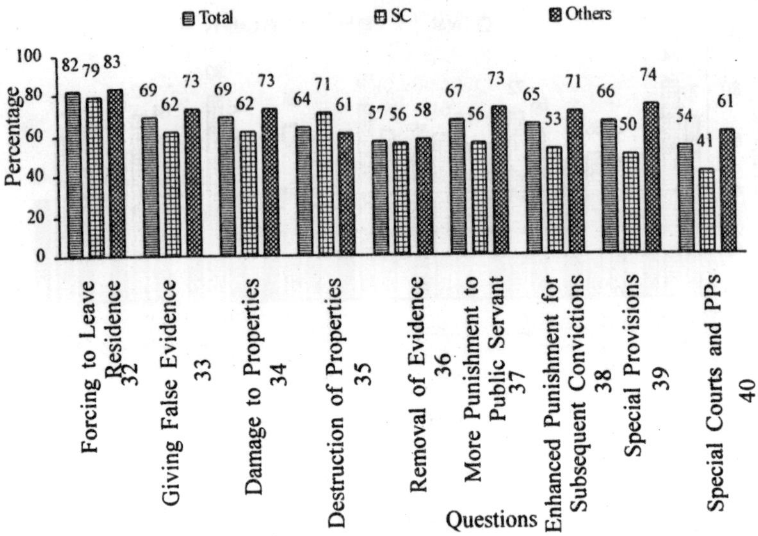

Graph No. 40 : Awareness of Provisions of the Act amongst I.A.S., P.C.S., Doctors and Other Officers

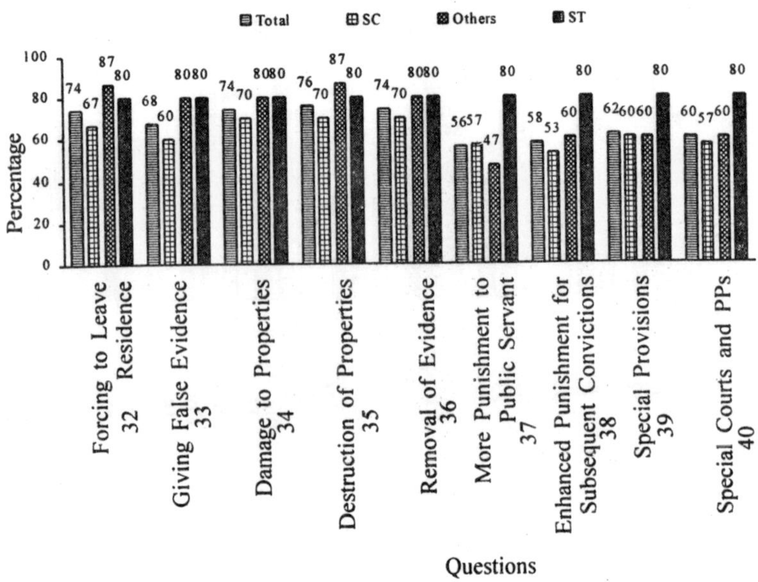

Graph No. 41 : Awareness of Provisions of the Act amongst Police Officials

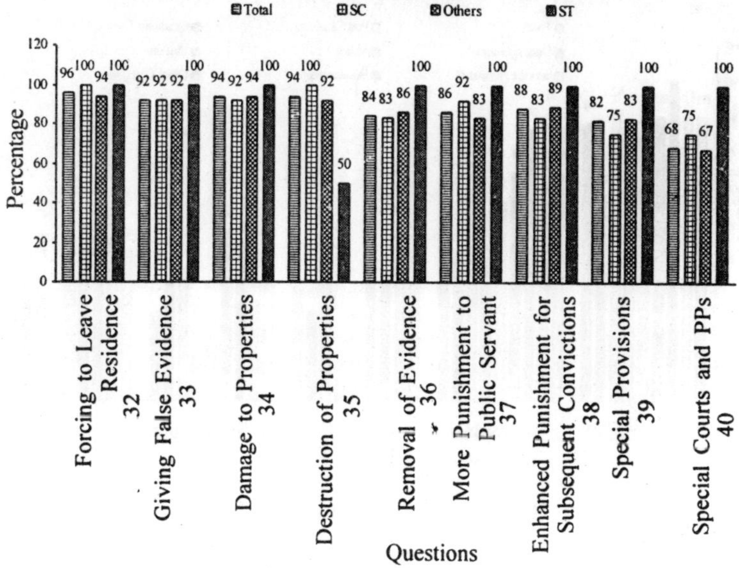

Graph No. 42 : Implementation of Provisions of the Act according to Target Group

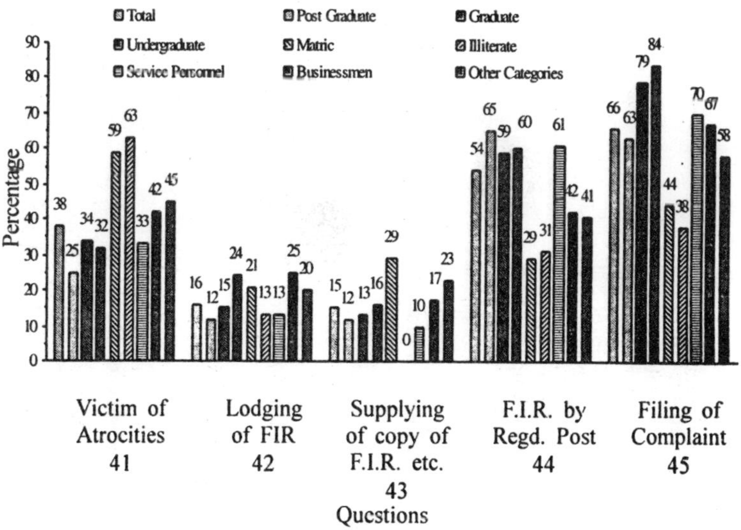

Graph No. 43 : Implementation of Provisions of the Act according to Target Group

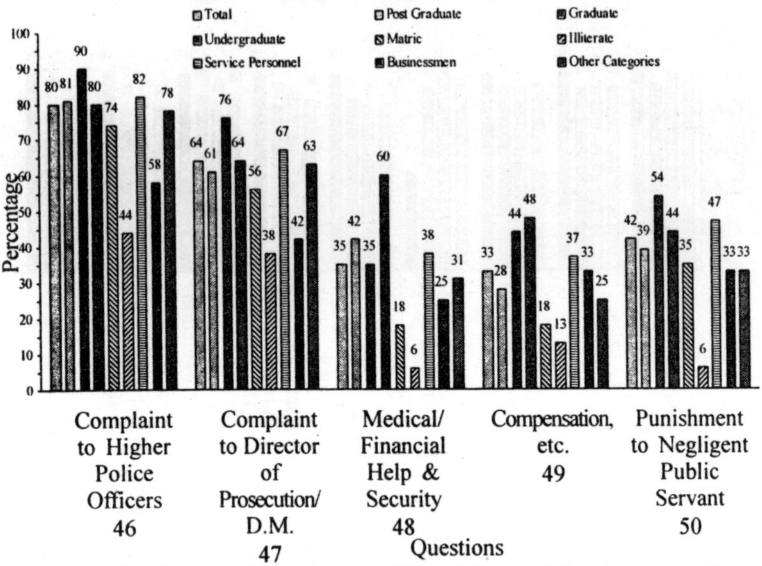

Graph No. 44 : Implementation of Provisions of the Act according to M.Ps., Legislators, Academicians, Media Persons, Social Activists and Members of N.G.Os, etc.

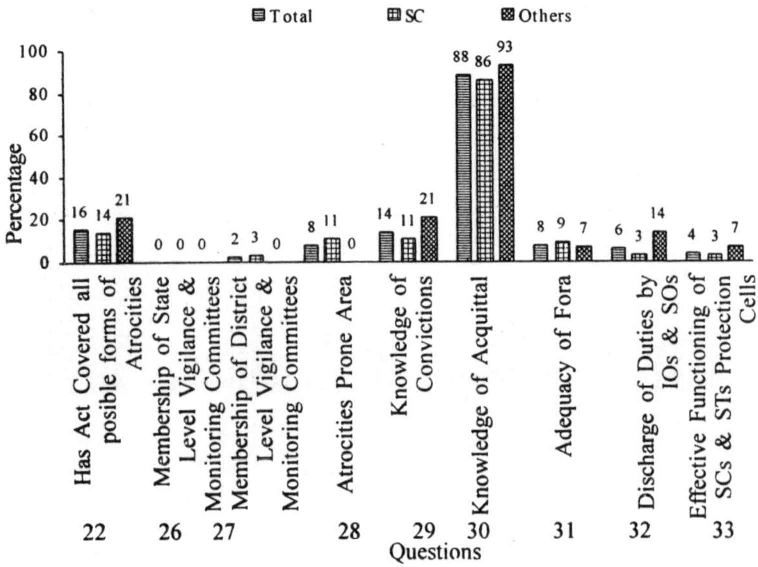

Graph No. 45 : Implementation of Provisions of the Act according to M.Ps., Legislators, Academicians, Media Persons, Social Activists and Members of N.G.Os., etc.

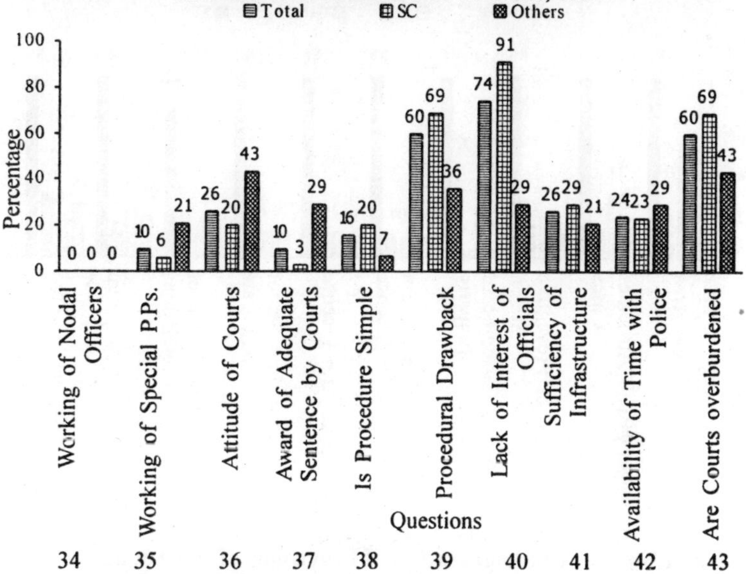

Graph No. 46 : Implementation of Provisions of the Act according to M.Ps., Legislators, Academicians, Media Persons, Social Activists and Members of N.G.Os. etc.

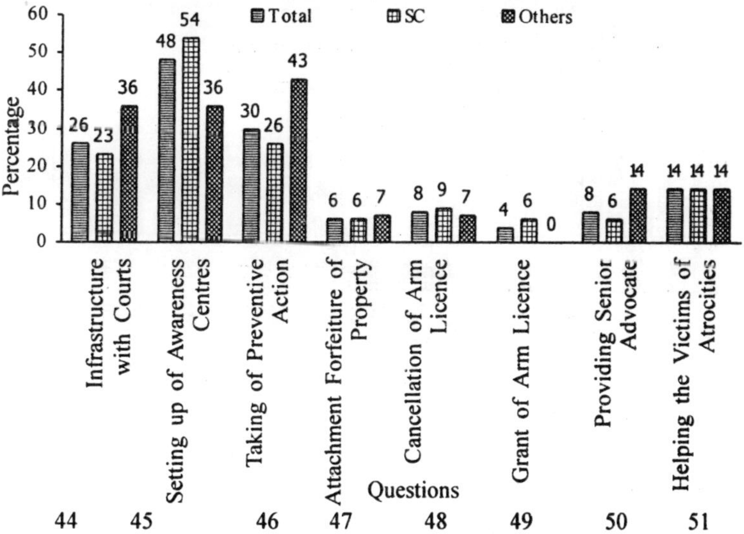

Graph No. 47 : Implementation of Provisions of the Act according to Judicial Officers, Public Prosecutors, Lawyers, Police Officials I.A.S., P.C.S., Doctors and other Officers

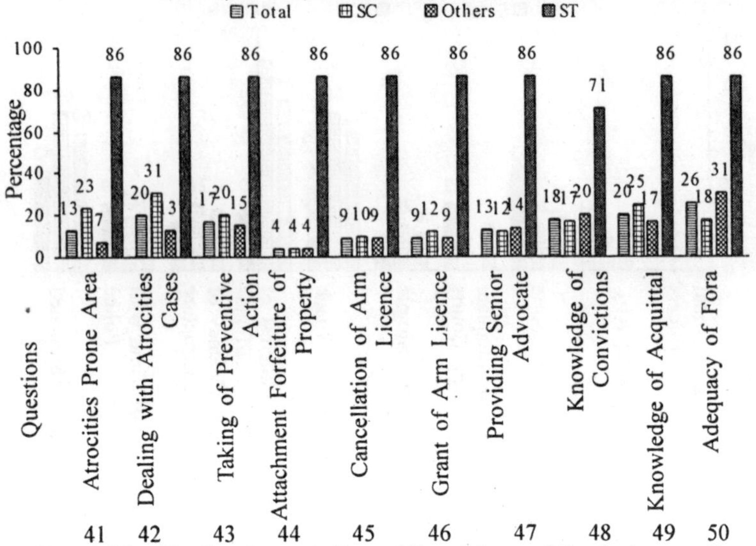

Graph No. 48 : Implementation of Provisions of the Act according to Judicial Officers

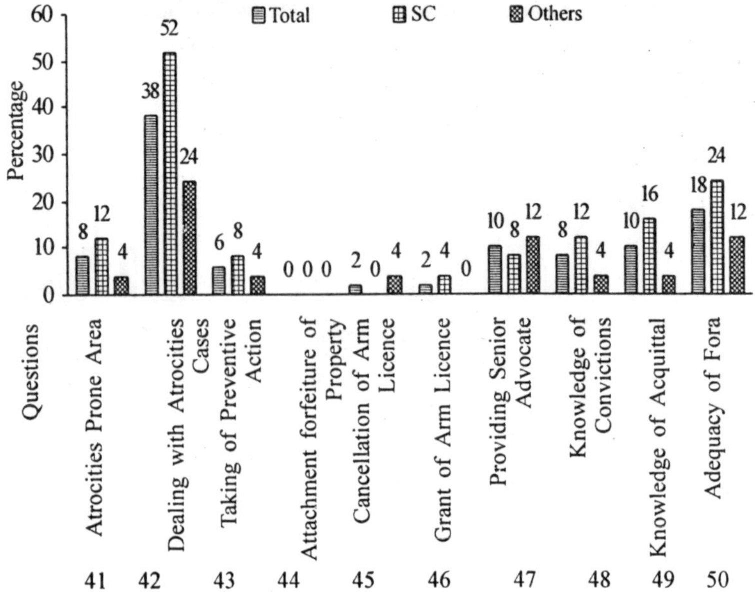

Graph No. 49 : Implementation of Provisions of the Act according to Public Prosecutors

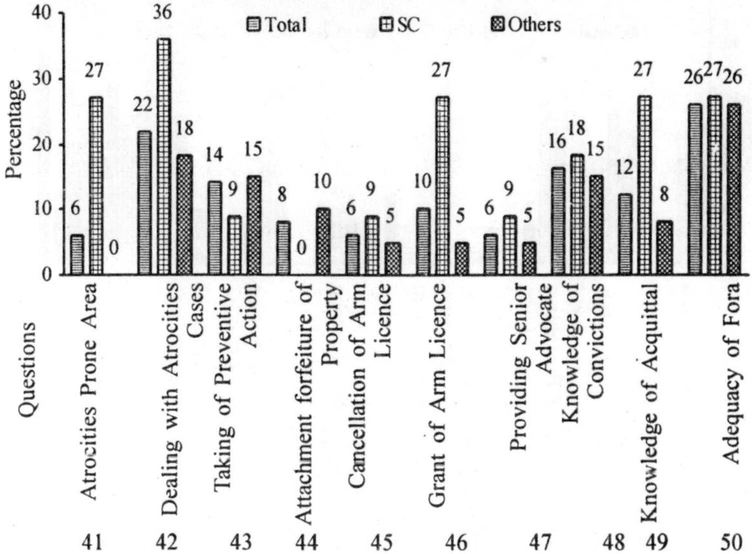

Graph No. 50 : Implementation of Provisions of the Act according to Lawyers

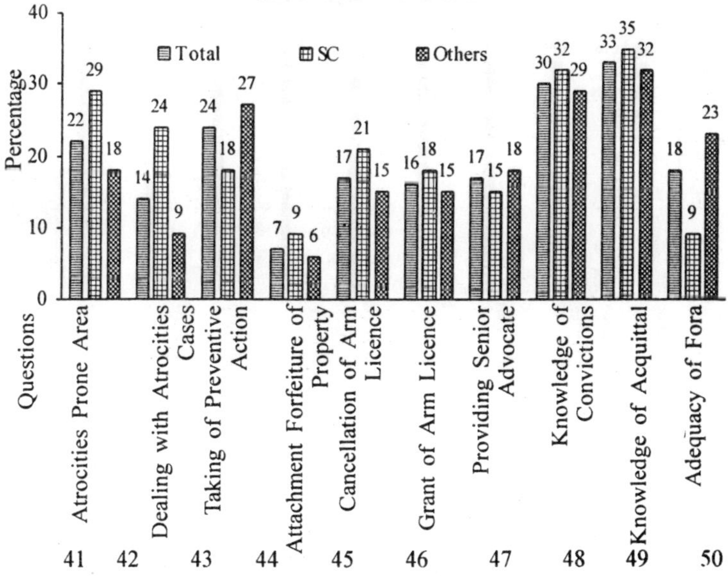

Graph No. 51 Implementation of Provisions of the Act amongst I.A.S., PCS, Doctors and Other Officers

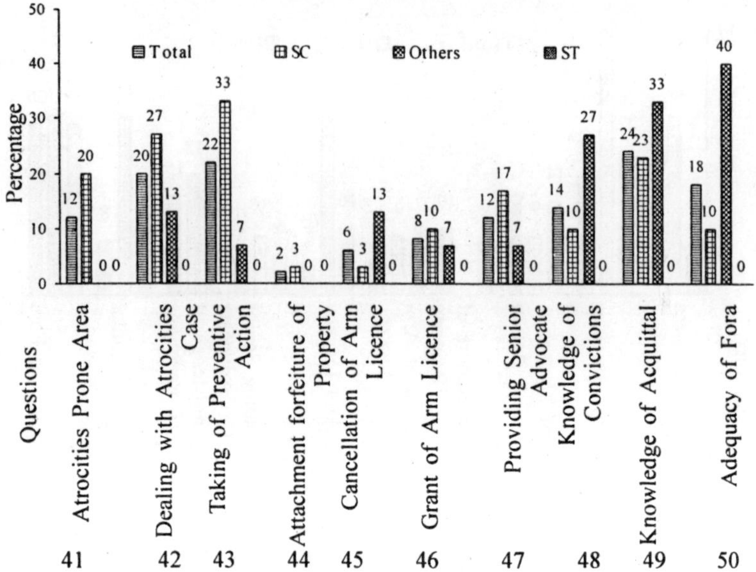

Graph No. 52 : Implementation of Provisions of the Act according to Police Officials

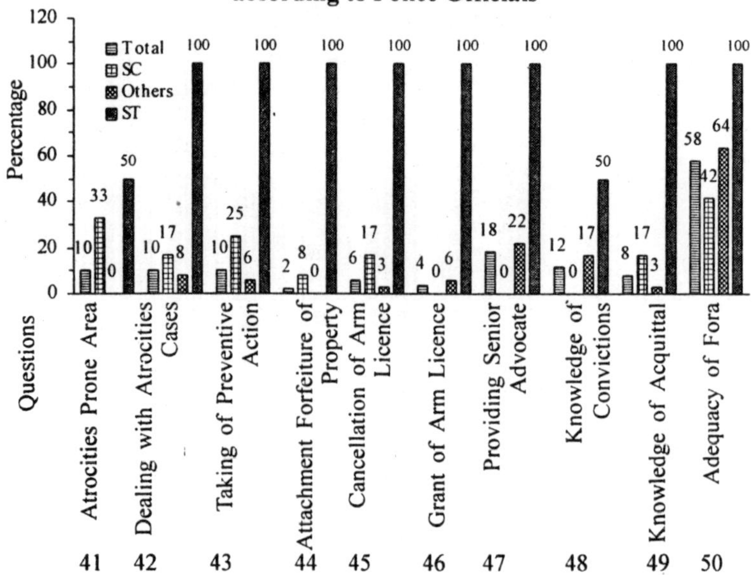

Graph No. 53 : Opinions of Judicial Officers, Public Prosecutors, Lawyers, Police Officials, I.A.S., P.C.S., Doctors and Other Officers about Provisions of the Act

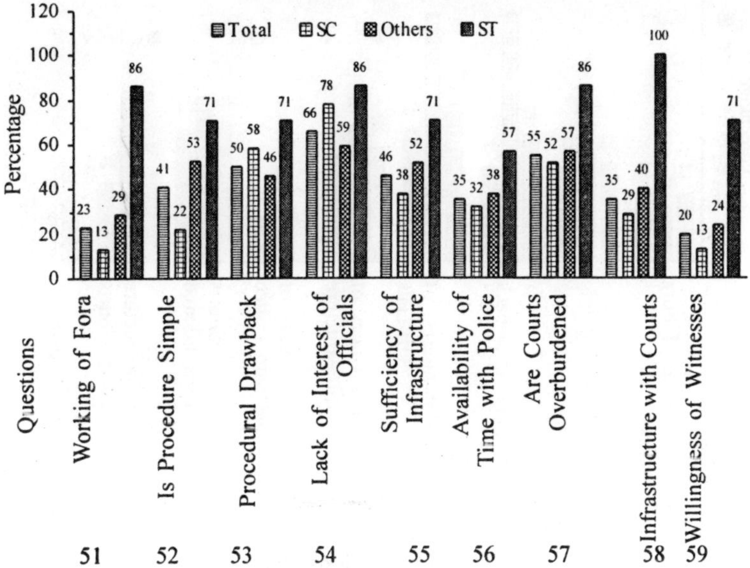

Graph No. 54 : Opinions of Judicial Officers about Provisions of the Act

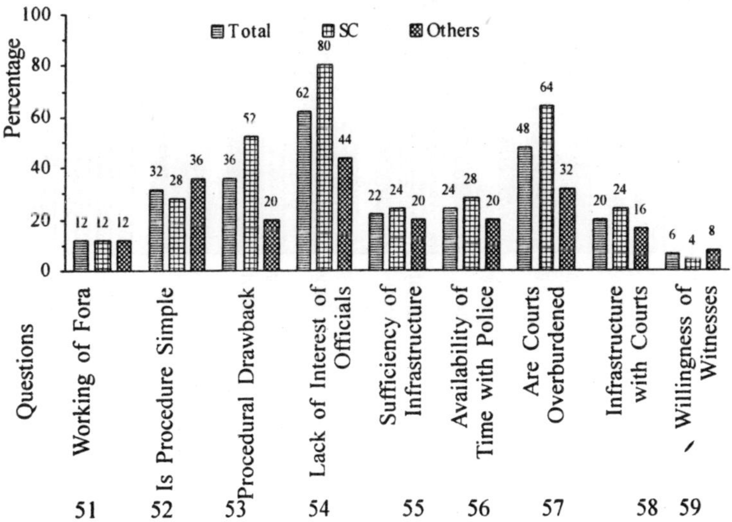

Graph No. 55 : Opinions of Public Prosecutors about Provisions of the Act

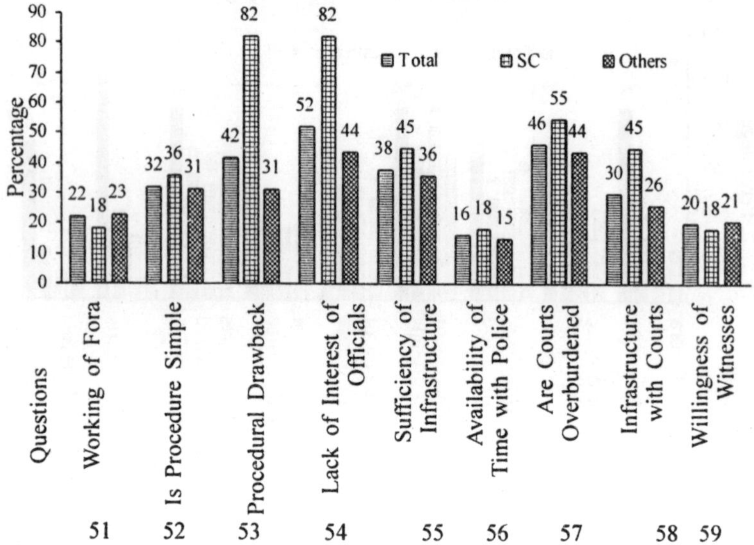

Graph No. 56 : Opinions of Lawyers about Provisions of the Act

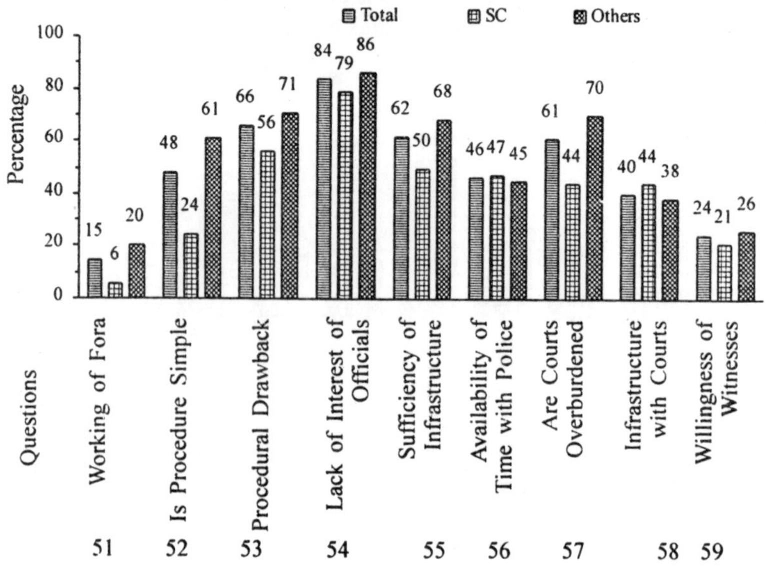

Graph No. 57 : Opinions of I.A.S., P.C.S., Doctors and Other Officers about Provisions of the Act

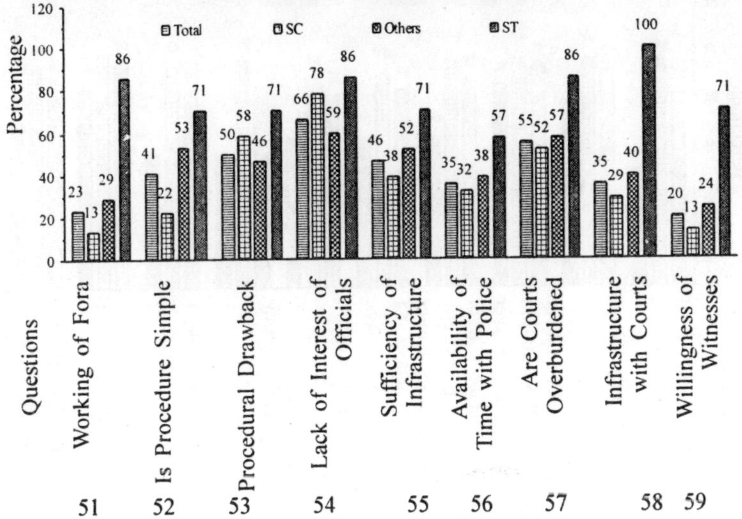

Graph No. 58 : Opinions of Police Officials about Provisions of the Act

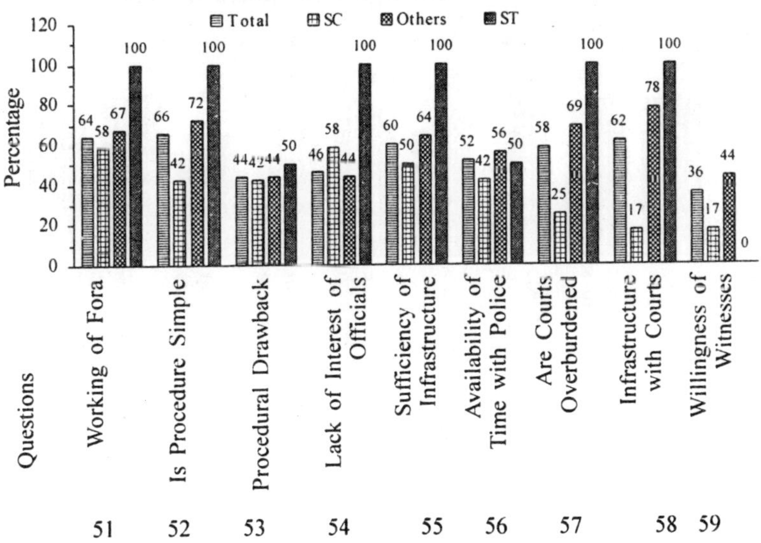

Graph No. 59 : Suggestions of M.Ps., Legislators, Academicians, Media Persons, Social Activists and Members of N.G.Os. etc.

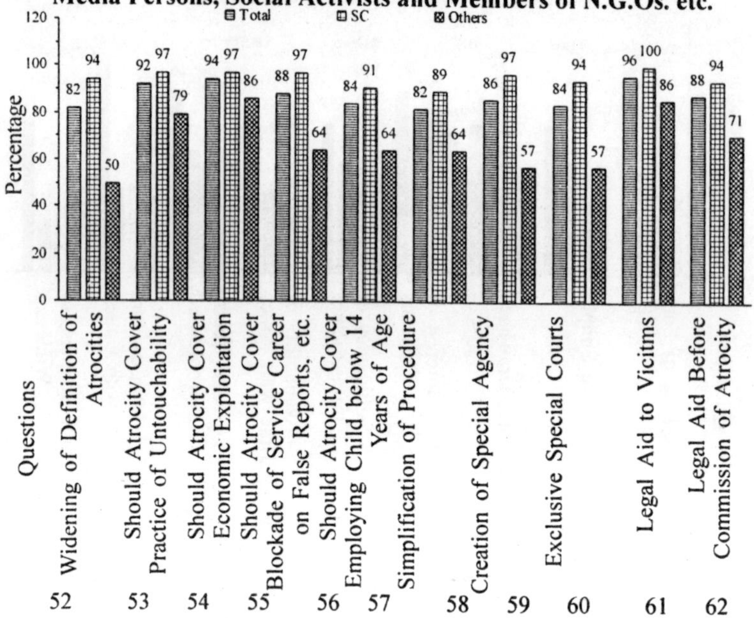

Graph No. 60 : Suggestions of M.Ps, Legislator, Academicians, Media Persons, Social Activists and Members of N.G.Os. etc.

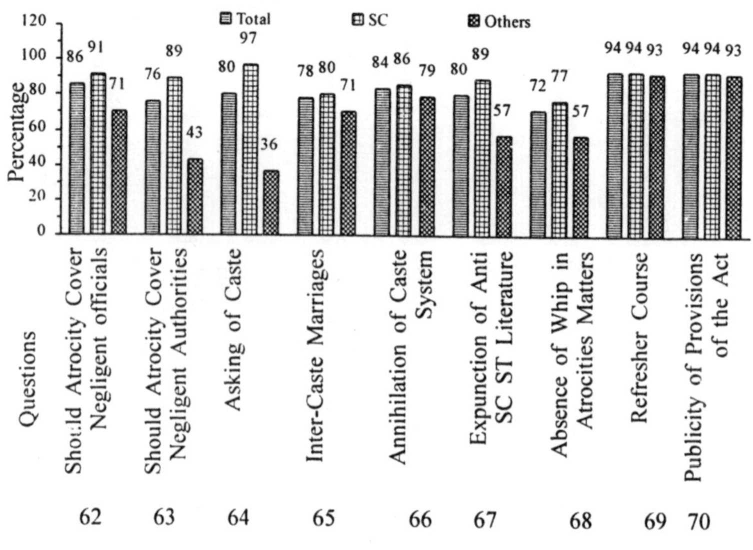

Graph No. 61 : Suggestions of Judicial Officers, Public Prosecutors, Lawyers, Police Officials, I.A.S., P.C.S., Doctors and Other Officers for Improvement of Provisions of the Act

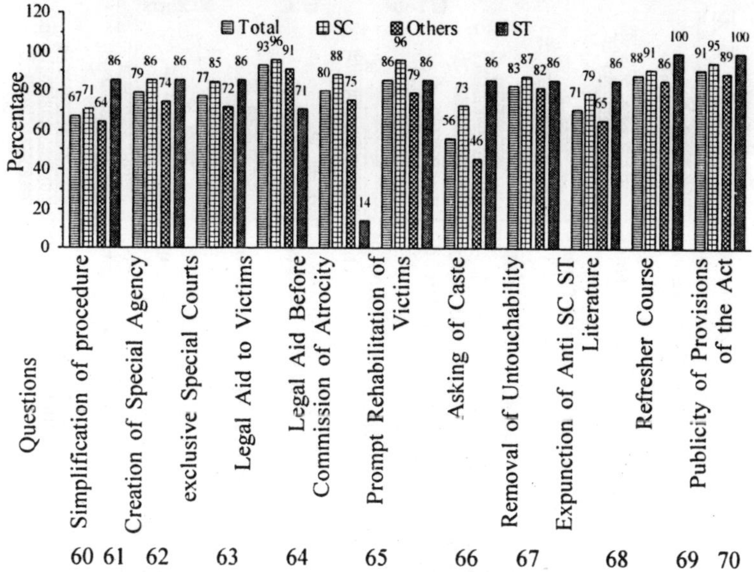

Graph No. 62 : Suggestions of Judicial Officers for Improvement of Provisions of the Act

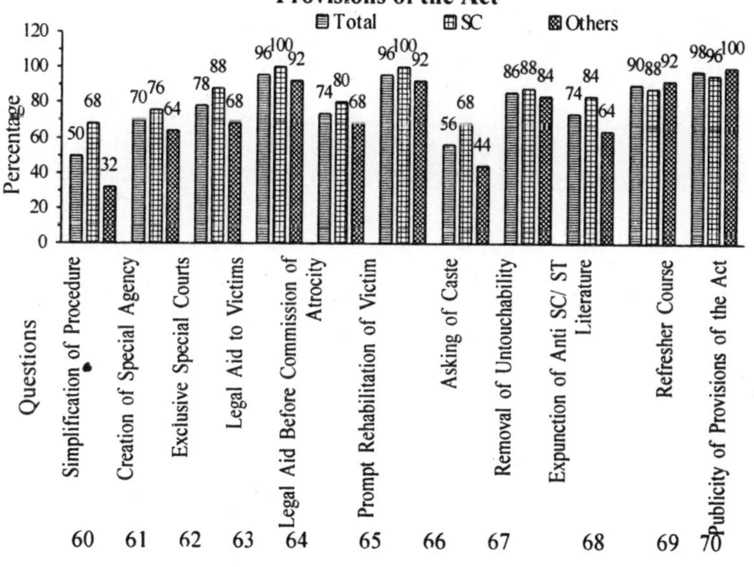

Graph No. 63 : Suggestions of Public Prosecutors for Improvement of Provisions of the Act

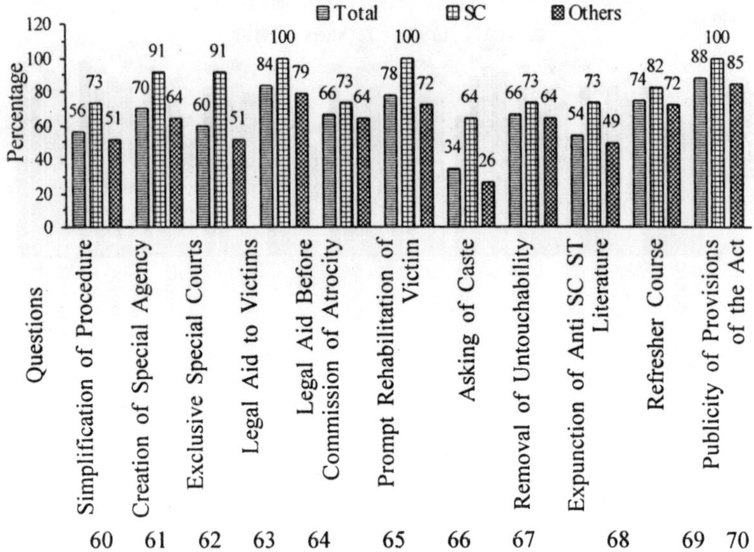

Graph No. 64 : Suggestions of Lawyers for Improvement of Provisions of the Act

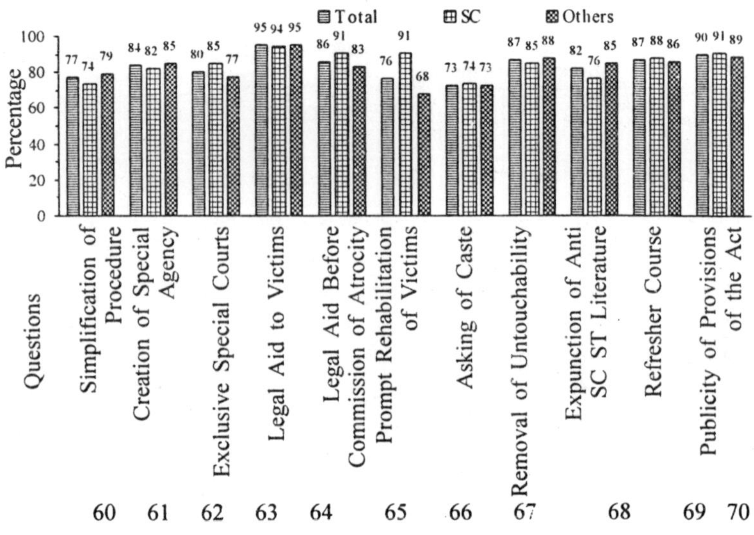

Graph No. 65 : Suggestions of I.A.S., P.C.S., Doctors and Other Officers for Improvement of Provisions of the Act

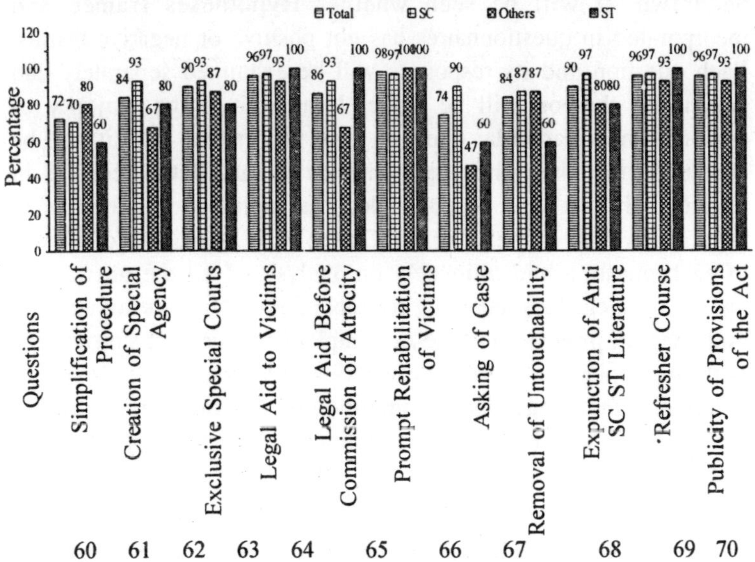

Graph No. 66 : Suggestions of Police Officials for Improvement of Provisions of the Act

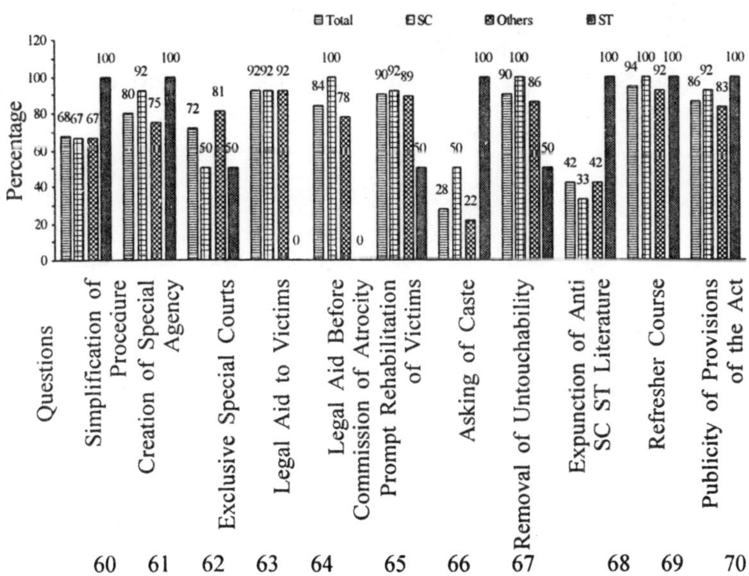

3.14 Conclusions and Suggestions

After completion of doctrinal and emperical work, conclusions will be drawn. It will be seen whether Hypotheses framed and incorporated in questionnaires has got positive or negative results. Each question and its responses will be examined separately and conclusion thereon will be made. If answer of the majority of responses of a particular question is in affirmative, then it will be concluded that the public opinion is in favour. If the result is in negative, then it will be concluded that opinion of public is in negative on that particular aspect. On the basis of analysis of answer of each question and ultimately on analysis of all the answers of question, conclusions regarding concept of atrocity, causes of atrocity, awareness of provisions of the Act, implementation of the provisions of the Act, opinion of different categories of persons on the provisions of the Act and suggestions to improve the Act in order to prevent the atrocities will be drawn, in addition to see the impact of the Act on the SCs.

On the basis of conclusions, suggestions for further improvement of the Act, for prevention of atrocities on the SCs will be made.

Notes and References

1. Blalock, H.M., *Sociological Theory and Research.*
2. *See*, *Encyclopædia Britannica* (1911) Cambridge Edition.
3. Chaire, Selltiz; Marie, J.; Morton, D.; and Cook, S.W., *Research Methods in Social Relations.*
4. *See,* Graph Nos. 1 to 66.

CHAPTER 4

EMPIRICAL STUDY OF THE PROVISIONS OF THE ACT

A. COMMISSION OF ATROCITIES ON THE SCHEDULED CASTES AND ITS IMPACT ON THE SOCIETY AND NATION

4.1 Awareness of Incidents of Atrocities on the Scheduled Castes

Question number 1 of all the questionnaires, *i.e.* questionnaire on the subject for Target Group,[1] Different Units of Legal System,[2] and Law Makers and Opinion Makers,[3] elicited information from the respondents, whether or not atrocities are still being committed on the members of SCs?

Table No. 1 : Awareness of Incidents of Atrocities on SCs

Categories		*Responses in*							
		Number				*Percentage*			
		Yes	*No*	*Und.*	*Total*	*Yes*	*No*	*Und.*	*Total*
Target Group 200		0	0	200	100	0	0	100	
Different Units of Legal System	*SCs*	111	1	0	112	99	1	0	100
	STs	7	0	0	7	100	0	0	100
	Others	143	33	5	181	79	18	3	100
	Total	261	34	5	300	87	11	2	100
L.M. & O.M.		48	2	0	50	96	4	0	100
Grand Total		509	36	5	550	93	6	1	100

550 respondents were examined on this question. Their responses are depicted in Graph No. 67 and Table Nos. 1, 1A, 1B and 1C.

Out of these, 509 replied in positive, 36 in negative and 5 did not give any specific reply.[4]

Graph No. 67 : Awareness of Incidents of Atrocities on the Scheduled Castes

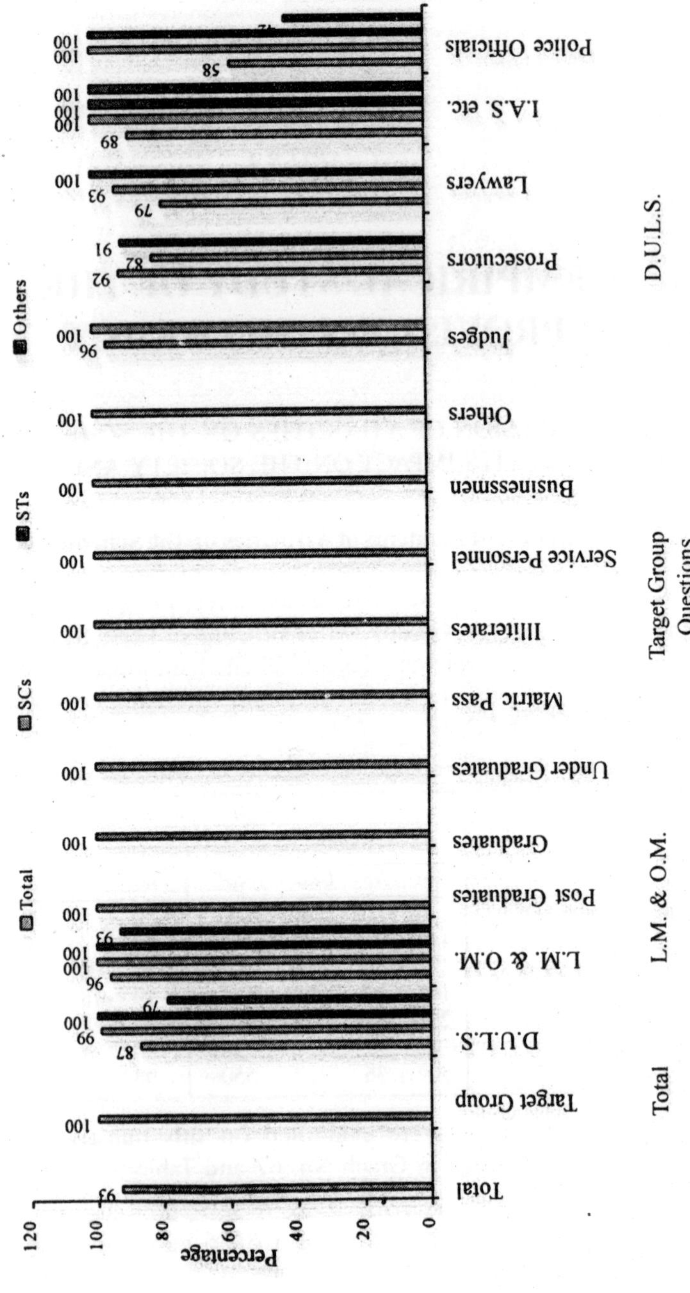

Table No. 1A : Target Group on Commission of Atrocities on SCs

Categories	*Responses in*							
	Number				*Percentage*			
	Yes	*No*	*Und.*	*Total*	*Yes*	*No*	*Und.*	*Total*
Post Graduates	57	0	0	57	100	0	0	100
Graduates	68	0	0	68	100	0	0	100
Under Graduates	25	0	0	25	100	0	0	100
Matric Pass	34	0	0	34	100	0	0	100
Illiterates	16	0	0	16	100	0	0	100
Service Personnel	124	0	0	124	100	0	0	100
Businessmen	12	0	0	12	100	0	0	100
Other Occupations	68	0	0	68	100	0	0	100

93% respondents replied in affirmative. 100% respondents of Target Group, 87% officials forming Different Units of Legal System and 96% Law Makers and Opinion Makers admitted commission of atrocities on SCs[5] All the persons belonging to SCs & STs, irrespective of the fact whether he is an illiterate or holding a post graduate degree, are of the view that atrocities are still being committed on the members of SCs[6]

Table No. 1B : Law Makers and Opinion Makers on Commission of Atrocities on SCs

Categories		*Responses in*							
		Number				*Percentage*			
		Yes	*No*	*Und.*	*Total*	*Yes*	*No*	*Und.*	*Total*
Law Makers & Opinion Makers	*SCs*	35	0	0	35	100	0	0	100
	STs	1	0	0	1	100	0	0	100
	Others	12	2	0	14	86	14	0	100

100% MPs, Legislators, Academicians, Media persons, Social activists and members of N.G.Os., *etc.*, belonging to SCs and 86% Non SC & ST are in conformity of this view.[7]

100% I.A.S., P.C.S., Doctors and other officers, irrespective of the fact whether they belong to SCs & STs or Non SC & ST, are of the view that atrocities are being committed on SCs 100% Judges, Lawyers and Policemen belonging to SC & ST are having the similar opinion.[8]

Table No. 1C : Different Units of Legal System on Commission of Atrocities on SCs

Categories		Responses in							
		Number				Percentage			
		Yes	No	Und.	Total	Yes	No	Und.	Total
Judges	SCs	25	0	0	25	100	0	0	100
	Others	23	1	1	25	92	4	4	100
	Total	48	1	1	50	96	2	2	100
Prosecutors	SCs	10	1	0	11	91	9	0	100
	Others	31	6	2	39	79	16	5	100
	Total	41	7	2	50	82	14	4	100
Lawyers	SCs	34	0	0	34	100	0	0	100
	Others	59	5	2	66	89	8	3	100
	Total	93	5	2	100	93	5	2	100
I.A.S., P.C.S., Doctors etc.	SCs	30	0	0	30	100	0	0	100
	STs	5	0	0	5	100	0	0	100
	Others	15	0	0	15	100	0	0	100
	Total	50	0	0	50	100	0	0	100
Police Officials	SCs	12	0	0	12	100	0	0	100
	STs	2	0	0	2	100	0	0	100
	Others	15	21	0	36	42	58	0	100
	Total	29	21	0	50	58	42	0	100
Grand Total		261	34	5	300	87	11	2	100

96% Judges, 82% Public Prosecutors, 93% Lawyers, and 58% Police Officers are of the view that atrocities are still being committed on SCs. Percentage of officials belonging to Non-SC & ST under these categories are 92, 79, 89 and 42, respectively. 91% Prosecutors belonging to SCs are having the same opinion.[9]

On the basis of above discussion and percentage, it is concluded that most of the people are of the view that atrocities are still being committed on the SCs

4.2 Atrocities on the Scheduled Castes : Whether a Blot on Our Society?

Question number 2 of the questionnaire on the subject for Different Units of Legal System and Law Makers and Opinion Makers elicited information whether or not commission of atrocities on the SCs is a blot on our society?[10]

Table No. 2 : Impact of Atrocities on Society

Categories		*Responses in*							
		Number				*Percentage*			
		Yes	*No*	*Und.*	*Total*	*Yes*	*No*	*Und.*	*Total*
Different Units of Legal System	*SCs*	112	0	0	112	100	0	0	100
	STs	7	0	0	7	100	0	0	100
	Others	167	13	1	181	92	7	1	100
	Total	286	13	1	300	95	5	0	100
L.M. & O.M		49	1	0	50	98	2	0	100
Grand Total		335	14	1	350	96	4	0	100

350 respondents were examined on this question. Their responses are depicted in Graph No. 68 and Table Nos. 2, 2A and 2B. Out of these, 335 replied in affirmative, 14 in negative and one did not give any specific reply.[11]

Thus, 96% respondents replied in positive. Percentage of officials forming Different Units of Legal System is 95 and Law Makers and Opinion Makers is 98.[12]

Graph No. 68 : Atrocities on the Scheduled Castes Whether a Blot on Our Society?

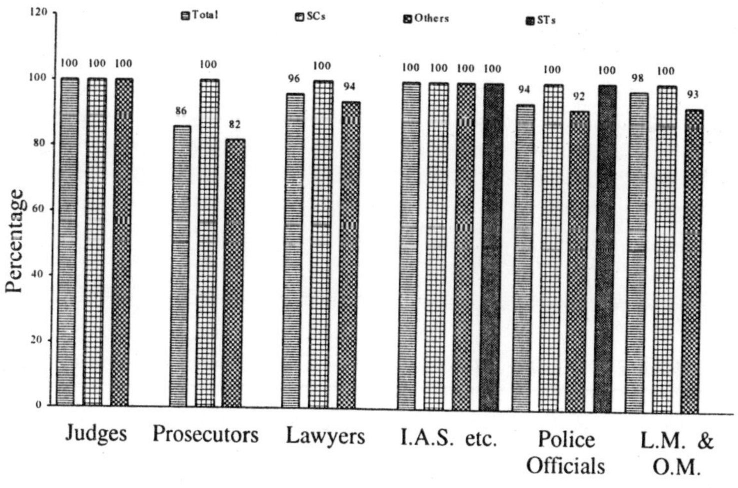

Table No. 2A : Law Makers and Opinion Makers on Impact of Atrocities on Society

Categories		Responses in							
		Number				Percentage			
		Yes	No	Und.	Total	Yes	No	Und.	Total
Law Makers & Opinion Makers	SCs	35	0	0	35	100	0	0	100
	STs	1	0	0	1	100	0	0	100
	Others	13	1	0	14	93	7	0	100

100% MPs, Legislators, Academicians, Media Persons, Social Activists, and members of N.G.Os, *etc.*, belonging to SCs and Judges belonging to SCs and Non SC & ST, Prosecutors, Lawyers, I.A.S., P.C.S., Doctors and other Officers and Policemen belonging to SCs are of the view that commission of atrocities on the SCs is a blot on our society.[13]

Table No. 2B : Different Units of Legal System on Impact of Atrocities on Society

Categories		Responses in							
		Number				Percentage			
		Yes	No	Und.	Total	Yes	No	Und.	Total
Judges	SCs	25	0	0	25	100	0	0	100
	Others	25	0	0	25	100	0	0	100
	Total	50	0	0	50	100	0	0	100
Prosecutors	SCs	11	0	0	11	100	0	0	100
	Others	32	7	0	39	82	18	0	100
	Total	43	7	0	50	86	14	0	100
Lawyers	SCs	34	0	0	34	100	0	0	100
	Others	62	3	1	66	94	5	1	100
	Total	96	3	1	100	96	3	1	100
I.A.S., P.C.S., Doctors, etc.	SCs	30	0	0	30	100	0	0	100
	STs	5	0	0	5	100	0	0	100
	Others	15	0	0	15	100	0	0	100
	Total	50	0	0	50	100	0	0	100
Police Officials	SCs	12	0	0	12	100	0	0	100
	STs	2	0	0	2	100	0	0	100
	Others	33	3	0	36	92	8	0	100
	Total	47	3	0	50	94	6	2	100
Grand Total		286	13	1	300	96	4	0	100

86% Public Prosecutors, 96% Lawyers and 94% Police Officials are having the same opinion. Percentages of respondents belonging to Non-SC & ST under these categories are 82, 94 and 92 respectively.[14]

It may, therefore, be concluded that most of the people are of the opinion that commission of atrocities on SCs is a blot on our society.

4.3 Atrocities on the Scheduled Castes : Whether an Impediment in Advancement and Development of Our Country ?

Question number 3 of the questionnaire on the subject for Different Units of the Legal System and Law Makers and Opinion Makers elicited information whether or not commission of atrocities on the SCs is an impediment in the advancement and development of our country.[15]

Table No. 3 : Impact of Atrocities on Development of Our Country

Categories		*Responses in*							
		Number				*Percentage*			
		Yes	*No*	*Und.*	*Total*	*Yes*	*No*	*Und.*	*Total*
Different Units of Legal System	*SCs*	107	5	0	112	96	4	0	100
	STs	6	1	0	7	86	14	0	100
	Others	155	23	3	181	86	13	1	100
	Total	268	29	3	300	89	10	1	100
L.M. & O.M		48	2	0	50	96	4	0	100
Grand Total		316	31	3	350	90	7	3	100

350 respondents were examined on these questions. Their responses are depicted in Graph No. 69 and Table Nos. 3, 3A and 3B. Out of these 316 replied in affirmative, 31 in negative and 3 did not give any specific reply.[16]

Thus, 90% in all, 89% officials forming Different Units of Legal System and 96% M.Ps., Legislators, Academicians, Media Persons, Social Activists and member of N.G.Os., *etc.*, opined that commission of atrocities on the SCs is an impediment in the advancement and development of our country.[17] Percentage of SC respondents under this category is 97 and Non SC & ST category is 93.

100% Judges belonging to SCs and Non SC & ST, I.A.S., P.C.S., Doctors and other officers both belonging to SCs and Non SC & ST and Policemen belonging to STs hold the same view. 80% Prosecutors, 90% Lawyers, 98% I.A.S., P.C.S., Doctors and other officers and 78% Policemen are having the same opinion.[18]

Table No. 3A : Law Makers and Opinion Makers on Impact of Atrocities on Development of Our Country

Categories		Responses in							
		Number				Percentage			
		Yes	No	Und.	Total	Yes	No	Und.	Total
Law Makers & Opinion Makers	SCs	34	1	0	35	97	3	0	100
	STs	1	0	0	1	100	0	0	100
	Others	13	1	0	14	93	7	0	100

Percentages of SCs under these categories are 91, 91, 100 and 92, respectively. 77% Prosecutors, 89% Lawyers, 100% I.A.S., P.C.S., Doctors and other officers and 72% Police officials belonging to Non SC & ST are of the same opinion.[19]

Graph No. 69 : Atrocities on the SCs : Whether an Impediment in Advancement and Development of Our Country?

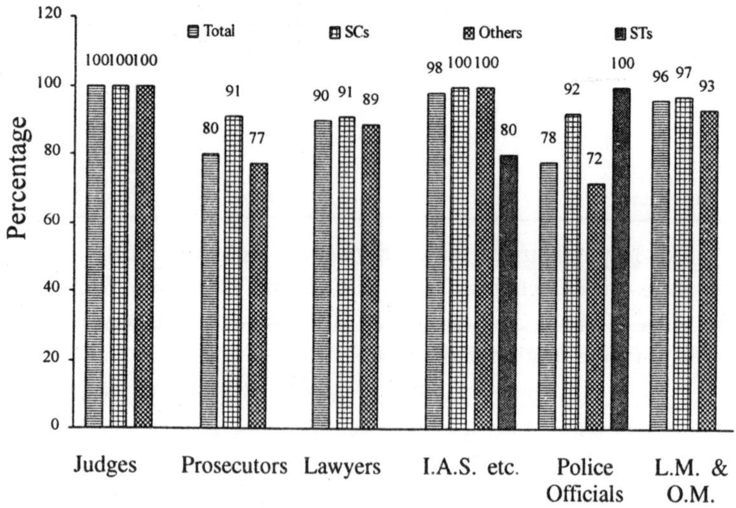

Since the percentage of all categories of respondents is above 78, which extended upto 100 in most of the categories, it may, therefore, be concluded that most of the respondents admitted that commission of atrocities on the SCs is an impediment in the advancement and development of our country.

Table No. 3B : Different Units of Legal System on Impact of Atrocities on Development of our Country

Categories		*Responses in*							
		Number				*Percentage*			
		Yes	*No*	*Und.*	*Total*	*Yes*	*No*	*Und.*	*Total*
Judges	*SCs*	25	0	0	25	100	0	0	100
	Others	25	0	0	25	100	0	0	100
	Total	50	0	0	50	100	0	0	100
Prosecutors	*SCs*	10	1	0	11	91	9	0	100
	Others	30	8	1	39	77	21	2	100
	Total	40	9	1	50	80	18	2	100
Lawyers	*SCs*	31	3	0	34	91	9	0	100
	Others	59	6	1	66	89	9	2	100
	Total	90	9	1	100	90	9	1	100
I.A.S., P.C.S., Doctors, etc.	*SCs*	30	0	0	30	100	0	0	100
	STs	4	1	0	5	100	0	0	100
	Others	15	0	0	15	100	0	0	100
	Total	49	1	0	50	98	2	0	100
Police Officials	*SCs*	11	1	0	12	92	8	0	100
	STs	2	0	0	2	10	0	0	100
	Others	26	9	1	36	72	25	3	100
	Total	39	10	1	50	78	20	2	100
Grand Total		268	29	3	300	89	10	1	100

B. CAUSES OF ATROCITIES ON THE SCHEDULED CASTES

4.4 Caste System

Question number 5 of the questionnaire on the subject for Law Makers and Opinion Makers, elicited information from M.Ps., Legislators, Academicians, Media Persons, Social Activists and members of N.G.Os., *etc.*, whether or not caste system is a factor for commission and continuation of practice of untouchability on the members of SCs?[20]

50 respondents were examined on this question. Their responses are depicted in Graph No. 70 and Table No. 4. Out of these 46 replied in affirmative, 3 in negative and one did not give any specific reply.[21] Thus, 92% replied in positive. Percentage of SCs respondents, who replied in positive, is 97 and Non SC & ST is 79.[22]

It is, therefore, concluded that caste system is responsible for commission and continuation of untouchability on the members of SCs

Table No. 4 : Law Makers and Opinion Makers on the Caste System as a Cause for Commission of Atrocities on SCs

Categories		*Responses in*							
		Number				*Percentage*			
		Yes	*No*	*Und.*	*Total*	*Yes*	*No*	*Und.*	*Total*
Law Makers & Opinion Makers	*SCs*	34	1	0	35	97	3	0	100
	STs	1	0	0	01	100	0	0	100
	Others	11	2	1	14	79	14	7	100
	Total	46	3	1	50	92	6	2	100

Graph Nos. 70 & 71 : Caste System and Endogamy : Causes of Commission of Atrocities on the SCs

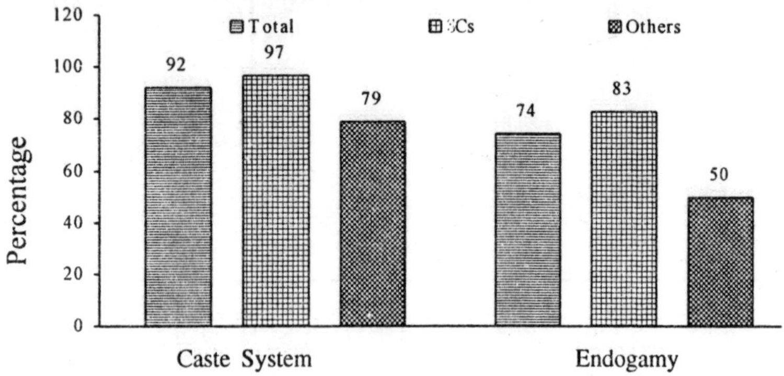

4.5 Endogamy

Question number 7 of the questionnaire on the subject for Law Makers and Opinion Makers, elicited information from M.Ps., Legislators, Academicians, Media Persons, Social Activists and members of N.G.Os., *etc.*, whether or not endogamy is one of the reason for continuation of caste system?[23]

Table No. 5 : Law Makers and Opinion Makers on Endogamy as a Cause for Commission of Atrocities on SCs

Categories		*Responses in*							
		Number				*Percentage*			
		Yes	*No*	*Und.*	*Total*	*Yes*	*No*	*Und.*	*Total*
Law Makers & Opinion Makers	SCs	29	6	0	35	83	17	0	100
	STs	1	0	0	01	100	0	0	100
	Others	7	4	3	14	50	29	21	100
	Total	37	10	3	50	74	20	6	100

50 respondents were examined on this question. Their responses are depicted in Graph No. 71 and Table No. 5. Out of these 37 replied in affirmative, 10 in negative and 3 did not give any specific reply.[24] Thus, 74% of the M.Ps., Legislators, Academicians, Media Persons, Social Activists and members of N.G.Os., *etc.*, are of the opinion that endogamy is one of the reason for continuation of caste system.[25]

Percentage of SCs respondents of these categories, who are having the same view, is 83%.[26]

It is, therefore, concluded that endogamy is one of the reason for continuation of caste system.

4.6 Caste Hatred

Question numbers 8, 6 and 8 of the questionnaire of the subject for Target Group,[27] Different Units of the Legal System,[28] and Law Makers and Opinion Makers,[29] respectively, elicited, opinion whether or not caste hatred with the members of SCs by persons of other communities, is a factor for commission or atrocities on them ?

Table No. 6 : Caste Hatred as a Factor for Commission of Atrocities on SCs

Categories		*Responses in*							
		Number				*Percentage*			
		Yes	*No*	*Und.*	*Total*	*Yes*	*No*	*Und.*	*Total*
Target Group 187		10	3	200	94	5	1	100	
Different Units of Legal System	*SCs*	110	1	1	112	98	1	1	100
	STs	6	1	0	7	86	14	0	100
	Others	145	29	7	181	80	16	4	100
	Total	261	31	8	300	87	10	3	100
L.M. & O.M		46	3	1	50	92	6	2	100
Grand Total		494	44	12	550	90	8	2	100

550 respondents were examined on this question. Their responses are depicted in Graph No. 72 and Table No. 6, 6A 6B and 6C. 494 replied in affirmative, 44 in negative and 12 did not give any specific reply.[30] Thus, 94% respondents of Target Group,[31] 87% respondents forming Different Units of the Legal System;[32] and 92% Law Makers and Opinion Makers opined in positive.[33] Thus, 90% respondents replied in affirmative.

Graph No. 72 : Caste Hatred : A Cause of Commission of Atrocities on the SCs

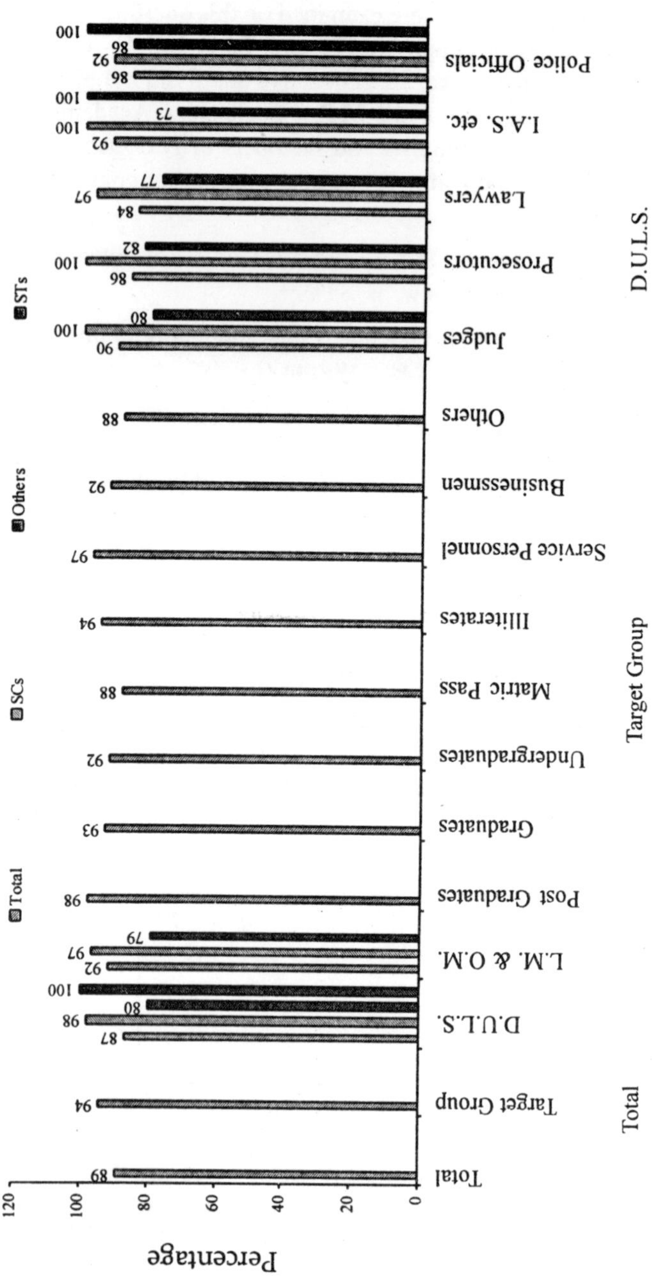

Table No. 6A : Target Group on Caste Hatred as a Factor for Commission of Atrocities on SCs

Categories	*Responses in*							
	Number				*Percentage*			
	Yes	*No*	*Und.*	*Total*	*Yes*	*No*	*Und.*	*Total*
Post Graduates	56	1	0	57	98	2	0	100
Graduates	63	5	0	68	93	7	0	100
Under Graduates	23	1	1	25	92	4	4	100
Matric Pass	30	2	2	34	88	6	6	100
Illiterates	15	1	0	16	94	6	0	100
Service Personnel	120	4	0	124	97	3	0	100
Businessmen	11	0	1	12	92	0	8	100
Other Occupations	56	6	2	68	88	9	3	100

98% Post Graduates, 93% Graduates, 92% Under Graduates, 88% Matric Pass, 94% Illiterates, 97% Service Personnel, 92% Businessmen and 88% carrying different occupations of the Target Group hold this view.[34]

Table No. 6B : Different Units of Legal System on Caste Hatred as a Factor for Commission of Atrocities on SCs

Categories		*Responses in*							
		Number				*Percentage*			
		Yes	*No*	*Und.*	*Total*	*Yes*	*No*	*Und.*	*Total*
Judges	*SCs*	25	0	0	25	100	0	0	100
	Others	20	4	1	25	80	16	4	100
	Total	45	4	1	50	90	8	2	100
Prosecutors	*SCs*	11	0	0	11	100	0	0	100
	Others	32	5	2	39	82	13	5	100
	Total	43	5	2	50	86	10	4	100
Lawyers	*SCs*	33	0	1	34	97	0	3	100
	Others	51	12	3	66	77	19	4	100
	Total	84	12	4	100	84	12	4	100
I.A.S., P.C.S., Doctors, etc.	*SCs*	30	0	0	30	100	0	0	100
	STs	5	0	0	5	100	0	0	100
	Others	11	4	0	15	73	17	0	100
	Total	46	4	0	50	92	8	0	100

Table No. 6B *Contd.*

		Yes	No	Und.	Total	Yes	No	Und.	Total
Police Officials	*SCs*	11	1	0	12	92	8	0	100
	STs	1	1	0	2	50	50	0	100
	Others	31	4	1	36	86	11	3	100
	Total	43	6	1	50	86	12	2	100
Grand Total		261	31	8	300	87	10	3	100

90% Judges, 86% Public Prosecutors, 84% Lawyers, 92% I.A.S., P.C.S., Doctors and other officers and 86% Police officials are of the same opinion. Percentages of SC respondents of these categories, agreeing to this view are 100, 100, 97, 100 and 92, respectively. Percentages of Non SC & ST officials having same view are 80, 82, 77, 73 and 86, respectively.[35]

Table No. 6C : Law Makers and Opinion Makers on Caste Hatred as a Factor for Commission of Atrocities on SCs

Categories		*Responses in*							
		Number				*Percentage*			
		Yes	*No*	*Und.*	*Total*	*Yes*	*No*	*Und.*	*Total*
Law Makers & Opinion Makers	*SCs*	34	1	0	35	97	3	0	100
	STs	01	0	0	01	100	0	0	100
	Others	11	2	1	14	79	14	7	100

92% M.Ps., Legislators, Academicians, Media Persons, Social Activists and members of N.G.Os., *etc.*, also hold this view. Percentage of SCs respondents of these categories having same opinion is 97 and Non SC & ST respondents having same view is 79.[36]

On the basis of above analysis, it is concluded that caste hatred is one of the main factors for commission of atrocities on the SCs.

4.7 Untouchability

Question numbers 7, 5 and 6 of the questionnaire on the subject for Target Group,[37] Different Units of the Legal System,[38] Law Makers and Opinion Makers,[39] respectively, elicited opinion, whether or not untouchability with the member of the SCs by the persons of other community is a factor for commission of atrocities on the member of the SCs?

Table No. 7 : Untouchability as a Factor for Commission of Atrocities on SCs

Categories		*Responses in*							
		Number				*Percentage*			
		Yes	*No*	*Und.*	*Total*	*Yes*	*No*	*Und.*	*Total*
Target Group		190	7	3	200	95	4	1	100
Different Units of Legal System	*SCs*	103	7	2	112	92	6	2	100
	STs	6	0	1	7	86	0	14	100
	Others	147	28	6	181	81	15	4	100
	Total	256	35	9	300	85	12	3	100
L.M. & O.M		47	2	1	50	94	4	2	100
Grand Total		493	44	13	550	90	8	2	100

550 respondents were examined on these questions. Their responses are depicted in Graph No. 73 and Table Nos. 7, 7A, 7B and 7C. Out of these 493 replied in affirmative, 44 in negative and 13 did not give any specific reply.[40] Thus, 90% replied in positive.

95% respondents of Target Group,[41] 85% officials forming Different Units of the Legal System[42] and 94% Law Makers and Opinion Makers[43] are of the view that untouchability with members of SC by persons of other communities is one of the factor for commission of atrocities on the SCs

Table No. 7A : Target Group on Untouchability as a Factor for Commission of Atrocities on SCs

Categories	*Responses in*							
	Number				*Percentage*			
	Yes	*No*	*Und.*	*Total*	*Yes*	*No*	*Und.*	*Total*
Post Graduates	55	2	0	57	96	4	0	100
Graduates	64	3	1	68	94	4	2	100
Under Graduates	24	1	0	25	96	4	0	100
Matric Pass	32	0	2	34	94	0	6	100
Illiterates	15	1	0	16	94	6	0	100
Service Personnel	118	5	1	124	95	4	1	100
Businessmen	12	0	0	12	100	0	0	100
Other Occupations	60	2	2	68	94	3	3	100

Graph No. 73 : Untouchability : A Cause for Commission of Atrocities on the SCs

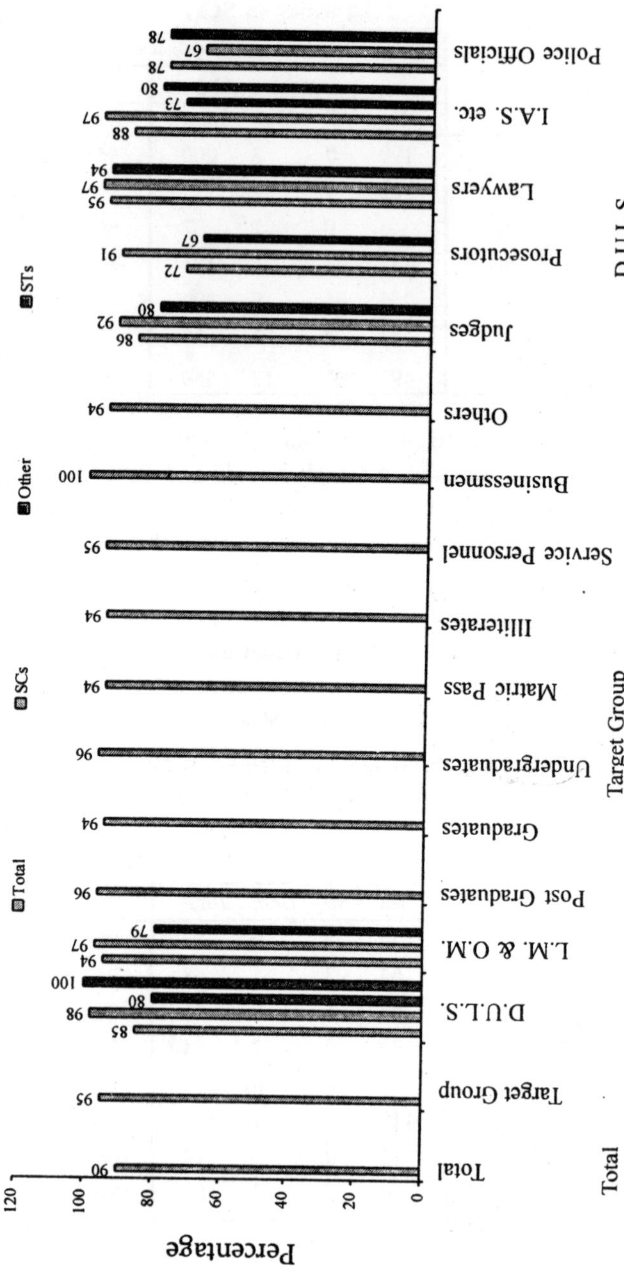

96% Post Graduates, 94% Graduates, 96% Under Graduates, 94% Matric Pass and Illiterates, 95% Service Personnel, 100% Businessmen and 94% carrying different occupations of the Target Group are having the same opinion.[44]

Table No. 7B : Different Units of Legal System on Untouchability as a Factor for Commission of Atrocities on SCs

Categories		*Responses in*							
		Number				*Percentage*			
		Yes	*No*	*Und.*	*Total*	*Yes*	*No*	*Und.*	*Total*
Judges	*SCs*	23	2	0	25	92	8	0	100
	Others	20	4	1	25	80	16	4	100
	Total	43	6	1	50	86	12	2	100
Prosecutors	*SCs*	10	1	0	11	91	9	0	100
	Others	26	8	5	39	67	21	12	100
	Total	36	9	5	50	72	18	10	100
Lawyers	*SCs*	33	0	1	34	97	0	0	100
	Others	62	4	0	66	94	6	0	100
	Total	95	4	1	100	95	4	1	100
I.A.S., P.C.S., Doctors, etc.	*SCs*	29	1	0	30	97	3	0	100
	STs	4	0	1	5	80	0	20	100
	Others	11	4	0	15	73	27	0	100
	Total	44	5	1	50	88	10	2	100
Police Officials	*SCs*	8	3	1	12	67	25	8	100
	STs	2	0	0	2	100	0	0	100
	Others	28	8	0	36	78	22	0	100
	Total	38	11	1	50	76	22	4	100
Grand Total		256	35	9	300	85	12	3	100

86% Judges, 72% Public Prosecutors, 95% Lawyers, 88% I.A.S., P.C.S., Doctors and others officers and 76% Police officials are having the same view.[45]

92% officials forming Different Units of the Legal System belonging to SCs, comprises of 92% Judges, 91% Public Prosecutors, 97% Lawyers, 97% I.A.S., P.C.S., Doctors and other officers and 67% Police Personnel are of the same opinion.[46]

80% I.A.S., P.C.S., Doctors and other officers and 100% Police officers belonging to STs, hold the same view.[47]

81% officials forming Different Units of the Legal System belonging to Non SC & ST comprises of 80% Judges, 67% Public Prosecutors, 94% Lawyers, 73% I.A.S., P.C.S., Doctors and other officers and 78% Police officials are in conformity of this view.[48]

Table No. 7C : Law Makers and Opinion Makers on Untouchability as a Factor for Commission of Atrocities on SCs

Categories		*Responses in*							
		Number				*Percentage*			
		Yes	*No*	*Und.*	*Total*	*Yes*	*No*	*Und.*	*Total*
Law Makers & Opinion Makers	*SCs*	34	1	0	35	97	3	0	100
	STs	1	0	0	01	100	0	0	100
	Others	12	1	1	14	86	7	7	100

94% M.Ps., Legislators, Academicians, Media Persons, Social Activists and members of N.G.Os., *etc.*, in all and 97% belonging to SCs and 86% belonging to Non SC & ST are having the similar views.[49]

It is, therefore, concluded that practice of untouchability with the members of SCs, by members of other communities is one of the main reasons for commission of atrocities on the SCs.

4.8 Religion

Question numbers 9, 7 and 9 of the questionnaire on the subject for Target Group,[50] Different Units of the Legal System[51] and Law Makers and Opinion Makers,[52] respectively, elicited opinion whether or not having no separate religion by the members of the SCs is a factor for commission of atrocities on them?

Table No. 8 : Religion as a Factor for Commission of Atrocities on SCs

Categories		*Responses in*							
		Number				*Percentage*			
		Yes	*No*	*Und.*	*Total*	*Yes*	*No*	*Und.*	*Total*
Target Group	109	84	7	200	55	42	3	100	
Different Units of Legal System	*SCs*	45	58	9	112	40	52	8	100
	STs	1	5	1	7	14	72	14	100
	Others	40	128	13	181	22	71	7	100
	Total	86	191	23	300	29	64	7	100
L.M. & O.M		23	26	1	50	46	52	2	100
Grand Total		218	301	31	550	40	55	5	100

Graph No. 74 : Having no Separate Religion by the SCs : A Cause for Commission of Atrocities on the SCs

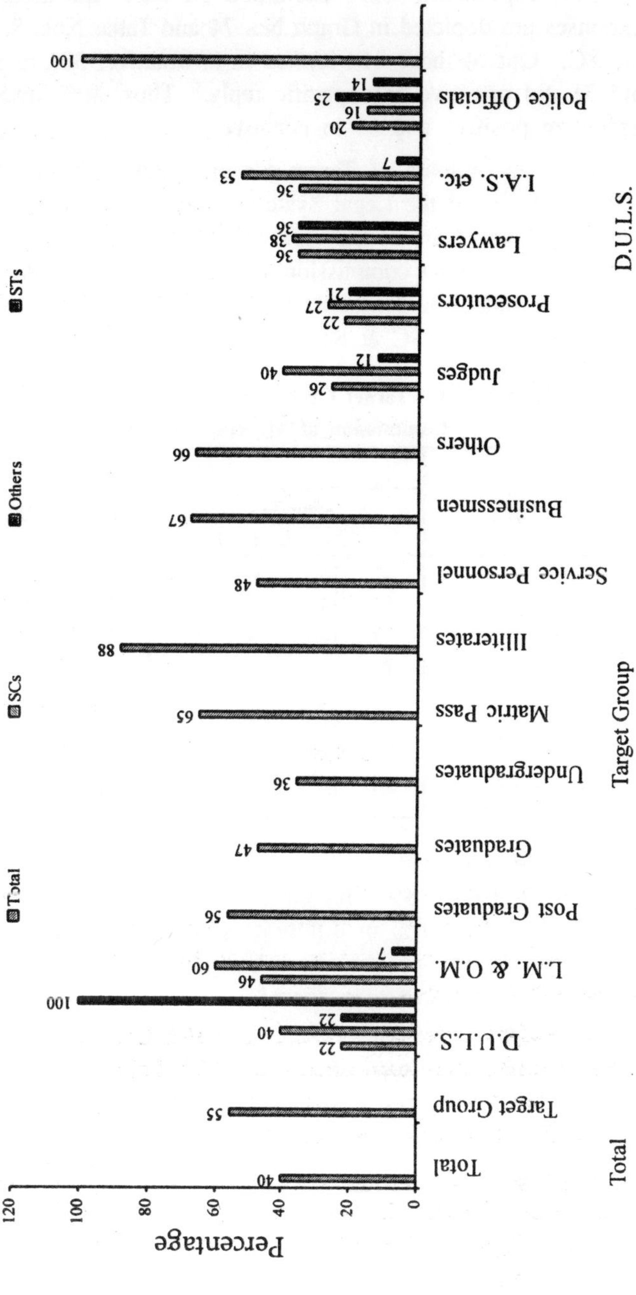

550 respondents were examined on these questions. Their responses are depicted in Graph No. 74 and Table Nos. 8, 8A, 8B and 8C. Out of these 218 replied in affirmative, 301 in negative and 31 did not give any specific reply.[53] Thus, 40% respondents replied in positive and 55 in negative.

55% respondents of Target Group,[54] 22% officials forming Different Units of the Legal System,[55] and 46% Law Makers and Opinion Makers[56] are of the view that having no separate religion by SCs is a reason for commission of atrocities on them. Percentages of SCs respondents under these categories are 40 and 60 respectively. Percentage of Non SC & ST are 22 and 7, respectively.[57]

Table No. 8A : Target Group on Religion as a Factor for Commission of Atrocities on SCs

Categories	*Responses in*							
	Number				*Percentage*			
	Yes	*No*	*Und.*	*Total*	*Yes*	*No*	*Und.*	*Total*
Post Graduates	32	25	0	57	56	44	0	100
Graduates	32	34	2	68	47	50	3	100
Under Graduates	9	16	0	25	36	64	0	100
Matric Pass	22	7	5	34	65	21	14	100
Illiterates	14	2	0	16	88	12	0	100
Service Personnels	59	61	4	124	48	49	3	100
Businessmen	8	3	1	12	67	25	8	100
Other Occupations	46	20	2	68	68	29	3	100

56% Post Graduates, 47% Graduates, 36% Under Graduates, 65% Matric Pass, 88% Illiterates, 48% Service Personnel, 67% Businessmen and 66% in different occupations of Target Group opined that having no separate religion by them is a reason for commission of atrocities on them.[58]

26% Judges, 22% Public Prosecutors, 36% Lawyers, 36% I.A.S., P.C.S., Doctors, and other officers and 16% Police officials are of the view that having no separate religion by SCs is a reason for commission of atrocities on the SCs[59]

Percentages of officials belonging to SCs of these categories are 40, 27, 38, 53 and 25, respectively. 20% I.A.S., P.C.S., Doctors and other officers and 100% Police personnel belonging to STs categories hold the same view.[60]

Table No. 8B : Different Units of Legal System on Religion as a Factor for Commission of Atrocities on SCs

Categories		Responses in							
		Number				Percentage			
		Yes	No	Und.	Total	Yes	No	Und.	Total
Judges	SCs	10	14	1	25	40	56	4	100
	Others	3	20	2	25	12	80	8	100
	Total	13	34	3	50	26	68	6	100
Prosecutors	SCs	3	7	1	11	27	64	9	100
	Others	8	28	3	39	21	71	8	100
	Total	11	35	4	50	22	70	8	100
Lawyers	SCs	13	16	5	34	38	47	15	100
	Others	23	38	5	66	35	57	8	100
	Total	36	54	10	100	36	54	10	100
I.A.S., P.C.S., Doctors, etc.	SCs	16	13	1	30	53	43	4	100
	STs	1	3	1	5	20	60	20	100
	Others	1	12	2	15	7	80	13	100
	Total	18	28	4	50	36	56	8	100
Police officials	SCs	3	8	1	12	25	67	8	100
	STs	0	2	0	2	0	100	0	100
	Others	5	30	1	36	13	83	4	100
	Total	8	40	2	50	16	80	4	100
Grand Total		86	191	23	300	29	63	8	100

22% officials forming Different Units of the Legal System belonging to Non SC & ST comprises of 12% Judges, 21% Public Prosecutors, 35% Lawyers, 7% I.A.S., P.C.S., Doctors, and other officers and 14% Police officials are in conformity of this view.[61]

Table No. 8C : Law Makers and Opinion Makers on Religion as a Factor for Commission of Atrocities on SCs

Categories		Responses in							
		Number				Percentage			
		Yes	No	Und.	Total	Yes	No	Und.	Total
Law Makers & Opinion Makers	SCs	21	14	0	35	60	40	0	100
	STs	1	0	0	01	100	0	0	100
	Others	1	12	1	14	7	86	7	100

46% M.Ps., Legislators, Academicians, Media Persons, Social Activists and members of N.G.Os., *etc.,* in all and 60% belonging to SCs and 7% belonging to Non SC & ST are having the similar opinion.[62]

On the basis of above discussions and percentage, it may be concluded that majority of population of SCs, I.A.S., P.C.S., Doctors and other officials of SCs and Police officials of STs are of the view that having no separate religion by SC is a reason for commission of atrocities on them. M.Ps., Legislators, Academicians, Media Persons, Social Activists and members of N.G.Os., *etc.*, of SC categories also agreed to this opinion.

The opinion of all other respondents are that having no separate religion by SCs is not a reason for commission of atrocities on them.

4.9 Cultural Backwardness

Question numbers 15, 11 and 13 of the questionnaire of this subject for Target Group,[63] Different Units of Legal System,[64] Law Makers and Opinion Makers,[65] respectively, elicited opinion whether or not cultural backwardness of the member of SCs, a factor for commission and continuation of atrocities on them?

Table No. 9 : Cultural Backwardness as a Factor for Commission of Atrocities on SCs

Categories		*Responses in*							
		Number				*Percentage*			
		Yes	*No*	*Und.*	*Total*	*Yes*	*No*	*Und.*	*Total*
*Target Group*149		45	6	200	75	22	3	100	
Different Units of Legal System	*SCs*	85	25	2	112	76	22	2	100
	STs	6	1	0	7	86	14	0	100
	Others	101	67	13	181	56	37	7	100
	Total	192	93	15	300	64	31	5	100
L.M. & O.M		35	12	3	50	70	24	6	100
Grand Total		376	150	24	550	68	27	4	100

550 respondents were examined on these questions. Their responses are depicted in Graph No. 75 and Table Nos. 9, 9A, 9B and 9C. Out of these, 376 replied in positive, 150 in negative and

24 did not give any specific reply.[66] Thus, 68% replied in positive. 75% respondents of Target Group,[67] 58% officials forming Different Units of the Legal System[68] and 70% Law Makers and Opinion Makers[69] opined that cultural backwardness of SCs is a factor for commission of atrocities on them.

Table No. 9A Target Group on Cultural Backwardness as a Factor for Commission of Atrocities on SCs

Categories	*Responses in*							
	Number				*Percentage*			
	Yes	*No*	*Und.*	*Total*	*Yes*	*No*	*Und.*	*Total*
Post Graduates	38	18	1	57	67	31	2	100
Graduates	48	18	2	68	71	26	3	100
Under Graduates	18	7	0	25	72	28	0	100
Matric Pass	30	1	3	34	88	3	9	100
Illiterates	15	1	0	16	94	6	0	100
Service Personnel	91	32	1	124	74	26	0	100
Businessmen	10	1	1	12	84	8	8	100
Other Occupations	51	12	5	68	75	18	7	100

67% Post-Graduates, 71% Graduates, 72% Under-Graduates, 88% Matric Pass, 94% Illiterate, 73% Service Personnel, 83% Businessmen and 75% persons of Target Group engaged in different occupations replied in affirmative.[70]

Table No. 9B : Different Units of Legal System on Cultural Backwardness as a Factor for Commission of Atrocities on SCs

Categories		*Responses in*							
		Number				*Percentage*			
		Yes	*No*	*Und.*	*Total*	*Yes*	*No*	*Und.*	*Total*
Judges	SCs	21	4	0	25	84	16	0	100
	Others	19	5	1	25	76	20	4	100
	Total	40	9	1	50	80	18	2	100
Prosecutors	SCs	5	6	0	11	45	55	0	100
	Others	24	13	2	39	62	33	5	100
	Total	29	19	2	50	58	38	4	100
Lawyers	SCs	23	9	2	34	68	26	6	100
	Others	35	21	10	66	53	32	15	100
	Total	58	30	12	100	58	30	12	100

TABLE No. 9B *Contd.*

		Yes	No	Und.	Total	Yes	No	Und.	Total
I.A.S.,P.C.S., Doctors, etc.	SCs	25	5	0	30	83	17	0	100
	STs	4	1	0	5	80	20	0	100
	Others	8	7	0	15	53	47	0	100
	Total	37	13	0	50	74	26	0	100
Police officials	SCs	11	1	0	12	92	8	0	100
	STs	2	0	0	2	100	0	0	100
	Others	15	21	0	36	42	58	0	100
	Total	28	22	0	50	56	44	0	100
Grand Total		192	93	15	300	64	31	5	100

80% Judges, 58% Public Prosecutors and Lawyers, 74% I.A.S., P.C.S., Doctors and other officers and 54% Police officials are of the same opinion. Percentages of SCs officials under these categories are 84, 45, 68, 83 and 92, respectively.[71]

Table No. 9C : Law Makers and Opinion Makers on Cultural Backwardness as a Factor for Commission of Atrocities on SCs

Categories		*Responses in*							
		Number				*Percentage*			
		Yes	*No*	*Und.*	*Total*	*Yes*	*No*	*Und.*	*Total*
Law Makers & Opinion Makers	SCs	25	8	2	35	71	23	6	100
	STs	1	0	0	01	100	0	0	100
	Others	9	4	1	14	64	29	7	100

70% MPs, Legislators, Academicians, Media Persons, Social Activists and Members of N.G.Os., *etc.*, answered in positive.[72]

71% respondents of these categories belonging to SCs and 64% Non SC & ST are having the similar views.[73]

On the basis of above discussion and percentage, it is concluded that cultural backwardness of the members of SCs is one of the main factors for commission of atrocities on the SCs

4.10 Illiteracy

Question numbers 10, 8 and 10 of the questionnaire of the subject for Target Group,[74] Different Units of Legal System,[75] Law Makers and Opinion Makers,[76] respectively, elicited opinion whether or not illiteracy is a factor for commission of atrocities on SCs?

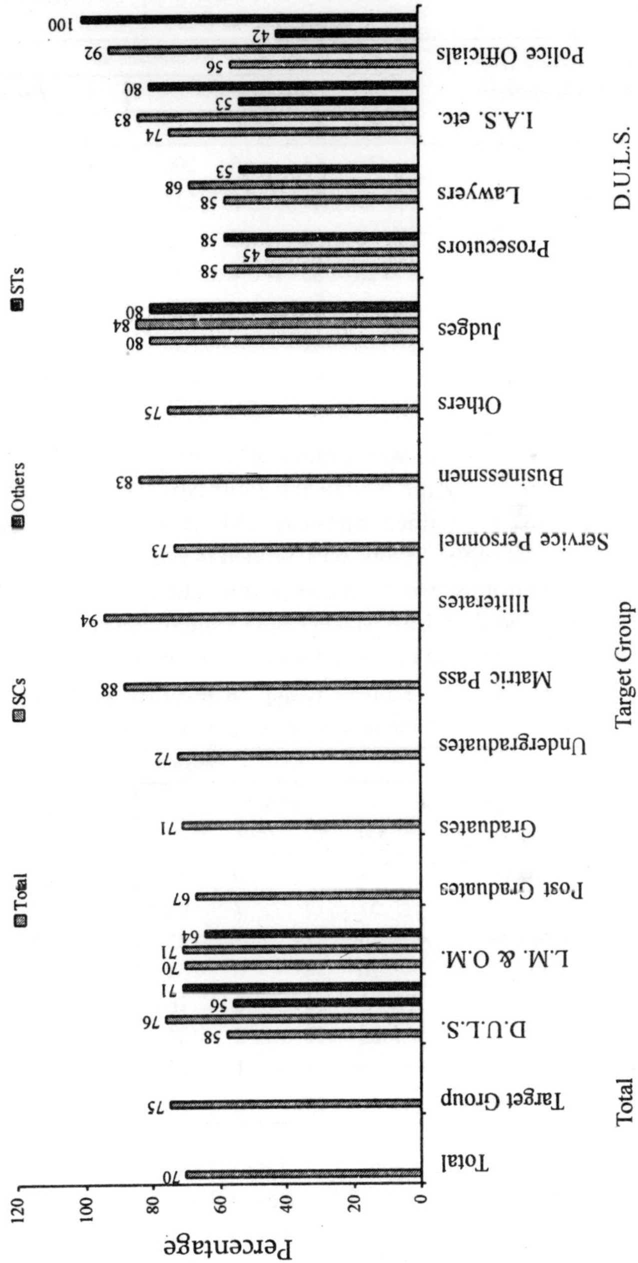

Graph No. 75 : Cultural Backwardness : A Cause for Commission of Atrocities on the SCs

Table No. 10 : Illiteracy as a Factor for Commission of Atrocities on SCs

Categories		*Responses in*							
		Number				*Percentage*			
		Yes	*No*	*Und.*	*Total*	*Yes*	*No*	*Und.*	*Total*
Target Group		130	65	5	200	65	33	2	100
Different Units of Legal System	SCs	90	21	1	112	81	19	0	100
	STs	5	2	0	7	71	29	0	100
	Others	122	55	4	181	68	30	2	100
	Total	217	78	5	300	72	26	2	100
L.M. & O.M		10	38	2	50	20	76	4	100
Grand Total		357	181	12	550	65	33	2	100

550 respondents were examined on this question. Their responses are depicted in Graph No. 76 and Table Nos. 10, 10A, 10B and 10C. Out of these 357 replied in positive, 181 in negative and 12 did not give any specific reply.[77] Thus, 65% replied in positive. 65% respondents of Target Groups,[78] 68% officials forming Different Units of the Legal System[79] and 20% Law Makers and Opinion Makers[80] are of the view that illiteracy is one of the factors for commission of atrocities on SCs

Table No. 10A : Target Group on Illiteracy as a Factor for Commission of Atrocities on SCs

Categories	*Responses in*							
	Number				*Percentage*			
	Yes	*No*	*Und.*	*Total*	*Yes*	*No*	*Und.*	*Total*
Post Graduates	39	18	0	57	68	32	0	100
Graduates	51	15	2	68	75	22	3	100
Under Graduates	15	7	3	25	60	28	12	100
Matric Pass	20	14	0	34	59	41	0	100
Illiterates	5	11	0	16	31	69	0	100
Service Personnel	85	37	2	124	68	30	2	100
Businessmen	6	5	1	12	50	42	8	100
Other Occupations	41	23	4	68	61	33	6	100

68% Post-Graduates, 75% Graduates, 60% Under Graduates, 59% Matric Pass, 31% Illiterates, 69% Service Personnel, 50% Businessmen and 61% persons of Target Group engaged in different occupations are having the same opinion.[81]

Graph No. 76 : Illiteracy : A Cause for Commission of Atrocities on the SCs

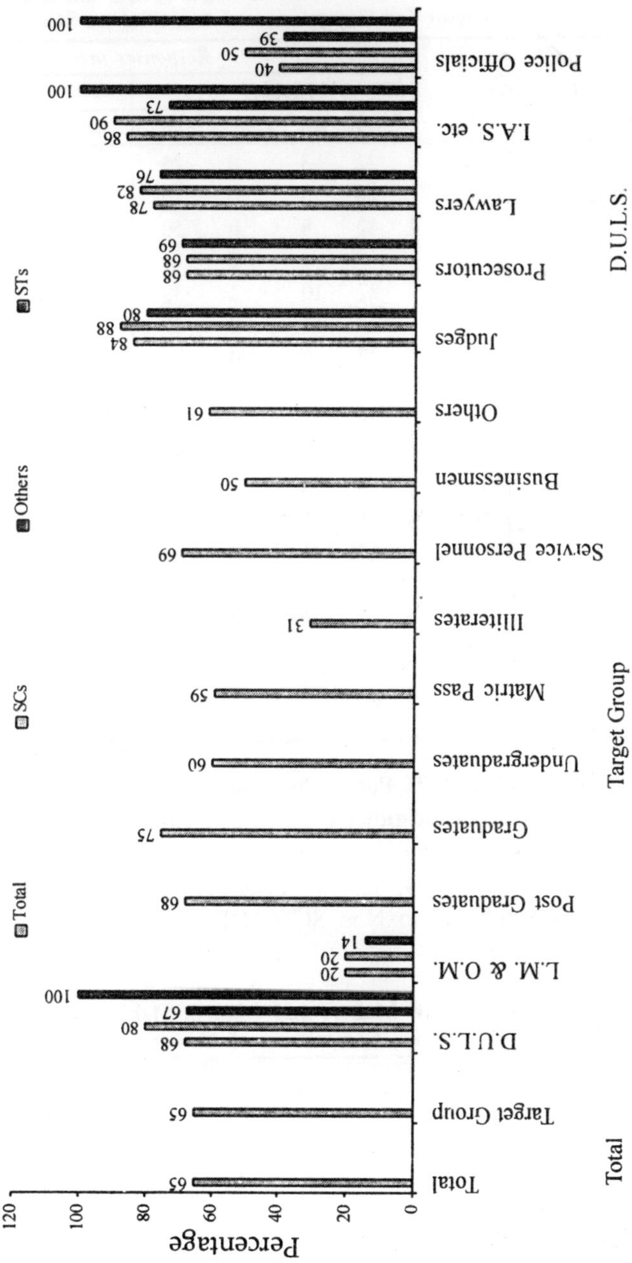

Table No. 10B : Different Units of Legal System on Illiteracy as a Factor for Commission of Atrocities on SCs

Categories		Responses in							
		Number				Percentage			
		Yes	No	Und.	Total	Yes	No	Und.	Total
Judges	SCs	22	3	0	25	88	12	0	100
	Others	20	5	0	25	80	20	0	100
	Total	42	8	0	50	84	16	0	100
Prosecutors	SCs	7	4	0	11	64	36	0	100
	Others	27	10	2	39	69	26	5	100
	Total	34	14	2	50	68	28	4	100
Lawyers	SCs	28	6	0	34	82	18	0	100
	Others	50	15	1	66	76	23	1	100
	Total	78	21	1	100	78	21	1	100
I.A.S.,P.C.S., Doctors, etc.	SCs	27	3	0	30	90	10	0	100
	STs	5	0	0	5	100	0	0	100
	Others	11	4	0	15	73	27	0	100
	Total	43	7	0	50	86	14	0	100
Police Officials	SCs	6	5	1	12	50	42	8	100
	STs	0	2	0	2	0	100	0	100
	Others	14	21	1	36	39	58	3	100
	Total	20	28	2	50	40	56	4	100
Grand Total		217	78	5	300	72	26	2	100

84% Judges, 68% Public Prosecutors, 78% Lawyers, 86% I.A.S., P.C.S., Doctors and other officers and 40% Police officials are in conformity of this opinion. Percentages of SC officials under these categories are 88, 64, 82, 90 and 50, respectively. Percentages of officials belonging to Non SC & ST are 80, 69, 76, 73 and 39, respectively.[82]

Table No. 10C : Law Makers and Opinion Makers on Illiteracy as a Factor for Commission of Atrocities on SCs

Categories		Responses in							
		Number				Percentage			
		Yes	No	Und.	Total	Yes	No	Und.	Total
Law Makers & Opinion Makers	SCs	7	27	1	35	20	77	3	100
	STs	1	0	0	01	100	0	0	100
	Others	2	11	1	14	14	79	7	100

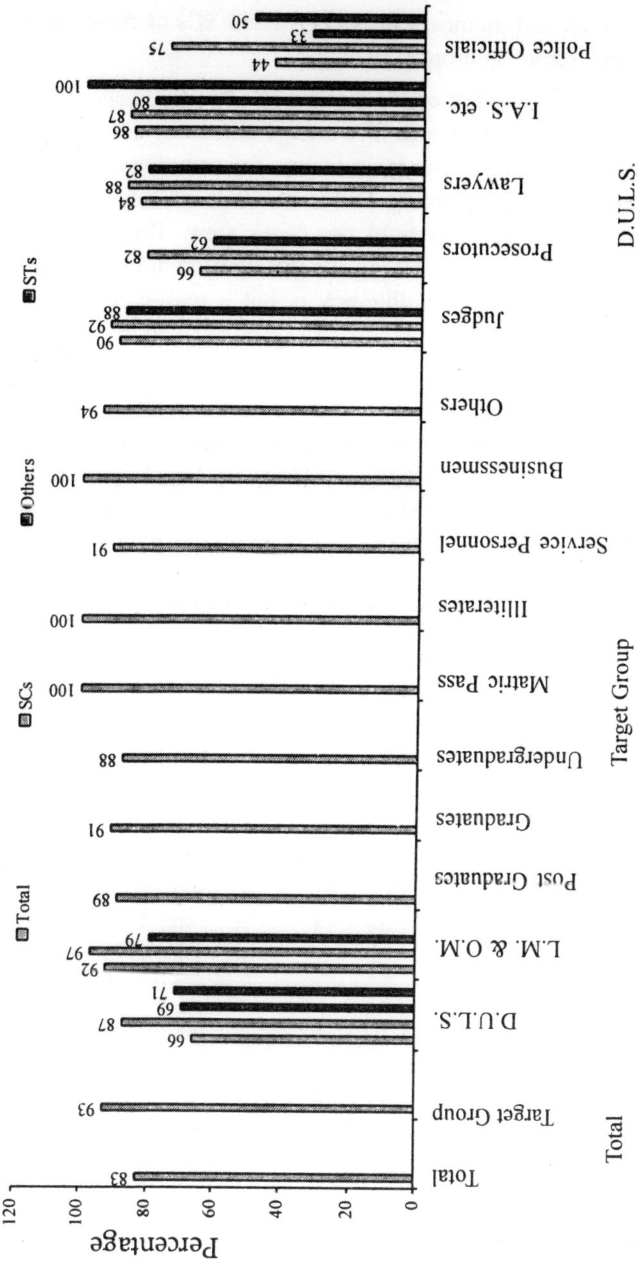

Graph No. 77: Poverty : A Cause for Commission of Atrocities on the SCs

20% MPs, Legislators, Academicians, Media persons, Social Activists and members of N.G.Os., and SCs of these categories are of the same opinion.[83]

On the basis of above discussion and percentage it is concluded that majority of SCs & STs except Illiterates are of the view that illiteracy is one of the main factors for commission of atrocities on them. Officials forming Different Units of Legal System except Police officials also hold the same view. The Law Makers and Opinion Makers are having the different opinion and most of them are of the view that illiteracy is not a reason for commission of atrocities on SCs.

4.11 Poverty

Question numbers 13, 9 and 11 of the questionnaire on the subject for Target Group,[84] Different Units of Legal System,[85] and Law Makers and Opinion Makers,[86] respectively, elicited opinion whether or not poverty is a factor for commission of atrocities on SCs?

Table No. 11 : Poverty as a Factor for Commission of Atrocities on SCs

Categories		Responses in							
		Number				Percentage			
		Yes	*No*	*Und.*	*Total*	*Yes*	*No*	*Und.*	*Total*
Target Group		185	13	2	200	93	6	1	100
Different Units of Legal System	SCs	97	14	1	112	87	12	1	100
	STs	6	0	1	7	86	0	14	100
	Others	124	53	4	181	69	29	2	100
	Total	227	67	6	300	76	22	2	100
L.M. & O.M		46	3	1	50	92	6	2	100
Grand Total		458	83	9	550	83	15	2	100

550 respondents were examined on these questions. Their responses are depicted in Graph No. 77 and Table Nos 11, 11A, 11B and 11C. Out of these 458 replied in positive, 83 in negative and 9 did not give any specific reply.[87] Thus, 83% replied in affirmative. 93% respondents of Target Group,[88] 76% officials forming Different Units of Legal System[89] and 92% Law Makers and Opinion Makers,[90] opined that poverty is a factor for commission of atrocities on them.

Table No. 11A : Target Group on Poverty as a Factor for Commission of Atrocities on SCs

Categories	*Responses in*							
	Number				*Percentage*			
	Yes	*No*	*Und.*	*Total*	*Yes*	*No*	*Und.*	*Total*
Post Graduates	51	4	2	57	89	7	4	100
Graduates	62	6	0	68	91	9	0	100
Under Graduates	22	3	0	25	88	12	0	100
Matric Pass	34	0	0	34	100	0	0	100
Illiterates	16	0	0	16	100	0	0	100
Service Personnel	113	10	1	124	91	9	0	100
Businessmen	12	0	0	12	100	0	0	100
Other Occupations	64	3	1	68	94	4	2	100

89% Post-Graduates, 91% Graduates, 88% Under Graduates, 100% Matric Pass and Illiterates, 91% Service Personnel, 100% Businessmen and 94% persons of Target Group engaged in different occupations are having the same view.[91]

Table No. 11B : Different Units of Legal System on Poverty as a Factor for Commission of Atrocities on SCs

Categories		*Responses in*							
		Number				*Percentage*			
		Yes	*No*	*Und.*	*Total*	*Yes*	*No*	*Und.*	*Total*
Judges	SCs	23	2	0	25	92	8	0	100
	Others	22	3	0	25	88	12	0	100
	Total	45	5	0	50	90	10	0	100
Prosecutors	SCs	9	2	0	11	82	18	0	100
	Others	24	14	1	39	62	36	2	100
	Total	33	16	1	50	66	32	2	100
Lawyers	SCs	30	4	0	34	88	12	0	100
	Others	54	10	2	66	82	15	3	100
	Total	84	14	2	100	84	14	2	100
I.A.S., P.C.S.	SCs	26	4	0	30	87	13	0	100
Doctors,	STs	5	0	0	5	100	0	0	100
etc.	Others	12	3	0	15	80	20	0	100
	Total	43	7	0	50	86	14	0	100

TABLE No. 11B *Contd.*

Categories		*Yes*	*No*	*Und.*	*Total*	*Yes*	*No*	*Und.*	*Total*
Police officials	SCs	9	2	1	12	75	17	8	100
	STs	2	0	0	2	100	0	0	100
	Others	12	23	1	36	33	64	3	100
	Total	22	25	3	50	44	50	6	100
Grand Total		227	67	6	300	76	22	2	100

90% Judges, 66% Public Prosecutors, 84% Lawyers, 86% I.A.S., P.C.S., Doctors and other officers and 44% Police officials are in conformity of this view. Percentages of SC officials under these categories are 92, 82, 88, 87 and 75 respectively. Percentages of Non SC & ST officials of these categories are 88, 62, 82, 80 and 33, respectively.[92]

Table No. 11C : Law Makers and Opinion Makers on Poverty as a Factor for Commission of Atrocities on SCs

Categories		*Responses in*							
		Number				*Percentage*			
		Yes	*No*	*Und.*	*Total*	*Yes*	*No*	*Und.*	*Total*
Law Makers & Opinion Makers	SCs	34	1	0	35	97	3	0	100
	STs	1	0	0	1	100	0	0	100
	Others	11	2	1	14	79	14	7	100

92% MPs, Legislators, Academicians, Media Persons, Social Activists and Members, of N.G.Os., *etc*., are having the same opinion. 97% respondents of these categories belonging to SCs and 79% Non SC & ST have the same opinion.[93]

On the basis of above discussion and percentage, it is concluded that most of the respondents, except Police officials are of the view that poverty is one of the main factors for commission of atrocities on SCs

4.12 Economic Dependence or Backwardness

Question numbers 14, 10 and 12 of the questionnaire for the Target Group,[94] Different Units of the Legal System[95] and Law Makers and the Opinion Makers,[96] respectively elicited information whether or not economic dependence/backwardness is a factor for commission of atrocities on the members of SCs?

Table No. 12 : Economic Dependence or Backwardness as a Factor for Commission of Atrocities on SCs

Categories		*Responses in*							
		Number				*Percentage*			
		Yes	*No*	*Und.*	*Total*	*Yes*	*No*	*Und.*	*Total*
Target Group		172	18	10	200	86	9	5	100
Different Units of Legal System	SCs	85	21	6	112	76	19	5	100
	STs	6	1	0	7	86	14	0	100
	Others	118	49	14	181	65	27	8	100
	Total	209	71	20	300	70	24	6	100
L.M. & O.M46		2	2	50	92	4	4	100	
Grand Total		427	91	32	550	78	16	6	100

All 550 respondents were examined on this question. Their responses are depicted in Graph No. 78 and Table Nos. 12, 12A, 12B and 12C. Out of these 427 replied in affirmative, 91 in negative and 32 did not give any specific reply.[97] Thus, 78% opined in favour. 86% respondents of Target Group,[98] 70% official forming Different Units of Legal System[99] and 92% Law Makers and Opinion Makers[100] agreed that economic dependence / backwardness is a factor for the commission of atrocities on the members of the SCs.

Table No. 12A : Target Group on Economic Dependence or Backwardness as a Factor for Commission of Atrocities on SCs

Categories	*Responses in*							
	Number				*Percentage*			
	Yes	*No*	*Und.*	*Total*	*Yes*	*No*	*Und.*	*Total*
Post Graduates	52	5	0	57	91	9	0	100
Graduates	55	7	6	68	81	10	9	100
Under Graduates	20	4	1	25	80	16	4	100
Matric Pass	29	2	3	34	85	6	9	100
Illiterates	16	0	0	16	100	0	0	100
Service Personnel	102	15	7	124	82	12	6	100
Businessmen	11	0	1	12	92	0	8	100
Other Occupations	63	3	2	68	92	4	4	100

Graph No. 78 : Economic Dependence or Backwardness : A Cause for Commission of Atrocities on the SCs

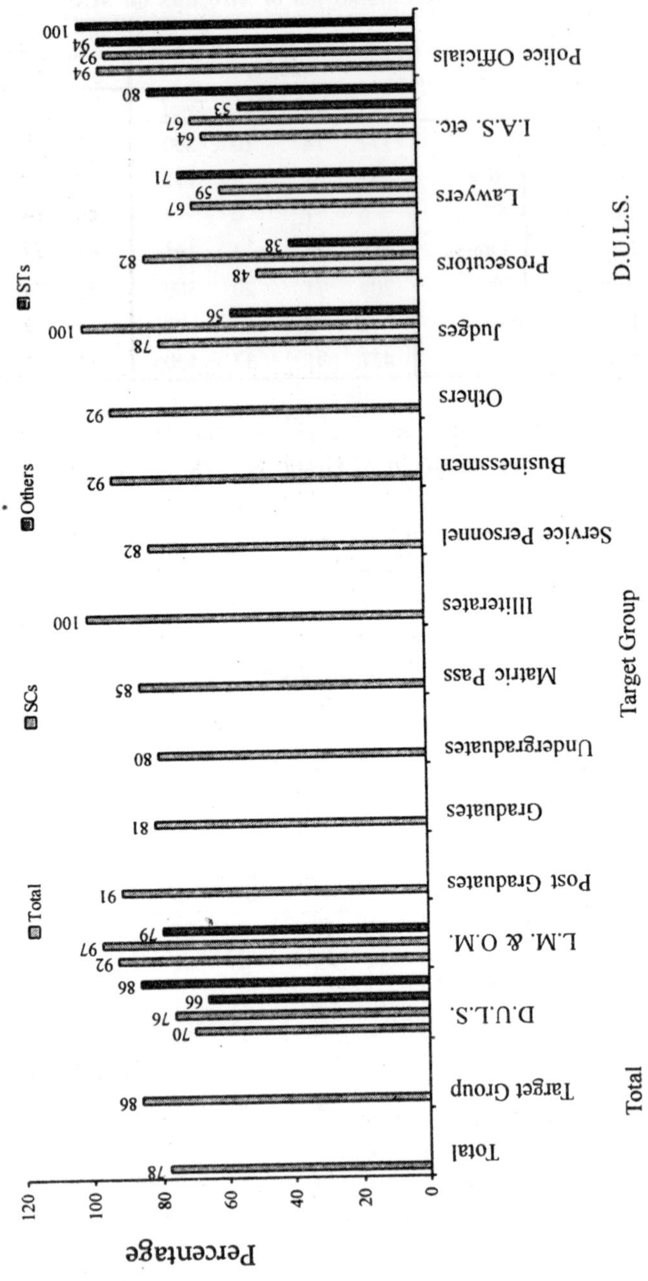

91% Post Graduates, 81% Graduates, 80% Under Graduates, 85% Matric Pass, 100% Illiterates, 82% Service Personnel, and 92% Businessmen and persons of Target Group engaged in different occupations replied in affirmative.[101]

Table No. 12B : Different Units of Legal System on Economic Dependence or Backwardness as a Factor for Commission of Atrocities on SCs

Categories		Number Yes	Number No	Number Und.	Number Total	Percentage Yes	Percentage No	Percentage Und.	Percentage Total
Judges	SCs	25	0	0	25	100	0	0	100
	Others	14	10	1	25	56	40	4	100
	Total	39	10	1	50	78	20	2	100
Prosecutors	SCs	9	1	1	11	82	9	9	100
	Others	15	17	7	39	38	44	18	100
	Total	24	18	8	50	48	36	16	100
Lawyers	SCs	20	10	4	34	59	29	12	100
	Others	47	17	2	66	71	26	3	100
	Total	67	27	6	100	67	27	6	100
I.A.S., P.C.S., Doctors, etc.	SCs	20	9	1	30	67	30	3	100
	STs	4	1	0	5	80	20	0	100
	Others	8	4	3	15	53	27	20	100
	Total	32	14	4	50	64	28	8	100
Police officials	SCs	11	1	0	12	92	8	0	100
	STs	2	0	0	2	100	0	0	100
	Others	34	1	1	36	94	3	3	100
	Total	47	2	1	50	94	4	2	100
Grand Total		209	71	20	300	70	24	6	100

78% Judges, 48% Public Prosecutors, 67% Advocates, 64% I.A.S., P.C.S., Doctors and other officers and 94% Police Personnel replied in affirmative. Percentages of SC officials of these categories are 100, 82, 59, 67 and 92, respectively.[102]

Table No. 12C : Law Makers and Opinion Makers on Economic Dependence or Backwardness as a Factor for Commission of Atrocities on SCs

Categories		Number Yes	Number No	Number Und.	Number Total	Percentage Yes	Percentage No	Percentage Und.	Percentage Total
Law Makers & Opinion Makers	SCs	34	0	1	35	97	0	3	100
	STs	1	0	0	1	100	0	0	100
	Others	11	2	1	14	79	14	7	100

92% M.Ps. Legislators, Academicians, Media Persons, Social Activists and members of N.G.Os., *etc.*, answered in positive. Percentage of SCs respondents under these categories is 97.[103]

On the basis of views narrated above, it is concluded that economic dependence/backwardness of SCs is one of the reasons for commission of atrocities on them.

4.13 Ignorance of Law

Question numbers 11, 13, and 18 of the questionnaire for the Target Group,[104] Different Units of the Legal System,[105] and Law Makers and Opinion Makers,[106] respectively, elicited informations whether or not ignorance of law is a factor for commission and continuation of atrocities on the members of the SCs?

Table No. 13 : Ignorance of Law as a Factor for Commission of Atrocities on SCs

Categories		*Responses in*							
		Number				*Percentage*			
		Yes	*No*	*Und.*	*Total*	*Yes*	*No*	*Und.*	*Total*
Target Group		151	40	9	200	75	20	5	100
Different Units of Legal System	SCs	90	22	0	112	80	20	0	100
	STs	7	0	0	7	100	0	0	100
	Others	107	71	3	181	59	39	2	100
	Total	204	93	3	300	68	31	1	100
L.M. & O.M35		14	1	50	70	28	2	100	
Grand Total		382	156	12	550	70	28	2	100

All 550 respondents examined on this question. Their responses are depicted in Graph No. 79 and Table Nos. 13, 13A, 13B and 13C. Out of these 382 replied in affirmative, 156 in negative and 12 did not give any specific reply.[107] Thus, 70% opined in favour. 75% respondents of Target Group,[108] 68% officials forming Different Units of Legal System,[109] and 70 % Law Makers and Opinion Makers[110] agreed that ignorance of law is a factor for commission and continuation of atrocities on the members of the SCs

Table No. 13A : Target Group on Ignorance of Law as a Factor for Commission of Atrocities on SCs

Categories	Responses in Number				Responses in Percentage			
	Yes	*No*	*Und.*	*Total*	*Yes*	*No*	*Und.*	*Total*
Post Graduates	40	16	1	57	70	28	2	100
Graduates	49	15	4	68	72	22	6	100
Under Graduates	19	4	2	25	76	16	8	100
Matric Pass	27	5	2	34	79	15	6	100
Illiterates	16	0	0	16	100	0	0	100
Service Personnel	84	34	6	124	68	27	5	100
Businessmen	11	0	1	12	92	0	8	100
Other Occupations	60	6	2	68	88	9	3	100

70% Post Graduates, 72% Graduates, 76% Under Graduates, 79% Matric Pass, 100% Illiterates, 68% Service Personnel, 92% Businessmen and 88% persons of Target Group engaged in different occupations are also having same view.[111]

Table No. 13B : Different Units of Legal System on Ignorance of Law as a Factor for Commission of Atrocities on SCs

Categories		Responses in Number				Responses in Percentage			
		Yes	*No*	*Und.*	*Total*	*Yes*	*No*	*Und.*	*Total*
Judges	SCs	19	6	0	25	76	24	0	100
	Others	16	9	0	25	64	36	0	100
	Total	35	15	0	50	70	30	0	100
Prosecutors	SCs	9	2	0	11	82	18	0	100
	Others	20	18	1	39	51	46	3	100
	Total	29	20	1	50	58	40	2	100
Lawyers	SCs	28	6	0	34	82	18	0	100
	Others	41	24	1	66	62	37	1	100
	Total	69	30	1	100	69	30	1	100
I.A.S., P.C.S., Doctors, etc.	SCs	26	4	0	30	87	13	0	100
	STs	5	0	0	5	100	0	0	100
	Others	12	3	0	15	80	20	0	100
	Total	43	7	0	50	86	14	0	100

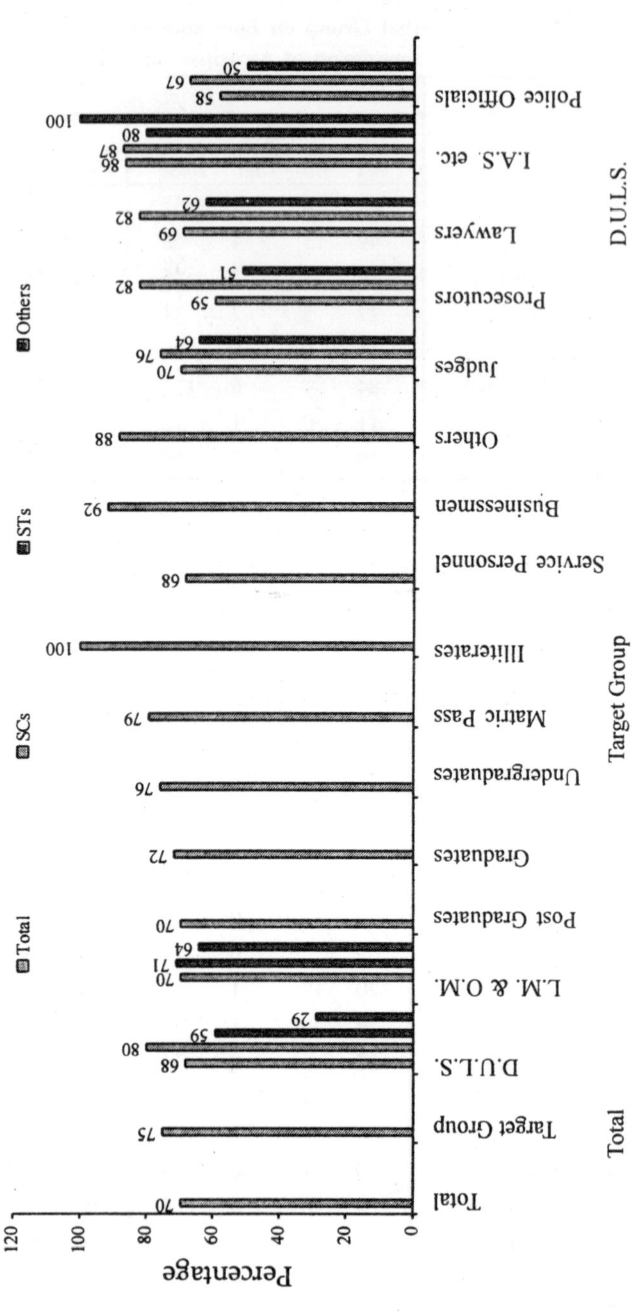

Graph No. 79 : Ignorance of Law : A Cause for Commission of Atrocities on the SCs

TABLE No. 13B *Contd.*

Categories		*Yes*	*No*	*Und.*	*Total*	*Yes*	*No*	*Und.*	*Total*
Police officials	SCs	8	4	0	12	67	33	0	100
	STs	2	0	0	2	100	0	0	100
	Others	18	17	1	36	50	47	3	100
	Total	28	21	1	50	56	42	2	100
Grand Total		204	93	3	300	68	31	1	100

70% Judges, 58% public prosecutors, 69% Lawyers, 86% I.A.S., P.C.S., Doctors and other officers and 56% Police officials replied in affirmative. Percentages of SC officials having same opinion under these categories are 76, 82, 82, 87 and 67, respectively.[112]

Table No 13C : Law Makers and Opinion Makers on Ignorance of Law as a Factor for Commission of Atrocities on SCs

Categories		*Responses in*							
		Number				*Percentage*			
		Yes	*No*	*Und.*	*Total*	*Yes*	*No*	*Und.*	*Total*
Law Makers & Opinion Makers	SCs	25	10	0	35	71	29	0	100
	STs	1	0	0	1	100	0	0	100
	Others	9	4	1	14	64	29	7	100

70% M.P., Legislators, Academicians, Media Persons, Social Activists and members of N.G.Os., *etc.*, answered in positive. Percentage of SC respondents under these categories is 71.[113]

On the basis of views narrated above, it is concluded that ignorance of law is a factor for commission of atrocities on the members of the SCs

4.14 Self-Assertion by the Scheduled Castes

In order to find out whether or not awakening of members of the SCs and resultant demand for their statutory rights and denial thereof by others has accelerated the commission of atrocities on them? Question Number 15 eliciting information on this aspect was fed to the Law Makers and Opinion Makers.[114] Their responses are depicted in Graph No. 80 and Table No. 14.

Graph No. 80 : Self-Assertion by the Secheduled Castes : A Cause for Commission of Atrocities on Them

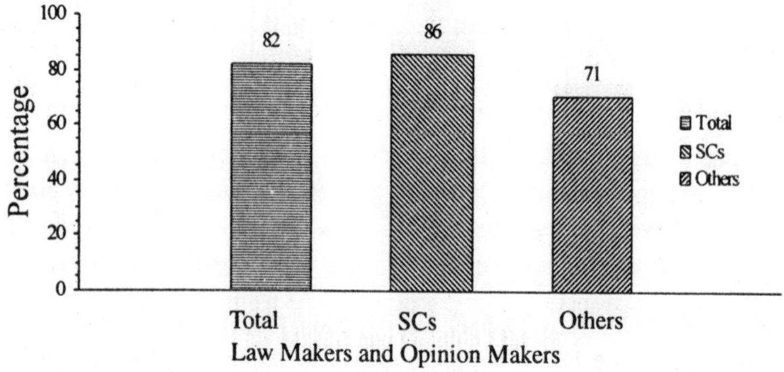

Table No. 14 : Law Makers and Opinion Makers on Self-Assertion by the Scheduled Caste as a Factor for Commission of Atrocities on SCs

Categories		*Responses in*							
		Number				*Percentage*			
		Yes	*No*	*Und.*	*Total*	*Yes*	*No*	*Und.*	*Total*
Law Makers & Opinion Makers	SCs	30	4	1	35	86	11	3	100
	STs	1	0	0	1	100	0	0	100
	Others	10	4	0	14	71	29	0	100
	Total	41	8	1	50	82	16	2	100

82% M.Ps., Legislators, Academicians, Media Persons, Social Activists and members of N.G.Os., *etc.,* opined that awakening of the members of SCs and resultant demand for their statutory rights and denial thereof by others has accelerated the commission of atrocities on them. Percentage of SC respondents under this category is 86.[115]

It is, therefore, concluded that awakening of the members of SCs and resultant demand of their statutory rights by them and denial thereof by others has accelerated the commission of atrocities on the SCs.

4.15 Lack of Political Will

Question numbers 12, 13 and 14 of the questionnaire for the Target Group,[116] Different Units of the Legal System[117] and Law Makers and the Opinion Makers,[118] respectively, elicited informations whether or not lack of political will is a factor for commission of atrocities on the members of SCs?

Table No. 15 : Lack of Political Will as a Factor for Commission of Atrocities on SCs

Categories		*Responses in*							
		Number				*Percentage*			
		Yes	*No*	*Und.*	*Total*	*Yes*	*No*	*Und.*	*Total*
Target Group		160	38	2	200	80	19	1	100
Different	SCs	79	27	6	112	71	24	5	100
Units of	STs	5	2	0	7	71	29	0	100
Legal	Others	95	76	10	181	52	42	6	100
System	Total	179	105	16	300	60	35	5	100
L.M. & O.M46		2	2	50	92	4	4	100	
Grand Total		385	145	20	550	70	26	4	100

All 550 respondents were examined on this question. Their responses are depicted in Graph No. 81 and Table No. 15, 15A, 15B and 15C. Out of these 385 replied in affirmative, 145 in negative and 20 did not give any specific reply.[119] Thus, 70% opined in favour, 80% respondents of Target Group,[120] 60% officials forming Different Units of the Legal System[121] and 92% Law Makers and Opinion Makers[122] agreed that lack of political will is a factor of continuation of atrocities on the members of SCs

Table No. 15A : Target Group on Lack of Political Will as a Factor for Commission of Atrocities on SCs

Categories	*Responses in*							
	Number				*Percentage*			
	Yes	*No*	*Und.*	*Total*	*Yes*	*No*	*Und.*	*Total*
Post Graduates	40	16	1	57	70	28	2	100
Graduates	54	14	0	68	79	21	0	100
Under Graduates	20	5	0	25	80	20	0	100
Matric Pass	32	1	1	34	94	3	3	100
Illiterates	14	2	0	16	88	12	0	100
Service Personnel	94	29	1	124	76	23	1	100
Businessmen	11	1	0	12	92	8	0	100
Other Occupations	59	8	1	68	88	11	1	100

70% Post-Graduates, 79% Graduates, 80% Under Graduates, 94% Matric Pass, 88% Illiterates, 76% Service Personnel, 92% Businessmen and 88% persons of Target Group engaged in different occupations replied in affirmative.[123]

Graph No. 81: Lack of Political Will : A Cause for Commission of Atrocities on the SCs

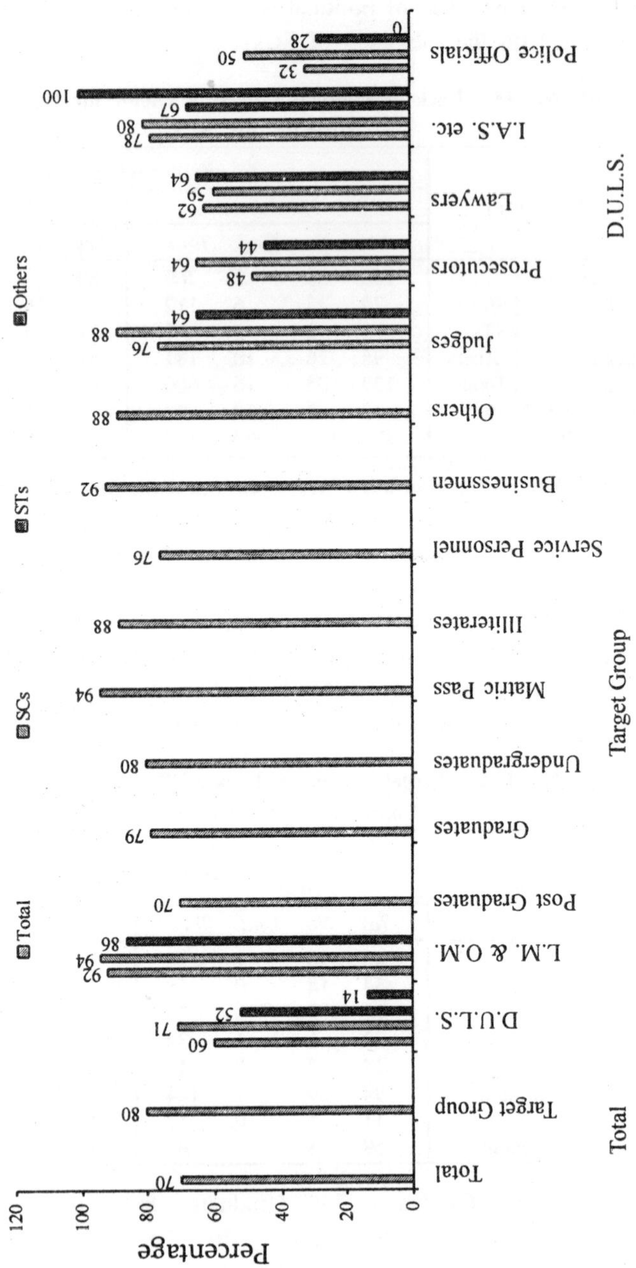

Table No. 15B : Different Units of Legal System on Lack of Political Will as a Factor for Commission of Atrocities on SCs

Categories		Responses in							
		Number				Percentage			
		Yes	*No*	*Und.*	*Total*	*Yes*	*No*	*Und.*	*Total*
Judges	SCs	22	3	0	25	88	12	0	100
	Others	16	9	0	25	64	36	0	100
	Total	38	12	0	50	76	24	0	100
Prosecutors	SCs	7	4	0	11	64	36	0	100
	Others	17	20	2	39	44	51	5	100
	Total	24	24	2	50	48	48	4	100
Lawyers	SCs	20	10	4	34	59	29	12	100
	Others	42	17	7	66	64	26	10	100
	Total	62	27	11	100	62	27	11	100
I.A.S.,P.C.S., Doctors, etc.	SCs	24	4	2	30	80	13	7	100
	STs	5	0	0	5	100	0	0	100
	Others	10	5	0	15	67	33	0	100
	Total	39	9	2	50	78	18	4	100
Police officials	SCs	6	6	0	12	50	50	0	100
	STs	0	2	0	2	0	100	0	100
	Others	10	25	1	36	28	69	3	100
	Total	16	33	1	50	32	66	2	100
Grand Total		179	105	16	300	60	35	5	100

76% Judges, 48% Public Prosecutors, 62% Advocates, 78% I.A.S., P.C.S., Doctors and other officers and 32% Police officials replied in affirmative. Percentages of SC officials under these categories are 88, 64, 59, 80 and 50, respectively.[124]

Table No. 15C : Law Makers and Opinion Makers on Lack of Political Will as a Factor for Commission of Atrocities on SCs

Categories		Responses in							
		Number				Percentage			
		Yes	*No*	*Und.*	*Total*	*Yes*	*No*	*Und.*	*Total*
Law Makers & Opinion Makers	SCs	33	0	2	35	94	0	6	100
	STs	1	0	0	1	100	0	0	100
	Others	12	2	0	14	86	14	0	100

92% M.Ps., Legislators, Academicians, Media Persons, Social Activists and members of N.G.Os., *etc.*, answered in positive. Percentage of SC respondents under these categories is 94.[125]

On the basis of opinion mentioned herein above, it is concluded that lack of political will is a reason for continuation of atrocities on the members of SCs

Notes and References

1. *See*, annexures 1 and 2. The question is, "Are you aware that atrocities still being committed on the members of the SCs?"
2. *Ibid.* and annexures 1 and 3.
3. *Ibid.* and annexures 1 and 4.
4. *See*, Table No. 1.
5. *See*, Table No.1A and Graph No. 1.
6. *See*, Graph Nos. 1 to 3.
7. *See*, Graph No. 2.
8. *See*, Graph Nos. 4 to 8.
9. *Supra,* note 8.
10. *See*, annexures 1, 3 and 4. The question is, "Do you think that commission and continuation of atrocities on the SCs is a blot on our society?"
11. *See*, Table No. 2.
12. *See*, Table No. 2 and Graph Nos. 3 and 2.
13. *See*, Table Nos. 2A and 2B and Graph Nos. 2 and 3.
14. *See*, Graph Nos. 4 to 8.
15. *See*, annexures 1, 3 and 4. The question is, "Do you think that commission and continuation of atrocities on the SCs is an impediment in the advancement and development of our country?"
16. *See*, Table No. 3.
17. *See*, Graph Nos. 3 and 2.
18. *See*, Graph Nos. 4 to 8 and 69.
19. *See*, Graph Nos. 6 to 8 and 69.
20. *See*, annexures 1 and 4. The question is, "Is caste system, a factor for commission and continuation of practice of untouchability on the members of SCs?"
21. *See*, Table No. 4.
22. *See*, Graph No. 11.
23. *See*, annexures 1 and 4. The question is, "Is endogamy, a reason for continuation of caste system?".
24. *See*, Table No. 5.
25. *See*, Graph No. 11.
26. *Ibid.*
27. *See*, annexures 1 and 2. The question is, "Is caste hatred, a cause for commission of atrocities on the members of the SCs?".
28. *Ibid.* and annexures 1 and 3.
29. *Ibid.* and annexures 1 and 4.
30. *See*, Table No. 6.
31. *See*, Graph No. 9.
32. *See*, Graph No. 12.
33. *See*, Graph No. 11.

34. *See*, Graph No. 9.
35. *See*, Graph Nos. 13 to 17.
36. *See*, Graph No. 11.
37. *See*, annexures 1 and 2. The question is, "Is practice of untouchability on the members of the SCs, a factor for commission of atrocities on them?"
38. *Ibid.* and annexures 1 and 3.
39. *Ibid.* and annexures 1 and 4.
40. *See*, Table No.7.
41. *See*, Graph No. 9.
42. *See*, Graph No. 12.
43. *See*, Graph No. 11.
44. *See*, Graph No. 9.
45. *See*, Graph Nos. 13 to 17.
46. *See*, Graph Nos. 13 to 17.
47. *Ibid.*
48. *Ibid.*
49. *See*, Graph No. 11.
50. *See*, annexures 1 and 2. The question is, "Is having no separate religion by the members of the SCs, a reason for commission of atrocities on them?"
51. *Ibid.* and annexures 1 and 3.
52. *Ibid.* and annexures 1 and 4.
53. *See*, Table No. 8.
54. *See*, Graph No. 9.
55. *See*, Graph No. 12.
56. *See*, Graph No. 11
57. *See*, Graph Nos. 11 and 12.
58. *See*, Graph No. 9.
59. *See*, Graph Nos. 13 to 17.
60. *Ibid.*
61. *Ibid.*
62. *See*, Graph No. 11.
63. *See*, annexures 1 and 2. The question is, "Is cultural backwardness of the members of SCs, a factor for commission and continuation of atrocities on them?"
64. *Ibid.* and annexures 1 and 3.
65. *Ibid.* and annexures 1 and 4.
66. *See*, Table No. 9.
67. *See*, Graph No. 10.
68. *See*, Graph No. 12.
69. *See*, Graph No. 11.
70. *Supra*, note 67.
71. *See*, Graph Nos. 13 to 17.
72. *See*, Graph No. 11.

73. *Ibid.*
74. *See*, annexures 1 and 2. The question is "Is illiteracy a factor for commission of atrocities on the member of the SCs".
75. *Ibid.* and annexures 1 and 3.
76. *Ibid.* and annexures 1 and 4.
77. *See*, Table No.10.
78. *See*, Graph No. 9.
79. *See*, Graph No. 12.
80. *See*, Graph No. 11.
81. *See*, Graph No. 9.
82. *See*, Graph Nos. 13 to 17.
83. *See*, Graph No. 11.
84. *See*, annexures 1 and 2. The question is, "Is poverty, a factor for commission and continuation of atrocities on the members of SCs?"
85. *Ibid.* and annexures 1 and 3.
86. *Ibid.* and annexures 1 and 4.
87. *See*, Table No. 11.
88. *See*, Graph No. 10.
89. *See*, Graph No. 12.
90. *See*, Graph No. 11.
91. *Supra,* note 88.
92. *See*, Graph Nos. 13 to 17.
93. *See*, Graph No. 11.
94. *See*, annexures 1 and 2. The question is, "Is economic dependence/ backwardness, a factor for commission of atrocities on the members of SCs?"
95. *Ibid.* and annexures 1 and 3.
96. *Ibid.* and annexures 1 and 4.
97. *See*, Table No. 12.
98. *See*, Graph No. 10.
99. *See*, Graph No. 12.
100. *See*, Graph No. 11.
101. *See*, Graph No. 10.
102. *See*, Graph Nos. 13 to 17.
103. *See*, Graph No. 11.
104. *See*, annexures 1 and 2. The question is, "Is ignorance of law, a factor for commission and continuation of atrocities on the members of the SCs?"
105. *Ibid.* and annexures 1 and 3.
106. *Ibid.* and annexures 1 and 4.
107. *See*, Table No.13.
108. *See*, Graph No. 9.
109. *See*, Graph No. 12.
110. *See*, Graph No. 11.
111. *See*, Graph No. 10.

112. *See*, Graph Nos. 13 to 17.
113. *See*, Graph No. 11.
114. *See*, annexures 1 and 4. The question is, "Is awakening of members of the SCs and resultant demand for their statutory rights and denial thereof by others has accelerated the commission of atrocities on them?"
115. *See*, Table No. 14 and Graph No. 11.
116. *See*, annexures 1 and 2. The question is, "Is lack of political will, a factor for continuation of atrocities on the members of SCs?"
117. *Ibid.* and annexures 1 and 3.
118. *Ibid.* and annexures 1 and 4.
119. *See*, Table No. 15.
120. *See*, Graph No. 10.
121. *See*, Graph No. 12.
122. *See*, Graph No. 11.
123. *Supra*, note 120.
124. *See*, Graph Nos. 13 to 17.
125. *See*, Graph No. 11.

CHAPTER 5

EMPIRICAL STUDY OF THE PROVISIONS OF THE ACT

Awareness

5.1 Awareness of the Act

Question numbers 16, 14 and 16 of the questionnaire for the Target Group,[1] Different Units of the Legal System[2] and Law Makers and Opinion Makers,[3] respectively, elicited information whether or not respondents have knowledge about the Scheduled Castes and the Scheduled Tribes (Prevention of Atrocities), Act 1989?

Table No. 16 : Awareness of the Act

Categories		Responses in							
		Number				Percentage			
		Yes	No	Und.	Total	Yes	No	Und.	Total
Target Group		67	122	11	200	34	61	5	100
Different Units of Legal System	SCs	89	21	2	112	79	19	2	100
	STs	6	1	0	7	86	14	0	100
	Others	138	37	6	181	76	21	3	100
	Total	233	59	8	300	77	20	3	100
L.M. & O.M27		23	0	50	54	46	0	100	
Grand Total		327	211	17	550	59	38	3	100

All 550 respondents were examined on this question. Their responses are depicted in Graph No. 82 and Table Nos. 16, 16A, 16B and 16C. Out of these 327 replied in affirmatives, 211 in negative and 17 did not give their replies.[4] Thus, 59% opined in positive. 34% respondents of Target Group,[5] 77% officials forming Different Units of the Legal System,[6] and 54% Law Makers and Opinion Makers[7] admitted that they have knowledge of the Scheduled Castes and the Scheduled Tribes (Prevention of Atrocities) Act, 1989.

Graph No. 82 : Awareness of the Act

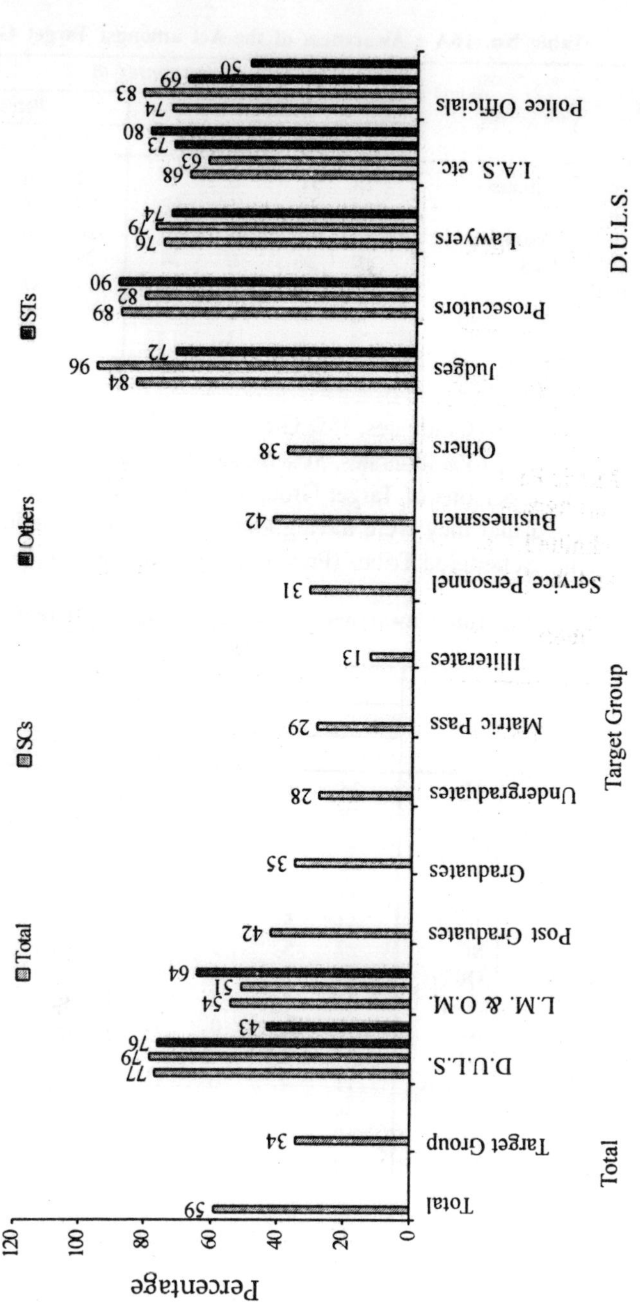

Table No. 16A : Awareness of the Act amongst Target Group

Categories	Responses in							
	Number				Percentage			
	Yes	No	Und.	Total	Yes	No	Und.	Total
Post Graduates	24	31	2	57	42	54	2	100
Graduates	24	39	5	68	35	58	7	100
Under Graduates	7	14	4	25	28	56	16	100
Matric Pass	10	24	0	34	29	71	0	100
Illiterates	2	14	0	16	13	87	0	100
Service Personnel	38	78	8	124	31	63	6	100
Businessmen	5	6	1	12	42	50	8	100
Other Occupations	26	40	2	68	38	59	3	100

42% Post Graduates, 35% Graduates, 28% Under Graduates, 29% Matric Pass, 13% Illiterates, 31% Service Personnel, 42% Businessmen and 38% persons of Target Group engaged in different occupations admitted that they were having knowledge of the Scheduled Castes and the Scheduled Tribes (Prevention of Atrocities) Act, 1989.[8]

Table No. 16B : Awareness of the Act amongst Different Units of Legal System

Categories		Responses in							
		Number				Percentage			
		Yes	No	Und.	Total	Yes	No	Und.	Total
Judges	SCs	24	1	0	25	96	4	0	100
	Others	18	7	0	25	72	28	0	100
	Total	42	8	0	50	84	16	0	100
Prosecutors	SCs	9	2	0	11	82	18	0	100
	Others	35	3	1	39	90	8	2	100
	Total	44	5	1	50	88	10	2	100
Lawyers	SCs	27	5	2	34	79	15	6	100
	Others	49	12	5	66	74	18	8	100
	Total	76	17	7	100	76	17	7	100
I.A.S., P.C.S., Doctors, etc.	SCs	19	11	0	30	63	37	0	100
	STs	4	1	0	5	80	20	0	100
	Others	11	4	0	15	73	27	0	100
	Total	34	16	0	50	68	32	0	100
Police officials	SCs	10	2	0	12	83	17	0	100
	STs	2	0	0	2	100	0	0	100
	Others	25	11	0	36	69	31	0	100
	Total	37	13	0	50	74	26	0	100
Grand Total		233	59	8	300	78	20	2	100

84% Judges, 88% Public Prosecutors, 76% Lawyers, 68% I.A.S.,

P.C.S., Doctors and other officers and 74% Police officials admitted that they have knowledge about the Act. Percentages of SCs officials under these categories are 96, 82, 79, 63 and 83, respectively.[9]

Table No. 16C : Awareness of the Act amongst Law Makers and Opinion Makers

Categories		*Responses in*							
		Number				*Percentage*			
		Yes	*No*	*Und.*	*Total*	*Yes*	*No*	*Und.*	*Total*
Law Makers & Opinion Makers	SCs	18	17	0	35	51	49	0	100
	STs	0	1	0	.1	0	100	0	100
	Others	9	5	0	14	64	36	0	100

54% M.Ps., Legislators, Academicians, Media Persons, Social Activists and members of N.G.Os., *etc.*, also admitted of their awareness about the Act. Percentage of SC respondents under this category is 51.[10]

Since, 34% respondents of Target Group are only aware about the Act and percentages of Under Graduates, Matric Pass, Illiterates and Service Personnel are much below this percentage, therefore, it is concluded that majority of the members of SCs are not aware about the provisions of the Scheduled Castes and the Scheduled Tribes (Prevention of Atrocities) Act, 1989.

On the basis of percentages enumerated hereinabove of the respondents forming part of the Different Units of the Legal System, it is concluded that all of them are not aware about the Act. It may be concluded about M.Ps., Legislators, Academicians, Media Persons, Social Activists and members of N.G.Os., *etc.*, that half of them are not aware about the Act.

5.2 Awareness of the Enforcement of the Act

Question numbers 17, 15 and 17 of the questionnaire for the Target Group,[11] Different Units of the Legal System,[12] and Law Makers and the Opinion Makers,[13] respectively, elicited information whether or not respondents were aware about the enforcement of the Act?

Table No. 17 : Awareness of the Enforcement of the Act

Categories	*Responses in*							
	Number				*Percentage*			
	Yes	*No*	*Und.*	*Total*	*Yes*	*No*	*Und.*	*Total*
Target Group	60	134	6	200	30	67	3	100
Different Units of Legal System — SCs	82	27	3	112	73	24	3	100
Different Units of Legal System — STs	4	3	0	7	57	43	0	100
Different Units of Legal System — Others	111	59	11	181	61	33	6	100
Different Units of Legal System — Total	197	89	14	300	66	30	4	100
L.M. & O.M19	31	0	50	38	62	0	100	
Grand Total	276	254	20	550	50	46	4	100

All 550 respondents were examined on this question. Their responses are depicted in Graph No. 83 and Table Nos. 17, 17A, 17B and 17C. Out of these, 276 replied in affirmative, 254 in negative and 20 did not express their opinions.[14] Thus, 50% replied in positive. 30% respondent of Target Group,[15] 66% officials forming Different Units of Legal System,[16] and 38% Law Makers and Opinion Makers[17] admitted that they were aware about the enforcement of the Act.

Table No. 17A : Awareness of the Enforcement of the Act amongst Target Group

Categories	*Responses in*							
	Number				*Percentage*			
	Yes	*No*	*Und.*	*Total*	*Yes*	*No*	*Und.*	*Total*
Post Graduates	22	34	1	57	39	60	1	100
Graduates	20	45	3	68	29	66	5	100
Under Graduates	8	15	2	25	32	60	8	100
Matric Pass	8	26	0	34	24	76	0	100
Illiterates	2	14	0	16	13	87	0	100
Service Personnel	33	87	4	124	27	70	3	100
Businessmen	5	6	1	12	42	50	8	100
Other Occupations	23	44	1	68	34	65	1	100

39% Post Graduates, 29% Graduates, 32% Under Graduates, 24% Matric Pass, 13% Illiterates, 27% Service Personnel, 42% Businessmen and 34% respondents of Target Group engaged in different occupations admitted that they were aware about the enforcement of the Act.[18]

Table No. 17B : Awareness of the Enforcement of the Act amongst Different Units of Legal System

Categories		*Responses in*							
		Number				*Percentage*			
		Yes	*No*	*Und.*	*Total*	*Yes*	*No*	*Und.*	*Total*
Judges	SCs	23	1	1	25	92	4	4	100
	Others	14	11	0	25	56	44	0	100
	Total	37	12	1	50	74	24	2	100
Prosecutors	SCs	10	1	0	11	91	9	0	100
	Others	28	9	2	39	72	23	5	100
	Total	38	10	2	50	76	20	4	100
Lawyers	SCs	21	11	2	34	62	32	6	100
	Others	41	21	4	66	62	32	6	100
	Total	62	32	6	100	62	32	6	100
I.A.S., P.C.S., Doctors, etc.	SCs	21	9	0	30	70	30	0	100
	STs	3	2	0	5	60	40	0	100
	Others	9	6	0	15	60	40	0	100
	Total	33	17	0	50	66	34	0	100
Police officials	SCs	7	5	0	12	58	42	0	100
	STs	1	1	0	2	50	50	0	100
	Others	19	12	5	36	53	33	14	100
	Total	27	18	5	50	54	36	10	100
Grand Total		197	89	14	300	65	30	5	100

74% Judges, 76% Public Prosecutors, 62% Lawyers, 66% I.A.S., P.C.S., Doctors and other officers and 54% Police officials admitted that they were aware about the enforcement of the Act. Percentages of SC officials under these categories are 92, 91, 62, 70 and 58 respectively.[19]

Table No. 17C ; Awareness of the Enforcement of the Act amongst Law Makers and Opinion Makers

Categories		*Responses in*							
		Number				*Percentage*			
		Yes	*No*	*Und.*	*Total*	*Yes*	*No*	*Und.*	*Total*
Law Makers & Opinion Makers	SCs	13	22	0	35	37	63	0	100
	STs	0	1	0	1	0	100	0	100
	Others	6	8	0	14	43	57	0	100

38% M.Ps., Legislators, Academicians, Media Persons, Social Activists and Members of N.G.Os., *etc.*, only are aware about the enforcement of the Act. Percentage of SC respondents under this

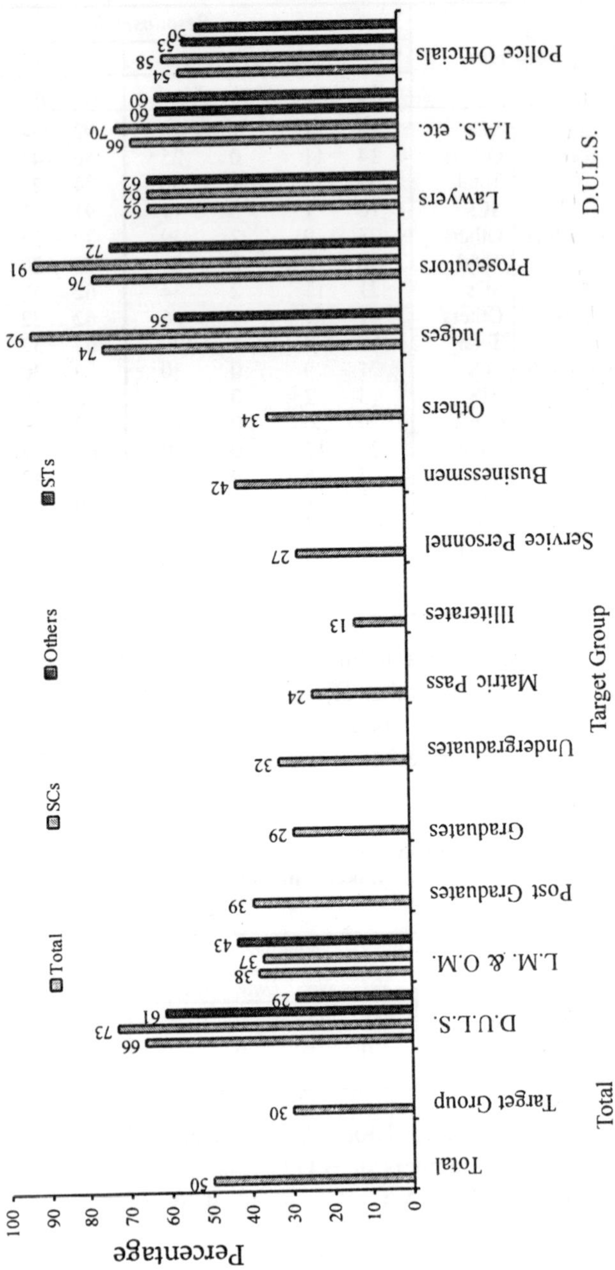

Graph No. 83 : Awareness of the Enforcement of the Act

category is 37.[20] Percentage of Non SC & ST respondents under this category is 43.

Since only 30% respondents of the Target Group are aware about the enforcement of the Act and percentage of Graduates, Under Graduates, Matric Pass, Illiterates, and Service Personnel of Target Groups is much below this percentage, therefore, it is concluded that majority of the people of SCs are not aware about the enforcement of the Act.

On the basis of percentage enumerated hereinabove of the respondents forming part of Different Units of Legal System, it is concluded that all of them are not aware about the enforcement of the Act. It can be concluded that majority of M.Ps., Legislators, Academicians, Media Persons, Social Activists and Members of N.G.Os., *etc.,* are not aware about the enforcement of the Act.

5.3 Awareness of Scheduled Castes and the Scheduled Tribes (Prevention of Atrocities) Rules, 1995

Question number 23 of the questionnaire for the Law Makers and the Opinion Makers,[21] elicited information whether or not M.Ps. Legislators, Academicians, Media Persons, Social Activists and members of N.G.Os., *etc.*, are aware about these rules?

Graph No. 84 : Awareness of the Scheduled Castes and the Scheduled Tribes (Prevention of Atrocities) Rules, 1995

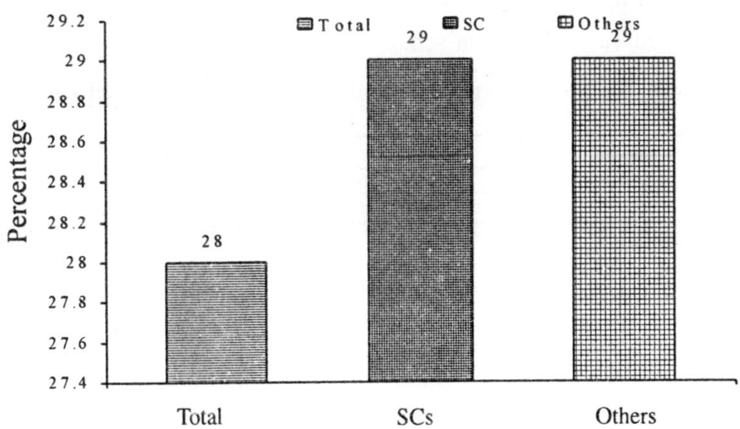

50 respondents were examined on this question. Their responses are depicted in Graph No.84 and Table No. 18.

Table No. 18 : Awareness of the Rules amongst Law Makers and Opinion Makers

Categories		Responses in							
		Number				*Percentage*			
		Yes	*No*	*Und.*	*Total*	*Yes*	*No*	*Und.*	*Total*
Law Makers & Opinion Makers	SCs	10	25	0	35	29	71	0	100
	STs	0	1	0	1	0	100	0	100
	Others	4	8	2	14	29	57	14	100
	Total	14	34	2	50	28	68	4	100

Out of these 14 replied in affirmative, 34 in negative and 2 did not give their replies.[22] Thus, only 28% of Law Makers and Opinion Makers are aware of the SC & ST (Prevention of Atrocities) Rules, 1995. Percentage of SC respondents under these categories is 20. It can be concluded that 72% respondents of these categories belonging, to non SC & ST and 80% respondents belonging to SCs are ignorant about the Rules.[23]

5.4 Awareness about the Applicability of the Act on Non Scheduled Caste and Non-Scheduled Tribe

Question numbers 19, 17 and 20 of the questionnaire for the Target Group[24], Different Units of the Legal System,[25] and Law Makers and the Opinion Makers,[26] respectively, elicited information whether or not respondents know that the Act is applicable against non-scheduled castes and non-scheduled tribes only?

Table No. 19 : Awareness about the Applicability of the Act on Non SC & ST

Categories		Responses in							
		Number				*Percentage*			
		Yes	*No*	*Und.*	*Total*	*Yes*	*No*	*Und.*	*Total*
Target Group		112	77	11	200	56	38	6	100
Different Units of Legal System	SCs	79	26	7	112	71	23	6	100
	STs	6	1	0	7	86	14	0	100
	Others	112	61	8	181	62	34	4	100
	Total	197	88	15	300	66	29	5	100
L.M. & O.M29		18	3	50	58	36	6	100	
Grand Total		338	183	29	550	61	34	5	100

Graph No. 85 : Awareness of Applicability of the Act on Non SC & ST

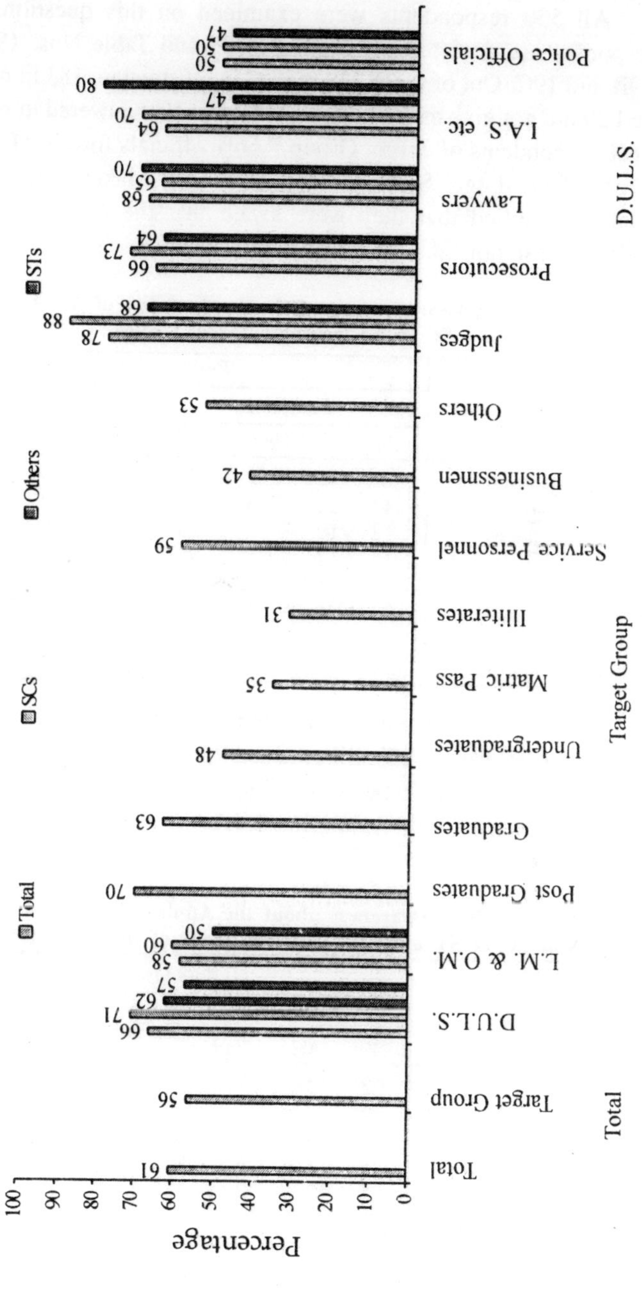

All 550 respondents were examined on this question. Their responses are depicted in Graph No. 85 and Table Nos. 19, 19A, 19B and 19C. Out of these 338 replied in affirmative, 183 in negative and 29 did not give their opinions.[27] Thus, 61% answered in positive. 56% respondents of Target Group,[28] 66% officials forming Different Units of the Legal System,[29] and 58% Law Makers and Opinion Makers[30] replied that they were aware that the Act is applicable only against non-SCs and Non-STs persons.

Table No. 19A : Awareness about the Applicability of the Act on Non SC & ST amongst Target Group

Categories	*Responses in*							
	Number				*Percentage*			
	Yes	*No*	*Und.*	*Total*	*Yes*	*No*	*Und.*	*Total*
Post Graduates	40	17	0	57	70	30	0	100
Graduates	43	22	3	68	63	32	5	100
Under Graduates	12	10	3	25	48	40	12	100
Matric Pass	12	17	5	34	35	50	15	100
Illiterates	5	11	0	16	31	69	0	100
Service Personnel	73	46	5	124	59	37	4	100
Businessmen	5	6	1	12	42	50	8	100
Other Occupations	36	26	6	68	53	38	9	100

70% Post Graduates, 63% Graduates, 48% Under Graduates, 35% Matric Pass, 31% Illiterates, 59% Service Personnel, 42% Businessmen, and 53% persons of Target Groups engaged in different occupations were only aware that the Act is applicable only against Non SC & ST persons.[31]

Table No. 19B : Awareness about the Applicability of the Act on Non SC & ST amongst Different Units of the Legal System

Categories		*Responses in*							
		Number				*Percentage*			
		Yes	*No*	*Und.*	*Total*	*Yes*	*No*	*Und*	*Total*
Judges	SCs	22	2	1	25	88	8	2	100
	Others	17	7	1	25	68	28	4	100
	Total	39	9	2	50	78	18	4	100
Prosecutors	SCs	8	1	2	11	73	9	18	100
	Others	25	12	2	39	64	31	5	100
	Total	33	13	4	50	66	26	8	100

TABLE No. 19B *Contd.*

Categories		*Yes*	*No*	*Und.*	*Total*	*Yes*	*No*	*Und.*	*Total*
Lawyers	SCs	22	10	2	34	65	29	6	100
	Others	46	15	5	66	70	23	7	100
	Total	68	25	7	100	68	25	7	100
I.A.S., P.C.S., Doctors, etc.	SCs	21	9	0	30	70	30	0	100
	STs	4	1	0	5	80	20	0	100
	Others	7	8	0	15	47	53	0	100
	Total	32	18	0	50	64	36	0	100
Police officials	SCs	6	4	2	12	50	30	20	100
	STs	2	0	0	2	100	0	0	100
	Others	17	19	0	36	47	53	0	100
	Total	25	23	2	50	50	46	4	100
Grand Total		197	88	15	300	66	29	5	100

78% Judges, 66% Public Prosecutors, 68% Lawyers, 64% I.A.S., P.C.S., Doctors and other officers and 50% Police officials are aware about the applicability of the Act only against Non SC & ST persons. Percentages of SC officials under these categories are 88, 73, 65, 70 and 50, respectively.[32]

Table No. 19C : Awareness about the Applicability of the Act on Non SC & ST amongst Law Makers and Opinion Makers

Categories		*Responses in*							
		Number				*Percentage*			
		Yes	*No*	*Und.*	*Total*	*Yes*	*No*	*Und.*	*Total*
Law Makers & Opinion Makers	SCs	21	12	2	35	60	34	6	100
	STs	1	0	0	1	100	0	0	100
	Others	7	6	1	14	50	43	7	100

58% MPs., Legislators, Academicians, Media Persons, Social Activists and members of N.G.Os., *etc.*, are only aware about this fact of applicability of the Act only against Non SC & ST persons. Percentage of SCs respondents under this category is 60.[33]

Since percentage of awareness amongst the persons of Target Group, except Matric Pass Illiterates and Businessmen is more than 50%, therefore, it is concluded that majority of the people of SCs are aware that this Act is applicable only against Non SC & ST persons. This is so because they know that atrocities are committed upon them by Non SC & ST persons.

On the basis of percentage, enumerated hereinabove, of the

respondents forming part of Different Units of the Legal System, it is concluded that all of them are not aware about the enforcement of the provision of the Act only against Non SC & ST persons. Same is the conclusion about M.Ps., Legislators, Academicians, Media Persons, Social Activists and members of N.G.Os., *etc.*

5.5 Offences of Atrocities

Question numbers 18, 16 and 19 of the questionnaire for the Target Group,[34] Different Units of the Legal System[35] and Law Makers and Opinion Makers,[36] respectively, elicited information whether or not respondents have knowledge about the inclusion of several categories of atrocities in the definition of atrocity offence?

Table No. 20 : Awareness about Offences of Atrocities

Categories		*Responses in*							
		Number				*Percentage*			
		Yes	*No*	*Und.*	*Total*	*Yes*	*No*	*Und.*	*Total*
Target Group		85	108	7	200	43	54	3	100
Different Units of Legal System	SCs	86	26	0	112	77	23	0	100
	STs	5	2	0	7	71	29	0	100
	Others	137	38	6	181	76	21	3	100
	Total	228	66	6	300	76	22	2	100
L.M. & O.M27		20	3	50	54	40	6	100	
Grand Total		340	194	16	550	62	35	3	100

All 550 respondents were examined on this question. Their responses are depicted in Graph No. 86 and Table Nos. 20, 20A, 20B and 20C. Out of these, 340 replied in affirmative, 194 in negative and 16 did not express their opinions.[37] Thus, 62% opined in positive. 43% respondents of Target Group,[38] 76% officials forming Different Units of Legal System[39] and 54% Law Makers and Opinion Makers[40] are aware about categorization of several atrocities and inclusion thereof in the definition of atrocities under the Act.

53% Post Graduates, 44% Graduates, 28% Under-Graduates, 41% Matric Pass, 25% Illiterates, 43% Service Personnel, 58% Businessmen, and 39% respondents of Target Group engaged in different occupations only admitted that they were aware about categorization of the offences of atrocities and inclusion thereof in the definition of atrocities.[41]

Graph No. 86 : Awareness of the Categorisation of the Atrocities on the SCs

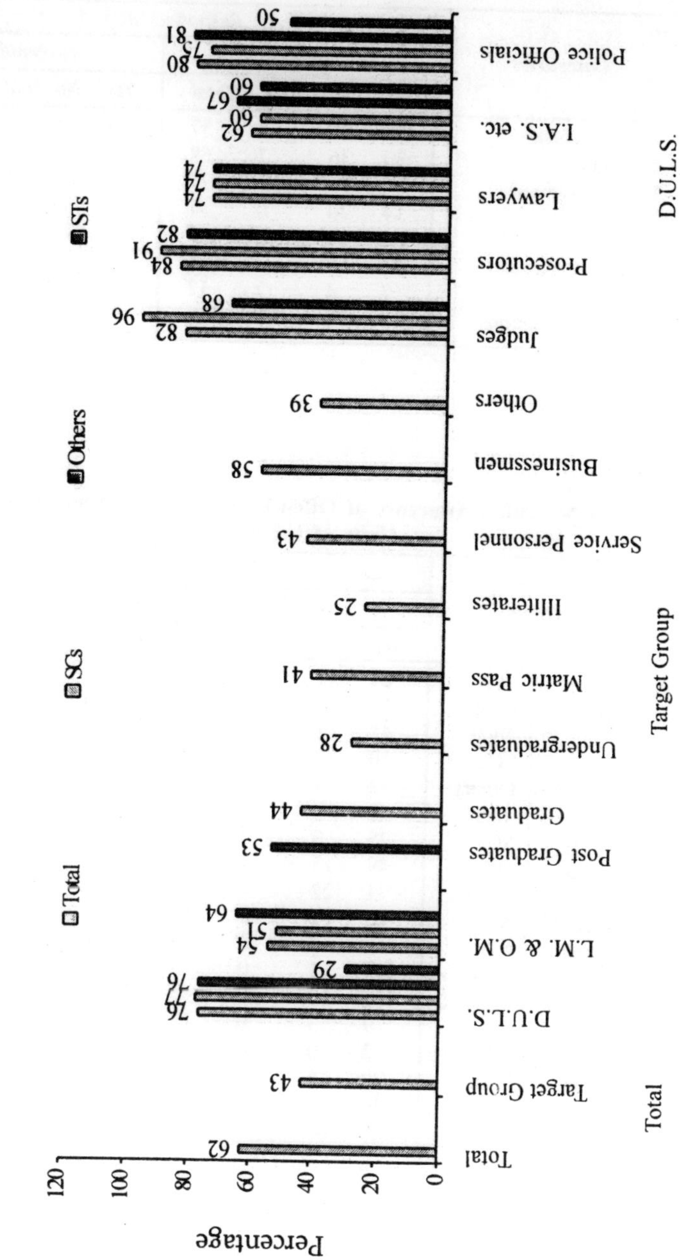

Table No. 20A : Awareness About offences of Atrocities Amongst Target Group

Categories	Responses in Number				Responses in Percentage			
	Yes	*No*	*Und.*	*Total*	*Yes*	*No*	*Und.*	*Total*
Post Graduates	30	25	2	57	53	44	3	100
Graduates	30	36	2	68	44	53	3	100
Under Graduates	7	15	3	25	28	60	12	100
Matric Pass	14	20	0	34	41	59	0	100
Illiterates	4	12	0	16	25	75	0	100
Service Personnel	53	68	3	124	43	55	2	100
Businessmen	7	4	1	12	58	34	8	100
Other Occupations	27	38	3	68	39	56	5	100

Table No. 20B : Awarenss of Offences of Atrocities Amongst Different Units of Legal System

Categories		Responses in Number				Responses in Percentage			
		Yes	*No*	*Und.*	*Total*	*Yes*	*No*	*Und.*	*Total*
Judges	SCs	24	1	0	25	96	4	0	100
	Others	17	7	1	25	68	28	4	100
	Total	41	8	1	50	82	16	2	100
Prosecutors	SCs	10	1	0	11	91	9	0	100
	Others	32	7	.0	39	82	18	0	100
	Total	42	8	0	50	84	16	0	100
Lawyers	SCs	25	9	0	34	74	26	0	100
	Others	49	13	4	66	74	20	6	100
	Total	74	22	4	100	74	22	4	100
I.A.S., P.C.S. Doctors, etc.	SCs	18	12	0	30	60	40	0	100
	STs	3	2	0	5	60	40	0	100
	Others	10	5	0	15	67	33	0	100
	Total	31	19	0	50	62	38	0	100
Police officials	SCs	9	3	0	12	75	25	0	100
	STs	2	0	0	2	100	0	0	100
	Others	29	6	1	36	81	17	3	100
	Total	40	9	1	50	80	18	2	100
Grand Total		228	66	6	300	76	22	2	100

82% Judges, 84% Public Prosecutors, 74% Lawyers, 62% I.A.S., P.C.S., Doctors and other officers and 80% Police officials are aware about this fact. Percentages of SCs respondents under these categories having knowledge in this regard are 96, 91, 74, 60 and 75, respectively.[42]

Table No. 20C : Awareness of Offences of Atrocities amongst Law Makers and Opinion Makers

Categories		*Responses in*							
		Number				*Percentage*			
		Yes	*No*	*Und.*	*Total*	*Yes*	*No*	*Und.*	*Total*
Law Makers & Opinion Makers	SCs	18	16	1	35	51	46	3	100
	STs	0	1	0	1	0	100	0	100
	Others	9	3	2	14	64	22	14	100

54% M.Ps., Legislators, Academicians, Media Persons, Social Activists and members of N.G.Os., *etc.*, have knowledge in this regard. Percentage of SCs respondents under these categories, who are of similar opinion, is 51.[43]

Since less than 50% respondents of Target Group, except Post Graduates and Businessmen, are only aware about categorization of atrocities and inclusion thereof as an offence of atrocities and all officials forming part of the Different Units of the Legal System, who are expected to know and implement the same, but they are found not aware about the provisions of the Act, therefore, it is concluded that level of awareness is much below than the expected level of awareness of both Target Group and officials forming part of Different Units of the Legal System.

5.6 Non-Availability of Anticipatory Bail and Benefit of Probation

Question number 39 of questionnaire on the subject for Target Group[44] elicited information whether or not persons of Target Group are aware about the special provision of the Act that neither accused of atrocity can be released on anticipatory bail nor convict can be released on probation?

Table No. 21 : Awareness of Non-Availability of Anticipatory Bail and Benefit of Probation

Categories	Responses in							
	Number				Percentage			
	Yes	No	Und.	Total	Yes	No	Und.	Total
Target Group	75	114	11	200	38	57	5	100

200 respondents were examined on this question. Their responses are depicted in Graph No. 87 and Table Nos. 21 and 21A. Out of these, 75 replied in affirmative, 114 in negative and 11 did not express their opinions.[45] Thus, 37.5% respondents of Target Group are aware of this provision.

Graph No. 87 : Awareness about Non Availability of Anticipatory Bail and Benefit of Probation

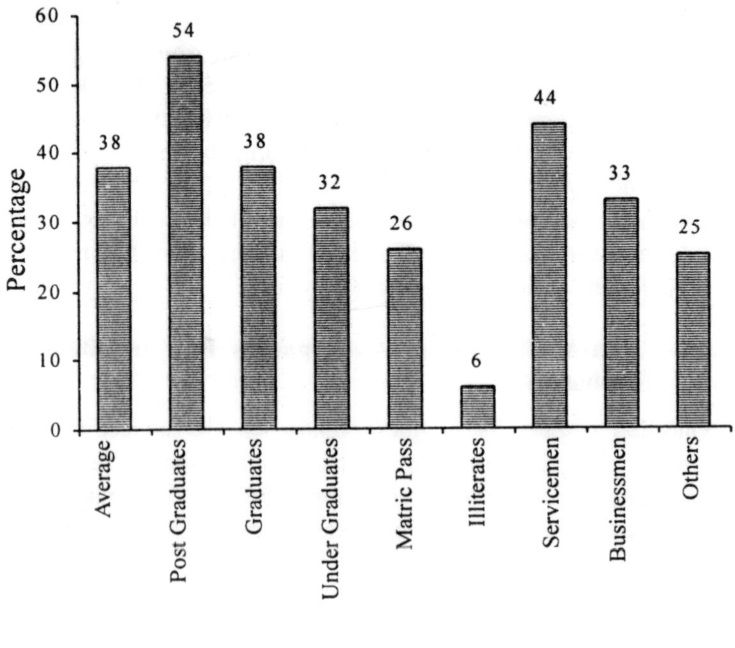

Table No. 21A : Awareness of Non-Availability of Anticipatory Bail and Benefit of Probation amongst Target Group

Categories	*Responses in*							
	Number				*Percentage*			
	Yes	*No*	*Und.*	*Total*	*Yes*	*No*	*Und.*	*Total*
Post Graduates	31	23	3	57	54	41	5	100
Graduates	26	39	3	68	38	58	4	100
Under Graduates	8	13	4	25	32	52	16	100
Matric Pass	9	24	1	34	26	71	3	100
Illiterates	1	15	0	16	6	94	0	100
Service Personnel	55	64	5	124	44	52	4	100
Businessmen	4	7	1	12	33	58	9	100
Other Occupations	17	46	5	68	25	68	7	100

54% Post Graduates, 38% Graduates, 32% Under-Graduates, 26% Matric pass, 6% Illiterates, 44% Service Personnel, 33% Businessmen, and 25% respondents of Target Group engaged in different occupations are only aware about these special provisions.[46]

On the basis of percentages narrated hereinabove, it is concluded that most of the Illiterates are not aware about these provisions. Matric Pass and persons of Target Groups engaged in different occupations are, negligibly, aware about these provisions. Awareness of Under Graduates and Businessmen is not up to expected level. Majority of SCs, except Post Graduates, whose level of awareness is just 54%, is not having awareness of these special provisions up to the desired level.

5.7 Awareness about Special Courts and Special Public Prosecutors

Question numbers 36 and 40 of the questionnaire on the subject for the Target Group[47] and Different Units of the Legal System,[48] respectively, elicited information, whether respondents were aware about creation of special courts and appointment of Special Public Prosecutors?

Table No. 22 : Awareness of Special Courts and Special Public Prosecutors

Categories		Responses in							
		Number				Percentage			
		Yes	No	Und.	Total	Yes	No	Und.	Total
Target Group		91	102	7	200	46	51	3	100
Different Units of Legal System	SCs	64	39	9	112	57	35	8	100
	STs	5	1	1	7	72	14	14	100
	Others	102	68	11	181	56	38	6	100
	Total	171	108	21	300	57	36	7	100
Grand Total		262	210	28	500	52	42	6	100

500 respondents were examined on this question. Their responses are depicted in Graph No 88 and Table Nos. 22, 22A and 22B. Out of these, 262 replied in affirmative, 210 in negative and 28 did not give their opinions.[49] Thus, 52% respondents replied in positive. 46% respondents of Target Group[50] and 57% officials forming Different Units of Legal System[51] are aware about creation of Special Courts and appointment of Special Public Prosecutors.

Table No. 22A : Awareness of Special Courts and Special Public Prosecutors amongst Target Group

Categories	Responses in							
	Number				Percentage			
	Yes	No	Und.	Total	Yes	No	Und.	Total
Post Graduates	29	26	2	57	51	46	3	100
Graduates	38	27	3	68	56	40	4	100
Under Graduates	12	11	2	25	48	44	8	100
Matric Pass	11	23	0	34	32	68	0	100
Illiterates	1	15	0	16	6	94	0	100
Service Personnel	64	56	4	124	52	45	3	100
Businessmen	6	5	1	12	50	42	8	100
Other Occupations	22	44	2	68	33	64	3	100

51% Post-Graduates, 56% Graduates, 48% Under Graduates, 32% Matric Pass, 6% Illiterates, 52% Service Personnel, 50% Businessmen and 33% respondents of Target Group engaged in different occupations are only aware about these special features of the Act.[52]

Graph No. 88 : Awareness of Special Courts and Special Public Prosecutors

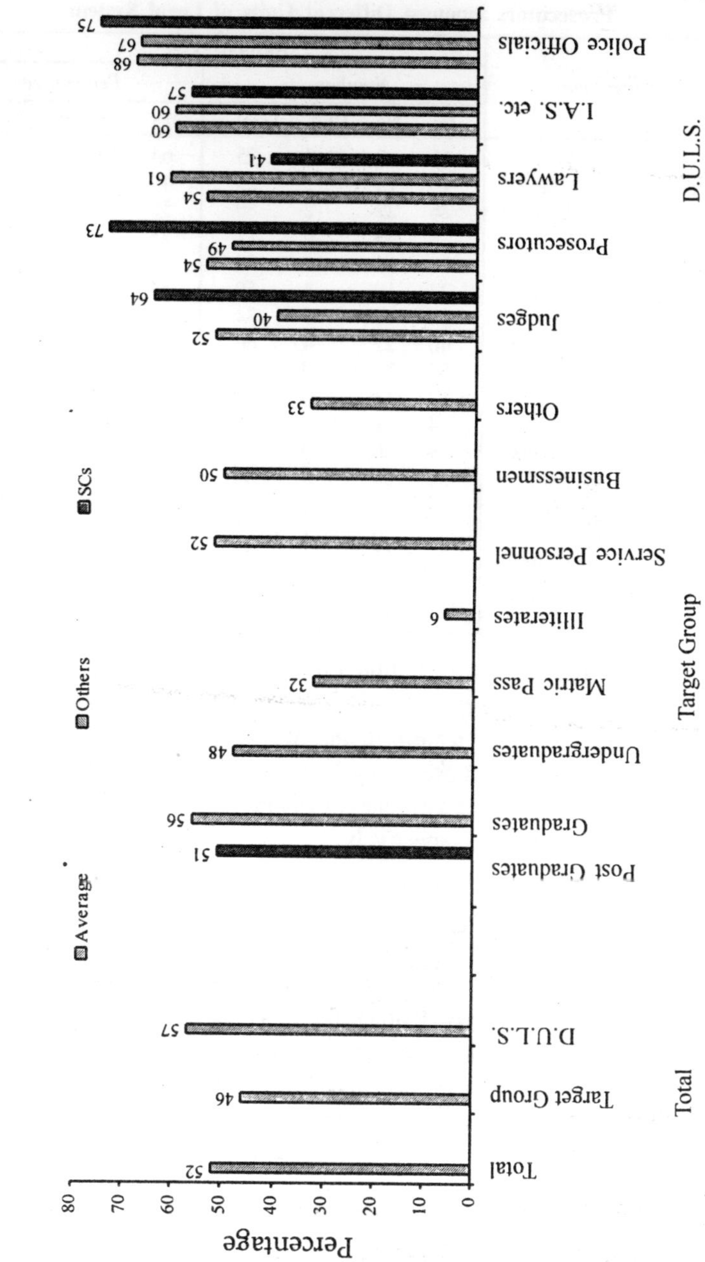

Table No. 22B : Awareness of Special Courts and Special Public Prosecutors amongst Different Units of Legal System

Categories		*Responses in*							
		Number				*Percentage*			
		Yes	*No*	*Und.*	*Total*	*Yes*	*No*	*Und.*	*Total*
Judges	SCs	16	9	0	25	64	36	0	100
	Others	10	13	2	25	40	52	8	100
	Total	26	22	2	50	52	44	4	100
Prosecutors	SCs	8	3	0	11	73	27	0	100
	Others	19	16	4	39	49	41	10	100
	Total	27	19	4	50	54	38	8	100
Lawyers	SCs	14	13	7	34	41	38	21	100
	Others	40	22	4	66	61	33	6	100
	Total	54	35	11	100	54	35	11	100
I.A.S., P.C.S., Doctors, etc.	SCs	17	13	0	30	57	43	0	100
	STs	4	1	0	5	80	20	0	100
	Others	9	6	0	15	60	40	0	100
	Total	30	20	0	50	60	40	0	100
Police officials	SCs	9	1	2	12	75	8	17	100
	STs	1	0	1	2	50	0	50	100
	Others	24	11	1	36	67	31	2	100
	Total	34	12	4	50	68	24	8	100
Grand Total		171	108	21	300	57	36	7	100

52% Judges, 54% Public Prosecutors, 54% Lawyers, 60% I.A.S., P.C.S., Doctors and other officers, and 68% Police officials are aware about this feature of the Act. Percentages of awareness of SC officials of these categories are 64, 73, 41, 57 and 75, respectively. Level of awareness of Non SC & ST officials are 40, 40, 61, 60 and 67, respectively.[53]

Since less than 50% respondents of Target Group, except Post Graduates, Graduates, and Service Personnel, whose level of awareness is just above 50%, are only aware about creation of Special Courts and appointment of Special Public Prosecutors, and all officials forming part of Different Units of the Legal System, who are expected to know *in toto*, are not aware about this, therefore, it is concluded that level of awareness is much below the expected level of awareness of both Target Group and officials forming part of Different Units of the Legal System.

5.8 Punishment to Public Servant

Question number 50 of the questionnaire on the subject for Target

Group[54] elicited information whether or not respondents are aware that even Non SC & ST public servant is liable for punishment of 6 to 12 months imprisonment, if he wilfully neglects his duties required to be performed under the Act?

Graph No. 89 : Awareness about Punishment to Negligent Public Servant

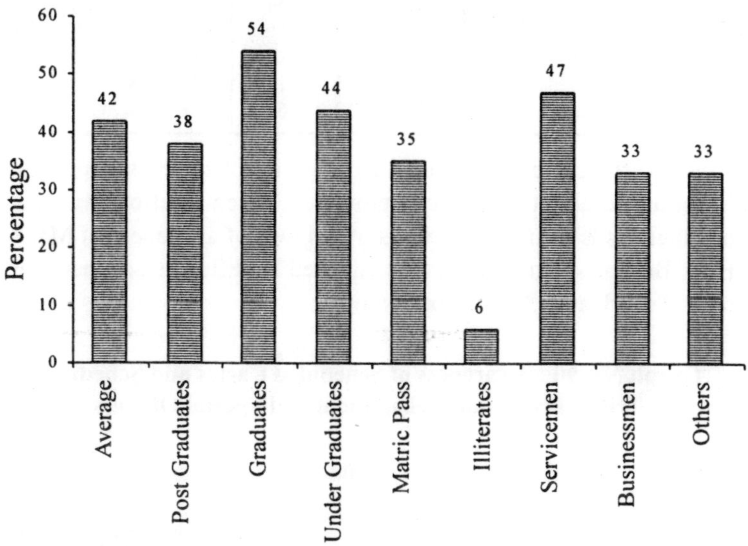

Table No. 23 : Awareness of Punishment to Public Servants

Categories	*Responses in*							
	Number				*Percentage*			
	Yes	*No*	*Und.*	*Total*	*Yes*	*No*	*Und.*	*Total*
Target Group	83	107	10	200	42	53	5	100

200 respondents were examined on this question. Their responses are depicted in Graph No. 89 and Table Nos. 23 and 23A. only 83 replied in affirmative, 107 in negative and 10 did not express any opinion.[55] Thus, 42% of SCs population is aware and 58% thereof are not aware that a Non SC & ST public servant is liable for punishment if he wilfully neglects his duties to be performed under this Act.[56]

Table No. 23A : Awareness of Punishment to Public Servants amongst Target Group

Categories	Responses in							
	Number				Percentage			
	Yes	*No*	*Und.*	*Total*	*Yes*	*No*	*Und.*	*Total*
Post Graduates	22	32	3	57	39	56	5	100
Graduates	37	29	2	68	54	43	3	100
Under Graduates	11	11	3	25	44	44	12	100
Matric Pass	12	20	2	34	35	59	6	100
Illiterates	1	15	0	16	6	94	0	100
Service Personnel	58	59	7	124	47	48	6	100
Businessmen	4	7	1	12	34	58	8	100
Other Occupations	22	44	2	68	33	64	3	100

It is, therefore, concluded that majority of the SCs population is not aware about this special provision. Even level of awareness of Illiterates is found as below as 6%. Level of awareness of Matric Pass, Businessmen and persons engaged in different occupation is only 35, 33 and 33% respectively.

Graph No. 90 : Awareness of Scheduled Castes and Scheduled Tribes Protection Cells, Nodal and Special Officers

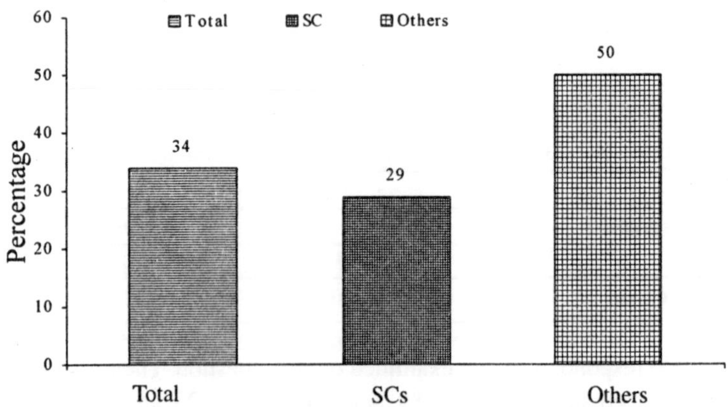

5.9 Awareness about Scheduled Castes and Scheduled Tribes Protection Cells, Nodal and Special Officers

Question number 24 of the questionnaire on the subject for Law Makers and Opinion Makers[57] elicited information from M.Ps.,

Legislators, Media Persons, Social Activists and members of N.G.Os., *etc.*, whether they are aware that rules framed under the Act, envisaged setting up of SCs and STs Protection Cells, nomination of Nodal officers and appointment of Special officers for effective implementation of the provision of the Act?

Table No. 24 : Awareness of SC & ST Protection Cells, Nodal and Special Officers amongst Law Makers and Opinion Makers

Categories		*Responses in*							
		Number				*Percentage*			
		Yes	*No*	*Und.*	*Total*	*Yes*	*No*	*Und.*	*Total*
Law Makers & Opinion Makers	SCs	10	24	1	35	29	69	2	100
	STs	0	1	0	1	0	100	0	100
	Others	7	4	3	14	50	29	21	100
	Total	17	29	4	50	34	58	8	100

50 respondents were examined on this question. Their responses are depicted in Graph No. 90 and Table No. 24. Out of these, 17 replied in affirmative, 29 in negative and 4 did not give any specific answers.[58] Thus, only 34% Law Makers and Opinion Makers are having awareness about setting up of SC & ST Protection Cells, nomination of Nodal officers and appointment of Special officers for effective implementation of the Act. Level of awareness of SCs respondents under this category is 29 per cent.[59]

It is, therefore, concluded that even two-third population of Law Makers and Opinion Makers is not aware about this provision of the Act and Rules framed thereunder.

5.10 Awareness of Salient Features of the Act

Question number 21 of the questionnaire on the subject for Law Makers and Opinion Makers[60] elicited information from M.Ps., Legislators, Academicians, Media Persons, Social Activists and members of N.G.Os, *etc.*, whether they were aware about the salient features of the Act?

50 respondents were examined on this question. Their responses are depicted in Graph No. 91 and Table No. 25. Out of these, 22 replied in affirmative, 27 in negative and 1 did not give any specific answer.[61] Thus, 44% Law Makers and Opinion Makers are

Table No. 25 : Awareness of Salient Features of the Act amongst Law Makers and Opinion Makers

Categories		*Responses in*							
		Number				*Percentage*			
		Yes	*No*	*Und.*	*Total*	*Yes*	*No*	*Und.*	*Total*
Law Makers & Opinion Makers	SCs	15	20	0	35	43	57	0	100
	STs	0	1	0	01	0	100	0	100
	Others	7	6	1	14	50	43	7	100
	Total	22	27	1	50	44	54	2	100

Graph No. 91 : Awareness of Salient Features of the Act

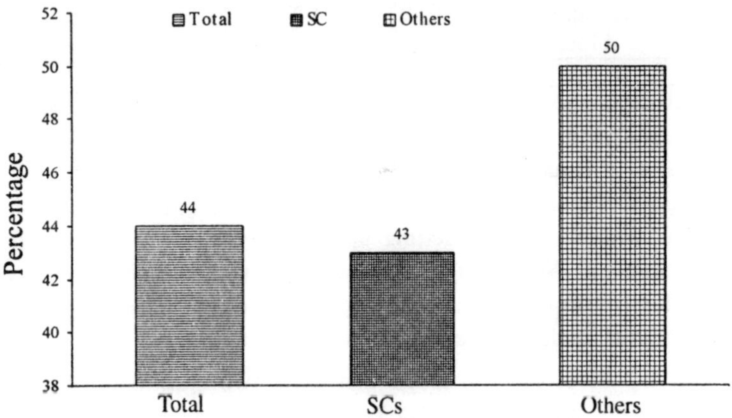

only having awareness about the salient features of the Act. Level of awareness of SC respondents under these categories is 43 per cent.[62]

It is, therefore, concluded that most of the MPs., Legislators, Academicians, Media Persons, Social Activists and members of N.G.Os., *etc.*, are not having awareness about the salient features, *i.e.*, special features of the Act.

5.11 Constitution of State and District Level Vigilance and Monitoring Committees

Question numbers 25, 26 and 27 of the questionnaire for Law Makers and Opinion Makers[63] elicited information as to how many respondents are aware that rules framed under the Act provide for constitution of State and District Level Vigilance and Monitoring Committees? And whether any respondent has ever been a member of either State Level Vigilance and Monitoring Committee or District Level Vigilance and Monitoring Committee for implementation of the provisions of the Act and reviewing the implementation of the provisions of the Act, respectively?

Graph No. 92 : Constitution of State and District Level Vigilance and Monitoring Committees

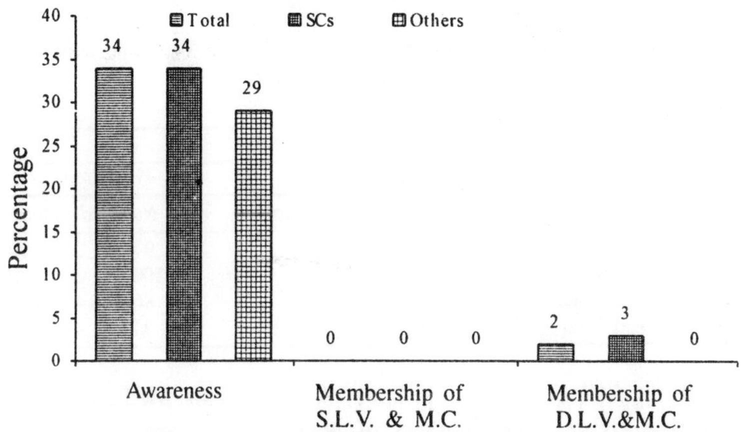

Table No. 26 : Awareness of District Level Vigilance and Monitoring Committee amongst Law Makers and Opinion Makers

Categories		*Responses in*							
		Number				*Percentage*			
		Yes	*No*	*Und.*	*Total*	*Yes*	*No*	*Und.*	*Total*
Law Makers & Opinion Makers	SCs	12	22	1	35	34	63	3	100
	STs	1	0	0	1	100	0	0	100
	Others	4	7	3	14	29	50	21	100
	Total	17	29	4	50	34	58	8	100

50 respondents on each question were examined. Their responses are depicted in Graph No. 92. Out of these, 17, 0 and 1, respectively, replied in affirmative. 29, 48 and 47, respectively, replied in negative. Rest did not express any opinion.[64]

Table No. 26A : Membership of State Level Vigilance and Monitoring Committee

Categories		Responses in							
		Number				Percentage			
		Yes	*No*	*Und.*	*Total*	*Yes*	*No*	*Und.*	*Total*
Law Makers & Opinion Makers	SCs	0	35	0	35	0	100	0	100
	STs	0	1	0	1	0	100	0	100
	Others	0	12	2	14	0	86	14	100
	Total	0	48	2	50	0	96	4	100

Table No. 26B : Membership of District Level Vigilance and Monitoring Committee

Categories		Responses in							
		Number				Percentage			
		Yes	*No*	*Und.*	*Total*	*Yes*	*No*	*Und.*	*Total*
Law Makers & Opinion Makers	SCs	1	34	0	35	3	97	0	100
	STs	0	1	0	1	0	100	0	100
	Others	0	12	2	14	0	86	14	100
	Total	1	47	2	50	2	94	4	100

Thus, 34% of M.Ps., Legislators, Academicians, Media Persons, Social Activists, and members of N.G.Os., *etc.*, are only aware about constitution of State and District Level Vigilance and Monitoring Committees. None of the respondent under these categories has ever been a member of State Level Vigilance and Monitoring Committees for implementation of the provision of the Act and only 2% of the respondents were found member of the District Level Vigilance and monitoring committee for reviewing the implementation of the Act. There is no difference between the opinion of SCs and Non SC & ST respondents in respect of awareness.[65]

On the basis of percentage narrated herein above, it is concluded that neither the public in general nor Law Makers and Opinion Makers are aware about the constitution of State and District Level Vigilance and Monitoring Committees nor these Committees have been doing any work for implementation of the provisions of the Act, for reviewing the implementation of the provisions of the Act.

5.12 Complaint against Prosecutor to the Director of Prosecution or District Magistrate

Question number 47 of the questionnaire on the subject for Target Group[66] elicited information whether or not respondents are aware, if they were not satisfied with the work of Special Public Prosecutor, then they should bring the same to the knowledge of Director of Prosecution or District Magistrate?

Graph No. 93 : Awareness about Complaint of Prosecutor to the Director of Prosecution or District Magistrate

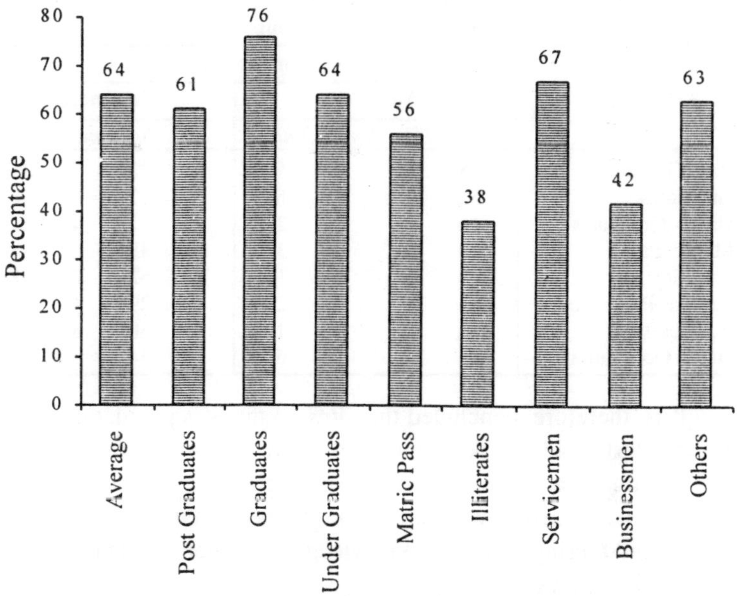

Table No. 27 : Complaint against Prosecutor to the Director of Prosecution or District Magistrate

Categories	*Responses in*							
	Number				*Percentage*			
	Yes	*No*	*Und.*	*Total*	*Yes*	*No*	*Und.*	*Total*
Target Group	128	64	8	200	64	32	4	100

200 respondents were examined on this question. Their responses are depicted in Graph No. 93 and Table Nos. 27 and 27A. Out of these 128 replied in affirmative, 64 in negative and 8 did not give any specific answers.[67] Thus, 64% of Target Group are aware and 36% are not aware that in case of unsatisfactory work of special public prosecutor, they should bring the same to the knowledge of either the Director of Prosecution or the District Magistrate. Level of awareness of Illiterates and Businessmen is found much below the average percentage and even below 50% as their level of awareness are only 38% and 42% respectively.[68]

Table No. 27A : Awareness regarding Filing of Complaint against Prosecutor to the Director of Prosecution or District Magistrate amongst Target Group

Categories	*Responses in*							
	Number				*Percentage*			
	Yes	*No*	*Und.*	*Total*	*Yes*	*No*	*Und.*	*Total*
Post Graduates	35	18	4	57	61	32	7	100
Graduates	52	15	1	68	77	22	1	100
Under Graduates	16	8	1	25	64	32	4	100
Matric Pass	19	13	2	34	56	38	6	100
Illiterates	6	10	0	16	38	62	0	100
Service Personnel	83	36	5	124	67	29	4	100
Businessmen	5	6	1	12	42	50	8	100
Other Occupations	43	23	2	68	63	34	3	100

It is, therefore, concluded that 36% of the SCs population even having Post Graduate degree are not aware of this and minority of the Illiterates and Businessmen are having knowledge that in case they are not satisfied with the work of Special Public Prosecutor, they should bring it to the knowledge of either the Director of prosecution or to the District Magistrate.

5.13 Complaint to Senior Police Officers

Question No. 46 of the questionnaire on the subject for Target Group,[69] elicited information whether or not respondents are aware that if they were not satisfied with the investigation of the police. then they should bring the same to the knowledge of higher police officers?

Table No. 28 : Complaint to Senior Police Officer

Categories	*Responses in*							
	Number				*Percentage*			
	Yes	*No*	*Und.*	*Total*	*Yes*	*No*	*Und.*	*Total*
Target Group	159	36	5	200	80	18	2	100

200 respondents were examined on this question. Their responses are depicted in Graph No. 94 and Table Nos. 28 and 28A. Out of these 159 replied in affirmative, 36 in negative and 5 did not give any specific answers.[70] Thus, the average level of awareness of Target Group is 80 per cent.[71]

Graph No. 94 : Awareness about Complaint of Investigating Officer to Senior Police Officers

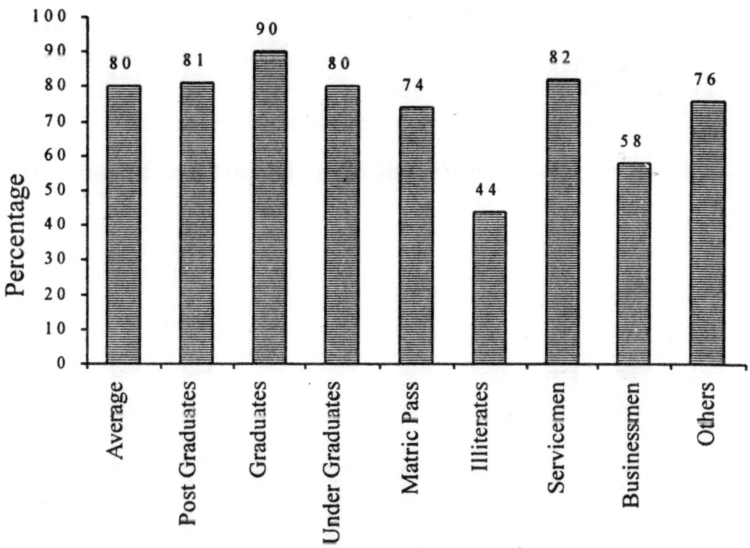

The level of awareness of Illiterates was found as below as 44% in comparison to average level of awareness. Level of awareness of Businessmen was found as 58 and Matric Pass as 74 per cent.[72]

It is, therefore, concluded that majority of Illiterate SCs are not aware of the provision that in case of unsatisfactory investigation by the police, they should bring the same to the knowledge of higher police officers.

Table No. 28A : Awareness regarding Complaint to Senior Police Officer amongst Target Group

Categories	*Responses in*							
	Number				*Percentage*			
	Yes	*No*	*Und.*	*Total*	*Yes*	*No*	*Und.*	*Total*
Post Graduates	46	9	2	57	81	16	3	100
Graduates	61	6	1	68	90	9	1	100
Under Graduates	20	3	2	25	80	12	8	100
Matric Pass	25	9	0	34	74	26	0	100
Illiterates	7	9	0	16	44	56	0	100
Service Personnel	102	20	2	124	82	16	2	100
Businessmen	7	3	2	12	58	25	17	100
Other Occupations	52	15	1	68	76	22	2	100

5.14 Filing of Complaint to the Court

Question number 45 of the questionnaire on the subject for Target Group,[73] elicited information from the respondents, if they are aware of the provision that in case they are not satisfied with the work of police, then they may file a complaint to the court?

Graph No. 95 : Awareness of Filing of Complaint Direct to the Court

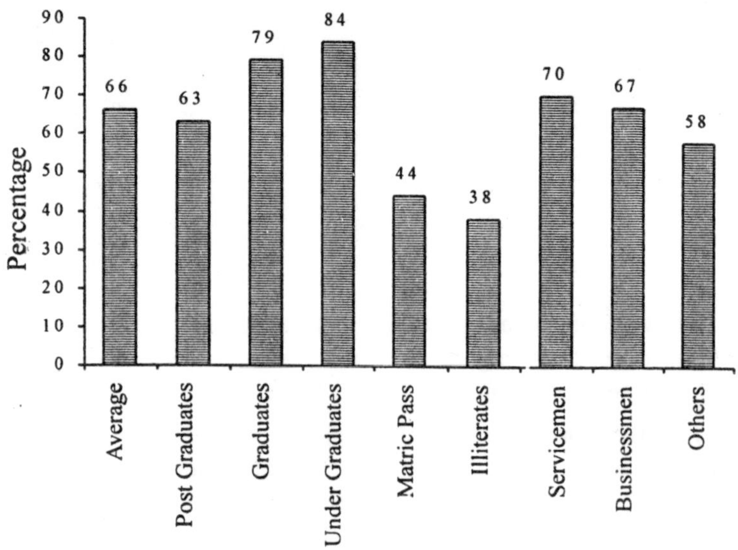

Table No. 29 : Awareness regarding Filing of Complaint to the Court

Categories	*Responses in*							
	Number				*Percentage*			
	Yes	*No*	*Und.*	*Total*	*Yes*	*No*	*Und.*	*Total*
Target Group	132	65	3	200	66	32	2	100

200 respondents were examined on this question. Their responses are depicted in Graph No. 95 and Table Nos. 29 and 29A. Out of these 132 replied in affirmative, 65 in negative and 3 did not give any specific answers.[74] Thus 66% of the respondents were found aware about this provisions. Level of awareness of Illiterates and Matric Pass was much less than average level, which is 36% and 44% respectively.[75]

Table No. 29A : Awareness regarding Filing of Complaint to the Court amongst Target Group

Categories	*Responses in*							
	Number				*Percentage*			
	Yes	*No*	*Und.*	*Total*	*Yes*	*No*	*Und.*	*Total*
Post Graduates	36	18	3	57	63	32	5	100
Graduates	54	14	0	68	79	21	0	100
Under Graduates	21	4	0	25	84	16	0	100
Matric Pass	15	19	0	34	44	56	0	100
Illiterates	6	10	0	16	38	62	0	100
Service Personnel	87	34	3	124	70	27	3	100
Businessmen	8	4	0	12	67	33	0	100
Other Occupations	39	29	0	68	58	42	0	100

It is, therefore, concluded that 32% population of SCs even Post Graduates and Graduates are not aware of this provision. Illiterates and Matric Pass in majority are not aware of the provision that in case of unsatisfactory work of police, they may file a complaint to the court directly.

5.15 First Information Report by Registered Post

Question number 44 of the questionnaire on the subject for Target Group,[76] elicited information from the respondents, whether or not they were aware if Police did not record their FIR then they may send it to the S.P./D.C.P. of the area by Registered Post?

Graph No. 96 : Awareness about Filing of F.I.R. by Registered Post

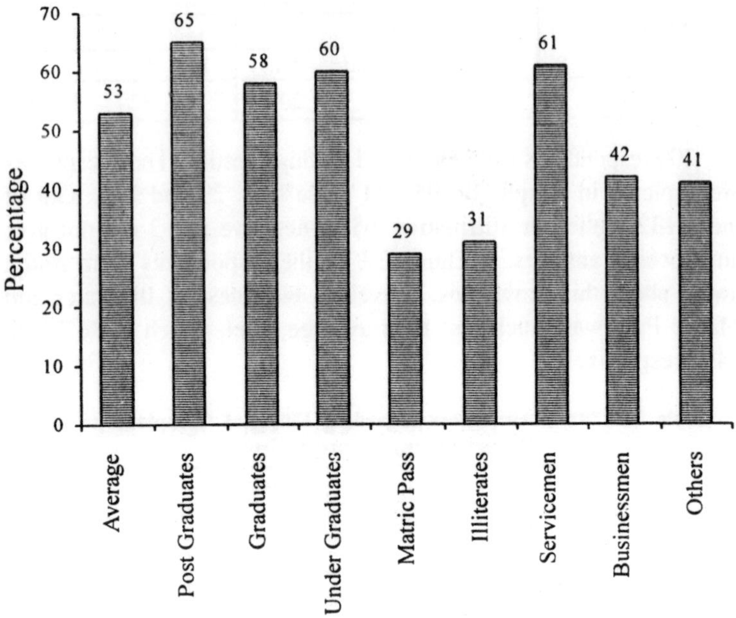

Table No. 30 : First Information Report by Registered Post

Categories	*Responses in*							
	Number				*Percentage*			
	Yes	*No*	*Und.*	*Total*	*Yes*	*No*	*Und.*	*Total*
Target Group	107	86	7	200	53	43	4	100

200 respondents were examined on this question. Their responses are depicted in Graph No. 96 and Table Nos. 30 and 30A. Out of these 107 replied in affirmative, 86 replied in negative and 7 did not express their opinions.[77] Thus, only 53% members of SCs are only aware that in case of refusal by Police they may get their report lodged by sending it to the S.P./D.C.P. of the area by Registered Post. Only 29% of Matric Pass, 31% Illiterates, 41% engaged in different occupations and 42% Businessmen have knowledge of this.[78]

Table No. 30A : Awareness of Lodging of F.I.R. by Registered Post amongst Target Group

Categories	*Responses in*							
	Number				*Percentage*			
	Yes	*No*	*Und.*	*Total*	*Yes*	*No*	*Und.*	*Total*
Post Graduates	37	19	1	57	65	33	2	100
Graduates	40	26	2	68	59	38	3	100
Under Graduates	15	8	2	25	60	32	8	100
Matric Pass	10	22	2	34	29	65	6	100
Illiterates	5	11	0	16	31	69	0	100
Service Personnel	76	45	3	124	61	36	3	100
Businessmen	5	6	1	12	42	50	8	100
Other Occupations	28	37	3	68	41	55	4	100

It is, therefore, concluded that negligible numbers of Illiterates and Matric Pass are aware that report to Police can be lodged by Registered Post. Majority of Businessmen and persons engaged in different occupations have this knowledge. Level of awareness of Post Graduates, Service Personnel, Under Graduates and Graduates are 65, 61, 60 and 59, respectively. Thus, they too, all are not aware of this provision.

5.16 Position of Illiterates of Target Group

Question numbers 16 to 35 of the questionnaire on the subject for Target Group,[79] elicited, information about the awareness of the Act and its provisions amongst the Target Group. 200 respondents under this category were examined consisting of right from Illiterate persons to persons holding Post Graduate degree. Their responses are depicted in Graph No. 97 and Table Nos. 16A, 17A, 19A, 20A, 21A, 22A, 23A, 27A, 28A, 29A and 30A. It revealed that only 13% Illiterates are aware about the Act and its enforcement.[80] It also emerged that 25% of the Illiterates are aware about the inclusion of certain categories of atrocities as offence.[81] Only 31% of them know that offences of atrocities can only be committed by Non SC & ST persons.[82] 25% are aware that denial of access to public place or use of customary passage is an offence of atrocity.[83] 31% of them know that fouling of water is an offence. 44% of them are aware that causing injury, insult or annoyance is an offence.[84] 38% of them are aware that forcing them to eat or drink inedible substance is an offence.[85] 31% of them know that stripping or parading naked or with painted face or painted body or by any other mode which is derogatory to the human dignity or subjecting them to indignities is an offence.[86] 38% of them are aware that outrage of modesty or sexual exploitation of their woman is an offence.[87] 38% of them are aware that wrongful occupation of their land and bonded labour are offences.[88] 19% of them are aware that instituting false, malicious or vexatious suit or criminal or other legal proceedings against them and giving false frivolous informations against them to public servants with the intention of causing injury or annoyance to them by such public servants is an offence.[89] only 13% of them have knowledge that giving false evidence against them or destroying evidence of atrocity or giving financial support to the offenders of atrocities is an offence.[90] As low as 6% of them are aware about special provisions of investigation, trial and rehabilitation of victims and creation of Special Courts and appointment of Special Public Prosecutors.[91] 13% of them are aware that they may get services of Senior Advocates for conducting their cases at Govt. expenses.[92] 19% of them are having knowledge of attachment and forfeiture of the properties of offenders and convicts, respectively.[93] As low as 6% of them are aware that offenders and convicts can neither be released on anticipatory bail nor they can be granted probation.[94]

Graph No. 97 : Awareness of the Act, its Provisions amongst Illiterates of Target Group

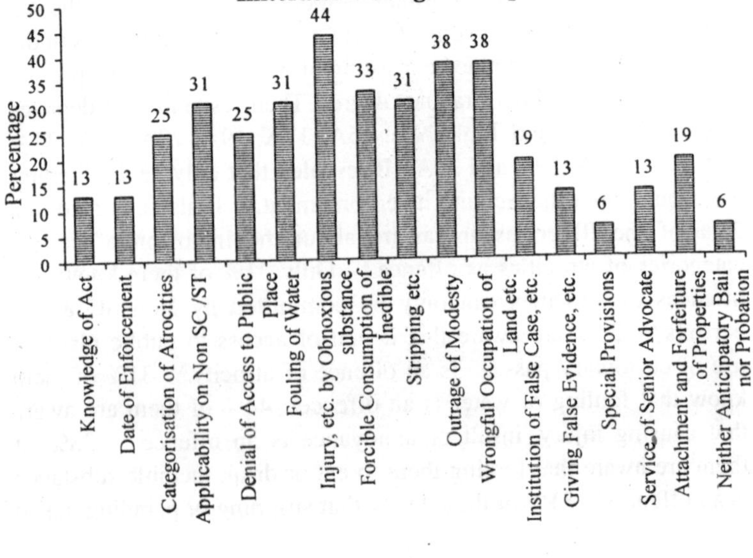

The literacy[95] level of SCs has always been lower than the general population. In the year 1931, the rate of literacy of SCs was as low as 1.9% while it was 9.5% for general population. In the year 1961, it rose to 10.27%; in the year 1971, 14.67%; in the year 1981, 21.38%; in the year 1991, it was 37.41%.[96] Thus, 62.59% population of SCs is illiterate.

As discussed above, only 13% illiterates are aware about the Act and its enforcement. Even level of awareness of some of the provisions of the Act is as low as 6%.

Thus, 13% population of 62.59% illiterates is aware about the Act and its enforcement. It follows that 70% population of SCs is not, absolutely, aware about the Act and its provisions.

About 23.51% of the country's population comprised the SCs and STs Population of SCs is 16.3% of the country's population.[97] Total population of India is 846,302,688.[98] Thus, the SCs population comes to about thirteen crores. Out of these, only 1.12 crores SCs are aware and 12.57 crores SCs are not aware about the present Act or its enforcement.

Notes and References

1. *See*, annexures 1 and 2. The question is, "Do you have knowledge about the Scheduled Castes and the Scheduled Tribes (Prevention of Atrocities) Act, 1989?"
2. *Ibid.* and annexures 1 and 3.
3. *Ibid.* and annexures 1 and 4.
4. *See*, Table No. 16.
5. *See*, Graph No. 18.
6. *See*, Graph No. 24.
7. *See*, Graph No. 23.
8. *See*, Graph No. 18.
9. *See*, Graph Nos. 19 to 25.
10. *See*, Graph No. 23.
11. *See*, annexures 1 and 2. The question is, "Are you aware that the Act has come into force *w.e.f.* 30th January, 1990?"
12. *Ibid.* and annexures 1 and 3.
13. *Ibid.* and annexures 1 and 4.
14. *See*, Table No. 17.
15. *See*, Graph No. 18.
16. *See*, Graph No. 24.
17. *See*, Graph No. 23.
18. *Supra,* note 15.

19. *See*, Graph Nos. 25 to 29.
20. *See*, Graph No. 23.
21. *See*, annexures 1 and 4. The question is, "Do you have knowledge of the Scheduled Castes and the Scheduled Tribes (Prevention of Atrocities) Rules, 1995?"
22. *See*, Table No. 18.
23. *See*, Graph No. 23.
24. *See*, annexures 1 and 2. The question is, "Do you know that an offence under the Act can only be committed by non-Scheduled Castes and Scheduled Tribes on the SCs and the Scheduled Tribes?"
25. *Ibid.* and annexures 1 and 3.
26. *Ibid.* and annexures 1 and 4.
27. *See*, Table No.19.
28. *See*, Graph No. 18.
29. *See*, Graph No. 24.
30. *See*, Graph No. 23.
31. *See*, Graph No. 18.
32. *See*, Graph Nos. 25 to 29.
33. *See*, Graph No. 23.
34. *See*, annexures 1 and 2. The question is, "Do you know that the Act has designated several categories of atrocities as offence?"
35. *Ibid.* and annexures 1 and 3.
36. *Ibid.* and annexures 1 and 4.
37. *See*, Table No.20.
38. *See*, Graph No. 18.
39. *See*, Graph No. 24.
40. *See*, Graph No. 23.
41. *See*, Graph No. 18.
42. *See*, Graph Nos. 25 to 29.
43. *See*, Graph No. 23.
44. *See*, annexures 1 and 2. The question is, "Do you know that accused of and convict of atrocity can neither be released on anticipatory bail nor on probation?"
45. *See*, Table No. 21.
46. *See*, Graph No. 22.
47. *See*, annexures 1 and 2. The question is, "Do you know that the special courts have been created and special public prosecutors have been appointed for trial of offence of atrocities?"
48. *Ibid.* and annexures 1 and 3.
49. *See*, Table No. 22.
50. *See*, Graph No. 22.
51. *See*, Graph No. 36.
52. *See*, Graph No. 22.
53. *See*, Graph Nos. 37 to 41.
54. *See*, annexures 1 and 2. The question is, "Do you know that a Non SC and ST public servant is liable for punishment of 6 to 12 months jail, if he wilfully neglects his duties required to be performed under the Act?"

55. *See*, Table No. 23.
56. *See*, Graph No. 43.
57. *See*, annexures 1 and 4. The question is, "Do you know that these Rules envisaged setting up of the SCs and Scheduled Tribes protection Cells, nomination of nodal officers and appointment of special officers for effective implementation of the provisions of the Act?"
58. *See*, Table No. 24.
59. *See*, Graph No. 23.
60. *See*, annexures 1 and 4. The question is, "Are you aware about the salient features of the Act?"
61. *See*, Table No. 25.
62. *See*, Graph No. 23.
63. *See*, annexures 1 and 4. The questions are, "Do you know that these Rules also provide for constitution of State and District Level Vigilance and Monitoring Committees?", "Have you ever been a member of the State Level Vigilance and Monitoring Committee for implementation of the provisions of the Act?", "Have you ever been a member of the District Level Vigilance and Monitoring Committee for reviewing the implementation of the provisions of the Act?"
64. *See*, Table Nos. 26, 26A and 26B.
65. *See*, Graph No. 23.
66. *See*, annexures 1 and 2. The question is, "Do you know that if you are not satisfied with the work of Special Public Prosecutor, you should bring it to the knowledge of the Director of Prosecution or the District Magistrate?"
67. *See*, Table No. 27.
68. *See*, Graph No. 43.
69. *See*, annexures 1 and 3. The question is, "Do you know that if you are not satisfied with the investigation by the police, you should bring it to the knowledge of higher Police officers?"
70. *See*, Table No. 28.
71. *See*, Graph No. 43.
72. *See*, Graph No. 43.
73. *See*, annexures 1 and 3. The question is, "Do you know that if you are not satisfied with the work of Police, then you may file a complaint to Court?"
74. *See*, Table No. 29.
75. *See*, Graph No. 42.
76. *See*, annexures 1 and 2. The question is, "Do you know that if your report is not recorded by the police then you should send it to S.P./D.C.P. by Registered Post?"
77. *See*, Table No. 30.
78. *See*, Graph No. 42.
79. *See*, annexures 1 and 2.
80. *See*, Graph No. 18.
81. *Ibid.*
82. *Id.*

83. *See*, Graph No. 18.
84. *See*, Graph No. 19.
85. *Ibid.*
86. *Id.*
87. *Id.*
88. *See*, Graph No. 20.
89. *See*, Graph No. 21.
90. *Ibid.*
91. *Id.*
92. *See*, Graph No. 22.
93. *Ibid.*
94. *Ibid.*
95. A person is deemed to be literate if he or she can read and write with understanding in any language.
96. Census of India, 1981, Series Ist at XXVI ; See, also First Report of N.C. SC and ST at 23.
97. Crime in India, 1994, National Crime Bureau, New Delhi at 246.
98. *Supra,* note 97.

CHAPTER 6

EMPIRICAL STUDY OF THE PROVISIONS OF THE ACT : Implementation Realities

6.1 Attachment of Properties of Offenders and Forfeiture of Properties of Convicts

Question number 38 of the questionnaire for the Target Group,[1] elicited information whether or not SC & ST persons are aware that under the Act, properties of offender may be attached and properties of convict may be forfeited?

Table No. 31 : Attachment of Properties of Offenders and Forfeiture of Properties of Convicts

Categories	*Responses in*							
	Number				*Percentage*			
	Yes	*No*	*Und.*	*Total*	*Yes*	*No*	*Und.*	*Total*
Target Group	86	104	10	200	43	52	5	100

200 respondents were examined on this question. Their responses are depicted in Graph No. 98 and Table Nos. 31 and 31A. Out of these, 86 replied in affirmative, 114 in negative and 10 did not give any opinion.[2] Thus, 43% respondents of SCs and STs were only aware about this provision of the Act.[3] Amongst them, 47% Post Graduates, 53% Graduates, 44% Under Graduates, 28% Matric Pass, 19% Illiterates, 50% Service Personnel, 33% Businessmen and 31% persons of Target Group engaged in different occupations are aware about the provision of attachment of property of offender and forfeiture of property of convict.[4]

Graph No. 98 : Awareness of Target Group regarding Attachment of Properties of Offenders and Forfeiture of Properties of Convicts

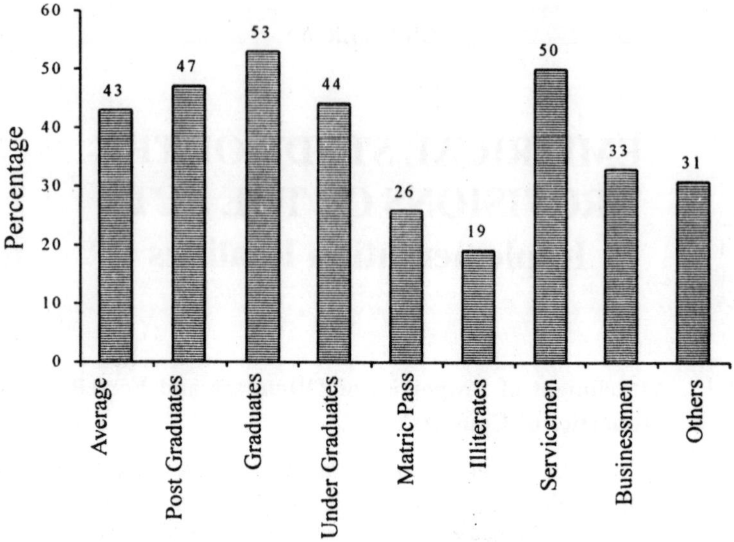

Table No. 31A : Attachment of Properties of Offenders and Forfeiture of Properties of Convicts : Awareness amongst Target Groups

Categories	*Responses in*							
	Number				*Percentage*			
	Yes	*No*	*Und.*	*Total*	*Yes*	*No*	*Und.*	*Total*
Post Graduates	27	28	2	57	47	49	4	100
Graduates	36	29	3	68	53	43	4	100
Under Graduates	11	11	3	25	44	44	12	100
Matric Pass	9	23	2	34	26	68	6	100
Illiterates	3	13	0	16	19	81	0	100
Service Personnel	62	57	5	124	50	46	4	100
Businessmen	4	7	1	12	33	57	8	100
Other Occupations	21	43	4	68	31	63	6	100

It is, therefore, concluded that most of the population of SCs is not aware about this special provision. Percentage of awareness of Illiterates and Matric Pass is much below the average percentage of rest of the group.

Question numbers 44 and 47 of the questionnaire for the Different Units of the Legal System[5] and Law Makers and Opinion

Makers,[6] respectively, elicited information whether respondents have ever attached or caused to be attached the properties of an offender or forfeited and caused to be forfeited the properties of a convict of offences of atrocity?

Table No. 31B : Attachment of Properties of Offenders and Forfeiture of Properties of Convicts: Implementation

Categories		*Responses in*							
		Number				*Percentage*			
		Yes	*No*	*Und.*	*Total*	*Yes*	*No*	*Und.*	*Total*
Different Units of Legal System	SCs	5	104	3	112	4	93	3	100
	STs	0	6	1	7	0	86	14	100
	Others	8	157	16	181	4	87	9	100
	Total	13	267	20	300	4	89	7	100
L.M. & O.M.		3	45	2	50	6	90	4	100
Grand Total		16	312	22	350	5	89	6	100

350 respondents were examined on this question. Their responses are depicted in Graph No. 99 and Table Nos. 31B, 31C and 31D. Out of these, only 16 replied in affirmative, 312 in negative and 22 did not give any opinion.[7] Thus, only 5% respondents of these categories replied that they have either attached or caused to be attached the properties of an offender or forfeited or caused to be forfeited the properties of a convict of an offence of atrocity.

Only 4% officials forming Different Units of Legal System[8] and 6% Law Makers and Opinion Makers discharged their duties in this regard.[9]

0% Judges, 8% Public Prosecutors, 7% Lawyers, 2% I.A.S., P.C.S., Doctors and other Officers and 2% Police Officials discharged their duties in this regard. Percentages of SC officials under these categories are 0, 0, 9, 3 and 8, respectively.[10]

6% M.Ps., Legislators, Academicians, Media Persons, Social Activists and members of N.G.Os., *etc.*, reportedly, discharged their duties for causing attachment of properties of offender and causing forfeiture of properties of convict of offences of atrocity. Percentage of SC respondents under these categories is similar to Non SC & ST persons.[11]

Table No. 31C : Attachment of Properties of Offenders and Forfeiture of Properties of Convicts: Implementation by Different Units of Legal System

Categories		Responses in							
		Number				*Percentage*			
		Yes	*No*	*Und.*	*Total*	*Yes*	*No*	*Und.*	*Total*
Judges	SCs	0	25	0	25	0	100	0	100
	Others	0	23	2	25	0	92	8	100
	Total	0	48	2	50	0	96	4	100
Prosecutors	SCs	0	10	1	11	0	91	9	100
	Others	4	30	5	39	10	77	13	100
	Total	4	40	6	50	8	80	12	100
Lawyers	SCs	3	30	1	34	9	88	3	100
	Others	4	54	8	66	6	82	12	100
	Total	7	84	9	100	7	84	9	100
I.A.S., P.C.S., Doctors, etc.	SCs	1	28	1	30	3	94	3	100
	STs	0	5	0	5	0	100	0	100
	Others	0	15	0	15	0	100	0	100
	Total	1	48	1	50	2	96	2	100
Police Officials	SCs	1	11	0	12	8	92	0	100
	STs	0	1	1	2	0	50	50	100
	Others	0	35	1	36	0	97	3	100
	Total	1	47	2	50	2	94	4	100
Grand Total		13	267	20	300	4	89	7	100

Graph No. 99 : Attachment of Properties of Offenders and Forfeiture of Properties of Convicts Implementation by D.U.L.S. and L.M. & O. M.

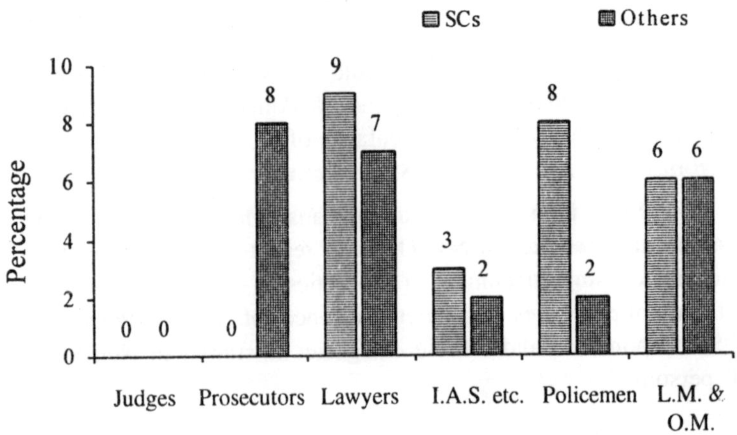

Table No. 31D Attachment of Properties of Offenders and Forfeiture of Properties of Convicts: Implementation in View of Law Makers and Opinion Makers

Categories		Responses in							
		Number				Percentage			
		Yes	No	Und.	Total	Yes	No	Und.	Total
Law Makers & Opinion Makers	SCs	2	31	2	35	6	88	6	100
	STs	0	1	0	1	0	100	0	100
	Others	1	13	0	14	7	93	0	100

On the basis of percentages narrated herein above, it is concluded that this special provision was exceptionally and negligibly used, both by officials forming Different Unit of Legal System and Law Makers and Opinion Makers. Thus, this remained on paper only and was not acted upon.

6.2 Services of Senior Advocate to the Victims

Question number 37 of the questionnaire for the Target Group[12] elicited information whether or not they are aware about the special provision that victim of atrocity may get services of Senior Advocate for conducting his case at government expenses?

Table No. 32 : Services of Senior Advocate to the Victims of Atrocities

Categories	Responses in							
	Number				Percentage			
	Yes	No	Und.	Total	Yes	No	Und.	Total
Target Group	83	105	12	200	42	52	6	100

200 respondents were examined on this question. Their responses are depicted in Graph No. 100 and Table Nos. 32 and 32A. Out of these, 83 replied in affirmative, 105 in negative and 12 did not give any specific replies.[13] Thus, 42% respondents under these categories are aware about this special provision. Amongst them, 54% Post Graduates, 49% Graduates, 28% Under Graduates, 29% Matric Pass, 13% Illiterates, 52% Service Personnel, 33% Businessmen, and 22% carrying on different occupations are aware about this special provision that victims of atrocities may get services of Senior Advocate of their choice for conducting their case at government expenses.[14]

Graph No. 100 : Services of Senior Advocate to the Victims : Awareness of Target Group

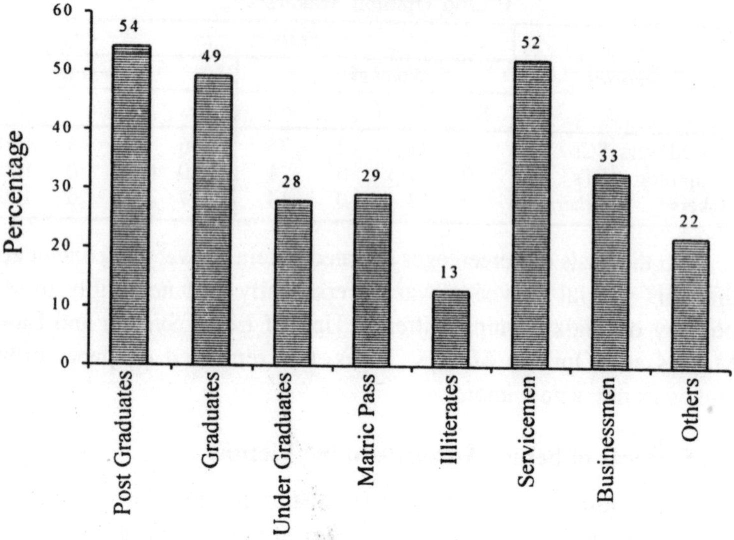

Table No. 32A : Services of Senior Advocate to the Victims: Awareness amongst Target Group

Categories	*Responses in*							
	Number				*Percentage*			
	Yes	*No*	*Und.*	*Total*	*Yes*	*No*	*Und.*	*Total*
Post Graduates	31	23	3	57	54	40	6	100
Graduates	33	31	4	68	49	46	5	100
Under Graduates	7	15	3	25	28	60	12	100
Matric Pass	10	22	2	34	29	65	6	100
Illiterates	2	14	0	16	13	87	0	100
Service Personnel	65	53	6	124	52	43	5	100
Businessmen	4	6	2	12	33	50	17	100
Other Occupations	15	49	4	68	22	72	6	100

It is, therefore, concluded that most of SCs population is not aware about this special provision except Post Graduates and Service Personnel of SCs. Percentages of awareness of Under Graduates, Matric Pass, Illiterates and persons engaged in different occupations are much below the average percentage of the rest of the group.

Question numbers 47 and 50 of the questionnaire for Different Units of the Legal System[15] and Law Makers and Opinion Makers,[16] respectively, elicited information whether they were ever given or caused to be given or seen giving the victim of atrocities, services of Senior Advocates of their choice for conducting their case at government expenses under the Act or Rules framed thereunder?

Table No. 32B : Services of Senior Advocate to the Victims: Implementation

Categories		*Responses in*							
		Number				*Percentage*			
		Yes	*No*	*Und.*	*Total*	*Yes*	*No*	*Und.*	*Total*
Different Units of Legal System	SCs	13	96	3	112	12	86	2	100
	STs	1	6	0	7	14	86	0	100
	Others	26	142	13	181	14	79	7	100
	Total	40	244	16	300	13	82	5	100
L.M. & O.M4		44	2	50	8	88	4	100	Grand
Total		44	288	18	350	13	82	5	100

350 respondents were examined on this question. Their responses are depicted in Graph No. 101 and Table Nos. 32B, 32C and 32D. Out of these, only 44 replied in affirmative, 288 in negative and

Table No. 32C : Services of Senior Advocate to the Victims: Implementation by Different Units of Legal System

Categories		*Responses in*							
		Number				*Percentage*			
		Yes	*No*	*Und.*	*Total*	*Yes*	*No*	*Und.*	*Total*
Judges	SCs	2	23	0	25	8	92	0	100
	Others	3	19	3	25	12	76	12	100
	Total	5	42	3	50	10	84	6	100
Prosecutors	SCs	1	10	0	11	9	91	0	100
	Others	2	31	6	39	5	80	15	100
	Total	3	41	6	50	6	82	12	100
Lawyers	SCs	5	27	2	34	15	79	6	100
	Others	12	51	3	66	18	77	5	100
	Total	17	78	5	100	17	78	5	100
I.A.S., P.C.S., Doctors, etc.	SCs	5	25	0	30	17	83	0	100
	STs	0	5	0	5	0	100	0	100
	Others	1	14	0	15	7	93	0	100
	Total	6	44	0	50	12	88	0	100
Police Officials	SCs	0	11	1	12	0	91	9	100
	STs	1	1	0	2	50	50	0	100
	Others	8	27	1	36	22	75	3	100
	Total	9	39	2	50	18	78	4	100
Grand Total		40	244	16	300	13	82	5	100

18 did not give any specific reply.[17] Thus, only 13% respondents of these categories used and 82% did not use this provision. Only 13% officials forming Different Units of the Legal System[18] and 8% Law Makers[19] and Opinion Makers brought this special provision into action.

Graph No. 101 : Services of Senior Advocate to the Victims Implementation by D.U.L.S. and L.M.&O.M.

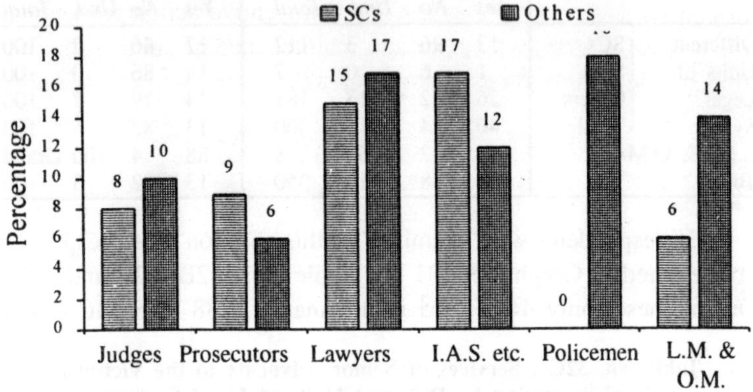

10% Judges, 6% Public Prosecutors, 17% Lawyers, 12% I.A.S., P.C.S., Doctors and other Officers and 18% Police Officials used this provision. Percentages of SC officials who used this provision are 8, 9, 15, 17 and 0, respectively.[20]

Table No. 32D : Services of Senior Advocate to the Victims: Implementation in View of Law Makers and Opinion Makers

Categories		Responses in							
		Number				Percentage			
		Yes	No	Und.	Total	Yes	No	Und.	Total
Law Makers & Opinion Makers	SCs	2	32	1	35	6	91	3	100
	STs	0	1	0	1	0	100	0	100
	Others	2	11	1	14	14	79	7	100

14% M.Ps., Legislators, Academicians, Media Persons, Social Activists, and members of N.G.Os., *etc.*, used this provision. Percentage of SCs respondent under this category is 6.[21]

On the basis of discussion and percentage narrated hereinabove, it is concluded that both officials forming Different Units of Legal

System and Law Makers and Opinion Makers too, rarely used this provision. Thus, this provision too, remained as a symbolic piece of legislation.

6.3 Taking of Preventive Action

Question numbers 43 and 46 of the questionnaire for the Different Units of the Legal System,[22] Law Makers and Opinion Makers,[23] respectively, elicited information whether respondents have ever taken or caused to be taken or seen taking preventive action for keeping the peace and good behaviour and maintenance of public order and tranquillity in the atrocity prone area?

Table No. 33 : Taking of Preventive Action

Categories		*Responses in*							
		Number				*Percentage*			
		Yes	*No*	*Und.*	*Total*	*Yes*	*No*	*Und.*	*Total*
Different Units of Legal System	SCs	22	87	3	112	20	78	2	100
	STs	0	7	0	7	0	100	0	100
	Others	28	138	15	181	15	77	8	100
	Total	50	232	18	300	17	77	6	100
L.M. & O.M.		15	32	3	50	30	64	6	100
Grand Total		65	264	21	350	19	75	6	100

Graph No. 102 : Taking of Preventive Action by D.U.L.S. and L.M. & O.M.

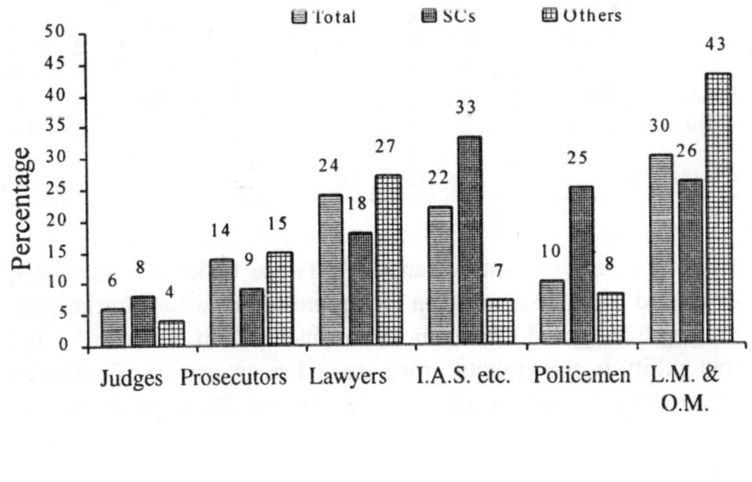

350 respondents were examined on this question. Their responses are depicted in Graph No. 102 and Table Nos. 33, 33A and 33B. Out of these, only 65 replied in affirmative, 264 in negative and 21 did not express any opinion.[24] Thus, only 19% respondents of these categories replied that they have either taken or caused to be taken or seen taking preventive action for keeping the peace and good behaviour and maintenance of public order and tranquillity in the atrocity prone area.

Only 17% officials forming Different Units of Legal System[25] and 30% Law Makers and Opinion Makers[26] brought this special provision in the action.

Table No. 33A : Taking of Preventive Action by Different Units of Legal System

Categories		*Responses in*							
		Number				*Percentage*			
		Yes	*No*	*Und.*	*Total*	*Yes*	*No*	*Und.*	*Total*
Judges	SCs	2	23	0	25	8	92	0	100
	Others	1	22	2	25	4	88	8	100
	Total	3	45	2	50	6	90	4	100
Prosecutors	SCs	1	8	2	11	9	73	18	100
	Others	6	26	7	39	15	67	18	100
	Total	7	34	9	50	14	68	18	100
Lawyers	SCs	6	28	0	34	18	82	0	100
	Others	18	43	5	66	27	65	8	100
	Total	24	71	5	100	24	71	5	100
I.A.S., P.C.S., Doctors, etc.	SCs	10	19	1	30	33	64	3	100
	STs	0	5	0	5	0	100	0	100
	Others	1	14	0	15	7	93	0	100
	Total	11	38	1	50	22	76	2	100
Police Officials	SCs	3	9	0	12	25	75	0	100
	STs	0	2	0	2	0	100	0	100
	Others	2	33	1	36	6	92	2	100
	Total	5	44	1	50	10	88	2	100
Grand Total		50	232	18	300	17	77	6	100

6% Judges, 14% Public Prosecutors, 24% Lawyers, 22% I.A.S., P.C.S., Doctors and Others and 10% Police Officials either taken or caused to be taken or seen taking preventive action for keeping the peace and good behaviour and maintenance of public order and tranquillity in the atrocity prone area. Percentages of SC officials under these categories are 8, 9, 18, 33 and 25, respectively.[27]

Table No. 33B : Law Makers and Opinion Makers on Taking of Preventive Action

Categories		*Responses in*							
		Number				*Percentage*			
		Yes	*No*	*Und.*	*Total*	*Yes*	*No*	*Und.*	*Total*
Law Makers & Opinion Makers	SCs	9	23	3	35	26	66	8	100
	STs	0	1	0	1	0	100	0	100
	Others	6	8	0	14	43	57	0	100

30% M.Ps., Legislators, Academicians, Media Persons, Social Activists and members of N.G.Os., *etc.*, used or seen the use of this provision. Percentage of SC respondents under this category is 26.[28]

On the basis of discussion and percentage narrated here in above, it is concluded that this provision was seldom used. Thus, it was not used up to the desired level that could have converted this legislation from symbolic peace of legislation into effective law.

6.4 Grant of Arm Licence

Question numbers 46 and 49 of the questionnaire for the Different Units of the Legal System[29] and Law Makers and Opinion Makers,[30] respectively, elicited information whether respondents ever granted or helped in grant or seen grant of an arm licence to the members of SCs under the Act or Rules framed thereunder?

Table No. 34 : Grant of Arm Licence

Categories		*Responses in*							
		Number				*Percentage*			
		Yes	*No*	*Und.*	*Total*	*Yes*	*No*	*Und.*	*Total*
Different Units of Legal System	SCs	13	95	4	112	12	85	3	100
	STs	0	7	0	7	0	100	0	100
	Others	15	152	14	181	8	84	8	100
	Total	28	254	18	300	9	85	6	100
L.M. & O.M.		2	46	2	50	4	92	4	100
Grand Total		30	300	20	350	9	86	5	100

350 respondents were examined on this question. Their responses are depicted in Graph No. 103 and Table Nos. 34, 34A and 34B. Out of these, 30 replied in affirmative 300 in negative and 20 did not give any specific reply.[31] Thus, only 9% respondents of these categories used and 87% did not use this provision. Only 9% officials forming

Different Units of Legal System[32] and 4% Law Makers and Opinion Makers[33] brought this special provision into action.

Table No. 34A : Grant of Arm Licence: Implementation by Different Units of Legal System

Categories		Responses in							
		Number				Percentage			
		Yes	No	Und.	Total	Yes	No	Und.	Total
Judges	SCs	1	24	0	25	4	96	0	100
	Others	0	24	1	25	0	96	4	100
	Total	1	48	1	50	2	96	2	100
Prosecutors	SCs	3	8	0	11	27	73	0	100
	Others	2	32	5	39	5	82	13	100
	Total	5	40	5	50	10	80	10	100
Lawyers	SCs	6	28	0	34	18	82	0	100
	Others	10	48	8	66	15	73	12	100
	Total	16	76	8	100	16	76	8	100
I.A.S., P.C.S., Doctors, etc.	SCs	3	24	3	30	10	80	10	100
	STs	0	5	0	5	0	100	0	100
	Others	1	14	0	15	7	93	0	100
	Total	4	43	3	50	8	86	6	100
Police Officials	SCs	0	11	1	12	0	92	8	100
	STs	0	2	0	2	0	100	0	100
	Others	2	34	0	36	6	94	0	100
	Total	2	47	1	50	4	94	2	100
Grand Total		28	254	18	300	9	85	6	100

2% Judges, 10% Public Prosecutors, 16% Lawyers, 8% I.A.S., P.C.S., Doctors and other Officers and 4% Police Officials used this provision. Percentages of SC officials who used this provision are 4, 27, 18, 10 and 0, respectively.[34]

Table No. 34B : Grant of Arm Licence: Action by Law Makers and Opinion Makers

Categories		Responses in							
		Number				Percentage			
		Yes	No	Und.	Total	Yes	No	Und.	Total
Law Makers & Opinion Makers	SCs	2	32	1	35	6	91	3	100
	STs	0	1	0	1	0	100	0	100
	Others	0	13	1	14	0	93	7	100

4% M.Ps., Legislators, Academicians, Media Persons, Social Activists and members of N.G.Os., *etc.*, used this provision. Percentage of SC respondents under this category is 6.[35]

Graph No. 103 : Grant of Arm Licence

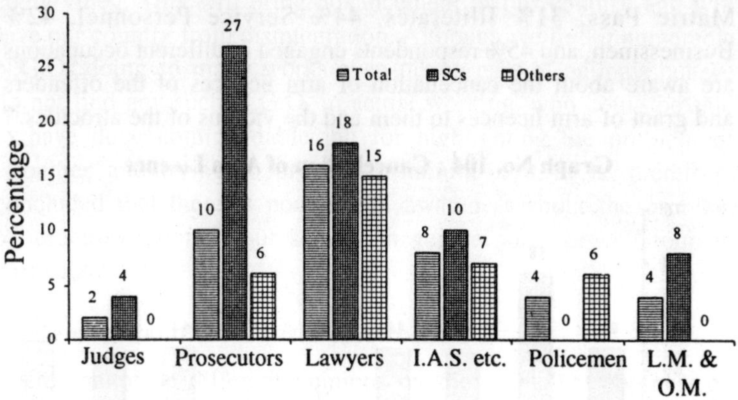

On the basis of discussion and percentage narrated hereinabove, it is concluded that only negligible officials forming part of Different Units of the Legal System used this provision. No different view can be taken regarding respondents of Law Makers and Opinion Makers. Thus, this provision too, remained as a symbolic piece of legislation.

6.5 Cancellation of Arm Licences

Question number 40 of the questionnaire on the subject for the Target Group[36] elicited information whether or not SCs are aware about the provisions of cancellation of arm licences of the offenders and grant of arm licence to the victims of atrocities and members of SCs?

Table No. 35 : Cancellation of Arm Licence

Categories	*Responses in*							
	Number				*Percentage*			
	Yes	*No*	*Und.*	*Total*	*Yes*	*No*	*Und.*	*Total*
Target Group	89	105	6	200	45	52	3	100

200 respondents were examined on this question. Their responses are depicted in Graph No. 104 and Table Nos. 35 and 35A. Out of these, 89 replied in affirmative, 105 in negative and 6 did not express any opinion.[37] Thus, 44.5% respondents under these categories were aware about this special provision. Amongst them,

58% Post Graduates, 43% Graduates, 44% Under Graduates, 32% Matric Pass, 31% Illiterates, 44% Service Personnel, 42% Businessmen, and 45% respondents engaged in different occupations are aware about the cancellation of arm licences of the offenders and grant of arm licences to them and the victims of the atrocities.[38]

Graph No. 104 : Cancellation of Arm Licence

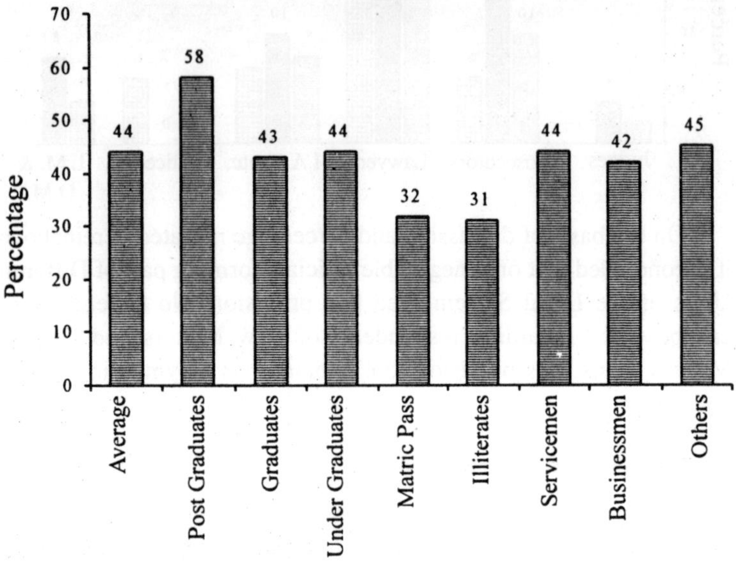

Table No. 35A : Cancellation of Arm Licence: Awareness of Target Group

Categories	*Responses in*							
	Number				*Percentage*			
	Yes	*No*	*Und.*	*Total*	*Yes*	*No*	*Und.*	*Total*
Post Graduates	33	24	0	57	58	42	0	100
Graduates	29	37	2	68	43	54	3	100
Under Graduates	11	11	3	25	44	44	12	100
Matric Pass	11	22	1	34	32	65	3	100
Illiterates	5	11	0	16	31	69	0	100
Service Personnel	55	67	2	124	44	54	2	100
Businessmen	5	6	1	12	42	50	8	100
Other Occupations	31	34	3	68	45	50	5	100

It is, therefore, concluded that most of the SCs population is not aware about this special provision except Post Graduates of

Target Group. Percentage of awareness of Matric Pass and Illiterates is much below the average percentage of the rest of the group.

Question numbers 45 and 48 of the questionnaire for the Different Units of the Legal System[39] and Law Makers and Opinion Makers,[40] respectively elicited information whether respondents ever cancelled or caused to be cancelled the arm licences of an accused of atrocity offences or any other person under the Act?

Table No. 35B : Cancellation of Arm Licence

Categories		*Responses in*							
		Number				*Percentage*			
		Yes	*No*	*Und.*	*Total*	*Yes*	*No*	*Und.*	*Total*
Different Units of Legal System	SCs	11	99	2	112	10	88	2	100
	STs	0	7	0	7	0	100	0	100
	Others	16	150	15	181	9	83	8	100
	Total	27	256	17	300	9	85	6	100
L.M. & O.M4		45	1	50	8	90	2	100	
Grand Total		31	301	18	350	9	86	5	100

Graph No. 105 : Cancellation of Arm Licence

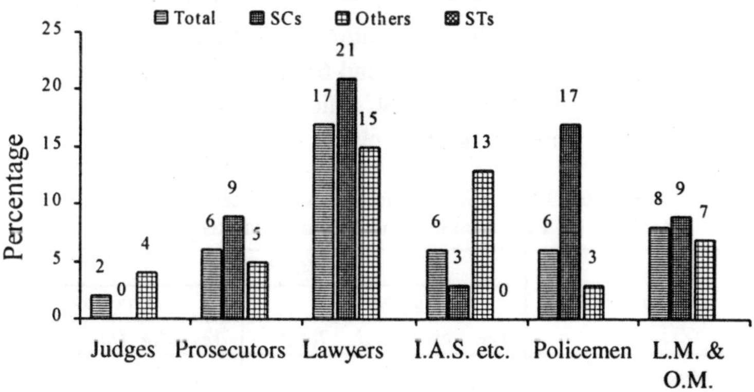

350 respondents were examined on this question. Their responses are depicted in Graph No. 105 and Table Nos. 35B, 35C and 35D. Out of these, 31 replied in affirmative, 301 in negative and 18 did not express any opinion.[41] Thus, only 9% respondents of these categories used and 86% did not use this provision. Only 9% officials forming Different Units of the Legal System[42] and 8% Law Makers and Opinion Makers[43] brought this special provision into action.

Table No. 35C : Cancellation of Arm Licence: Implementation by Different Units of Legal System

Categories		*Responses in*							
		Number				*Percentage*			
		Yes	*No*	*Und.*	*Total*	*Yes*	*No*	*Und.*	*Total*
Judges	SCs	0	25	0	25	0	100	0	100
	Others	1	22	2	25	4	88	8	100
	Total	1	47	2	50	2	94	4	100
Prosecutors	SCs	1	10	0	11	9	91	0	100
	Others	2	31	6	39	6	79	15	100
	Total	3	41	6	50	6	82	12	100
Lawyers	SCs	7	26	1	34	21	76	3	100
	Others	10	51	5	66	15	77	8	100
	Total	17	77	6	100	17	77	6	100
I.A.S., P.C.S., Doctors, etc.	SCs	1	28	1	30	3	94	3	100
	STs	0	5	0	5	0	100	0	100
	Others	2	11	2	15	13	74	13	100
	Total	3	44	3	50	6	88	6	100
Police Officials	SCs	2	10	0	12	17	83	0	100
	STs	0	2	0	2	0	100	0	100
	Others	1	35	0	36	3	97	0	100
	Total	3	47	0	50	6	94	0	100
Grand Total		27	256	17	300	9	85	6	100

2% Judges, 6% Public Prosecutors, 17% Lawyers, 6% I.A.S., P.C.S., Doctors and other Officers and 6% Police Officials used this special provision. Percentages of SC officials who used this provision are 0, 9, 21, 3 and 17, respectively.[44]

Table No. 35D : Cancellation of Arm Licence: Action by Law Makers and Opinion Makers

Categories		*Responses in*							
		Number				*Percentage*			
		Yes	*No*	*Und.*	*Total*	*Yes*	*No*	*Und.*	*Total*
Law Makers & Opinion Makers	SCs	3	32	0	35	9	91	0	100
	STs	0	1	0	1	0	100	0	100
	Others	1	12	1	14	7	86	7	100

8% M.Ps., Legislators, Academicians, Media Persons, Social Activists and members of N.G.Os., *etc.,* used this provision. Percentage of SC respondents under this category is 9.[45]

On the basis of discussion and percentage narrated hereinabove, it is concluded that both officials forming Different Units of the

Legal System and Law Makers and Opinion Makers, exceptionally and rarely used this provision. Thus, this provision too, remained as a symbolic piece of legislation.

6.6 Help to Victims of Atrocity

Question numbers 48 and 49 of the questionnaires for the Target Group[46] elicited information whether SC persons are aware that they may get medical and financial help and security from Police, District Magistrate, SCs & STs protection cells, Nodal Officers, *etc.*, and compensation as well as T.A/D.A./M.A./Transport facilities for attending court or Special Court?

Graph No. 106 : Awareness about Getting Security Medical and Financial Help

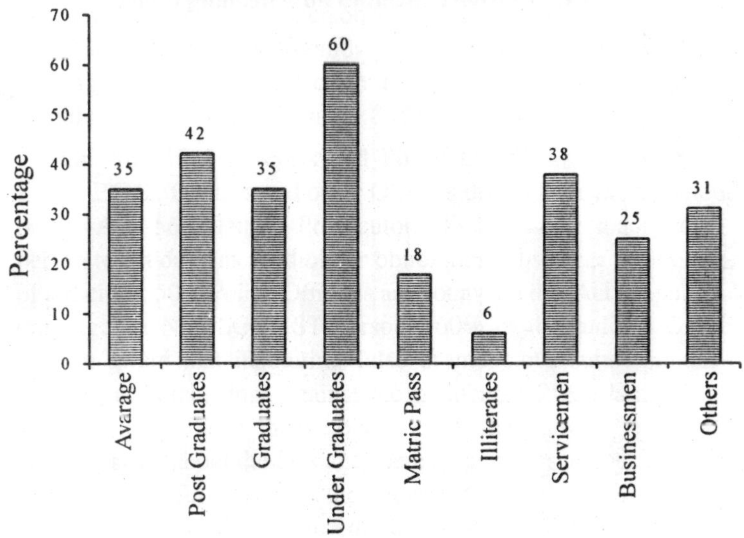

Table No. 36 : Medical and Financial Help to Victims of Atrocities

Categories	*Responses in*							
	Number				*Percentage*			
	Yes	*No*	*Und.*	*Total*	*Yes*	*No*	*Und.*	*Total*
Target Group	70	120	10	200	35	60	5	100

Table No. 36A : Compensation to Victims of Atrocities

Categories	*Responses in*							
	Number				*Percentage*			
	Yes	*No*	*Und.*	*Total*	*Yes*	*No*	*Und.*	*Total*
Target Group	66	125	9	200	33	62	5	100

200 respondents were examined on each of these questions. Their responses are depicted in Graphs Nos. 106 and 107 and Table Nos. 36, 36A, 36B and 36C. Out of these 70 and 66, respectively replied in affirmative, 120 and 125, respectively in negative and 10 and 9, respectively opted for no reply.[47] Thus 35% and 33%, respectively replied in positive and 60% and 62%, respectively replied in negative.[48]

Graph No. 107 : Awareness about getting Compensation, TA, DA, MA, Transport Facilities for Attending Court

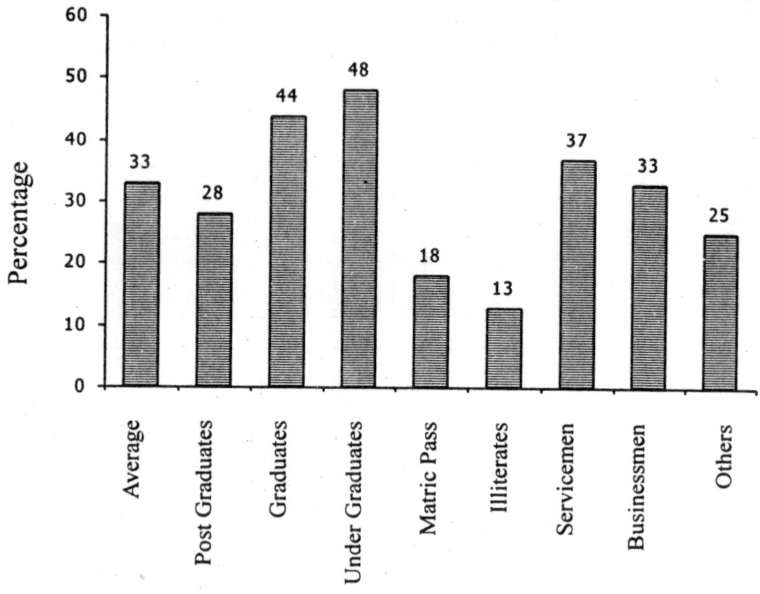

42% Post Graduates, 35% Graduates, 60% Under Graduates, 18% Matric Pass, 6% Illiterates, 38% Service Personnel, 25% Businessmen and 31% persons of Target Group engaged in different occupations are aware that they may get medical and financial help as well as security from Police, *etc.*[49]

Table No. 36B : Medical and Financial Help to Victims of Atrocities: Awareness of Target Group

Categories	Responses in							
	Number				Percentage			
	Yes	*No*	*Und.*	*Total*	*Yes*	*No*	*Und.*	*Total*
Post Graduates	24	28	5	57	42	49	9	100
Graduates	24	42	2	68	35	62	3	100
Under Graduates	15	8	2	25	60	32	8	100
Matric Pass	6	27	1	34	18	79	3	100
Illiterates	1	15	0	16	6	94	0	100
Service Personnels	47	72	5	124	38	58	4	100
Businessmen	3	7	2	12	25	58	17	100
Other Occupations	21	44	3	68	31	65	4	100

Table No. 36C : Compensation to Victims of Atrocities: Awareness of Target Group

Categories	Responses in							
	Number				Percentage			
	Yes	*No*	*Und.*	*Total*	*Yes*	*No*	*Und.*	*Total*
Post Graduates	16	37	4	57	28	65	8	100
Graduates	30	37	1	68	44	54	1	100
Under Graduates	12	11	2	25	48	44	8	100
Matric Pass	6	26	2	34	18	76	6	100
Illiterates	2	14	0	16	13	87	0	100
Service Personnel	46	74	4	124	37	60	3	100
Businessmen	4	7	1	12	33	59	8	100
Other Occupations	17	47	4	68	25	69	6	100

28% Post Graduates, 44% Graduates, 48% Under Graduates, 18% Matric Pass, 13% Illiterates, 37% Service Personnel, 33% Businessmen and 25% respondents of Target Group engaged in different occupations are aware that they may get compensation and T.A./D.A./M.A./Transport Facilities for the victims and their witnesses for attending the court or the Special Court, *etc.*[50]

It is, therefore, concluded that most of the SCs population is not aware about their rights in this regard. Even percentage of awareness of Matric Pass and Illiterates is much below the average percentage of rest of the group.

Question number 51 of the questionnaire for Law Maker and the Opinion Maker,[51] elicited information whether any of the MPs., Legislators, Academicians, Media Persons, Social Activists, members of N.G.Os., *etc.*, ever helped the victims of atrocities to obtain the compensation from the State?

Graph No. 108 : Help of Victims by Law Makers and Opinion Makers

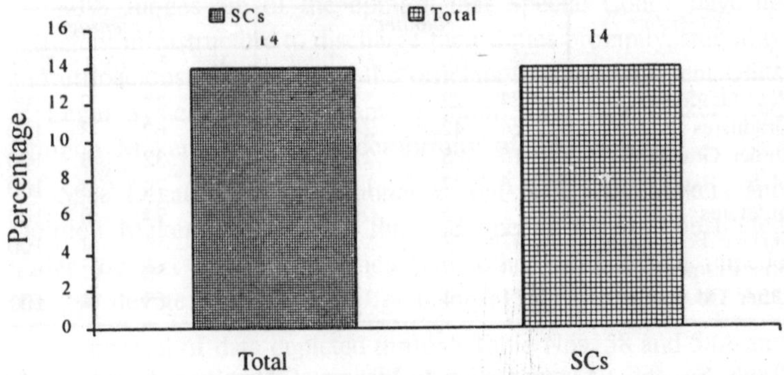

Table No. 36D : Compensation to Victims of Atrocities: Help by Law Makers and Opinion Makers

Categories		Responses in							
		Number				Percentage			
		Yes	*No*	*Und.*	*Total*	*Yes*	*No*	*Und.*	*Total*
Law Makers & Opinion Makers	SCs	5	28	2	35	14	80	6	100
	STs	0	1	0	1	0	100	0	100
	Others	2	11	1	14	14	79	7	100
	Total	7	40	3	50	14	80	6	100

50 respondents were examined on the question. Their responses are depicted in Graph No. 108 and Table No. 36D. Out of these, 7 replied in affirmative, 40 in negative and 3 did not give any specific answer.[52] Thus, only 14% reportedly, helped the victims of atrocities to get compensation from the State. There is no difference in percentage of SC respondents under this category.[53]

On the basis of this low percentage, it is concluded that very few victims of atrocities could get the compensation from the State. Thus, this provision too, remained on papers only as a piece of symbolic legislation.

6.7 Knowledge of Acquittal under the Act

Question numbers 49 and 30 of the questionnaire for Different Units of Legal System[54] and Law Makers and Opinion Makers,[55] respectively elicited information about the awareness of respondents regarding acquittal in atrocity cases?

Table No. 37 : Knowledge of Acquittal Under the Act

Categories		*Responses in*							
		Number				*Percentage*			
		Yes	*No*	*Und.*	*Total*	*Yes*	*No*	*Und.*	*Total*
Different Units of Legal System	SCs	28	79	5	112	25	71	4	100
	STs	1	5	1	7	14	72	14	100
	Others	31	135	15	181	17	75	8	100
	Total	60	219	21	300	20	73	7	100
L.M. & O.M44		5	1	50	88	10	2	100	Grand
Total		104	224	22	350	30	64	6	100

350 respondents were examined on these questions. Their responses are depicted in Graph No. 109 and Table No. 37, 37A and 37B. Out of these, 104 replied in affirmative, 224 in negative and 22 opted for giving no specific reply.[56] Thus, only 30% replied in affirmative and 64% in negative. 20% officials forming part of the Different Units of the Legal System[57] and 88% Law Makers and Opinion Makers replied in affirmative.[58]

Graph No. 109 : Knowledge of Acquittal under the Act

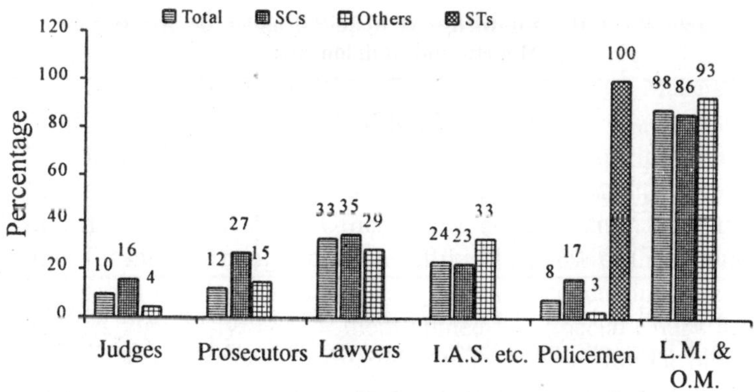

10% Judges, 12% Public Prosecutors, 33% Lawyers, 24% I.A.S., P.C.S., Doctors and other Officers, and 8% Police Officials replied in affirmative. Percentages of SC respondents under these categories are 16, 27, 35, 23 and 17 respectively.[59]

88% M.Ps., Legislators, Academicians, Media Persons, Social Activists, and members of N.G.Os., *etc.*, are found having knowledge

Table No. 37A : Knowledge of Acquittal under the Act to the Officials of Different Units of the Legal System

Categories		Responses in							
		Number				Percentage			
		Yes	No	Und.	Total	Yes	No	Und.	Total
Judges	SCs	4	20	1	25	16	80	4	100
	Others	1	22	2	25	4	88	8	100
	Total	5	42	3	50	10	84	6	100
Prosecutors	SCs	3	6	2	11	27	55	18	100
	Others	3	28	8	39	8	72	20	100
	Total	6	34	10	50	12	68	20	100
Lawyers	SCs	12	21	1	34	35	62	3	100
	Others	21	40	5	66	32	61	7	100
	Total	33	61	6	100	33	61	6	100
I.A.S.P.C.S., Doctors, etc.	SCs	7	23	0	30	23	77	0	100
	STs	0	4	1	5	0	80	20	100
	Others	5	10	0	15	33	67	0	100
	Total	12	37	1	50	24	74	2	100
Officials Police	SCs	2	9	1	12	17	75	8	100
	STs	1	1	0	2	50	50	0	100
	Others	1	35	0	36	3	97	0	100
	Total	4	45	1	50	8	90	2	100
Grand Total		60	219	21	300	20	73	7	100

Table No. 37B : Knowledge of Acquittal under the Act to Law Makers and Opinion Makers

Categories		Responses in							
		Number				Percentage			
		Yes	No	Und.	Total	Yes	No	Und.	Total
Law Makers & Opinion Makers	SCs	30	5	0	35	86	14	0	100
	STs	1	0	0	1	100	0	0	100
	Others	13	0	1	14	93	0	7	100

of acquittal in trials of atrocity cases. Percentages of SCs and Non SC & ST persons under these categories are 86 and 93, respectively.[60]

It is, therefore, concluded that M.Ps., Legislators, Academicians, Media Persons, Social Activists, and member of N.G.Os., *etc.*, are of the view that most of the atrocity trials ended in acquittal. Comparative study of awareness amongst that officials forming part of Different Units of the Legal System regarding acquittal and conviction has also established that more cases ended in acquittals than convictions.

6.8 Role of Concerned Officials

Question numbers 54 and 40 on the questionnaire for Different Units of the Legal System,[61] and Law Makers and Opinion Makers,[62] respectively, elicited information whether or not there is lack of interest in concerned official to implement the Act in letter and spirit?

Table No. 38 : Lack of Interest of Concerned Officials

Categories		*Responses in*							
		Number				*Percentage*			
		Yes	*No*	*Und.*	*Total*	*Yes*	*No*	*Und.*	*Total*
Different Units of Legal System	SCs	87	14	11	112	78	12	10	100
	STs	4	2	1	7	57	29	14	100
	Others	106	38	37	181	59	21	20	100
	Total	197	54	49	300	66	18	16	100
L.M. & O.M37		8	5	50	74	16	10	100 Grand	
Total		234	62	54	350	67	18	15	100

Graph No. 110 : Lack of Interest in Concerned Officials to Implement the Act

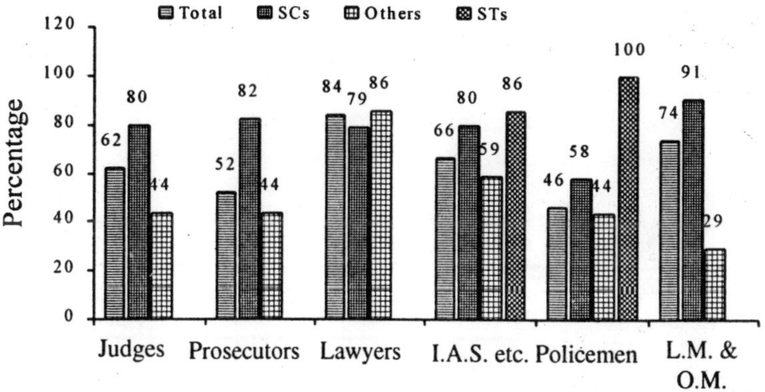

350 respondents were examined on this question. Their responses are depicted in Graph No. 110 and Table Nos. 38, 38A and 38B. Out of these, 234 replied in affirmative, 62 in negative and 54 did not give any specific reply.[63] Thus, 67% respondents replied in affirmative, 18% in negative and 15% did not express any opinion on this aspect. 66% officials forming part of Different Units of Legal System[64] and 74% Law Makers and Opinion Makers[65] are of the view that there is lack of interest on the part of concerned officials to implement the provisions of the Act in letter and spirit.

Table No. 38A : Different Units of the Legal System on Lack of Interest in Concerned Officials to Implement the Act

Categories		*Responses in*							
		Number				*Percentage*			
		Yes	*No*	*Und.*	*Total*	*Yes*	*No*	*Und.*	*Total*
Judges	SCs	20	2	3	25	80	8	12	100
	Others	11	2	12	25	44	8	48	100
	Total	31	4	15	50	62	8	30	100
Prosecutors	SCs	9	1	1	11	82	9	9	100
	Others	17	14	8	39	44	36	20	100
	Total	26	15	9	50	52	30	18	100
Lawyers	SCs	27	4	3	34	79	12	9	100
	Others	57	2	7	66	86	3	11	100
	Total	84	6	10	100	84	6	10	100
I.A.S., P.C.S., Doctors, etc.	SCs	24	3	3	30	80	10	10	100
	STs	4	1	0	5	80	20	0	100
	Others	5	3	7	15	33	20	47	100
	Total	33	7	10	50	66	14	20	100
Police Officials	SCs	7	4	1	12	58	34	8	100
	STs	0	1	1	2	0	50	50	100
	Others	16	17	3	36	44	48	8	100
	Total	23	22	5	50	46	44	10	100
Grand Total		197	54	49	300	66	18	16	100

62% Judges, 52% Public Prosecutors, 84% Lawyers, 66% I.A.S., P.C.S., Doctors and other Officers, 46% Police Officials also hold this view. Percentages of SC officials having similar opinion in this regard are 80, 82, 79, 80 and 58, respectively.[66]

Table No. 38B : Law Makers and Opinion Makers on Lack of Interest in Concerned Officials to Implement the Act

Categories		*Responses in*							
		Number				*Percentage*			
		Yes	*No*	*Und.*	*Total*	*Yes*	*No*	*Und.*	*Total*
Law Makers & Opinion Makers	SCs	32	2	1	35	91	6	3	100
	STs	1	0	0	1	100	0	0	100
	Others	4	6	4	14	29	42	29	100

74% M.Ps., Legislators, Academicians, Media Persons, Social Activists and members of N.G.Os., *etc.*, opined the same. Percentage of SC respondents in these categories is 91.[67]

On the basis of discussion and percentage narrated hereinabove, it is concluded that most of the respondents examined are of the view that there is lack of interest in concerned officials to implement the provisions of the Act in letter and spirit.

6.9 Attitude of the Investigating Officers

Question number 32 of the questionnaire for the Law Makers and the Opinion Makers,[68] elicited information as to what is the opinion of M.Ps., Legislators, Academicians, Media Persons, Social Activists, member of N.G.Os., *etc.,* in respect of attitude of the investigating officers and special officers? Whether or not they have been discharging their duties for giving effect to the provisions of the Act in letter and spirit?

Graph No. 111 : Attitude of the Investigating Officers and Special Public Prosecutors

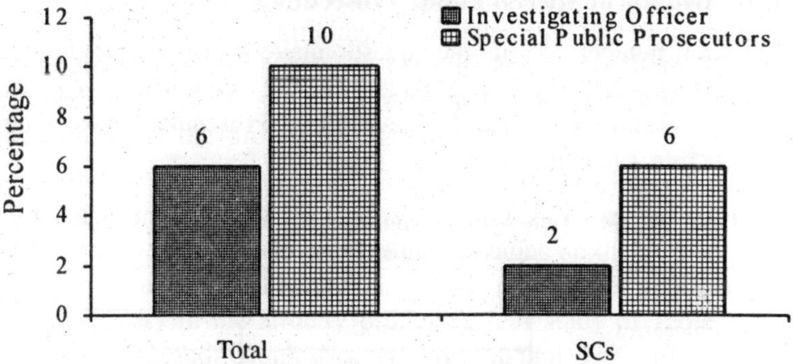

Table No. 39 : Law Makers and Opinion Makers on Attitude of Investigating Officers to Implement the Act

Categories		*Responses in*							
		Number				*Percentage*			
		Yes	*No*	*Und.*	*Total*	*Yes*	*No*	*Und.*	*Total*
Law Makers & Opinion Makers	SCs	1	30	4	35	3	86	11	100
	STs	1	0	0	1	100	0	0	100
	Others	13	0	1	14	93	0	7	100
	Total	3	38	9	50	6	76	18	100

50 respondents were examined on this question. Their responses are depicted in Graph No. 111 and Table No. 39. Out of these, 3 replied in affirmative, 38 in negative and 9 did not express any opinion.[69] Thus, 6% of the respondents under these categories are

of the view that Investigating Officers and Special Police Officers have been discharging their duties in letter and spirit.[70] Percentage of SC respondents under this category is only 3.[71]

76% of the respondents under these categories replied definitely that the Investigating Officer and Special Officer have not been discharging their duties for giving effect to the provisions of the Act in letter and spirit.[72] 18% did not express any opinion on this aspect.[73]

On the basis of discussion and percentage narrated hereinabove, it is concluded that the officials entrusted with the task of giving effect to provisions of the Act are not doing their duties to the best of their capacities and abilities. Thus, their role and attitude in implementing this Act was found negative.

6.10 Attitude of Special Public Prosecutors

Question number 35 of the questionnaire on the subject for the Law Makers and Opinion Makers[74] elicited information on the issue whether or not Special Public Prosecutors have been conducting cases under the Act vigorously?

Table No. 40 : Law Makers and Opinion Makers on Attitude of Special Public Prosecutors

Categories		*Responses in*							
		Number				*Percentage*			
		Yes	*No*	*Und.*	*Total*	*Yes*	*No*	*Und.*	*Total*
Law Makers & Opinion Makers	SCs	2	30	3	35	6	86	8	100
	STs	0	1	0	1	0	100	0	100
	Others	3	7	4	14	21	50	29	100
	Total	5	38	7	50	10	76	14	100

50 respondents were examined on this question. Their responses are depicted in Graph No. 111 and Table No. 40. Out of these, only 5 replied in positive, 38 in negative and 7 did not give any specific reply.[75] Thus, only 10% M.Ps., Legislators, Academicians, Media Persons, Social Activists, and members of N.G.Os., *etc.*, are of the view that Special Public Prosecutors have been conducting the cases under the Act vigorously. Percentage of SC respondents holding this view is only 6.[76]

Thus, negligible numbers of respondents have opined that Special Public Prosecutors have been conducting their cases vigorously under the Act.

It is, therefore, concluded that the Special Public Prosecutors have not been conducting their cases under the Act vigorously. Resultantly, their attitude towards implementation of this Act is not positive.

6.11 Willingness of Witnesses

Question number 59 of the questionnaire for the Different Units of the Legal System[77] elicited information whether the witnesses of the offences under the Act easily appear and depose before the Special Court?

Table No. 41 : Willingness of Witnesses of Atrocities

Categories		*Responses in*							
		Number				*Percentage*			
		Yes	*No*	*Und.*	*Total*	*Yes*	*No*	*Und.*	*Total*
Different Units of Legal System	SCs	15	82	15	112	13	74	13	100
	STs	1	6	0	7	14	86	0	100
	Others	43	83	55	181	24	46	30	100
	Total	59	171	70	300	20	57	23	100

Graph No. 112 : Willingness of Witnesses to Depose before Special Court

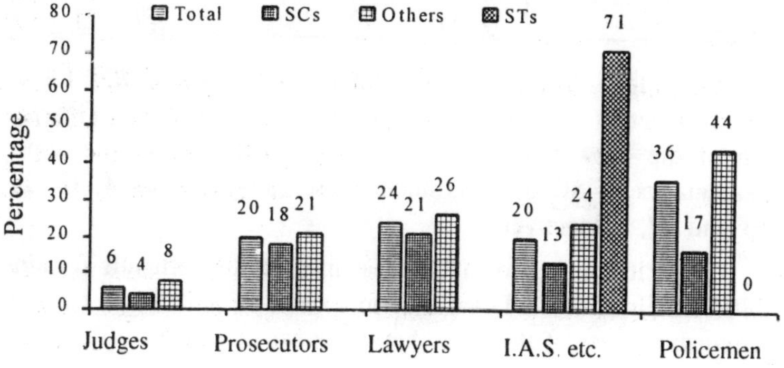

300 respondents were examined on this question. Their responses are depicted in Graph No. 112 and Table Nos. 41and 41A. Out of these, 59 replied in affirmative, 171 in negative and 70 did not express any opinion.[78] Thus, less than 20% respondents of these categories are of the view that witnesses easily appear whereas 57% of the respondents think that witnesses of offences of atrocities do not appear easily before the Special Court for giving their statements.[79]

Table No. 41A : Different Units of Legal System on Willingness of Witnesses of Atrocities

Categories		*Responses in*							
		Number				*Percentage*			
		Yes	*No*	*Und.*	*Total*	*Yes*	*No*	*Und.*	*Total*
Judges	SCs	1	17	7	25	4	78	28	100
	Others	2	8	15	25	8	32	60	100
	Total	3	25	22	50	6	50	44	100
Prosecutors	SCs	2	6	3	11	18	55	27	100
	Others	8	17	14	39	20	44	36	100
	Total	10	23	17	50	20	46	34	100
Lawyers	SCs	7	26	1	34	21	76	3	100
	Others	17	34	15	66	26	52	22	100
	Total	24	60	16	100	24	60	16	100
I.A.S., P.C.S., Doctors, etc.	SCs	4	24	2	30	13	80	7	100
	STs	1	4	0	5	20	80	0	100
	Others	0	8	7	15	0	53	47	100
	Total	10	36	4	50	20	72	8	100
Police Officials	SCs	2	9	1	12	17	75	8	100
	STs	0	2	0	2	0	100	0	100
	Others	16	16	4	36	44	44	12	100
	Total	18	27	5	50	36	54	10	100
Grand Total		59	171	70	300	20	57	23	100

6% Judges, 20% Public Prosecutors, 24% Lawyers, 20% I.A.S., P.C.S., Doctors and other Officers, *etc.*, and 36% Police Officials are of the view that witnesses appear easily before the court. Percentages of SC officials under these categories are 4, 18, 21, 13 and 17, respectively.[80]

Thus, it can be concluded that most of the officials forming Different Units of the Legal System, except the percentage narrated hereinabove, are of the view that witnesses of atrocity offences do not appear easily to give their statements before the court.

6.12 Identification of Atrocities Prone Area

Question numbers 41 and 28 of the questionnaires for Different Units of the Legal System[81] and Law Makers and Opinion Makers,[82] respectively, elicited information from the respondents whether or not any part of their district has been identified as atrocities prone area?

Table No. 42 : Identification of Atrocities Prone Area

Categories		*Responses in*							
		Number				*Percentage*			
		Yes	*No*	*Und.*	*Total*	*Yes*	*No*	*Und.*	*Total*
Different Units of Legal System	SCs	26	75	11	112	23	67	10	100
	STs	1	6	0	7	14	86	0	100
	Others	13	140	28	181	7	78	15	100
	Total	40	221	39	300	13	74	13	100
L.M. & O.M.		4	40	6	50	8	80	12	100
Grand Total		44	261	45	350	12	75	13	100

350 respondents were examined on this question. Their responses are depicted in Graph No. 113 and Table Nos. 42, 42A and 42B. Out of these, 44 replied in affirmative, 261 in negative and 45 did not give any specific answer.[83] Thus, 12% respondents replied in positive and 75% in negative.

13% officials forming part of Different Units of Legal System[84] and 8% Law Makers and Opinion Makers[85] have knowledge of identification of atrocities prone area in their district.

Graph No. 113 : Identification of Atrocities Prone Area

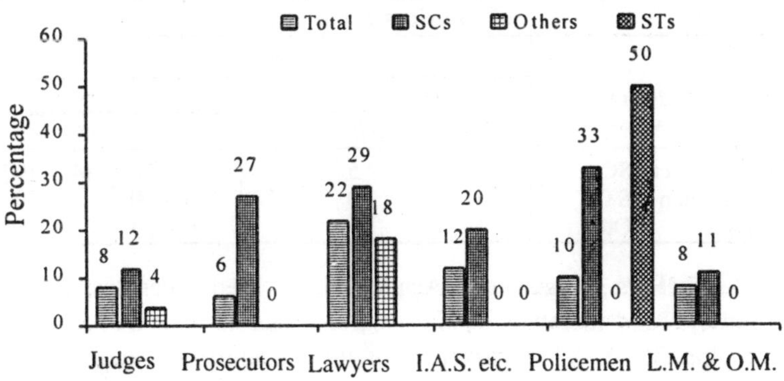

Table No. 42A : Different Units of Legal System on Identification of Atrocities Prone Area

Categories		*Responses in*							
		Number				*Percentage*			
		Yes	*No*	*Und.*	*Total*	*Yes*	*No*	*Und.*	*Total*
Judges	SCs	3	20	2	25	12	80	8	100
	Others	1	18	6	25	4	72	24	100
	Total	4	38	8	50	8	76	16	100
Prosecutors	SCs	3	7	1	11	27	64	9	100
	Others	0	27	12	39	0	69	31	100
	Total	3	34	13	50	6	68	26	100
Lawyers	SCs	10	20	4	34	29	59	12	100
	Others	12	48	6	66	18	73	9	100
	Total	22	68	10	100	22	68	10	100
I.A.S., P.C.S., Doctors, etc.	SCs	6	21	3	30	20	70	10	100
	STs	0	5	0	5	0	100	0	100
	Others	0	13	2	15	0	87	13	100
	Total	6	39	5	50	12	78	10	100
Police Officials	SCs	4	7	1	12	33	59	8	100
	STs	1	1	0	2	50	50	0	100
	Others	0	34	2	36	0	94	6	100
	Total	5	42	3	50	10	84	6	100
Grand Total		40	221	39	300	13	74	13	100

8% Judges, 6% Public Prosecutors, 22% Lawyers, 12% I.A.S., P.C.S., Doctors and other Officers and 10% Police Officials are aware about atrocities prone area. Percentages of SC respondents having this awareness are 12, 27, 29, 20 and 33, respectively. Level of awareness of Non SC & ST respondents in this regard is 4, 0, 18, 0 and 0 per cent, respectively.[86]

Table No. 42B : Law Makers and Opinion Makers on Identification of Atrocities Prone Area

Categories		*Responses in*							
		Number				*Percentage*			
		Yes	*No*	*Und.*	*Total*	*Yes*	*No*	*Und.*	*Total*
Law Makers & Opinion Makers	SCs	4	26	5	35	11	75	14	100
	STs	0	1	0	1	0	100	0	100
	Others	0	13	1	14	0	93	7	100

8% MPs., Legislators, Academicians, Media Persons, Social Activists and members of N.G.Os., *etc.*, and 11% of SCs and 0% of Non SC & ST respondents of this category are aware about atrocities prone area in their districts.[87]

6.13 Working of Scheduled Castes and Scheduled Tribes Protection Cells

Question number 33 of the questionnaire for Law Makers and Opinion Makers[88] elicited information whether or not SCs and STs Protection Cells are functioning effectively in combating atrocities on the members of SCs?

Table No. 43 : Law Makers and Opinion Makers on Working of SCs and STs Protection Cells

Categories		Responses in							
		Number				Percentage			
		Yes	*No*	*Und.*	*Total*	*Yes*	*No*	*Und.*	*Total*
Law Makers & Opinion Makers	SCs	1	31	3	35	3	89	8	100
	STs	0	1	0	1	0	100	0	100
	Others	1	8	5	14	7	57	36	100
	Total	2	40	8	50	4	80	16	100

50 respondents were examined on this question. Their responses are depicted in Graph No. 114 and Table No. 43. Out of these, only 2 replied in affirmative, 40 replied in negative and 8 did not express any opinion.[89] Thus, only 4% are of the view and 80% are not of the view that SCs & STs Protection Cells are functioning effectively in combating atrocities on SCs Percentage of SCs respondents who replied in affirmative is only 3.[90]

Graph No. 114 : Working of SCs & STs Protection Cell Co-ordination amongst Nodal Officer/DM/SP/IO Etc.

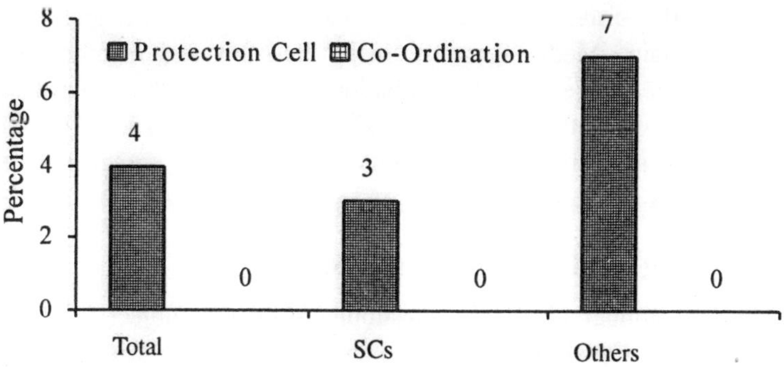

It is, therefore, concluded that M.Ps., Legislators, Academicians, Media Persons, Social Activists and members of N.G.Os., *etc.*, in total, except 4%, are of the view that SCs & STs Protection Cells are not functioning effectively in combating atrocities on the members of SCs

6.14 Co-ordination amongst Nodal Officer, District Magistrate, Superintendent of Police, Investigating Officer, etc.

Question number 34 of the questionnaire for Law Makers and Opinion Makers[91] elicited information whether or not the Nodal Officers have been effectively coordinating the functioning of the District Magistrate, Superintendent of Police, Investigating Officer, *etc.,* for real implementation of the provisions of the Act?

Table No. 44 : Law Makers and Opinion Makers on Co-ordination amongst Nodal Officer, D.M., S.P. and I.O.

Categories		Responses in							
		Number				Percentage			
		Yes	No	Und.	Total	Yes	No	Und.	Total
Law Makers & Opinion Makers	SCs	0	32	3	35	0	91	9	100
	STs	0	1	0	1	0	100	0	100
	Others	0	8	6	14	0	57	43	100
	Total	0	41	9	50	0	82	18	100

50 respondents were examined on this question. Their responses are depicted in Graph No. 114 and Table No. 44. Out of these, none replied in affirmative, 41 replied in negative and 9 did not express any opinion.[92]

It is, therefore, concluded that in view of the M.Ps., Legislators, Academicians, Media Persons, Social Activists and members of N.G.Os., *etc.,* there is no co-ordination amongst the above narrated officials to give effect to the provisions of the Act. There is total agreement on this view between SCs and other categories of respondents.

6.15 Setting up of Awareness Centres, etc.

Question number 45 of the questionnaire on the subject for Law Makers and Opinion Makers,[93] elicited information from M.Ps., Legislators, Media Persons, Social Activists and members of N.G.Os., *etc.*, whether they have ever set up any awareness centre and organized workshop to educate members of SCs about the rights and protections available to them?

Table No. 45 : Setting up of Awareness Centres by Law Makers and Opinion Makers

Categories		Responses in							
		Number				Percentage			
		Yes	*No*	*Und.*	*Total*	*Yes*	*No*	*Und.*	*Total*
Law Makers & Opinion Makers	SCs	19	15	1	35	54	43	3	100
	STs	0	1	0	1	0	100	0	100
	Others	5	9	0	14	36	64	0	100
	Total	24	25	1	50	48	50	2	100

Graph No. 115 : Setting up of Awareness Centres by Law Makers and Opinion Makers

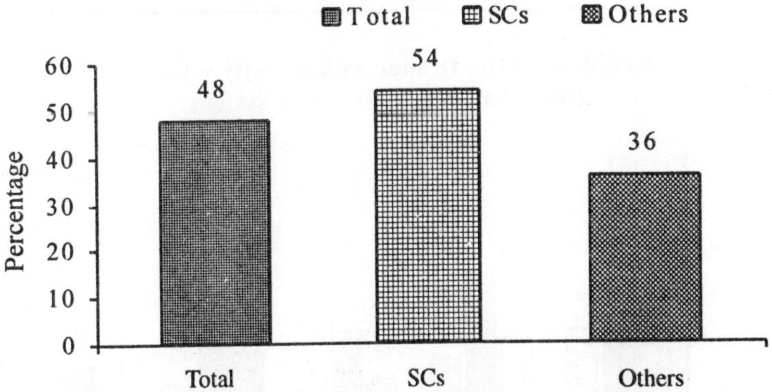

50 respondents were examined on this question. Their responses are depicted in Graph No. 115 and Table No. 45. Out of these, 24 replied in affirmative, 25 in negative and one did not give any specific answer.[94] Thus, only 48% respondents of these groups organized workshop and set up awareness centres to educate the members of SCs about the rights and protections available to them. Percentage of SC respondents is 54 and Non-SC & ST is 36.[95]

On the basis of above percentage, it is concluded that majority of the M.Ps., Legislators, Media Persons, Social Activists and members of N.G.Os. have not set up any awareness centres and not organized any workshops to educate the members of SCs about the rights and protections available to them.

6.16 Dealing with Atrocity Cases

Question number 42 of the questionnaire on the subject for Different Units of Legal System[96] elicited information from Police Personnel, Prosecútors, Lawyers, Doctors, Judges and Magistrates whether or not they ever dealt with any case of atrocity under the Act?

Table No. 46 : Dealing with Atrocity Cases

Categories		*Responses in*							
		Number				*Percentage*			
		Yes	*No*	*Und.*	*Total*	*Yes*	*No*	*Und.*	*Total*
Different Units of Legal System	SCs	35	73	4	112	31	65	4	100
	STs	0	7	0	7	0	100	0	100
	Others	24	147	10	181	13	81	6	100
	Total	59	227	14	300	20	75	5	100

Graph No. 116 : Dealing with Atrocity Case by Different Units of the Legal System

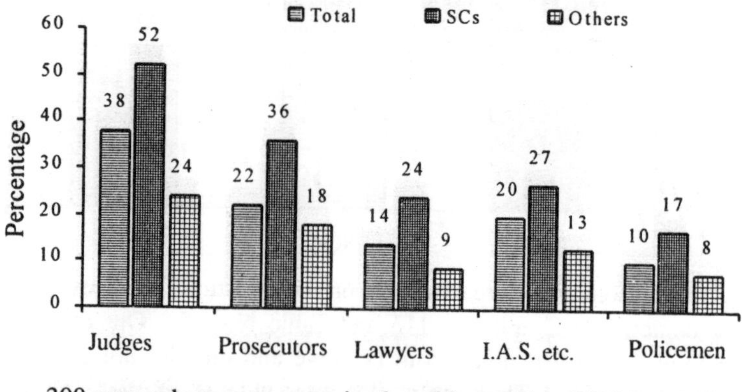

300 respondents were examined on this question. Their responses are depicted in Graph No. 116 and Table Nos. 46 and 46A. Out of these, 59 replied in affirmative, 227 in negative and 14 did not give any specific answer.[97] Thus, only about 20% of the respondents were found who have dealt with atrocity cases.[98]

Table No. 46A : Dealing With Atrocity Cases by Officials of Different Units of Legal System

Categories		Responses in Number				Responses in Percentage			
		Yes	*No*	*Und.*	*Total*	*Yes*	*No*	*Und.*	*Total*
Judges	SCs	13	12	0	25	52	48	0	100
	Others	6	18	1	25	24	72	4	100
	Total	19	30	1	50	38	60	2	100
Prosecutors	SCs	4	5	2	11	37	45	18	100
	Others	7	27	5	39	18	69	13	100
	Total	11	32	7	50	22	64	14	100
Lawyers	SCs	8	26	0	34	24	76	0	100
	Others	6	56	4	66	9	85	6	100
	Total	14	82	4	100	14	82	4	100
I.A.S. P.C.S., Doctors, etc.	SCs	8	21	1	30	26	70	4	100
	STs	0	5	0	5	0	100	0	100
	Others	2	13	0	15	13	87	0	100
	Total	10	39	1	50	20	78	2	100
Police Officials	SCs	2	9	1	12	17	75	8	100
	STs	0	2	0	2	0	100	0	100
	Others	3	33	0	36	8	92	0	100
	Total	5	44	1	50	10	88	2	100
Grand Total		59	227	14	300	20	75	5	100

38% Judges, 22% Public Prosecutors, 14% Lawyers, 20% I.A.S., P.C.S., Doctors and other Officers and 10% Police Officers have dealt with atrocity cases.[99]

On the basis of above percentage, it is concluded that very minimum percentage of atrocities were reported to police and resultantly, very few officials forming Different Units of Legal System had occasion to deal with atrocity cases.

Notes and References

1. *See*, annexures 1 and 2. The question is, "Do you know that under the Act, properties of offender may be attached and properties of convict may be forfeited?"
2. *See*, Table No. 31.
3. *See*, Graph No. 22.
4. *Ibid.*
5. *See*, annexures 1 and 3. The question is, "Have you ever attached or caused to be attached the properties of an offender and forfeited and caused to be forfeited the properties of a convict of offence of atrocity?"
6. *Ibid.* and annexures 1 and 4.

7. *See*, Table No. 31B.
8. *See*, Graph No. 47.
9. *See*, Graph No. 46.
10. *See*, Graph Nos. 48 to 52.
11. *See*, Graph No. 46.
12. *See*, annexures 1 and 2. The question is, "Do you know that victim of atrocity may get services of senior advocate for conducting his case at government expenses?"
13. *See*, Table No. 32.
14. *See*, Graph No. 22.
15. *See*, annexures 1 and 3. The question is, "Have you given or caused to be given or seen giving the victim of atrocity, service of senior Advocate of his choice for conducting his case at Government expenses under the Act or Rules framed thereunder?"
16. *Ibid.* and annexures 1 and 4.
17. *See*, Table No. 32B.
18. *See*, Graph No. 47.
19. *See*, Graph No. 46.
20. *See*, Graph Nos. 48 to 52.
21. *See*, Graph No. 46.
22. *See*, annexures 1 and 3. The question is, "Have you taken or caused to be taken or seen taking preventive action for keeping the peace and good behaviour and maintenance of public order and tranquillity in the atrocity prone area?"
23. *Ibid.* and annexures 1 and 4.
24. *See*, Table No. 33.
25. *See*, Graph No. 47.
26. *See*, Graph No. 46.
27. *See*, Graph Nos. 48 to 52.
28. *See*, Graph No. 46.
29. *See*, annexures 1 and 3. The question is, "Have you ever granted or helped in grant or seen grant of an arm licence to members of the SCs under the Act or Rules framed thereunder?"
30. *Ibid.* and annexures 1 and 4.
31. *See*, Table No. 34.
32. *See*, Graph No. 47.
33. *See*, Graph No. 46.
34. *See*, Graph Nos. 48 to 52.
35. *See*, Graph No. 46.
36. *See*, annexures 1 and 2. The question is, "Do you know that arm lieence of accused of atrocity, *etc.* may be cancelled and arm licence to victim of atrocity and members of SCs may be given?"
37. *See*, Table No. 35.
38. *See*, Graph No. 22.
39. *See*, annexures 1 and 3. The question is, "Have you ever cancelled or caused to be cancelled or seen cancellation of the arm licence of an accused or any other person under the Act or Rules framed thereunder?"

40. *Ibid.* and annexures 1 and 4.
41. *See*, Table No. 35B.
42. *See*, Graph No. 47.
43. *See*, Graph No. 46.
44. *See*, Graph Nos. 48 to 52.
45. *See*, Graph No. 46.
46. *See*, annexures 1 and 2. The questions are, "Do you know that you should get medical and financial help as well as security from police D.M./SC and ST Protection Cell/Nodal Officer, etc.?" and "Do you know that you should get compensation and you and your witnesses should get TA/DA/MA/Transport facilities for attending court?"
47. *See*, Table Nos. 36 and 36A.
48. *See*, Graph No. 43.
49. *Ibid.*
50. *Ibid.*
51. *See*, annexures 1 and 4. The question is, "Have you ever helped the victim of atrocities to obtain compensation from the State?"
52. *See*, Table No. 36D.
53. *See*, Graph No. 46.
54. *See*, annexures 1 and 2. The question is, "Do you know any case of atrocities trial which ended in acquittal?"
55. *Ibid.* and annexures 1 and 4.
56. *See*, Table No. 37.
57. *See*, Graph No. 47.
58. *See*, Graph No. 44.
59. *See*, Graph Nos. 48 to 52.
60. *See*, Graph No. 44.
61. *See*, annexures 1 and 3. The question is, "Do you think that there is lack of interest in concerned officials to implement the Act in letter and spirit?"
62. *Ibid.* and annexures 1 and 4.
63. *See*, Table No. 38.
64. *See*, Graph No. 53.
65. *See*, Graph No. 45.
66. *See*, Graph Nos. 54 to 58.
67. *See*, Graph No. 45.
68. *See*, annexures 1 and 4. The question is, "Do you think that the investigating officers and special officers have been discharging their duties for giving effect to the provisions of the Act in letter and spirit?"
69. *See*, Graph No. 39.
70. *See*, Graph No. 44.
71. *Ibid.*
72. *Supra*, note 69.
73. *Ibid.*
74. *See*, annexures 1 and 4. The question is, "Do you think that the special public prosecutors have been conducting cases under the Act vigorously?"

75. *See*, Table No. 31.
76. *See*, Graph No. 40.
77. *See*, annexures 1 and 3. The question is, "Do you think that witnesses of the offences under the Act easily appear and depose before the special court?"
78. *See*, Table No. 41.
79. *See*, Graph No. 53.
80. *See*, Graph Nos. 54 to 58.
81. *See*, annexures 1 and 3. The question is, "Whether any part of your District is identified as atrocities prone area?"
82. *Ibid.* and annexures 1 and 4.
83. *See*, Table No. 42.
84. *See*, Graph No. 47.
85. *See*, Graph No. 44.
86. *See*, Graph Nos. 48 to 52.
87. *See*, Graph No. 44.
88. *See*, annexures 1 and 4. The question is, "Do you think that the SCs and the Scheduled Tribes Protection Cells have been functioning effectively in combating atrocities on the members of SCs?"
89. *See*, Table No. 43.
90. *See*, Graph No. 44.
91. *See*, annexures 1 and 4. The question is, "Do you think that the Nodal officers have been effectively co-ordinating the functioning of the DMs, SPs and investigating officers, *etc.*, for real implementation of the provisions of the Act?"
92. *See*, Table No. 44.
93. *See*, annexures 1 and 4. The question is, "Have you ever set up Awareness Centres and organised workshops to educate members of SCs about the rights and protections available to them?"
94. *See*, Table No. 45.
95. *See*, Graph No. 46.
96. *See*, annexures 1 and 3. The question is, "Have you ever dealt with any case of atrocities under the Act in the capacity of police personnel or prosecutor or lawyer or doctor or judge or magistrate or in any other capacity?"
97. *See*, Table No. 46.
98. *See*, Graph No. 47.
99. *See*, Graph Nos. 48 to 52.

CHAPTER 7

EMPIRICAL STUDY OF THE PROVISIONS OF THE ACT : Reasons For Its Failure

7.1 Non-Coverage of All Possible Forms of the Atrocities

Question number 22 of the questionnaire for the Law Makers and the Opinion Makers,[1] elicited information whether or not M.Ps., Legislators, Academicians, Media Persons, Social Activists and member of N.G.Os., *etc.*, think that the Act has covered all the possible forms of atrocities?

Table No. 47 : Non-Coverage of All Possible Forms of Atrocities

Categories		*Responses in*							
		Number				*Percentage*			
		Yes	*No*	*Und.*	*Total*	*Yes*	*No*	*Und.*	*Total*
Law Makers & Opinion Makers	SCs	5	24	6	35	14	69	17	100
	STs	0	0	1	1	0	0	100	100
	Others	3	6	5	14	21	43	36	100
	Total	8	30	12	50	16	60	24	100

50 respondents were examined on this question. Their responses are depicted in Graph No. 117 and Table No. 47. Out of these, 8 replied in positive, 30 in negative and 12 did not give any specific reply.[2] Thus, only 16% of the Law Makers and Opinion Makers are of the view that Act has covered all the possible forms of atrocities.[3] Percentage of SC respondents under this category is 14.

60% Law Makers and Opinion Makers are of the definite view that the Act has not covered all the possible forms of atrocities. 24% respondents of these categories remained neutral.[4]

It is, therefore, concluded that the Act is not complete in itself, as all possible forms of atrocities have not been dealt with under the Act.

Graph No. 117 : Non-Converage of All Possible Forms of the Atrocities

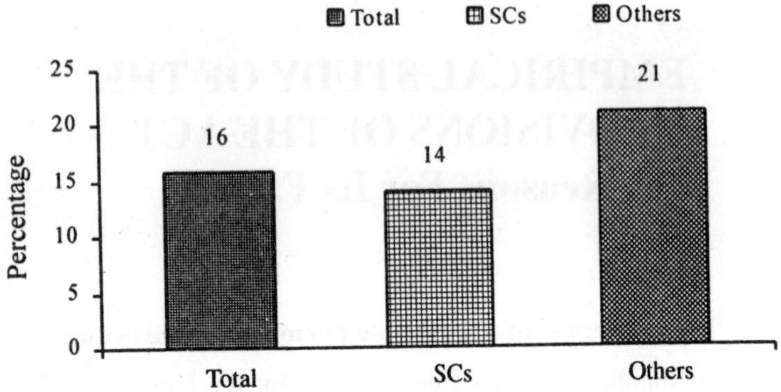

7.2 Facing Atrocities but not Reporting them to Police

Question numbers 41 and 42 of the questionnaire on the subject for Target Group[5] elicited information from SC respondents whether they have ever faced atrocities and whether they had lodged F.I.R. to the police about the commission of atrocities, respectively?

Table No. 48 : Facing Atrocities by Target Group

Categories	*Responses in*							
	Number				*Percentage*			
	Yes	*No*	*Und.*	*Total*	*Yes*	*No*	*Und.*	*Total*
Target Group	75	117	8	200	38	58	4	100

Table No. 48A : Reporting of Atrocities by Target Group

Categoris	*Responses in*							
	Number				*Percentage*			
	Yes	*No*	*Und.*	*Total*	*Yes*	*No*	*Und.*	*Total*
Target Group	32	138	30	200	16	69	15	100

On both the questions, 200 respondents were examined. Their responses are depicted in Graph No. 118 and Table Nos. 48, 48A, 48B and 48C. Out of these, 75 and 32 respectively, replied in affirmative, 117 and 138 respectively, replied in negative and 8 and

30 respectively, did not give any specific reply.[6] Thus, 38% and 16%, respectively, replied in affirmative.[7]

Graph No. 118 : Facing Atrocities, Reporting of Atrocities to Police

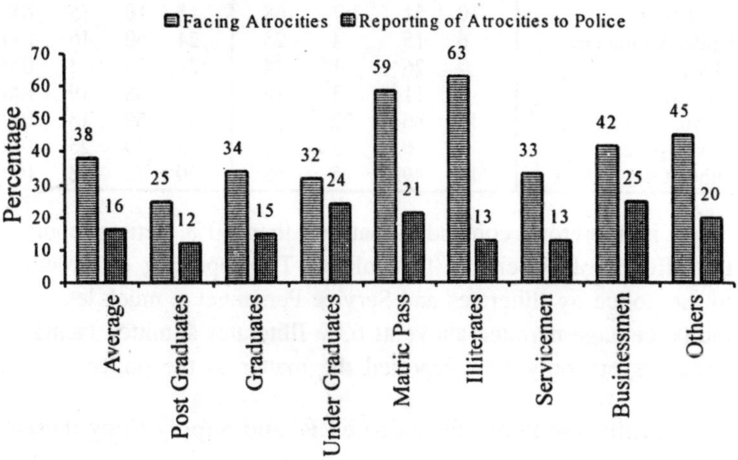

Table No. 48B : Facing of Atrocities by Target Group

Categories	Responses in: Number				Percentage			
	Yes	No	Und.	Total	Yes	No	Und.	Total
Post Graduates	14	43	0	57	25	75	0	100
Graduates	23	39	6	68	34	57	9	100
Under Graduates	8	16	1	25	32	64	4	100
Matric Pass	20	14	0	34	59	41	0	100
Illiterates	10	5	1	16	63	31	6	100
Service Personnel	41	78	5	124	33	63	4	100
Businessmen	5	6	1	12	42	50	8	100
Other Occupations	30	36	2	68	45	53	2	100

25% Post Graduates, 34% Graduates, 32% Under Graduates, 59% Matric Pass, 63% Illiterates, 33% Service Personnel, 42% Businessmen, and 45% respondents engaged in different occupations suffered the atrocities. Out of these, only 12% Post Graduates, 15% Graduates, 24% Under Graduates, 21% Matric Pass, 13% Illiterates, 13% Service Personnel, 25% Businessmen and 20% respondents of Target Group engaged in different occupations respectively, reported commission of atrocities on them to the police.[8]

Table No. 48C : Reporting of Atrocities by Target Group

Categories	Responses in							
	Number				Percentage			
	Yes	No	Und.	Total	Yes	No	Und.	Total
Post Graduates	7	35	15	57	12	61	26	100
Graduates	10	51	7	68	15	10	75	100
Under Graduates	6	15	4	25	24	60	16	100
Matric Pass	7	26	1	34	21	76	3	100
Illiterates	2	11	3	16	13	68	19	100
Service Personnel	16	86	22	124	13	69	18	100
Businessmen	3	6	3	12	25	50	25	100
Other Occupations	14	49	5	68	20	72	8	100

It is, therefore, concluded that less than 50% victims reported the offence of atrocity to the police. The reporting of atrocities to the police by Illiterates and Service Personnel is much less than the percentage narrated above as 63% Illiterates admitted facing of atrocities but only 13% reported the matter to the police.

7.3 Failure of Police to Lodge F.I.R. and Supply Copy thereof to Victim

Question number 43 of questionnaire on the subject for Target Group[9] elicited information from SC respondents whether or not police lodge their report and supply them a copy of F.I.R. free of cost?

Table No. 49 : Failure of Police to Lodge F.I.R. and Supply Copy thereof to Victim

Categories	Responses in							
	Number				Percentage			
	Yes	No	Und.	Total	Yes	No	Und.	Total
Target Group	30	110	60	200	15	55	30	100

200 respondents were examined on this question. Their responses are depicted in Graph No. 119 and Table No. 49. Out of these, 30 replied in affirmative, 110 in negative and 60 did not give any specific answer.[10] Thus, 15% SC respondents replied that police lodge their report and supply them a copy of F.I.R. free of cost. The percentages of Post Graduates, Graduates, Illiterates and Service Personnel are even lessor, which are 12, 13, 0 and 10, respectively. Percentages of Matric Pass, Businessmen and respondents engaged in different occupations are 29, 17 and 28, respectively.[11]

Graph No. 119 : Lodging of F.I.R. and Supplying Copy thereof by Police

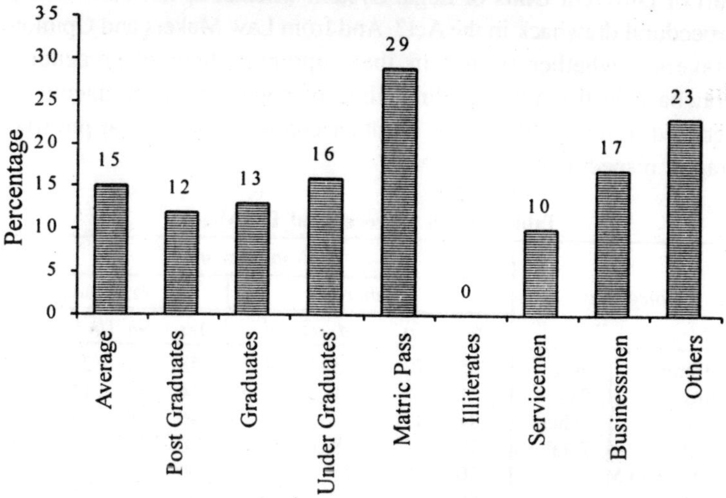

Table No. 49A : Failure of Police to Lodge F.I.R. and Supply Copy thereof to Victim: Responses of Target Group

Categories	*Responses in*							
	Number				*Percentage*			
	Yes	*No*	*Und.*	*Total*	*Yes*	*No*	*Und.*	*Total*
Post Graduates	7	31	19	57	12	55	33	100
Graduates	9	42	17	68	13	62	25	100
Under Graduates	4	14	7	25	16	56	28	100
Matric Pass	10	15	9	34	29	45	26	100
Illiterates	0	8	8	16	0	50	50	100
Service Personnel	13	72	39	124	10	58	32	100
Businessmen	2	6	4	12	17	50	33	100
Other Occupations	16	35	17	68	23	52	25	100

It is, therefore, concluded that in the opinion of the Illiterates, police neither lodge their reports nor supply them copy of F.I.R. free of cost. In view of remaining respondents, the police in rare and exceptional cases lodge their report and supply them a copy thereof free of cost. In view of 85% of respondents police did not lodge their report and give them copy of F.I.R. free of cost.

7.4 Procedural Drawback

Question numbers 53 and 39 of the questionnaire for Different

Units of Legal System[12] elicited information from officials forming part of Different Units of Legal System whether or not there is any procedural drawback in the Act? And from Law Makers and Opinion Makers,[13] whether or not in their opinion, there is procedural drawback in the Act regarding filing of complaint or producing of accused in the court and for all other connected matters at pre-trial stages respectively?

Table No. 50 : Procedural Drawback

Categories		*Responses in*							
		Number				*Percentage*			
		Yes	*No*	*Und.*	*Total*	*Yes*	*No*	*Und.*	*Total*
Different Units of Legal System	SCs	65	22	25	112	58	20	22	100
	STs	1	5	1	7	14	72	14	100
	Others	84	45	52	181	46	25	29	100
	Total	150	72	78	300	50	24	26	100
L.M. & O.M.		30	10	10	50	60	20	20	100
Grand Total		180	82	88	350	51	24	25	100

350 respondents were examined on these questions. Their responses are depicted in Graph No. 120 and Table Nos. 50, 50A and 50B. Out of these, 180 replied in affirmative, 82 in negative and 88 did not give any specific answer.[14] Thus, 51% respondents are of the view that there is procedural drawback in the Act.

50% officials forming part of Different Units of Legal System and 60% Law Makers and Opinion Makers are in conformity of this view.[15]

Table No. 50A : Responses of Law Makers and Opinion Makers on Procedural Drawback

Categories		*Responses in*							
		Number				*Percentage*			
		Yes	*No*	*Und.*	*Total*	*Yes*	*No*	*Und.*	*Total*
Law Makers & Opinion Makers	SCs	24	6	5	35	69	17	14	100
	STs	1	0	0	1	100	0	0	100
	Others	5	4	5	14	36	28	36	100

69% M.Ps., Legislators, Academicians, Media Persons, Social Activists and members of N.G.Os., *etc.*, belonging to SCs and 36% Non SC & ST respondents of this category hold this view.[16]

Graph No. 120 : Procedural Drawback : A Reason for Failure of the Act

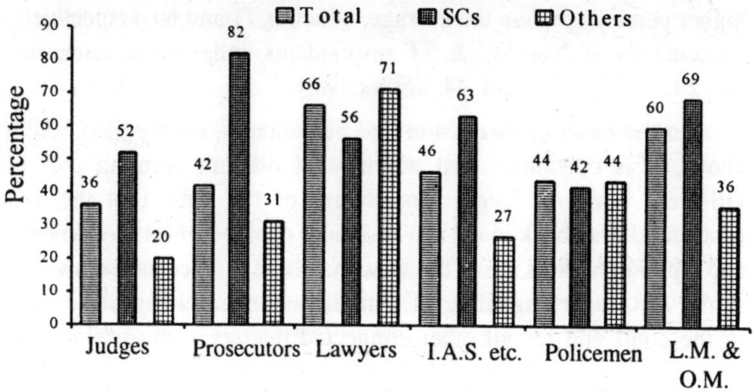

Table No. 50B : Responses of Different Units of Legal System on Procedural Drawback

Categories		*Responses in*							
		Number				*Percentage*			
		Yes	*No*	*Und.*	*Total*	*Yes*	*No*	*Und.*	*Total*
Judges	SCs	13	3	9	25	52	12	36	100
	Others	5	6	14	25	20	24	56	100
	Total	18	9	23	50	36	18	46	100
Prosecutors	SCs	9	1	1	11	82	9	9	100
	Others	12	11	16	39	31	28	41	100
	Total	21	12	17	50	42	24	34	100
Lawyers	SCs	19	6	9	34	56	18	26	100
	Others	47	6	13	66	71	9	20	100
	Total	66	12	22	100	66	12	22	100
I.A.S.,P.C.S., Doctors, etc.	SCs	19	5	6	30	63	17	20	100
	STs	0	4	1	5	0	80	20	100
	Others	4	4	7	15	27	27	46	100
	Total	23	13	14	50	46	26	28	100
Police Officials	SCs	5	7	0	12	42	58	0	100
	STs	1	1	0	2	50	50	0	100
	Others	16	18	2	36	44	50	6	100
	Total	22	26	2	50	44	52	4	100
Grand Total		150	72	78	300	50	24	26	100

36% Judges, 42% Public Prosecutors, 66% Lawyers, 46% I.A.S., P.C.S., Doctors, and other Officers and 44% Police Officials are of the view that there is procedural drawback in the Act. Percentages of SC respondents under these categories are 52, 82, 56, 63 and

42, respectively. ST respondents examined under the category of I.A.S., P.C.S., Doctors and other Officers and Police Officials have higher percentage than the average, which is 71 and 60, respectively. Percentages of Non-SC & ST respondents under these categories are 20, 31, 71, 27 and 44, respectively.[17]

On the basis of discussion and percentages, enumerated herein above, it is concluded that majority of officials forming part of Different Units of Legal System are of the view that there is procedural drawback in the Act and more then two-third Law Makers and Opinion Makers are of the view that there is procedural drawback in the Act, regarding filing of complaints or producing of accused in the court and for all other connected matters at pre-trial stages.

7.5 Lack of Infrastructure with Investigating Agencies

Question numbers 55 and 41 of the questionnaire for Different Units of the Legal System[18] and Law Makers and Opinion Makers[19] respectively, elicited information from respondents whether in their opinion, there is sufficient infrastructure with the investigating agencies to meet the requirements under the Act?

Table No. 51 : Lack of Infrastructure with Investigating Agencies

Categories		*Responses in*							
		Number				*Percentage*			
		Yes	*No*	*Und.*	*Total*	*Yes*	*No*	*Und.*	*Total*
Different Units of Legal System	SCs	42	56	14	112	38	50	12	100
	STs	2	4	1	7	29	57	14	100
	Others	95	48	38	181	42	27	21	100
	Total	139	108	53	300	46	36	18	100
L.M. & O.M.		13	30	7	50	26	60	14	100
Grand Total		152	138	60	350	43	39	18	100

350 respondents were examined on this question. Their responses are depicted in Graph No. 121 and Table Nos. 51, 51A and 51B. Out of these, 152 replied in affirmative, 138 in negative and 60 did not give any specific answer.[20] Thus, 43% respondents replied in positive and 39% in negative.

46% officials forming part of Different Units of Legal System[21] and 26% Law Makers and Opinion Makers are of the view that there is sufficient infrastructure with the investigating officers to perform their duties under the Act.[22]

Graph No. 121 : Lack of Infrastructure with Investigating Agencies : A Reason for Failure of the Act

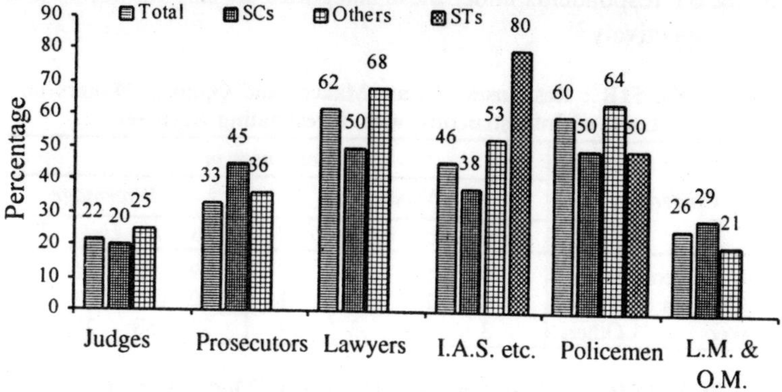

Table No. 51A : Responses of Different Units of Legal System on Lack of Infrastructure with Investigating Agencies

Categories		*Responses in*							
		Number				*Percentage*			
		Yes	*No*	*Und.*	*Total*	*Yes*	*No*	*Und.*	*Total*
Judges	SCs	5	14	6	25	20	56	24	100
	Others	5	9	11	25	25	36	44	100
	Total	11	22	17	50	22	44	34	100
Prosecutors	SCs	5	5	1	11	45	45	10	100
	Others	14	12	13	39	36	31	33	100
	Total	19	17	14	50	38	34	28	100
Lawyers	SCs	17	15	2	34	50	44	6	100
	Others	45	12	9	66	68	18	14	100
	Total	62	27	11	100	62	27	11	100
I.A.S., P.C.S., Doctors, etc.	SCs	11	15	4	30	38	50	12	100
	STs	4	0	1	5	80	0	20	100
	Others	8	5	2	15	53	34	13	100
	Total	23	20	7	50	46	40	14	100
Police Officials	SCs	6	5	1	12	50	42	8	100
	STs	1	1	0	2	50	50	0	100
	Others	23	10	3	36	64	28	8	100
	Total	30	16	4	50	60	32	8	100
Grand Total		139	108	53	300	46	36	18	100

22% Judges, 38% Public Prosecutors, 62% Lawyers, 46% I.A.S., P.C.S., Doctors and other Officers and 60% Police Officials hold this view. Percentages of SC respondent under these categories are 20, 45, 50, 38 and 50, respectively.[23]

80% I.A.S., P.C.S., Doctors, and other Officers and 50% Police Officials of ST categories replied in positive. Percentages of Non-SC & ST respondents under these categories are 25, 36, 68, 53 and 64, respectively.[24]

Table No. 51B : Responses of Law Makers and Opinion Makers on Lack of Infrastructure with Investigating Agencies

Categories		*Responses in*							
		Number				*Percentage*			
		Yes	*No*	*Und.*	*Total*	*Yes*	*No*	*Und.*	*Total*
Law Makers & Opinion Makers	SCs	10	21	4	35	29	60	11	100
	STs	0	1	0	1	0	100	0	100
	Others	3	8	3	14	21	58	21	100

26% M.Ps., Legislators, Academicians, Media Persons, Social Activists and member of N.G.Os., *etc.*, are in conformity with this view. Percentage of SCs respondents under these categories is 29.[25]

It is, therefore, concluded that majority of the Judges, Public Prosecutors, Lawyers, I.A.S., P.C.S., Doctors, M.Ps., Legislators, Academicians, Media Persons, Social Activists and members of N.G.Os. are having this view that there is no sufficient infrastructure with the investigating agencies to meet the requirements under the Act.

7.6 Non-Availability of Time with Police Personnel

Question numbers 56 and 42 of the questionnaire for Different Units of Legal System[26] and Law Makers and Opinion Makers,[27] respectively, elicited information from respondents whether or not the Police Personnel have sufficient time to perform their duties entrusted under the Act, *vis-à-vis,* their other duties under various laws?

Table No. 52 : Non-Availability of Time with Police Personnel

Categories		*Responses in*							
		Number				*Percentage*			
		Yes	*No*	*Und.*	*Total*	*Yes*	*No*	*Und.*	*Total*
Different Units of Legal System	SCs	36	67	9	112	32	60	8	100
	STs	2	5	0	7	29	71	0	100
	Others	68	89	24	181	38	49	13	100
	Total	106	161	33	300	35	54	11	100
L.M. & O.M.		12	34	4	50	24	68	8	100
Grand Total		118	195	37	350	34	55	11	100

350 respondents were examined on this question. Their responses are depicted in Graph No. 122 and Table Nos. 52, 52A and 52B. Out of these, 118 replied in affirmative, 195 in negative and 37 did not give any specific answer.[28] Thus, 34% replied in affirmative and 56% in negative.35% officials forming part of Different Units of the Legal System[29] and 24% Law Makers and Opinion Makers[30] are of the view that Police Personnel have sufficient time to perform their duties under the Act, *vis-a-vis,* their other duties under various laws.

Graph No. 122 : Non-Availability of Time with Police Personnel A Reason for Failure of the Act

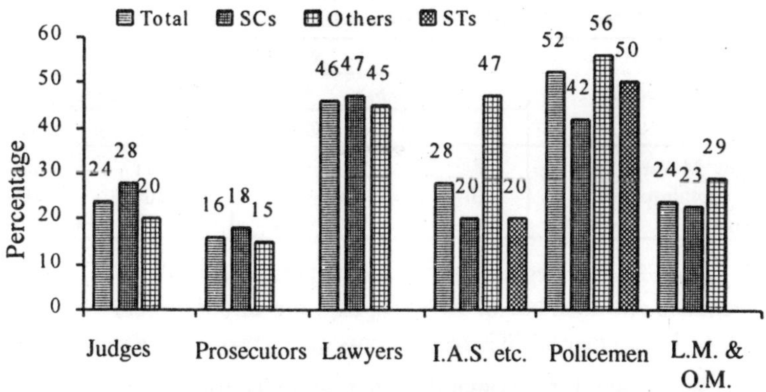

Table No. 52A : Different Units of Legal System on Non-Availability of Time with Police Personnel

Categories		*Responses in*							
		Number				*Percentage*			
		Yes	*No*	*Und.*	*Total*	*Yes*	*No*	*Und.*	*Total*
Judges	SCs	7	15	3	25	28	60	12	100
	Others	5	13	7	25	20	52	28	100
	Total	12	28	10	50	24	56	20	100
Prosecutors	SCs	2	8	1	11	18	73	9	100
	Others	6	26	7	39	15	67	18	100
	Total	8	34	8	50	16	68	16	100
Lawyers	SCs	16	16	2	34	47	47	6	100
	Others	30	29	7	66	45	44	11	100
	Total	46	45	9	100	46	45	9	100
I.A.S., P.C.S., Doctors, etc.	SCs	6	21	3	30	20	70	10	100
	STs	1	4	0	5	20	80	0	100
	Others	7	6	2	15	47	40	13	100
	Total	14	31	5	50	28	62	10	100

TABLE No. 52A (Contd.)

Police Officials	SCs.	5	7	0	12	42	58	0	100
	STs.	1	1	0	2	50	50	0	100
	Others	20	15	1	36	56	42	2	100
	Total	26	23	1	50	52	46	2	100
Grand Total		106	161	33	300	35	54	11	100

24% Judges, 16% Public Prosecutors, 46% Lawyers, 28% I.A.S., P.C.S., Doctors and other Officers and 52% Police Officials hold this view. Percentages of SC respondents having same opinion are 28, 18, 47, 20 and 42, respectively.[31]

Table No. 52B : Law Makers and Opinion Makers on Non-Availability of Time with Police Personnel

Categories		*Responses in*							
		Number				*Percentage*			
		Yes	*No*	*Und.*	*Total*	*Yes*	*No*	*Und.*	*Total*
Law Makers & Opinion Makers	SCs	8	25	2	35	23	71	6	100
	STs	0	1	0	1	0	100	0	100
	Others	4	8	2	14	29	57	14	100

24% M.Ps., Legislators, Academicians, Media Persons, Social Activists and member of N.G.Os., *etc.*, are in conformity with this view. Percentage of SCs respondents under these categories is 23.[32]

It is, therefore, concluded that officials forming part of the Different Units of the Legal System and Law Makers and Opinion Makers in majority are of the view that Police Personnel do not have sufficient time to perform their duties entrusted under the Act, *vis-à-vis*, their duties under other laws.

It is pertinent to high light here that majority of Police Officers are not in agreement with this view as 52% Police Officers replied that Police Personnel have sufficient time. Views of the police tally with the views of STs and Non SC & ST Police Officials, as their percentages under these categories are 50 and 56, respectively.

7.7 Insufficient Infrastructure with Special Courts

Question numbers 58 and 44 of the questionnaire for Different Units of Legal System[33] and Law Makers and Opinion Makers,[34] respectively, elicited information from respondents whether in their opinion, the Special Courts have sufficient infrastructure to discharge its duties promptly, smoothly and efficaciously?

Graph No. 123 : Insufficient Infrastructure with Special Courts : A Reason for Failure of the Act

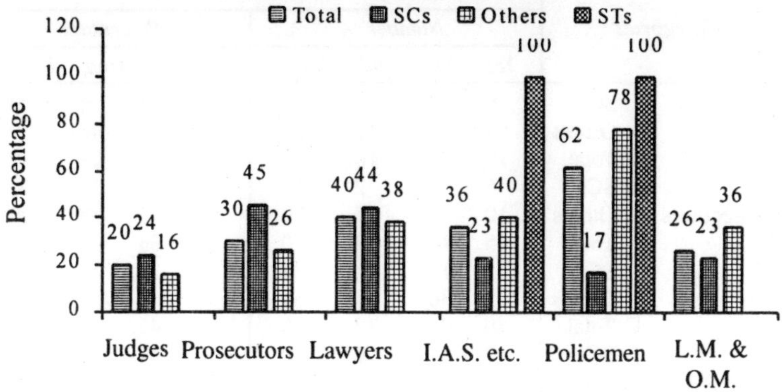

Table No. 53 : Sufficiency of Infrastructure with Special Courts

Categories		*Responses in*							
		Number				*Percentage*			
		Yes	*No*	*Und.*	*Total*	*Yes*	*No*	*Und.*	*Total*
Different Units of Legal System	SCs	32	63	17	112	29	56	15	100
	STs	2	5	0	7	29	71	0	100
	Others	72	64	45	181	40	35	25	100
	Total	106	132	62	300	35	44	21	100
L.M. & O.M.		13	31	6	50	26	62	12	100
Grand Total		119	163	68	350	34	47	19	100

350 respondents were examined on this question. Their responses are depicted in Graph No. 123 and Table Nos. 53, 53A and 53B. Out of these, 119 replied in affirmative, 163 in negative and 68 did not give any specific answer.[35] Thus, 34% respondents replied in positive, and 47% in negative.

35% officials forming part of Different Units of the Legal System[36] and 26% Law Makers and Opinion Makers[37] are of the view that there is sufficient infrastructure with the Special Court for discharging its duties promptly, smoothly and efficaciously.

Table No. 53A : Different Units of Legal System on Sufficiency of Infrastructure with Special Courts

Categories		*Responses in*							
		Number				*Percentage*			
		Yes	*No*	*Und.*	*Total*	*Yes*	*No*	*Und.*	*Total*
Judges	SCs	6	17	2	25	24	68	8	100
	Others	4	9	12	25	16	36	48	100
	Total	10	26	14	50	20	52	28	100
Prosecutors	SCs	5	4	2	11	45	37	18	100
	Others	10	14	15	39	26	36	38	100
	Total	15	18	17	50	30	36	34	100
Lawyers	SCs	15	13	6	34	44	38	18	100
	Others	25	30	11	66	38	45	17	100
	Total	40	43	17	100	40	43	17	100
I.A.S.,P.C.S., Doctors, etc.	SCs	7	17	6	30	23	57	20	100
	STs	5	0	0	5	100	0	0	100
	Others	6	5	4	15	40	33	34	100
	Total	18	21	11	50	36	42	22	100
Police Officials	SCs	2	9	1	12	17	75	8	100
	STs	1	1	0	2	50	50	0	100
	Others	28	6	2	36	78	17	5	100
	Total	31	16	3	50	62	32	6	100
Grand Total		106	132	62	300	35	44	21	100

20% Judges, 30% Public Prosecutors, 40% Lawyers, 36% I.A.S., P.C.S. and Doctors and other Officers and 62% Police Officials hold this view. Percentages of SC respondents having same view are 24, 45, 44, 23 and 17, respectively.[38]

Table No. 53B : Law Makers and Opinion Makers on Sufficiency of Infrastructure with Special Courts

Categories		*Responses in*							
		Number				*Percentage*			
		Yes	*No*	*Und.*	*Total*	*Yes*	*No*	*Und.*	*Total*
Law Makers & Opinion Makers	SCs	8	23	4	35	23	66	11	100
	STs	0	1	0	1	0	100	0	100
	Others	5	7	2	14	36	50	14	100

26% M.Ps., Legislators, Academicians, Media Persons, Social Activists and member of N.G.Os., *etc.,* are in conformity with this view. Percentage of SCs respondents under these categories is 23.[39]

It is, therefore, concluded that 80% Judges are of the view that Special Courts have no sufficient infrastructure to discharge its duties promptly, smoothly and efficaciously. Majority of the officials forming part of Different Units of the Legal System, except Police Officers of Non SC & ST categories are of the same view. More than two-third of Law Makers and Opinion Makers also opined that Special Courts have no sufficient infrastructure for discharging its duties promptly, smoothly and efficaciously.

7.8 Negative Attitude of Courts in Atrocity Cases

Question numbers 36 and 37 of the questionnaire for Law Makers and Opinion Makers[40] elicited opinion whether courts have been deciding cases of atrocities in commensurate with objects of the Act and awarding adequate sentences to the convicts of offences under the Act, respectively?

Table No. 54 : Attitude of Courts in Atrocity Cases

Categories		*Responses in*							
		Number				*Percentage*			
		Yes	*No*	*Und.*	*Total*	*Yes*	*No*	*Und.*	*Total*
Law Makers & Opinion Makers	SCs	7	23	5	35	20	66	14	100
	STs	0	1	0	1	0	100	0	100
	Others	6	5	3	14	43	36	21	100
	Total	13	29	8	50	26	58	16	100

50 respondents on each question were examined. Their responses are depicted in Graph No. 124 and Table Nos. 54 and 54A. Out of these, 13 and 5 replied in positive, 29 and 32 in negative and 8 and 13 respectively, did not give any specific answer.[41] Thus, only 26% respondents are of the view that courts have been deciding cases of atrocities commensurate with the objects of the Act. Opinion of SC respondents under these categories is only 20%. 10% Law Makers and Opinion Makers are of the view that adequate sentence by courts are being awarded to the convicts of atrocity offences. Percentage of SC respondents under these categories is only 3.[42]

Graph No. 124 : Negative Attitude of Courts in Atrocity Cases

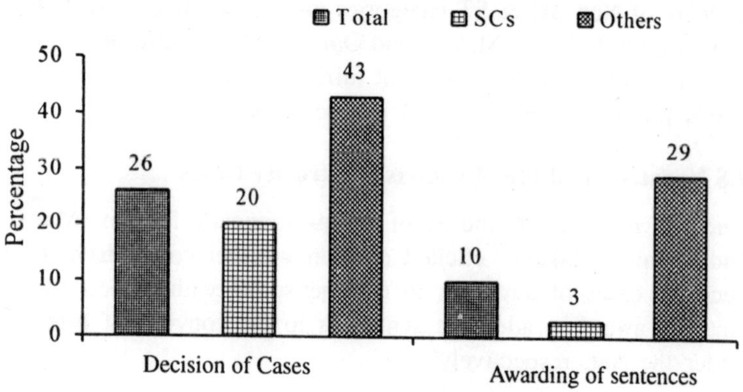

Table No. 54A : Awarding of Sentence by the Court in Atrocity Cases

Categories		*Responses in*							
		Number				*Percentage*			
		Yes	*No*	*Und.*	*Total*	*Yes*	*No*	*Und.*	*Total*
Law Makers & Opinion Makers	SCs	1	26	8	35	3	74	23	100
	STs	0	1	0	1	0	100	0	100
	Others	4	5	5	14	28	36	36	100
	Total	5	32	13	50	10	64	26	100

It is, therefore, concluded that majority of the respondents examined under these categories are of the view that courts have not been deciding cases of atrocities commensurate with the objects of the Act. Since 64% replies in regard to awarding adequate sentence to the convicts of atrocities by the courts are in negative, therefore, it is further concluded that the courts have not been awarding adequate sentences to the convicts of atrocity offences.

7.9 Overburdening of Special Courts

Question numbers 57 and 43 of the questionnaire for Different Units of the Legal System[43] and Law Makers and Opinion Makers[44] respectively, elicited information whether or not the court constituted under the Act are overburdened with other work which impede them to devote sufficient time for disposal of cases under the Act?

Table No. 55 : Overburdening of Special Courts

Categories		Responses in Number				Responses in Percentage			
		Yes	*No*	*Und.*	*Total*	*Yes*	*No*	*Und.*	*Total*
Different Units of Legal System	SCs	58	33	21	112	52	29	19	100
	STs	3	3	1	7	43	43	14	100
	Others	104	37	40	181	58	20	22	100
	Total	165	73	62	300	55	24	21	100
L.M. & O.M.		30	14	6	50	60	28	12	100
Grand Total		195	87	68	350	56	25	19	100

350 respondents were examined on this question. Their responses are depicted in Graph No.125 and Table Nos.55, 55A and 55B. Out of these, 195 respondents replied in affirmative, 87 in negative and 68 did not give any specific reply.[45] Thus, 56% officials forming part of Different Units of the Legal System and Law Makers and Opinion Makers are of the opinion that Special Courts constituted under the Act are overburdened with other work which impede them to give sufficient time for disposal of cases under the Act.

Table No. 55A : Different Units of Legal System on Overburdening of Special Courts

Categories		Responses in Number				Responses in Percentage			
		Yes	*No*	*Und.*	*Total*	*Yes*	*No*	*Und.*	*Total*
Judges	SCs	16	6	3	25	64	24	12	100
	Others	8	4	13	25	32	16	52	100
	Total	24	10	16	50	48	20	32	100
Prosecutors	SCs	6	3	2	11	55	27	18	100
	Others	17	10	12	39	44	26	30	100
	Total	23	13	14	50	46	26	28	100
Lawyers	SCs	15	11	8	34	44	32	24	100
	Others	46	13	7	66	70	20	10	100
	Total	61	24	15	100	61	24	15	100
I.A.S.,P.C.S., Doctors, etc.	SCs	16	8	6	30	52	28	20	100
	STs	4	1	0	5	80	20	0	100
	Others	8	1	6	15	53	7	40	100
	Total	28	9	13	50	56	18	26	100
Police Officials	SCs	3	7	2	12	25	58	17	100
	STs	2	0	0	2	100	0	0	100
	Others	25	9	2	36	69	25	6	100
	Total	29	17	4	50	58	34	8	100
Grand Total		165	73	62	300	55	24	21	100

55% officials forming part of Different Units of the Legal System,[46] and 60% Law Makers and Opinion Makers[47] hold this opinion.

Graph No. 125 : Overburdening of Special Courts : A Reason for Failure of the Act

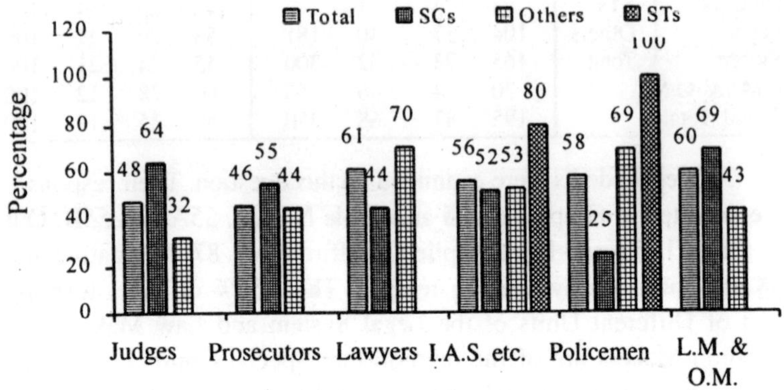

48% Judges, 46% Public Prosecutors, 61% Lawyers, 56% I.A.S., P.C.S., Doctors and other Officers and 58% Police Officials are of this opinion. Percentages of SC respondents under these categories are 64, 55, 44, 52 and 25 respectively. 80% STs I.A.S., P.C.S., Doctors and other Officers and 100% Police Officials of STs are also in conformity of this view.[48]

Table No. 55B : Law Makers and Opinion Makers on Overburdening of Special Courts

Categories		*Responses in*							
		Number				*Percentage*			
		Yes	*No*	*Und.*	*Total*	*Yes*	*No*	*Und.*	*Total*
Law Makers & Opinion Makers	SCs	24	8	3	35	69	23	8	100
	STs	0	1	0	1	0	100	0	100
	Others	6	5	3	14	43	36	21	100

60% M.Ps., Legislators, Academicians, Media Persons, Social Activists and member of N.G.Os., *etc.,* also opined that Special Courts are overburdened. Percentage of SC respondents under these categories is even higher than the average, which is 69.[49]

On the basis of above discussion, it is concluded that majority of the population is of the view that Special Courts are overburdened with other work which impede them to devote sufficient time for disposal of cases of atrocities.

7.10 Cumbersome Procedure

Question numbers 52 and 38 of the questionnaire for the Different Units of the Legal System[50] and Law Makers and Opinion Makers, respectively,[51] elicited information whether the procedure provided under the Act for imparting justice is simple?

Table No. 56 : Procedure

Categories		*Responses in*							
		Number				*Percentage*			
		Yes	*No*	*Und.*	*Total*	*Yes*	*No*	*Und.*	*Total*
Different Units of Legal System	SCs	25	66	21	112	22	59	19	100
	STs	2	3	2	7	29	42	29	100
	Others	96	40	45	181	53	22	25	100
	Total	123	109	68	300	41	36	23	100
L.M. & O.M.		8	32	10	50	16	64	20	100
Grand Total		131	141	78	350	37	41	22	100

350 respondents were examined on this question. Their responses are depicted in Graph No.126 and Table Nos.56, 56A and 56B. Out of these, 131 replied in affirmative, 141 in negative and 78 did not give any specific reply.[52] Thus, 37% respondents replied that procedure is simple. 41% officials forming Different Units of the Legal System[53] and 16% M.Ps., Legislators, Academicians, Media Persons, Social Activists and members of N.G.Os., *etc.*, replied in affirmative.[54]

Graph No. 126 : Cumbersome Procedure : A Reason for Failure of the Act

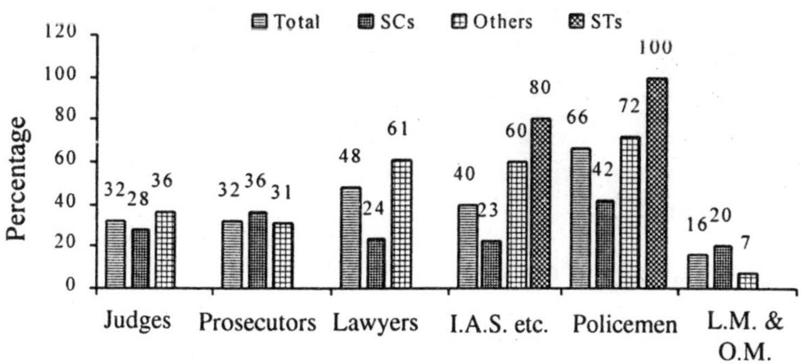

Table No. 56A : Law Makers and Opinion Makers on Procedure

Categories		Responses in Number				Responses in Percentage			
		Yes	*No*	*Und.*	*Total*	*Yes*	*No*	*Und.*	*Total*
Law Makers & Opinion Makers	SCs	7	22	6	35	20	63	17	100
	STs	0	1	0	1	0	100	0	100
	Others	1	9	4	14	7	65	28	100

32% Judges, and Public Prosecutors, 48% Lawyers, 40% I.A.S., P.C.S., Doctors and other Officers and 66% Police Officials are of the view that procedure is simple. Percentages of SC officials under these categories are 28, 36, 24, 23 and 42, respectively.[55]

Table No. 56B : Different Units of Legal System on Procedure

Categories		Responses in Number				Responses in Percentage			
		Yes	*No*	*Und.*	*Total*	*Yes*	*No*	*Und.*	*Total*
Judges	SCs	7	14	4	25	28	56	16	100
	Others	9	3	13	25	36	12	52	100
	Total	16	17	17	50	32	34	34	100
Prosecutors	SCs	4	7	0	11	36	64	0	100
	Others	12	14	13	39	31	36	33	100
	Total	16	21	13	50	32	42	26	100
Lawyers	SCs	8	15	11	34	24	44	32	100
	Others	40	11	15	66	61	17	22	100
	Total	48	26	26	100	48	26	26	100
I.A.S.,P.C.S., Doctors, etc.	SCs	7	17	6	30	23	57	20	100
	STs	4	1	0	5	80	20	0	100
	Others	9	4	2	15	60	27	13	100
	Total	20	30	10	50	40	60	20	100
Police Officials	SCs	5	7	0	12	42	58	0	100
	STs	2	0	0	2	100	0	0	100
	Others	26	8	2	36	72	22	6	100
	Total	33	15	2	50	66	30	4	100
Grand Total		123	109	68	300	41	36	23	100

Thus, minority view of the respondent is that procedure is simple whereas majority view is that procedure for imparting justice is cumbersome.

7.11 Low Rate of Convictions

Question numbers 48 and 29 of the questionnaire for Different

Units of the Legal System[56] and Law Makers and Opinion Makers[57] elicited information whether they know any case of atrocity trial, which ended in conviction?

Table No. 57 : Low Rate of Convictions

Categories		*Responses in*							
		Number				*Percentage*			
		Yes	*No*	*Und.*	*Total*	*Yes*	*No*	*Und.*	*Total*
Different Units of Legal System	SCs	19	89	4	112	17	79	4	100
	STs	0	6	1	7	0	86	14	100
	Others	36	131	14	181	20	72	8	100
	Total	55	226	19	300	18	76	6	100
L.M. & O.M.		7	40	3	50	14	80	6	100
Grand Total		62	260	22	350	18	74	8	100

350 respondents were examined on this question. Their responses are depicted in Graph No. 127 and Table Nos. 57, 57A and 57B. Out of these, 62 replied in affirmative, 260 in negative and 22 did not give any specific reply.[58] Thus, 18% respondents replied in positive and 74% replied in negative. 18% officials forming part of Different Units of the Legal System[59] and 14%, Law Makers and Opinion Makers are of this opinion.

Graph No. 127 : Low Rate of Convictions under the Act : A Reason for Failure of the Act

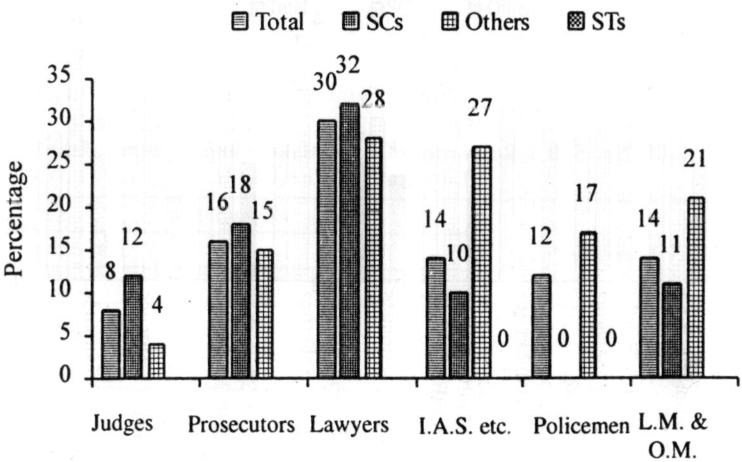

Table No. 57A : Different Units of Legal System on Low Rate of Convictions

Categories		Responses in Number				Responses in Percentage			
		Yes	No	Und.	Total	Yes	No	Und.	Total
Judges	SCs	3	21	1	25	12	84	4	100
	Others	1	22	2	25	4	88	8	100
	Total	4	43	3	50	8	86	6	100
Prosecutors	SCs	2	8	1	11	18	73	9	100
	Others	6	26	7	39	15	67	18	100
	Total	8	34	8	50	16	68	16	100
Lawyers	SCs	11	22	1	34	32	65	3	100
	Others	19	42	5	66	28	64	8	100
	Total	30	64	6	100	30	64	6	100
I.A.S., P.C.S., Doctors, etc.	SCs	3	27	0	30	10	90	0	100
	STs	0	5	0	5	0	100	0	100
	Others	4	11	0	15	27	73	0	100
	Total	7	43	0	50	14	86	0	100
Police Officials	SCs	0	11	1	12	0	92	8	100
	STs	0	1	1	2	0	50	50	100
	Others	6	30	0	36	17	83	0	100
	Total	6	42	2	50	12	84	4	100
Grand Total		55	226	19	300	18	76	6	100

8% Judges, 16% Public Prosecutors, 30% Lawyers, 14% I.A.S., P.C.S. and Doctors and other Officers and 12% Police Officials replied in affirmative to say that they have knowledge about convictions under the Act. Percentages of SC respondents under these categories are 12, 18, 32, 10 and 0, respectively. Percentage of ST I.A.S., P.C.S., Doctors and other Officers is also 0.[60]

Table No. 57B : Responses of Law Makers and Opinion Makers on Low Rate of Convictions

Categories		Responses in Number				Responses in Percentage			
		Yes	No	Und.	Total	Yes	No	Und.	Total
Law Makers & Opinion Makers	SCs	4	30	1	35	11	86	3	100
	STs	0	1	0	1	0	100	0	100
	Others	3	9	2	14	21	65	14	100

14% M.Ps., Legislators, Academicians, Media Persons, Social Activists and members of N.G.Os., *etc.*, are having knowledge of conviction under the Act. Percentage of SC respondents under this category is only 11.[61]

On the basis of discussion and percentage narrated herein above, it is concluded that negligible cases of atrocities end in the convictions.

7.12 Inadequacy of Fora

Question numbers 50 and 31 of the questionnaire for Different Units of Legal System[62] and Law Makers and Opinion Makers[63] elicited information from the respondents whether the Special Courts, machineries and fora provided under the Act, are adequate?

Table No. 58 : Adequacy of Fora

Categories		*Responses in*							
		Number				*Percentage*			
		Yes	*No*	*Und.*	*Total*	*Yes*	*No*	*Und.*	*Total*
Different Units of Legal System	SCs.	20	72	20	112	18	64	18	100
	STs.	1	5	1	7	14	72	14	100
	Others	57	72	52	181	31	40	29	100
	Total	78	149	73	300	26	50	24	100
L.M. & O.M.		4	36	10	50	8	72	20	100
Grand Total		82	185	83	350	23	53	24	100

350 respondents were examined on this question. Their responses are depicted in Graph No.128 and Table Nos.58, 58A and 58B. Out of these, only 82 respondents replied in affirmative, 185 replied in

Graph No. 128 : Inadequacy of Special Courts, Machineries and Fora : A Reason for Failure of the Act

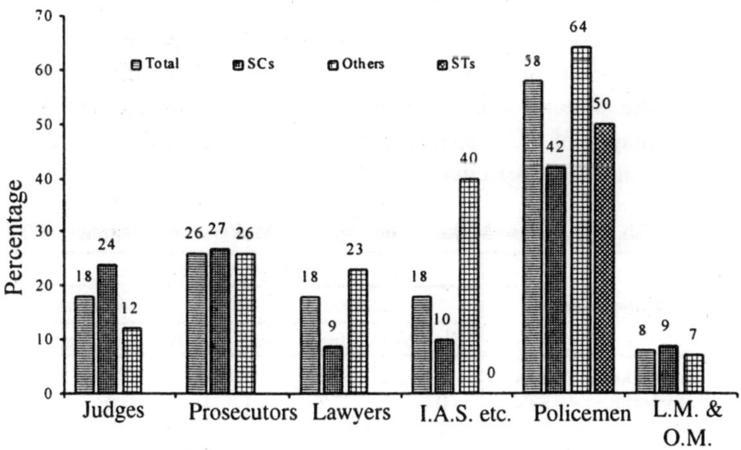

negative and 83 did not give any specific reply.[64] Thus, 23% respondents of both these categories replied in affirmative. Only 26% officials forming Different Units of Legal System[65] and 8% Law Makers and Opinion Makers[66] stated that the Special Courts, machineries and fora provided under the Act are adequate.

Table No. 58A : Different Units of Legal System on Adequacy of Fora

Categories		*Responses in*							
		Number				*Percentage*			
		Yes	*No*	*Und.*	*Total*	*Yes*	*No*	*Und.*	*Total*
Judges	SCs	6	16	3	25	24	64	12	100
	Others	3	9	13	25	12	36	52	100
	Total	9	25	16	50	18	50	32	100
Prosecutors	SCs	3	7	1	11	27	64	9	100
	Others	10	13	16	39	26	33	41	100
	Total	13	20	17	50	26	40	34	100
Lawyers	SCs	3	23	8	34	9	67	24	100
	Others	15	36	15	66	23	54	23	100
	Total	18	59	23	100	18	59	23	100
I.A.S., P.C.S., Doctors, etc.	SCs	3	19	8	30	10	63	27	100
	STs	0	4	1	5	0	80	20	100
	Others	6	4	5	15	40	27	33	100
	Total	9	27	14	50	18	54	28	100
Police Officials	SCs	5	7	0	12	42	58	0	100
	STs	1	1	0	2	50	50	0	100
	Others	23	10	3	36	64	28	8	100
	Total	29	18	3	50	58	36	6	100
Grand Total		78	149	73	300	26	50	24	100

18% Judges, 26% Public Prosecutors, 18% Lawyers and I.A.S., P.C.S., Doctors and other Officers and 58% Police Officials opined that the special courts, machineries and fora are adequate. Percentages of SC respondents under these categories are 24, 27, 9, 10 and 42, respectively.[67]

Table No. 58B : Law Makers and Opinion Makers on Adequacy of Fora

Categories		*Responses in*							
		Number				*Percentage*			
		Yes	*No*	*Und.*	*Total*	*Yes*	*No*	*Und.*	*Total*
Law Makers & Opinion Makers	SCs	3	26	6	35	9	74	17	100
	STs	0	1	0	1	0	100	0	100
	Others	1	8	5	14	7	57	36	100

8% M.Ps., Legislators, Academicians, Media Persons, Social Activists and members of N.G.Os., *etc.*, stated that provisions under the Act regarding Special Courts, machineries and fora are adequate. Percentage of SC respondents under these categories is 9.[68]

On the basis of discussion and percentages narrated hereinabove, it is concluded that a large number of respondents admitted that the Special Courts, machineries and fora provided under the Act are not adequate.

Notes and References

1. *See*, annexures 1 and 4. The question is, "Do you think that the Act has covered all the possible forms of atrocities?"
2. *See*, Table No. 47.
3. *See*, Graph No.. 44.
4. *Ibid.*
5. *See*, annexures 1 and 2. The questions are, "Have you ever faced atrocities of above kind or any other kind?" And, "Did you lodge F.I.R. about the commission of atrocity?"
6. *See*, Table Nos. 48 and 48A.
7. *See*, Graph No. 42.
8. *Ibid.*
9. *See*, annexures 1 and 2. The question is, "Did the police lodge your report and supplied you a copy of F.I.R. free of cost?"
10. *See*, Table No. 49.
11. *See*, Graph No. 42.
12. *See*, annexures 1 and 3. The question is, "Do you think that there is procedural drawback in the Act?"
13. *See*, annexures 1 and 4. The question is "Do you think that there is procedural drawback in the Act regarding filing of complaints, or producing accused in court and for all other connected matters at pre-trial stages?"
14. *See*, Table No. 50.
15. *See*, Graph No. 53.
16. *See*, Graph No. 45.
17. *See*, Graph Nos. 54 to 58.
18. *See*, annexures 1 and 3. The question is, "Do you think that there is sufficient infrastructure with the investigating agencies to meet the requirements under the Act?"
19. *Ibid.* and annexures 1 and 4.
20. *See*, Table No. 51.
21. *See*, Graph No. 53.
22. *See*, Graph No. 45.
23. *See*, Graph Nos. 54 to 58.
24. *Ibid.*

25. *See*, Graph No. 45.
26. *See*, annexures 1 and 3. The question is, "Do the police personnel have sufficient time to perform their duties entrusted under the Act. *vis-à-vis,* their other duties under various laws?"
27. *Ibid.* and annexures 1 and 4.
28. *See*, Table No. 52.
29. *See*, Graph No. 53.
30. *See*, Graph No. 45.
31. *See*, Graph Nos. 54 to 58.
32. *See*, Graph No. 45.
33. *See*, annexures 1 and 3. The question is, "Do you think that the special court has sufficient infrastructure to discharge its duties promptly, smoothly and efficaciously?"
34. *Ibid.* and annexures 1 and 4.
35. *See*, Table No. 53.
36. *See*, Graph No. 53.
37. *See*, Graph No. 46.
38. *See*, Graph Nos. 54 to 58.
39. *See*, Graph No. 46.
40. *See*, annexures 1 and 4. The questions are, "Do you think that Courts have been deciding cases of atrocities in commensurate with the objects of the Act?" And, "Do you think that the courts have been awarding adequate sentences to the convicts of offences under the Act?"
41. *See*, Table No. 54.
42. *See*, Graph No. 45.
43. *See*, annexures 1 and 3. The question is, "Do you think the courts constituted under the Act are overburdened with other work which impede them to devote sufficient time for disposal of cases under the Act?"
44. *Ibid.* and annexures 1 and 4.
45. *See*, Table No. 55.
46. *See*, Graph No. 53.
47. *See*, Graph No. 45.
48. *See*, Graph Nos. 54 to 58.
49. *See*, Graph No. 45.
50. *See*, annexures 1 and 3. The question is, "Do you think that the procedure for imparting justice under the Act is simple?"
51. *Ibid.* and annexure 1 and 4.
52. *See*, Table No. 56.
53. *See*, Graph No. 53.
54. *See*, Graph No. 45.
55. *See*, Graph Nos. 54 to 58.
56. *See*, annexures 1 and 3. The question is, "Do you know any case of atrocity trial which ended in convictions?"
57. *Ibid.* and annexures 1 and 4.
58. *See*, Table No. 57.
59. *See*, Graph No. 47.

60. *See*, Graph Nos. 48 to 52.
61. *See*, Graph No. 44.
62. *See*, annexures 1 and 3. The question is, "Do you think that the special courts, machineries and fora provided under the Act, are adequate?"
63. *Ibid.* and annexures 1 and 4.
64. *See*, Table No. 58.
65. *See*, Graph No. 47.
66. *See*, Graph No. 44.
67. *See*, Graph Nos. 48 to 52.
68. *See*, Graph No. 44.

CHAPTER 8

EMPIRICAL STUDY OF THE PROVISIONS OF THE ACT : Reform Suggestions

8.1 WIDENING OF DEFINITION OF ATROCITIES

8.1.1 Asking of Questions relating to Caste

Question numbers 66 and 64 of the questionnaire for Different Units of the Legal System[1] and Law Makers and Opinion Makers,[2] respectively, elicited information whether or not asking questions relating to caste from any person, when it was not required for giving any benefit to the members of SCs, should be deemed to be an atrocity punishable under the Act?

Table No. 59 : Asking of Questions relating to Caste

Categories		*Responses in*							
		Number				*Percentage*			
		Yes	*No*	*Und.*	*Total*	*Yes*	*No*	*Und.*	*Total*
Different Units of Legal System	SCs	82	25	5	112	73	22	5	100
	STs	3	4	0	7	43	57	0	100
	Others	84	80	17	181	46	44	10	100
	Total	169	109	22	300	56	36	8	100
L.M. & O.M.		40	10	0	50	80	20	0	100
Grand Total		209	119	22	350	60	34	6	100

350 respondents were examined on this question. Their responses are depicted in Graph No. 129 and Table Nos. 59, 59A and 59B. Out of these, 209 replied in affirmative, 119 in negative and 22 did not give any specific reply.[3] Thus, 60% suggested that asking of a caste by a person to any other person when it was not required for giving any benefit to a member of SCs should be made an

offence of atrocity under the Act. 56% officials forming part of Different Units of Legal System[4] and 80% of Law Makers and Opinion Makers opined in positive.[5]

Graph No. 129 : Suggestion : Widening of Definition of Atrocities : asking Questions relating to Caste

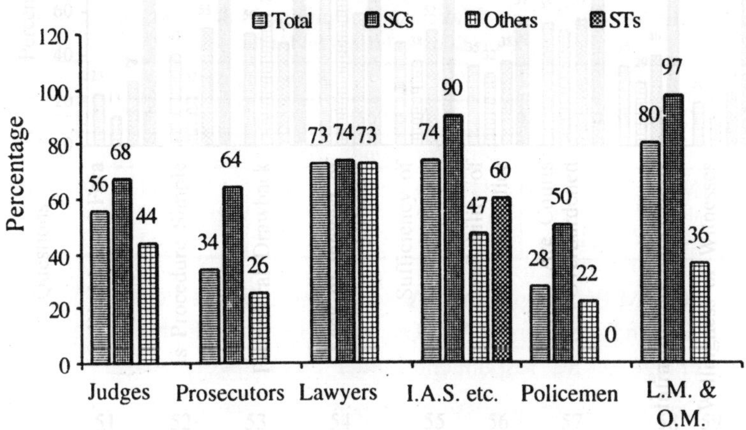

Table No. 59A : Different Units of Legal System on asking of Questions relating to Caste

Categories		*Responses in*							
		Number				*Percentage*			
		Yes	*No*	*Und.*	*Total*	*Yes*	*No*	*Und.*	*Total*
Judges	SCs	17	7	1	25	68	28	4	100
	Others	11	13	1	25	44	52	4	100
	Total	28	20	2	50	56	40	4	100
Prosecutors	SCs	7	4	0	11	64	46	0	100
	Others	10	19	10	39	26	48	26	100
	Total	17	23	10	50	34	46	20	100
Lawyers	SCs	25	6	3	34	74	18	18	100
	Others	48	16	2	66	73	24	3	100
	Total	73	22	5	100	73	22	5	100
I.A.S., P.C.S., Doctors, etc.	SCs	27	2	1	30	90	7	3	100
	STs	3	2	0	5	60	40	0	100
	Others	7	5	3	15	47	33	20	100
	Total	37	9	4	50	74	18	8	100
Police Officials	SCs	6	6	0	12	50	50	0	100
	STs	0	2	0	2	0	100	0	100
	Others	8	27	1	36	22	75	3	100
	Total	14	35	1	50	28	70	2	100
Grand Total		169	109	22	300	56	37	7	100

56% Judges, 34% Public Prosecutors, 73% Lawyers, 74% I.A.S., P.C.S., Doctors and other Officers and 28% Police Officials agreed to this suggestion.

Percentages of SCs officials under these categories are 68, 64, 74, 90 and 50, respectively. 60% ST I.A.S., P.C.S., Doctors and other Officers also replied in positive.[6]

Table No. 59B : Law Makers and Opinion Makers on asking of Questions relating to Caste

Categories		*Responses in*							
		Number				*Percentage*			
		Yes	*No*	*Und.*	*Total*	*Yes*	*No*	*Und.*	*Total*
Law Makers & Opinion Makers	SCs	34	1	0	35	97	3	0	100
	STs	1	0	0	1	100	0	0	100
	Others	5	9	0	14	36	64	0	100

80% M.Ps., Legislators, Academicians, Media Persons, Social Activists and members of N.G.Os., *etc.*, also agreed to this suggestion. Percentage of SC respondents under this category is 97.[7]

On the basis of discussion and percentage narrated herein above, it is concluded that majority of the respondents are in favour of this suggestion. All the SC respondents, barring few, suggested that asking of caste by a person to any other person when it was not required for giving any benefit to a member of SC should be made an offence of atrocities under the Act.

8.1.2 Employment of Children

Question number 56 of the questionnaire for Law Makers and Opinion Makers[8] elicited information, whether or not employing any child of the SCs below the age of 14 years, should be made an offence of atrocities under the Act?

Table No. 60 : Law Makers and Opinion Makers on Employment of Children

Categories		*Responses in*							
		Number				*Percentage*			
		Yes	*No*	*Und.*	*Total*	*Yes*	*No*	*Und.*	*Total*
Law Makers & Opinion Makers	SCs	32	3	0	35	91	9	0	100
	STs	1	0	0	1	100	0	0	100
	Others	9	3	2	14	64	22	14	100
Total		42	6	2	50	84	12	4	100

50 respondents were examined on this question. Their responses are depicted in Graph No. 130 and Table No. 60. Out of these, 42 replied in affirmative, 6 in negative and 2 did not express any opinion.[9] Thus, 84% M.Ps., Legislators, Academicians, Media Persons, Social Activists and members of N.G.Os., *etc.*, are of the opinion that employing any child of the SCs below the age of 14 years should be made an offence of atrocities under the Act. Even percentage of SC respondents examined under these categories is higher than average percentage, which is 91.[10]

It is, therefore, concluded that it is the opinion of general public, barring negligible, that employing any child of the SCs below the age of 14 years should be made an offence of atrocities under the Act.

Graph No. 130 : Suggestion : Widening of Definition of Atrocity, Employment of Children, Blockade of Service Career, Economic Exploitation, Untouchability

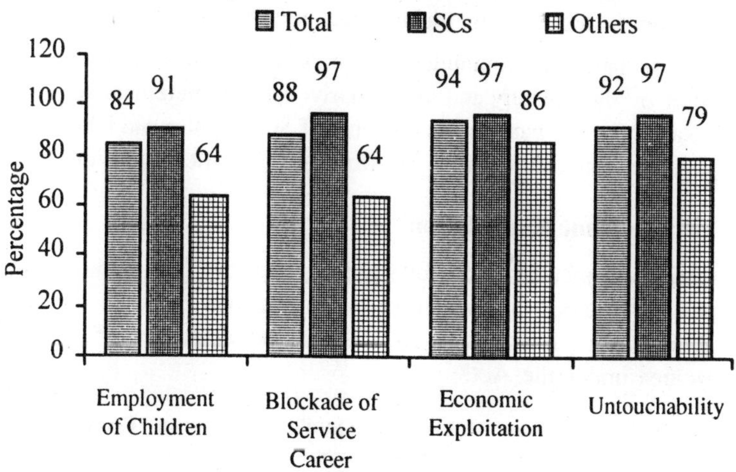

8.1.3 Blockade of Service Career

Question number 55 of the questionnaire for Law Makers and Opinion Makers[11] elicited information whether or not blockade of service career of member of SCs on false or fabricated report, *etc.*, should be made an offence of atrocities under the Act?

Table No. 61 : Law Makers and Opinion Makers on Blockade of Service Career

Categories		*Responses in*							
		Number				*Percentage*			
		Yes	*No*	*Und.*	*Total*	*Yes*	*No*	*Und.*	*Total*
Law Makers & Opinion Makers	SCs	34	1	0	35	97	3	0	100
	STs	1	0	0	1	100	0	0	100
	Others	9	4	1	14	64	29	7	100
	Total	44	5	1	50	88	10	2	100

50 respondents were examined on this question. Their responses are depicted in Graph No. 130 and Table No. 61. Out of these, 44 replied in affirmative, 5 in negative and one did not express any opinion.[12] Thus, 88% M.Ps., Legislators Academicians, Media Persons, Social Activists and members of N.G.Os., *etc.*, are of the opinion that blockade of service career of member of SCs on false and fabricated report, *etc.*, should be made an offence of atrocities under the Act. Percentage of SC respondents examined under these categories is higher than the average percentage, which is 97.[13]

It is, therefore, concluded that it is the opinion of the cross-section of the society and particularly detailed hereinabove, that blockade of service career of a member of SCs on false and fabricated report, *etc.*, should be made an offence of atrocities under the Act.

8.1.4 Economic Exploitation

Question number 54 of the questionnaire for the Law Makers and Opinion Makers,[14] elicited information whether or not economic exploitation of member of SCs should be made an offence of atrocities under the Act?

Table No. 62 : Law Makers and Opinion Makers on Economic Exploitation

Categories		*Responses in*							
		Number				*Percentage*			
		Yes	*No*	*Und.*	*Total*	*Yes*	*No*	*Und.*	*Total*
Law Makers & Opinion Makers	SCs	34	1	0	35	97	3	0	100
	STs	1	0	0	1	100	0	0	100
	Others	12	2	0	14	86	14	0	100
	Total	47	3	0	50	94	6	0	100

50 respondents were examined on this question. Their responses are depicted in Graph No. 130 and Table No. 62. Out of these, 47 replied in affirmative and 3 in negative.[15] Thus, 94% M.Ps., Legislators, Academicians, Media Persons, Social Activists and members of N.G.Os., *etc.*, are of the opinion that economic exploitation of a member of SCs should be made an offence of atrocities under the Act.[16] 97% SC respondents of these categories are of the same view.[17]

It is, therefore, concluded that large number of public are of the opinion that economic exploitation of a member of SCs should be covered under the Act.

8.1.5 Untouchability

Question number 53 of the questionnaire for the Law Makers and Opinion Makers,[18] elicited information whether or not practice of untouchability in any form with the member of SCs should be made an offence of atrocity under the Act?

Table No. 63 : Law Makers and Opinion Makers on Untouchability

Categories		*Responses in*							
		Number				*Percentage*			
		Yes	*No*	*Und.*	*Total*	*Yes*	*No*	*Und.*	*Total*
Law Makers & Opinion Makers	SCs	34	1	0	35	97	3	0	100
	STs	1	0	0	1	100	0	0	100
	Others	11	2	1	14	19	14	7	100
	Total	46	3	1	50	92	6	2	100

50 respondents were examined on this question. Their responses are depicted in Graph No. 130 and Table No. 63. Out of these, 46 replied in affirmative, 3 in negative and one did not express his view.[19] Thus, 92% M.Ps., Legislators, Academicians, Media Persons, Social Activists and members of N.G.Os., *etc.*, are of the view that practice of untouchability in any form with the member of SCs should be made an offence under the Act. The percentage of SC respondents under these categories is as high as 97 and the percentage of Non SC & ST respondents under these categories is 79.[20]

It is, therefore, concluded that all the people, except negligible percentage as below as 3%, are of the opinion that the practice of untouchability with a member of SCs should be made an offence of atrocities under the Act.

8.1.6 Negligence by Public Servant

Question numbers 62 and 63 of the questionnaire on the subject for Law Makers and Opinion Makers[21] elicited opinion whether omission on the part of concerned authorities to promptly rehabilitate the victims of atrocities or failure to make payment of compensation amount to them within a month from the due date should also be made an offence under the Act? And, whether omission on the part of concerned authorities to perform their duties under rules 3 to 18 of the Rules should also be made an offence under the Act ?

Table No. 64 : Law Makers and Opinion Makers on Negligence by Public Servant

Categories		Responses in							
		Number				Percentage			
		Yes	No	Und.	Total	Yes	No	Und.	Total
Law Makers & Opinion Makers	SCs	32	3	0	35	91	9	0	100
	STs	1	0	0	1	100	0	0	100
	Others	10	1	3	14	71	7	22	100
	Total	43	4	3	50	86	8	6	100

Graph No. 131 : Suggestion : Widening of Definition of Atrocity : Negligence of Public Servant

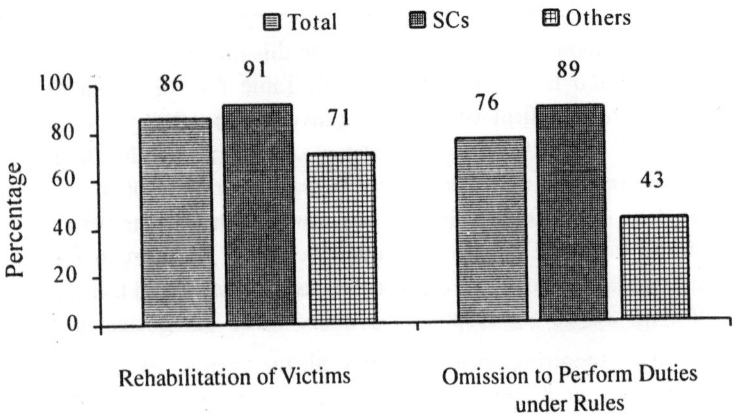

50 respondents on each question were examined. Their responses are depicted in Graph No. 131 and Table Nos. 64 and 64A. Out of these, 43 and 38 replied in positive, 4 and 2 in negative and 3 and 10, respectively did not give any specific reply.[22] Thus, 86% and 76% respectively, replied in affirmative.[23]

Table No. 64A : Law Makers and Opinion Makers on Negligence of Public Servant under the Rules

Categories		*Responses in*							
		Number				*Percentage*			
		Yes	*No*	*Und.*	*Total*	*Yes*	*No*	*Und.*	*Total*
Law Makers & Opinion Makers	SCs	31	1	3	35	89	3	8	100
	STs	1	0	0	1	100	0	0	100
	Others	6	1	7	14	43	7	50	100
	Total	38	2	10	50	76	4	20	100

It is, therefore, concluded that most of the respondents are of the view that omission on the part of the concerned authorities to promptly rehabilitate the victims of atrocities or failure to make payment of compensation amount to them within a month from the due date should also be made an offence under the Act and omission on the part of concerned authorities to perform their duties under rules 3 to 18 of the Rules should also be made an offence under the Act ?

8.1.7 Concept of Atrocities

Question numbers 2, 3 and 4 of the questionnaire on the subject for Target Group[24] elicited information whether or not people belonging to SCs consider invasion on body or property or reputation, respectively, as atrocities?

Table No. 65 : Invasion on Body

Categories	*Responses in*							
	Number				*Percentage*			
	Yes	*No*	*Und.*	*Total*	*Yes*	*No*	*Und.*	*Total*
Target Group	190	10	0	200	95	5	0	100

Table No. 65A : Invasion on Property

Categories	Responses in							
	Number				*Percentage*			
	Yes	*No*	*Und.*	*Total*	*Yes*	*No*	*Und.*	*Total*
Target Group	190	10	0	200	95	5	0	100

Table No. 65B : Invasion on Reputation

Categories	Responses in							
	Number				*Percentage*			
	Yes	*No*	*Und.*	*Total*	*Yes*	*No*	*Und.*	*Total*
Target Group	191	9	0	200	96	4	0	100

200 respondents were examined on these questions. Their responses are depicted in Graph No. 132 and Table Nos. 65, 65A, 65B, 65C, 65D and 65E. Out of these, 190, 190 and 191 answered in affirmative and 10, 10 and 9 respectively, in negative.[25]

Table No. 65C : Target Group on Invasion on Body

Categories	Responses in							
	Number				*Percentage*			
	Yes	*No*	*Und.*	*Total*	*Yes*	*No*	*Und.*	*Total*
Post Graduates	52	5	0	57	91	9	0	100
Graduates	63	5	0	68	93	7	0	100
Under Graduates	25	0	0	25	100	0	0	100
Matric Pass	34	0	0	34	100	0	0	100
Illiterates	16	0	0	16	100	0	0	100
Service Personnel	117	7	0	124	94	6	0	100
Businessmen	12	0	0	12	100	0	0	100
Other Occupations	65	3	0	68	95	5	0	100

Thus, 95% population of SCs is of the opinion that invasion on their bodies, properties and reputations amounts to atrocities. 91% Post Graduates, 93% Graduates, 100% Under Graduates, Matric Pass and Illiterates, 94% Service Personnel, 100% Businessmen and 95% engaged in different occupations are of the view that invasion on their bodies amounts to atrocities.[26]

Graph No. 132 : Suggestion : Widening of Definition of Atrocities, Invasion on the Body or Reputation or Property : Whether Atrocities?

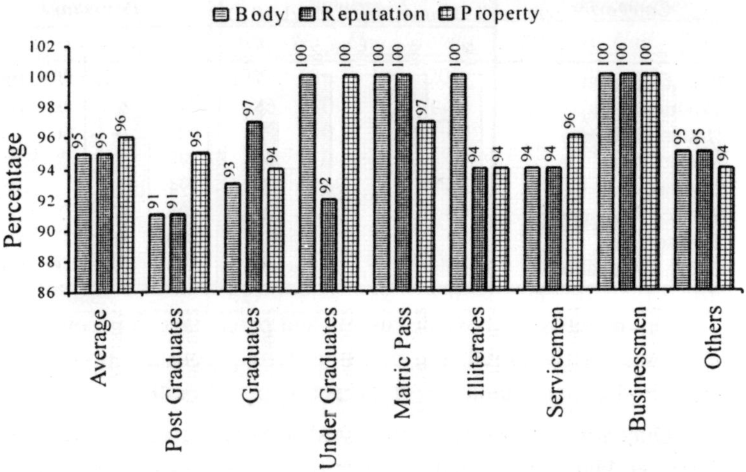

Table No. 65D : Target Group on Invasion on Property

Categories	*Responses in*							
	Number				*Percentage*			
	Yes	*No*	*Und.*	*Total*	*Yes*	*No*	*Und.*	*Total*
Post Graduates	52	5	0	57	91	9	0	100
Graduates	66	3	0	68	97	3	0	100
Under Graduates	23	2	0	25	92	8	0	100
Matric Pass	34	0	0	34	100	0	0	100
Illiterates	15	1	0	16	94	6	0	100
Service Personnel	117	7	0	124	94	6	0	100
Businessmen	12	0	0	12	100	0	0	100
Other Occupations	65	3	0	68	95	5	0	100

91% Post Graduates, 97% Graduates, 92% Under Graduates, 100% Matric Pass, 94% Illiterates and Servicemen, 100% Businessmen and 95% engaged in different occupations of the Target Group are of the view that invasion on their property amounts to atrocity. Percentages of respondents who opined that invasion on reputation is also atrocity are 95, 94, 100, 97, 94, 96, 100 and 94, respectively.[27]

Table No. 65E : Target Group on Invasion on Reputation

Categories	Responses in							
	Number				Percentage			
	Yes	No	Und.	Total	Yes	No	Und.	Total
Post Graduates	54	3	0	57	95	5	0	100
Graduates	64	4	0	68	94	6	0	100
Under Graduates	25	0	0	25	100	0	0	100
Matric Pass	33	1	0	34	97	3	0	100
Illiterates	15	1	0	16	94	6	0	100
Service Personnel	119	5	0	124	96	4	0	100
Businessmen	12	0	0	12	100	0	0	100
Other Occupations	64	4	0	68	94	6	0	100

On the basis of above discussion and percentage, it is concluded that most of the population of Target Group consider invasion on their bodies, or reputation or properties as atrocities.

Question number 52 of the questionnaire for Law Makers and Opinion Makers[28] elicited information whether or not invasion on the body or reputation or property of the member of SCs should be made an offence of atrocity under the Act?

Table No. 65F : Law Makers and Opinion Makers on Concept of Atrocities

Categories		Responses in							
		Number				Percentage			
		Yes	No	Und.	Total	Yes	No	Und.	Total
Law Makers & Opinion Makers	SCs	33	2	0	35	94	6	0	100
	STs	1	0	0	1	100	0	0	100
	Others	7	4	3	14	50	29	21	100
	Total	41	6	3	50	82	12	6	100

50 respondents were examined on this question. Their responses are depicted in Table No. 65F. Out of these, 41 replied in affirmative, 6 in negative and 3 did not express any opinion.[29] Thus, 82% of M.Ps., Legislators, Academicians, Media Persons, Social Activists and members of N.G.Os., *etc.*, are of the opinion that invasion on the body or reputation or property of member of SCs should be made an offence of atrocity under the Act. Percentage of SC respondents of these categories is much higher, *i.e.*, 94% as compared to average percentage of 82.[30]

On the basis of percentage enumerated hereinabove, it is concluded that there is desirability for widening the definition of atrocities given under section 3 of the Act. It is the view of most of the respondents that invasion on body or reputation or property of member of SCs should also be covered under the definition of the atrocity.

8.1.8 Indignities, Humiliations and Harassment

Question number 5 of the questionnaire on the subject for Target Group[31] elicited opinion whether or not indignities, humiliations and harassment of SCs amount to atrocities on them?

Table No. 66 : Indignities, Humiliation and Harassment

Categories	*Responses in*							
	Number				*Percentage*			
	Yes	*No*	*Und.*	*Total*	*Yes*	*No*	*Und.*	*Total*
Target Group	196	4	0	200	98	2	0	100

200 respondents were examined on this question. Their responses are depicted in Graph No. 133 and Table Nos. 66 and 66A. Out of these, 196 replied in affirmative and four in negative.[32] Thus, 98% population of Target Group are of the view that indignities, humiliations and harassment of SCs are atrocities.[33]

Graph No. 133 : Suggestion : Indignities, Humilations, Harrassment : Whether Atrocities ?

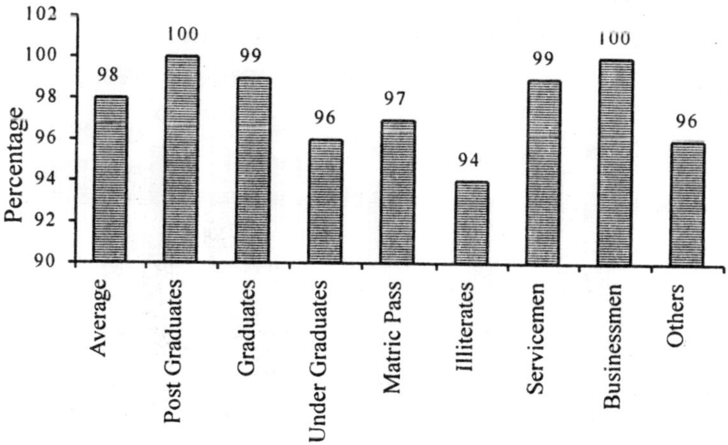

Table No. 66A : Target Group on Indiginities, Humiliation and Harassment

Categories	*Responses in*							
	Number				*Percentage*			
	Yes	*No*	*Und.*	*Total*	*Yes*	*No*	*Und.*	*Total*
Post Graduates	57	0	0	57	100	0	0	100
Graduates	67	1	0	68	99	1	0	100
Under Graduates	24	1	0	25	96	4	0	100
Matric Pass	33	1	0	34	97	3	0	100
Illiterates	15	1	0	16	94	6	0	100
Service Personnel	123	1	0	124	99	1	0	100
Businessmen	12	0	0	12	100	0	0	100
Other Occupations	61	3	0	68	90	10	0	100

100% Post Graduates, 99% Graduates, 96% Under Graduates, 97% Matric Pass, 94% Illiterates, 99% Servicemen, 100% Businessmen and 92% engaged in different occupations are of the same opinion.[34]

It is, therefore, concluded that people of Target Group consider indignities, humiliations and harassment as atrocities.

8.2 FEASIBILITY OF SENSITIZING THE FUNCTIONARIES

Question number 69 of the questionnaire for Different Units of the Legal System[35] and Law Makers and Opinion Makers[36] elicited information whether or not conducting refresher courses for all those who are in any way connected in giving effect to the provisions of the Act, may help in eradication of atrocities on the members of SCs?

Graph No. 134 : Suggestion : Refresher Course

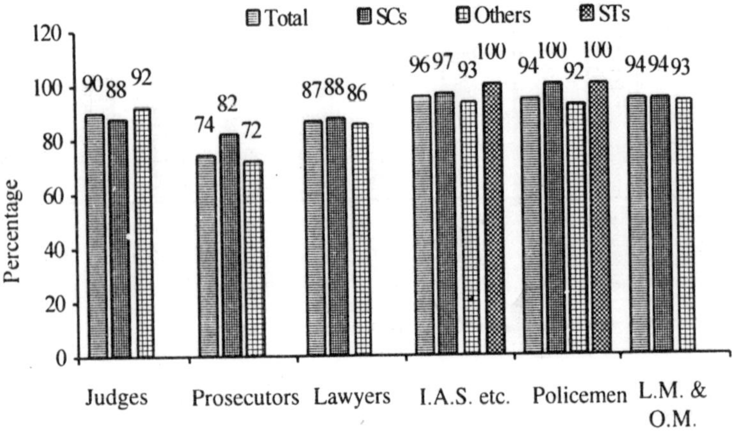

Table No. 67 : Sensitizing the Functionaries

Categories		*Responses in*							
		Number				*Percentage*			
		Yes	*No*	*Und.*	*Total*	*Yes*	*No*	*Und.*	*Total*
Different Units of Legal System	SCs	102	9	1	112	91	8	1	100
	STs	7	0	0	7	100	0	0	100
	Others	155	12	14	181	85	7	8	100
	Total	264	21	15	300	88	7	5	100
L.M. & O.M.		47	2	1	50	94	4	2	100
Grand Total		311	23	16	350	89	7	4	100

350 respondents were examined on this question. Their responses are depicted in Graph No. 134 and Table Nos. 67, 67A and 67B. Out of these, 311 replied in affirmative, 23 in negative and 16 did not give any specific reply.[37] Thus, 88% respondents replied in positive. 88% officials forming part of Different Units of Legal System[38] and 94% Law Makers and Opinion Makers replied in affirmative.[39]

Table No. 67A : Different Units of Legal System on Sensitizing the Functionaries

Categories		*Responses in*							
		Number				*Percentage*			
		Yes	*No*	*Und.*	*Total*	*Yes*	*No*	*Und.*	*Total*
Judges	SCs	22	3	0	25	88	12	0	100
	Others	23	1	1	25	92	4	4	100
	Total	45	4	1	50	90	8	2	100
Prosecutors	SCs	9	2	0	11	82	18	0	100
	Others	28	3	8	39	72	8	20	100
	Total	37	5	8	50	74	10	16	100
Lawyers	SCs	30	3	1	34	88	9	3	100
	Others	57	6	3	66	86	9	5	100
	Total	87	9	4	100	87	9	4	100
I.A.S., P.C.S., Doctors, etc.	SCs	29	1	0	30	97	3	0	100
	STs	5	0	0	5	100	0	0	100
	Others	14	0	1	15	93	0	7	100
	Total	48	1	1	50	96	2	2	100
Police Officials	SCs	12	0	0	12	100	0	0	100
	STs	2	0	0	2	100	0	0	100
	Others	33	2	1	36	92	5	3	100
	Total	47	2	1	50	94	4	2	100
Grand Total		264	21	15	300	88	7	5	100

90% Judges, 74% Public Prosecutors, 87% Lawyers, 96% I.A.S., P.C.S., Doctors and Officers and 94% Police Officials answered in affirmative. Percentages of SCs officials under these categories are 88, 82, 88, 97 and 100, respectively. 100% ST I.A.S., P.C.S., Doctors and other Officers and Police Officials replied in positive.[40]

Table No. 67B : Law Makers and Opinion Makers on Sensitizing the Functionaries

Categories		*Responses in*							
		Number				*Percentage*			
		Yes	*No*	*Und.*	*Total*	*Yes*	*No*	*Und.*	*Total*
Law Makers & Opinion Makers	SCs	33	2	0	35	94	6	0	100
	STs	1	0	0	1	100	0	0	100
	Others	13	0	1	14	93	0	7	100

94% M.Ps., Legislators, Academicians, Media Persons, Social Activists and members of N.G.Os., *etc.*, replied in affirmative. Same is the percentage of SC respondents under these categories. Percentage of Non SC & ST is 93.[41]

On the basis of discussion and percentage narrated hereinabove, it is concluded that conducting of refresher course for all those who are in any way connected in giving effect to the provisions of the Act will be of much help in eradication of atrocities on the members of SCs.

8.3 PUBLICITY OF PROVISIONS OF THE ACT

Question number 70 of the questionnaire for Different Units of the Legal System[42] and Law Makers and Opinion Makers[43] elicited

Graph No. 135 : Suggestion : Publicity of the Provisions of the Act

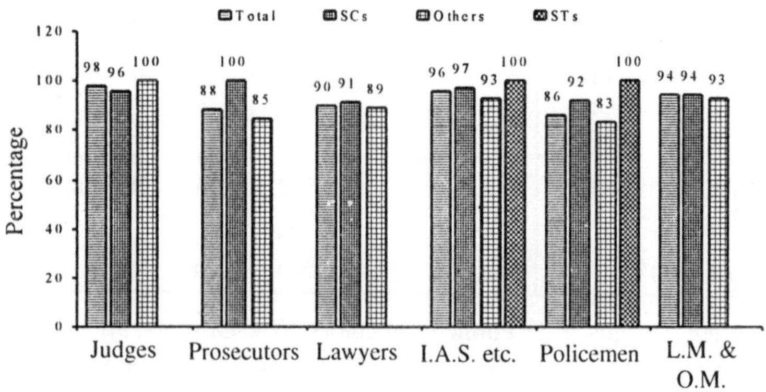

information whether or not publicity of the provisions of the Act through *Doordarshan,* Radio and all other public media may help in eradication of the atrocities on the members of the SCs.

Table No. 68 : Publicity of Provisions of the Act

Categories		*Responses in*							
		Number				*Percentage*			
		Yes	*No*	*Und.*	*Total*	*Yes*	*No*	*Und.*	*Total*
Different Units of Legal System	SCs	106	5	1	112	95	4	1	100
	STs	7	0	0	7	100	0	0	100
	Others	161	14	6	181	89	8	3	100
	Total	274	19	7	300	92	6	2	100
L.M. & O.M.		47	2	1	50	94	4	2	100
Grand Total		321	21	8	350	92	6	2	100

350 respondents were examined on this question. Their responses are depicted in Graph No. 135 and Table Nos. 68, 68A and 68B. Out of these, 321 replied in affirmative, 21 in negative and 8 did not give any specific reply.[44] Thus, 92% respondents replied in positive. 91% officials forming part of Different Units of the Legal System[45] and 94% Law Makers and Opinion Makers replied in affirmative.

Table No. 68A : Publicity of the Provisions of the Act

Categories		*Responses in*							
		Number				*Percentage*			
		Yes	*No*	*Und.*	*Total*	*Yes*	*No*	*Und.*	*Total*
Judges	SCs	24	1	0	25	96	4	0	100
	Others	25	0	0	25	100	0	0	100
	Total	49	1	0	50	98	2	0	100
Prosecutors	SCs	11	0	0	11	100	0	0	100
	Others	33	3	3	39	85	8	7	100
	Total	44	3	3	50	88	6	6	100
Lawyers	SCs	31	2	1	34	91	6	3	100
	Others	59	6	1	66	89	9	2	100
	Total	90	8	2	100	90	8	2	100
I.A.S., P.C.S. Doctors, etc.	SCs	29	1	0	30	97	3	0	100
	STs	5	0	0	5	100	0	0	100
	Others	14	0	1	15	93	0	7	100
	Total	48	1	1	50	96	2	2	100
Police Officials	SCs	11	1	0	12	92	8	0	100
	STs	2	0	0	2	100	0	0	100
	Others	30	5	1	36	83	14	3	100
	Total	43	6	1	50	86	12	2	100
Grand Total		274	19	7	300	92	6	2	100

98% Judges, 88% Public Prosecutors, 90% Lawyers, 96% I.A.S., P.C.S., Doctors and other Officers and 86% Police Officials supported this view. Percentages of SC officials under these categories are 96, 100, 91, 97 and 92, respectively.[46]

100% ST, I.A.S., P.C.S., Doctors and other Officers[47] and Police Officials[48] replied in positive.

Table No. 68B : Law Makers and Opinion Makers on Publicity of Provisions of the Act

Categories		*Responses in*							
		Number				*Percentage*			
		Yes	*No*	*Und.*	*Total*	*Yes*	*No*	*Und.*	*Total*
Law Makers & Opinion Makers	SCs	33	1	1	35	94	3	3	100
	STs	1	0	0	1	100	0	0	100
	Others	13	1	0	14	93	7	0	100

94% M.Ps., Legislators, Academicians, Media Persons, Social Activists and members of N.G.Os., *etc.*, opined the same. Percentage of SC responds is also 94 and percentage of Non SC & ST persons who agreed to this suggestion is 93.[49]

On the basis of discussion and percentage narrated hereinabove, it is concluded that publicity of the provisions of the Act through *Doordarshan*, Radio and all other public media may help in eradication of the atrocities on the members of the SCs.

8.4 SIMPLIFICATION OF PROCEDURE

Question numbers 60 and 57 of the questionnaire for Different Units of the Legal System[50] and Law Makers and Opinion Makers,[51] respectively elicited information about the desirability of simplification of procedure under the Act.

Table No. 69 : Simplification of Procedure

Categories		*Responses in*							
		Number				*Percentage*			
		Yes	*No*	*Und.*	*Total*	*Yes*	*No*	*Und.*	*Total*
Different Units of Legal System	SCs	79	17	16	112	71	15	14	100
	STs	5	2	0	7	71	29	0	100
	Others	116	33	32	181	64	18	18	100
	Total	200	52	48	300	67	17	16	100
L.M. & O.M41		2	7	50	82	4	14	100 Grand	
Total		241	54	55	350	69	15	16	100

350 respondents were examined on this question. Their responses are depicted in Graph No. 136 and Table Nos. 69, 69A and 69B. Out of these, 241 replied in positive, 54 in negative and 55 did not give

Graph No. 136 : Suggestion : Simplification of Procedure

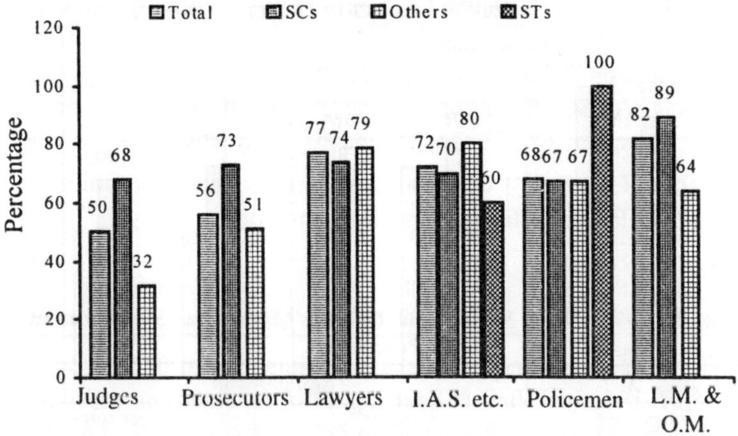

Table No. 69A : Different Units of Legal System on Simplification of Procedure

Categories		Responses in							
		Number				Percentage			
		Yes	No	Und.	Total	Yes	No	Und.	Total
Judges	SCs	17	3	5	25	68	12	20	100
	Others	8	4	13	25	32	16	52	100
	Total	25	7	18	50	50	14	36	100
Prosecutors	SCs	8	1	2	11	73	9	18	100
	Others	20	11	8	39	51	28	21	100
	Total	28	12	10	50	56	24	20	100
Lawyers	SCs	25	5	4	34	74	15	11	100
	Others	52	8	6	66	79	12	9	100
	Total	77	13	10	100	77	13	10	100
I.A.S., P.C.S., Doctors, etc.	SCs	21	4	5	30	70	13	17	100
	STs	3	2	0	5	60	40	0	100
	Others	12	1	2	15	80	7	13	100
	Total	36	7	7	50	72	14	14	100
Police Officials	SCs	8	4	0	12	67	33	0	100
	STs	2	0	0	2	100	0	0	100
	Others	24	9	3	36	67	25	8	100
	Total	34	13	3	50	68	26	6	100
Grand Total		200	52	48	300	67	17	16	100

any specific reply.[52] Thus, 69% respondents replied in affirmative. 67% officials forming part of the Different Units of the Legal System[53] and 82% Law Makers and Opinion Makers[54] expressed their opinion in affirmative about desirability of simplification of procedure.

50% Judges, 56% Public Prosecutor, 77% Lawyers, 72% I.A.S., P.C.S., Doctors other Officers and 68% Police Officials are of the opinion that procedure provided under the Act should be simplified. Percentages of SC officials of these categories, who are in conformity of this view, are 68, 73, 74, 70 and 67 respectively.[55]

60% STs, I.A.S., P.C.S., Officers, Doctors and other Officers[56] and 100% Police Officers[57] also hold this view.

Table No. 69B : Law Makers and Opinion Makers on Simplification of Procedure

Categories		*Responses in*							
		Number				*Percentage*			
		Yes	*No*	*Und.*	*Total*	*Yes*	*No*	*Und.*	*Total*
Law Makers & Opinion Makers	SCs	31	2	2	35	89	6	5	100
	STs	1	0	0	1	100	0	0	100
	Others	9	0	5	14	64	0	36	100

82% M.Ps., Legislators, Academicians, Media Persons, Social Activists and member of N.G.Os., *etc.*, are also of the same opinion. Percentage of SC respondents under this category is as high as 89.[58]

On the basis of discussion and percentage narrated hereinabove, it is concluded that there is suggestion of large number of public for simplification of procedure under the Act.

8.5 ESTABILISHMENT OF EXCLUSIVE SPECIAL COURTS

Question numbers 62 and 59 of the questionnaire for Different Units of the Legal System[59] and Law Makers and Opinion Makers,[60] respectively, elicited opinion from the respondents whether Special Courts under the Act should not be burdened with any other work except the cases under the Act?

Graph No. 137 : Suggestion : Establishment of Exclusive Special Courts

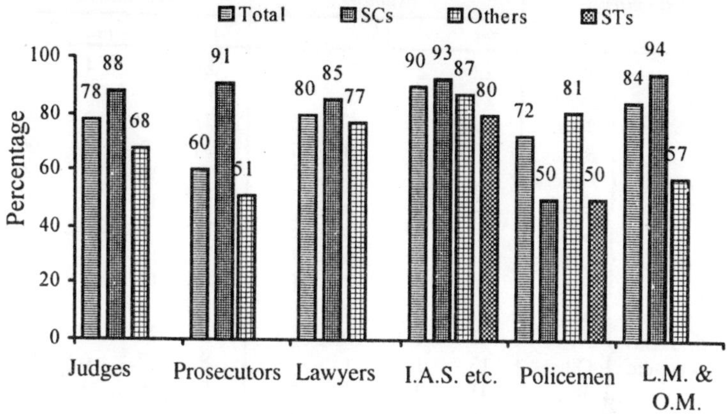

Table No. 70 : Establishment of Exclusive Special Courts

Categories		*Responses in*							
		Number				*Percentage*			
		Yes	*No*	*Und.*	*Total*	*Yes*	*No*	*Und.*	*Total*
Different Units of Legal System	SCs	95	13	4	112	85	12	3	100
	STs	5	2	0	7	71	29	0	100
	Others	130	36	15	181	72	20	8	100
	Total	230	51	19	300	77	17	6	100
L.M. & O.M.		42	4	4	50	84	8	8	100
Grand Total		272	55	23	350	78	16	6	100

350 respondents were examined on this question. Their responses are depicted in Graph No. 137 and Table Nos. 70, 70A and 70B. Out of these, 272 replied in affirmative, 55 in negative and 23 did not reply specifically.[61] Thus, 78% respondents replied in positive and 16% replied in negative. 77% officials forming part of Different Units of Legal System[62] and 84% Law Makers and Opinion Makers[63] are of the view that Special Courts should not be burdened with any other work except the cases under the Act.

Table No.70A : Different Units of Legal System on Establishment of Exclusive Special Courts

Categories		Responses in							
		Number				Percentage			
		Yes	No	Und.	Total	Yes	No	Und.	Total
Judges	SCs	22	2	1	25	88	8	4	100
	Others	17	3	5	25	68	12	20	100
	Total	39	5	6	50	78	10	12	100
Prosecutors	SCs	10	1	0	11	91	9	0	100
	Others	20	15	4	39	51	38	11	100
	Total	30	16	4	50	60	32	8	100
Lawyers	SCs	29	3	2	34	85	9	6	100
	Others	51	10	5	66	77	15	8	100
	Total	80	13	7	100	80	13	7	100
I.A.S., P.C.S., Doctors, etc.	SCs	28	1	1	30	93	4	3	100
	STs	4	1	0	5	80	20	0	100
	Others	13	1	1	15	87	7	6	100
	Total	45	3	2	50	90	6	4	100
Police Officials	SCs	6	6	0	12	50	50	0	100
	STs	1	1	0	2	50	50	0	100
	Others	29	7	0	36	81	19	0	100
	Total	36	14	0	50	72	28	0	100
Grand Total		230	51	19	300	77	17	6	100

78% Judge, 60% Public Prosecutors, 80% Lawyers, 90% I.A.S., P.C.S., Doctors and other Officers and 72% Police Officials hold this view. Percentages of SC respondents having similar opinion are 88, 91, 85, 93 and 50 respectively. Percentages of Non SC and ST respondents having conformity with this opinion are 68, 51, 77, 87 and 81, respectively.[64]

Percentages of STs respondents under the categories of I.A.S., P.C.S., Doctors and other Officers and Police Officials are 80 and 50, respectively.[65]

Table No. 70B : Law Makers and Opinion Makers on Establishment of Exclusive Special Courts

Categories		Responses in							
		Number				Percentage			
		Yes	No	Und.	Total	Yes	No	Und.	Total
Law Makers & Opinion Makers	SCs	33	1	1	35	94	3	3	100
	STs	1	0	0	1	100	0	0	100
	Others	8	3	3	14	57	22	21	100

84% M.Ps., Legislators, Academicians, Media Persons, Social Activists and members on N.G.Os., *etc.,* and 94% of SCs and 57% of Non SC & ST respondents of this category are having the same view.[66]

It is, therefore, concluded that more than three-fourth respondents are of the opinion that Special Courts created under the Act should not be burdened with any other work except the cases of atrocities, *etc.,* under the Act. All sections of the respondents are in agreement with this opinion.

8.6 PROMPT REHABILITATION OF THE VICTIMS OF ATROCITIES

Question number 65 of the questionnaire for Different Units of the Legal System[67] elicited opinion from the respondents whether victims of atrocities should be rehabilitated promptly by the State?

Table No. 71 : Prompt Rehabilitation of Victims of Atrocities

Categories		*Responses in*							
		Number				*Percentage*			
		Yes	*No*	*Und.*	*Total*	*Yes*	*No*	*Und.*	*Total*
Different Units of Legal System	SCs	107	3	2	112	95	3	2	100
	STs	7	0	0	7	100	0	0	100
	Others	143	21	17	181	79	12	9	100
	Total	257	24	19	300	86	8	6	100

300 respondents were examined on this question. Their responses are depicted in Graph No. 138 and Table No. 71. Out of these, 257 replied in affirmative, 24 in negative and 19 did not give any specific answer.[68] Thus, 86% replied in affirmative and 8% in negative.[69]

96% Judges, 78% Public Prosecutors, 76% Lawyers, 98% I.A.S., P.C.S., Doctors, and other Officers and 90% Police Officials are also of the opinion that victims of atrocities should be rehabilitated by the State promptly. Percentages of SC respondents under these categories are 100, 100, 91, 97 and 92, respectively. Percentages of Non SC & ST respondents under these categories are 92, 72, 68, 100 and 89, respectively. Percentages of ST I.A.S., P.C.S., Doctors and other Officers and Police Officials are 100 and 100, respectively.[70]

Table No. 71A : Different Units of Legal System on Prompt Rehabilitation of Victims of Atrocities

Categories		*Responses in*							
		Number				*Percentage*			
		Yes	*No*	*Und.*	*Total*	*Yes*	*No*	*Und.*	*Total*
Judges	SCs	25	0	0	25	100	0	0	100
	Others	23	0	2	25	92	0	8	100
	Total	48	0	2	50	96	0	4	100
Prosecutors	SCs	11	0	0	11	100	0	0	100
	Others	28	5	6	39	72	13	15	100
	Total	39	5	6	50	78	10	12	100
Lawyers	SCs	31	1	2	34	91	3	6	100
	Others	45	14	7	66	68	21	11	100
	Total	76	15	9	100	76	15	9	100
I.A.S., P.C.S. Doctors, etc.	SCs	29	1	0	30	97	3	0	100
	STs	5	0	0	5	100	0	0	100
	Others	15	0	0	15	100	0	0	100
	Total	49	1	0	50	98	2	0	100
Officials Police	SCs	11	1	0	12	92	8	0	100
	STs	2	0	0	2	100	0	0	100
	Others	32	2	2	36	89	6	5	100
	Total	45	3	2	50	90	6	4	100
Grand Total		257	24	19	300	86	8	8	100

Graph No. 138 : Suggestion : Prompt Rehabilitation of the Victims of Atrocities

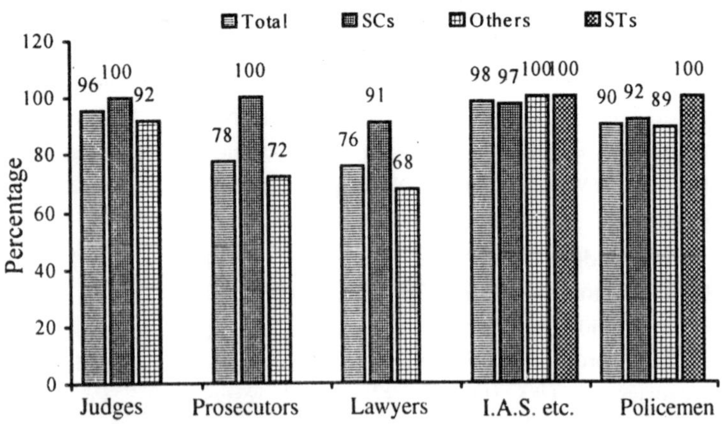

It is, therefore, concluded that majority of the people are of the opinion that victims of atrocities should be rehabilitated by the State promptly.

8.7 LEGAL AID TO THE VICTIMS

Question numbers 63 and 60 of the questionnaire for the Different Units of the Legal System[71] and Law Makers and Opinion Makers,[72] respectively, elicited information whether or not legal aid should be given to the victims of atrocities since the time and day of the commission of offences?

Table No. 72 : Legal Aid to Victims of Atrocities

Categories		*Responses in*							
		Number				*Percentage*			
		Yes	*No*	*Und.*	*Total*	*Yes*	*No*	*Und.*	*Total*
Different Units of Legal System	SCs	108	3	1	112	96	3	1	100
	STs	7	0	0	7	100	0	0	100
	Others	164	9	8	181	91	5	4	100
	Total	279	12	9	300	93	4	3	100
L.M. & O.M.		48	0	2	50	96	0	4	100
Grand Total		327	12	11	350	93	4	3	100

Table No. 72A : Different Units of Legal System on Legal Aid to Victims of Atrocities

Categories		*Responses in*							
		Number				*Percentage*			
		Yes	*No*	*Und.*	*Total*	*Yes*	*No*	*Und.*	*Total*
Judges	SCs	25	0	0	25	100	0	0	100
	Others	23	1	1	25	92	4	4	100
	Total	48	1	1	50	96	2	2	100
Prosecutors	SCs	11	0	0	11	100	0	0	100
	Others	31	4	4	39	80	10	10	100
	Total	42	4	4	50	84	8	8	100
Lawyers	SCs	32	2	0	34	94	6	0	100
	Others	63	2	1	66	95	3	2	100
	Total	95	4	1	100	95	4	1	100
I.A.S., P.C.S., Doctors, etc.	SCs	29	0	1	30	97	0	3	100
	STs	5	0	0	5	100	0	0	100
	Others	14	1	0	15	93	7	0	100
	Total	48	1	1	50	96	2	2	100
Police Officials	SCs.	11	1	0	12	92	8	0	100
	STs.	2	0	0	2	100	0	0	100
	Others	33	1	2	36	92	3	5	100
	Total	46	2	2	50	92	4	4	100
Grand Total		279	12	9	300	93	4	3	100

350 respondents were examined on this question. Their responses are depicted in Graph No. 139 and Table Nos. 72, 72A & 72B. Out of these, 327 replied in affirmative, 12 in negative and 11 did not give any specific reply.[73] 93% officials forming part of Different Units of Legal System[74] and 96% Law Makers and Opinion Makers[75] replied in positive.

Graph No. 139 : Suggestion : Legal Aid to SCs since Commission of Atrocities

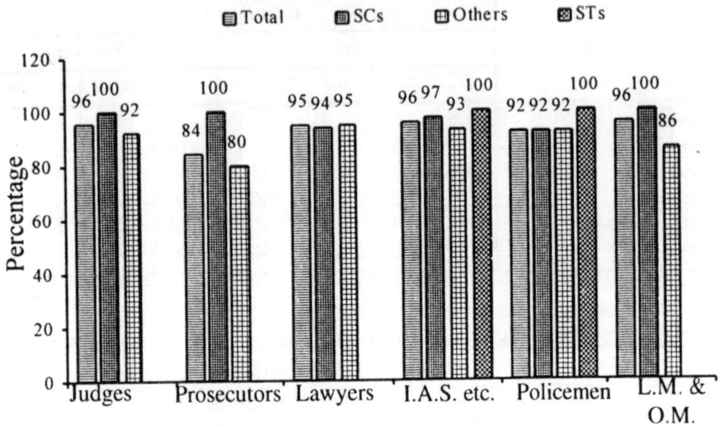

96% Judges, 84% Public Prosecutors, 95% Lawyers, 96% I.A.S., P.C.S., Doctors and other Officers and 92% Police Officers suggested for giving the legal aid to the victims of atrocities since the time and day of the commission of offence. Percentages of SC officials, who are in conformity of this view, are 100, 100, 94, 97 and 92 respectively.[76]

Table No. 72B : Law Makers and Opinion Makers on Legal Aid to Victims of Atrocities

Categories		*Responses in*							
		Number				*Percentage*			
		Yes	*No*	*Und.*	*Total*	*Yes*	*No*	*Und.*	*Total*
Law Makers & Opinion Makers	SCs	35	0	0	35	100	0	0	100
	STs	1	0	0	1	100	0	0	100
	Others	12	0	2	14	86	0	14	100

96% M.Ps., Legislators, Academicians, Media Persons, Social Activists and members of N.G.Os., *etc.*, are of the same opinion. 100% SC respondents under these categories replied in affirmative.[77]

Question numbers 64 and 61 of the questionnaire for the Different Units of the Legal System[78] and Law Makers and Opinion Makers,[79] respectively, elicited information whether or not legal aid should be given to the SCs even before commission of atrocities under the Act in atrocities prone area?

Table No. 72C : Legal Aid to SCs before Subjugation of Atrocities

Categories		*Responses in*							
		Number				*Percentage*			
		Yes	*No*	*Und.*	*Total*	*Yes*	*No*	*Und.*	*Total*
Different Units of Legal System	SCs.	99	12	1	112	88	11	1	100
	STs.	7	0	0	7	100	0	0	100
	Others	135	31	15	181	75	17	15	100
	Total	241	43	16	300	80	14	6	100
L.M. & O.M.		44	5	1	50	88	10	2	100
Grand Total		285	48	17	350	81	14	5	100

Table No. 72D : Different Units of Legal System on Providing Legal Aid to SCs before Commission of Atrocities

Categories		*Responses in*							
		Number				*Percentage*			
		Yes	*No*	*Und.*	*Total*	*Yes*	*No*	*Und.*	*Total*
Judges	SCs	20	5	0	25	80	20	0	100
	Others	17	7	1	25	68	28	4	100
	Total	37	12	1	50	74	24	2	100
Prosecutors	SCs	8	3	0	11	73	27	0	100
	Others	25	8	6	39	64	21	15	100
	Total	33	11	6	50	66	22	12	100
Lawyers	SCs	31	3	0	34	91	9	0	100
	Others	55	7	4	66	83	11	6	100
	Total	86	10	4	100	86	10	4	100
I.A.S., P.C.S., Doctors, etc.	SCs	28	1	1	30	93	4	3	100
	STs	5	0	0	5	100	0	0	100
	Others	10	2	3	15	67	13	20	100
	Total	43	3	4	50	86	6	8	100
Police Officials	SCs	12	0	0	12	100	0	0	100
	STs	2	0	0	2	100	0	0	100
	Others	28	7	1	36	78	19	3	100
	Total	42	7	1	50	84	14	2	100
Grand Total		241	43	16	300	80	14	6	100

350 respondents were examined on this question. Their responses are depicted in Graph No. 140 and Table Nos. 72C, 72D and 72E.

Out of these, 285 replied in affirmative, 48 in negative and 17 did not give any specific reply.[80] Thus, 81% replied in affirmative. Only 14% replied in negative. 80% officials forming part of Different Units of Legal System[81] and 88% Law Makers and Opinion Makers[82] replied in positive.

Graph No. 140 : Suggestion : Legal Aid to SCs before Commission of Atrocities

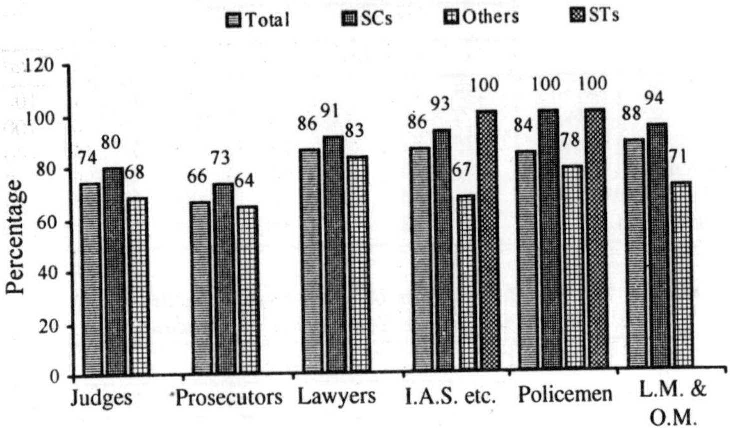

74% Judges, 66% Public Prosecutors, 86% Lawyers and I.A.S., P.C.S., Doctors and other Officers and 84% Police Officials are of the view that legal aid should be provided to the SCs in the atrocities prone area even before the commission of atrocities on them. Percentages of SC officials who are in conformity with this view are 80, 73, 91, 93 and 100, respectively. Percentage of ST I.A.S., P.C.S., Doctors and other Officers agreeing to this view is 100.[83]

Table No. 72E : Law Makers and Opinion Makers on Providing Legal Aid to SCs before Commission of Atrocities

Categories		*Responses in*							
		Number				*Percentage*			
		Yes	*No*	*Und.*	*Total*	*Yes*	*No*	*Und.*	*Total*
Law Makers & Opinion Makers	SCs	33	2	0	35	94	6	0	100
	STs	1	0	0	1	100	0	0	100
	Others	10	3	1	14	71	21	8	100

88% M.Ps., Legislators, Academicians, Media Persons, Social

Activists and members of N.G.Os., *etc.*, are of the same opinion. Percentage of SC respondents under these categories, who replied in affirmative, is 94.[84]

On the basis of discussion and percentage narrated hereinabove, it is concluded that people are of the view that legal aid should be provided to the victims and potential victims of atrocities, not only since the time and date of the commission of atrocities on them but also even before the commission of atrocities on them, in the atrocities prone areas.

8.8 CREATION OF CENTRALISED SPECIAL ENFORCEMENT AGENCY

Question numbers 61 and 58 of the questionnaire for Different Units of the Legal System[85] and Law Makers and Opinion Makers,[86] respectively, elicited information about the desirability of creation of centralized special enforcement agency for effective implementation of the Act.

Table No. 73 : Creation of Centralised Special Enforcement Agency

Categories		*Responses in*							
		Number				*Percentage*			
		Yes	*No*	*Und.*	*Total*	*Yes*	*No*	*Und.*	*Total*
Different Units of Legal System	SCs	96	10	6	112	86	9	5	100
	STs	6	1	0	7	86	14	0	100
	Others	134	24	23	181	74	13	13	100
	Total	236	35	29	300	79	11	10	100
L.M. & O.M.		43	4	3	50	86	8	6	100
Grand Total		279	39	32	350	80	11	9	100

350 respondents were examined on this question. Their responses are depicted in Graph No. 141 and Table Nos. 73, 73A and 73B. Out of these, 279 replied in affirmative, 39 in negative and 32 did not give any specific reply.[87] Thus, 80% agreed to the creation of centralized special enforcement agency for effective implementation of the Act. 79% officials forming part of Different Units of the Legal System[88] and 86% Law Makers and Opinion Makers[89] opined in favour of it.

Graph No. 141 : Suggestion : Creation of Centralised Special Enforcement Agency

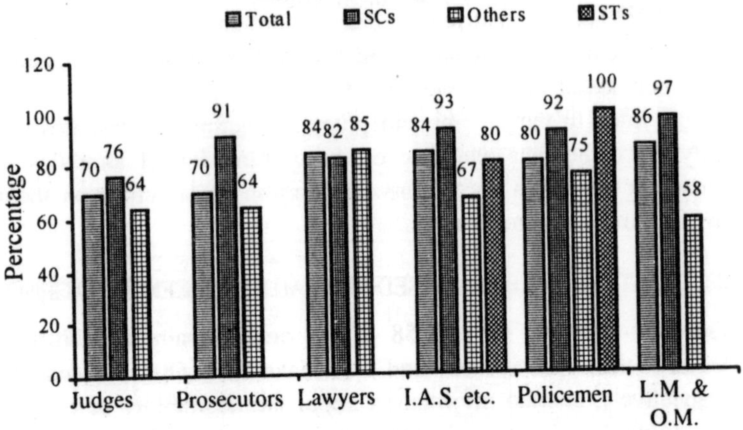

Table No. 73A : Different Units of Legal System on Creation of Centralised Special Enforcement Agency

Categories		*Responses in*							
		Number				*Percentage*			
		Yes	*No*	*Und.*	*Total*	*Yes*	*No*	*Und.*	*Total*
Judges	SCs	19	4	2	25	76	16	8	100
	Others	16	1	8	25	64	4	32	100
	Total	35	5	10	50	70	10	20	100
Prosecutors	SCs	10	1	0	11	91	9	0	100
	Others	25	8	6	39	64	20	16	100
	Total	35	9	6	50	70	18	12	100
Lawyers	SCs	28	4	2	34	82	12	6	100
	Others	56	6	4	66	85	9	6	100
	Total	84	10	6	100	84	10	6	100
I.A.S.,P.C.S., Doctors, etc.	SCs	28	1	1	30	93	4	3	100
	STs	4	1	0	5	80	20	0	100
	Others	10	1	4	15	67	7	26	100
	Total	42	3	5	50	84	6	10	100
Police Officials	SCs	11	0	1	12	92	0	8	100
	STs	2	0	0	2	100	0	0	100
	Others	27	8	1	36	75	22	3	100
	Total	40	8	2	50.	80	16	4	100
Grand Total		236	35	29	300	79	11	10	100

70% Judges, and Public Prosecutors, 84% Lawyers, I.A.S., P.C.S., Doctors and other Officers and 80% Police Officials desired for creation of centralized special enforcement agency. Percentages of SC officials in this regard are 76, 91, 82, 93 and 92, respectively.[90]

Table No. 73B : Law Makers and Opinion Makers on Creation of Centralised Special Enforcement Agency

Categories		Responses in							
		Number				Percentage			
		Yes	No	Und.	Total	Yes	No	Und.	Total
Law Makers & Opinion Makers	SCs	34	1	0	35	97	3	0	100
	STs	1	0	0	1	100	0	0	100
	Others	8	3	3	14	58	21	21	100

86% M.Ps., Legislators, Academicians, Media Persons, Social Activists and members of N.G.Os., *etc.*, also expressed their opinion in favour of this suggestion. Percentage of SC respondents in this regard is 97.[91]

On the basis of discussion and percentage narrated hereinabove, it is concluded that almost all the respondents, barring negligible, are of the view that centralized special enforcement agency should be created for effective implementation of the Act.

8.9 REMOVAL OF UNTOUCHABILITY

Question number 66 of the questionnaire for Law Makers and Opinion Makers[92] elicited information whether or not annihilation of caste system may result into removal of untouchability which in turn may lead to decline in atrocities on the members of SCs ?

Table No. 74 : Law Makers and Opinion Makers on Removal of Untouchability

Categories		Responses in							
		Number				Percentage			
		Yes	No	Und.	Total	Yes	No	Und.	Total
Law Makers & Opinion Makers	SCs	30	5	0	35	86	14	0	100
	STs	1	0	0	1	100	0	0	100
	Others	11	1	2	14	79	7	14	100
	Total	42	6	2	50	84	12	4	100

50 respondents were examined on this question. Their responses are depicted in Graph No. 142 and Table No. 74. Out of these, 42 replied in positive, 6 in negative and 2 did not give any specific reply.[93] Thus, 84% M.Ps., Legislators, Academicians, Media Persons, Social Activists and members of N.G.Os., *etc.*, are of the view that annihilation of caste system may result into removal of untouchability

Graph No. 142 : Suggestion : Annhilation of Caste System for Removal of Untouchability

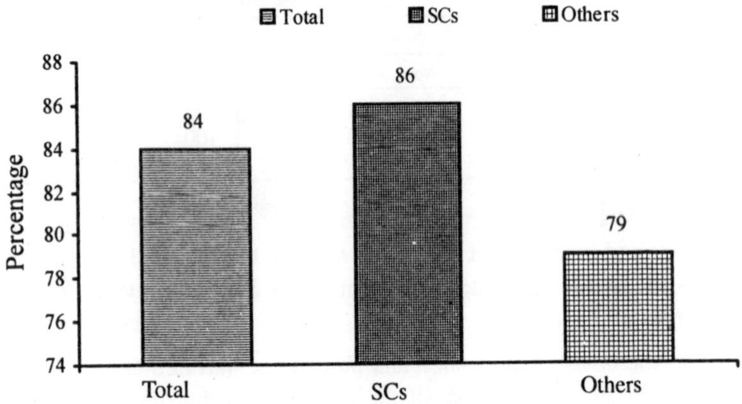

which in turn may lead to decline in atrocities on the members of the SCs. Percentage of SC respondents under this category is 86.[94]

Question No. 67 of the questionnaire for Different Units of the Legal System[95] also elicited information whether or not removal of untouchability may lead to eradication of atrocities on the members of SCs?

Table No. 74A : Removal of Untouchability for Prevention of Atrocities on SCs

Categories		*Responses in*							
		Number				*Percentage*			
		Yes	*No*	*Und.*	*Total*	*Yes*	*No*	*Und.*	*Total*
Different Units of Legal System	SCs.	97	12	3	112	87	11	2	100
	STs.	5	2	0	7	71	39	0	100
	Others	148	21	12	181	82	12	6	100
	Total	250	35	15	300	83	12	5	100

300 respondents were examined on this question. Their responses are depicted in Graph No. 143 and Table Nos. 74A and 74B. Out of these, 250 replied in affirmative, 35 in negative and 15 did not give any specific reply.[96] Thus, 83% officials forming part of Different Units of the Legal System replied in positive.[97]

Graph No. 143 : Suggestion : Annihilation of Caste System for Removal of Untouchability

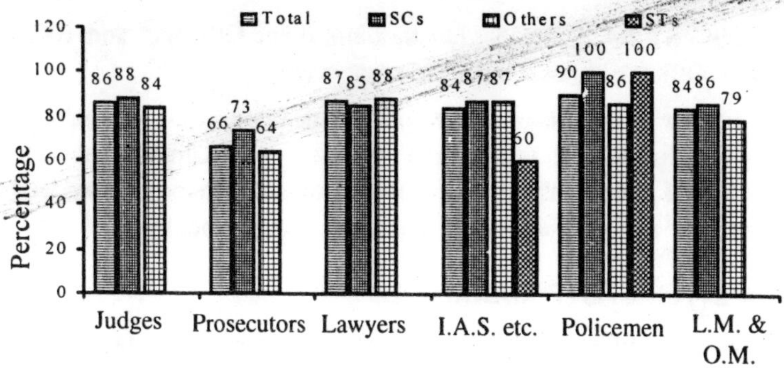

Table No. 74B : Different Units of Legal System on Removal of Untouchability for Prevention of Atrocities on SCs

Categories		Responses in							
		Number				Percentage			
		Yes	*No*	*Und.*	*Total*	*Yes*	*No*	*Und.*	*Total*
Judges	SCs	22	3	0	25	88	12	0	100
	Others	21	3	1	25	84	12	4	100
	Total	43	6	1	50	86	12	2	100
Prosecutors	SCs	8	2	1	11	73	18	9	100
	Others	25	7	7	39	64	18	18	100
	Total	33	9	8	50	66	18	16	100
Lawyers	SCs	29	4	1	34	85	12	3	100
	Others	58	5	3	66	88	8	4	100
	Total	87	9	4	100	87	9	4	100
I.A.S., P.C.S., Doctors, etc.	SCs	26	3	1	30	87	10	3	100
	STs	3	2	0	5	60	40	0	100
	Others	13	2	0	15	87	13	0	100
	Total	42	7	1	50	84	14	2	100
Police Officials	SCs	12	0	0	12	100	0	0	100
	STs	2	0	0	2	100	0	0	100
	Others	31	4	1	36	86	11	3	100
	Total	45	4	1	50	90	8	2	100
Grand Total		250	35	15	300	83	12	5	100

86% Judges, 66% Public Prosecutors, 87% Lawyers, 84% I.A.S., P.C.S., Doctors and other Officers and 90% Police Officials are of the opinion that removal of untouchability may lead to eradication of atrocities on the members of SC. Percentages of SC respondents who are in conformity of the view are 88, 73, 85, 87 and 100, respectively.[98]

60% ST I.A.S., P.C.S., Doctors and other Officers[99] and 100% Police Officials[100] also hold the same view.

In view of the discussion and percentage enumerated hereinabove, it is concluded that annihilation of caste system may result into removal of untouchability and removal of untouchability may lead to decline and eradication of atrocities on the members of SCs.

8.10 INTER-CASTE MARRIAGES

Question number 65 of the questionnaire for Law Makers and Opinion Makers,[101] elicited information whether or not inter-caste marriages at large scale may destroy the impregnable caste barrier?

Table No. 75 : Law Makers and Opinion Makers on Inter-Caste Marriages

Categories		*Responses in*							
		Number				*Percentage*			
		Yes	*No*	*Und.*	*Total*	*Yes*	*No*	*Und.*	*Total*
Law Makers & Opinion Makers	SCs	28	6	0	35	80	20	0	100
	STs	1	0	0	1	100	0	0	100
	Others	10	3	1	14	72	21	7	i00
	Total	39	9	2	50	78	18	4	100

50 respondents were examined on this question. Their responses are depicted in Graph No. 144 and Table No. 75. Out of these, 39 replied in affirmative, 9 in negative and 2 did not express any opinion.[102] Thus, 78% M.Ps., Legislators, Academicians, Media Persons, Social Activists and member of N.G.Os., *etc.*, are of the view that inter-caste marriages at large scale may destroy the impregnable caste barrier. The percentage of SC respondents of these categories is as high as 80.[103]

It is, therefore, concluded that a large number of people are of the view that inter-caste marriage at large scale may destroy the caste system which may result into decline of atrocities on the SCs.

Graph No. 144 : Suggestion : Inter Caste Marriages : Issuance of the Whip

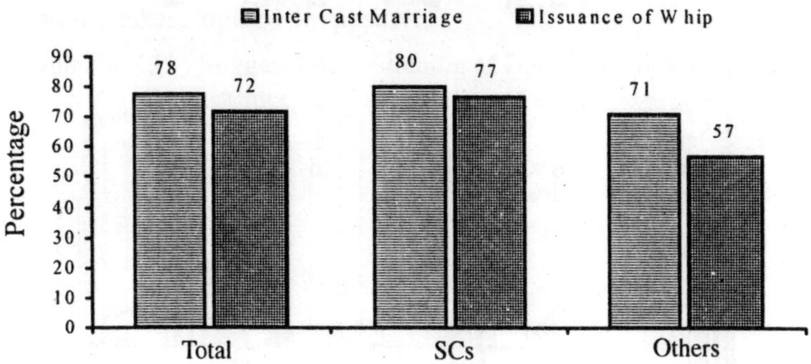

8.11 EXPUNCTION OF ANTI SCS & STS LITERATURE

Question number 67 of the questionnaire for Law Makers and Opinion Makers[104] elicited information whether or not expunction of literary verses in *Ramayana* or other Literature against SCs on ground of repugnancy with Constitutional ethos would be an effective way for the eradication of atrocities on the members of SCs?

Question number 68 of the questionnaire for Different Units of the Legal System[105] also elicited opinion whether or not expunction of those portions of literature which are contrary to Constitutional ethos, may help eradication of atrocities on the members of SCs?

Table No. 76 : Expunction of Anti SCs & STs Literature

Categories		*Responses in*							
		Number				*Percentage*			
		Yes	*No*	*Und.*	*Total*	*Yes*	*No*	*Und.*	*Total*
Different Units of Legal System	SCs	88	19	5	112	79	17	4	100
	STs	6	1	0	7	86	14	0	100
	Others	118	40	23	181	65	22	13	100
	Total	212	60	28	300	71	20	9	100
L.M. & O.M.		40	7	3	50	80	14	6	100
Grand Total		252	67	31	350	72	19	9	100

350 respondents were examined on these questions. Their responses are depicted in Graph No. 145 and Table Nos. 76, 76A

Graph No. 145 : Suggestion : Expunction of Anti SC & ST Literature

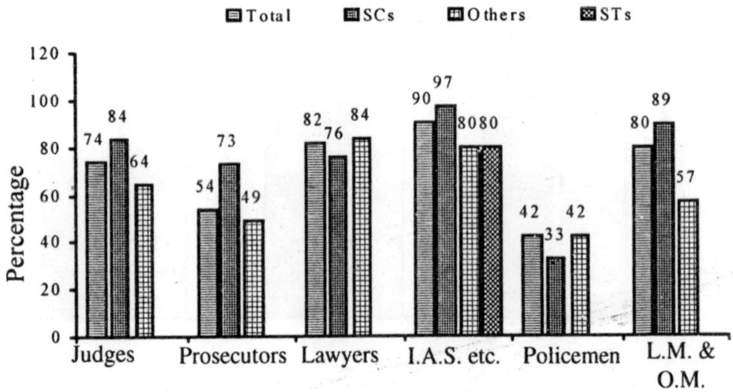

and 76B. Out of these, 252 replied in affirmative, 67 in negative and 31 did not give any specific reply.[106] Thus, 72% of the

Table No. 76A : Different Units of Legal System on Expunction of Anti SCs & STs Literature

Categories		Responses in							
		Number				Percentage			
		Yes	*No*	*Und.*	*Total*	*Yes*	*No*	*Und.*	*Total*
Judges	SCs	21	3	1	25	84	12	4	100
	Others	16	7	2	25	64	28	8	100
	Total	37	10	3	50	74	20	6	100
Prosecutors	SCs	8	2	1	11	73	18	9	100
	Others	19	9	11	39	49	23	28	100
	Total	27	11	12	50	54	22	24	100
Lawyers	SCs	26	7	1	34	76	21	3	100
	Others	56	5	5	66	84	8	8	100
	Total	82	12	6	100	82	12	6	100
I.A.S., P.C.S., Doctors, etc.	SCs	29	0	1	30	97	0	3	100
	STs	4	1	0	5	80	20	0	100
	Others	12	2	1	15	80	13	7	100
	Total	45	3	2	50	90	6	4	100
Police Officials	SCs	4	7	1	12	33	58	9	100
	STs	2	0	0	2	100	0	0	100
	Others	15	17	4	36	42	47	11	100
	Total	21	24	5	50	42	48	10	100
Grand Total		212	60	28	300	71	20	9	100

respondents favoured this suggestion. 80% Law Makers and Opinion Makers[107] and 71% Officials forming part of Different Units of the Legal System[108] are of the view that expunction of references derogatory of SC & ST from literature could be an effective way for eradication of atrocities on the member of SCs.

74% Judges, 54% Public Prosecutors, 82% Lawyers, 90% I.A.S. P.C.S., Doctors and other Officers and 42% Police Officials opined in favour of this suggestion. Percentages of SCs officials of these categories are 84, 73, 76, 97 and 33, respectively.[109]

Table No.76B : Law Makers and Opinion Makers on Expunction of Anti SCs & STs Literature

Categories		Responses in							
		Number				Percentage			
		Yes	*No*	*Und.*	*Total*	*Yes*	*No*	*Und.*	*Total*
Law Makers & Opinion Makers	SCs	31	2	2	35	89	6	5	100
	STs	1	0	0	1	100	0	0	100
	Others	8	5	1	14	57	36	7	100

80% M.Ps, Legislators, Academicians, Media Persons and Social Activists and members of N.G.Os., *etc.,* also hold this view. Percentage of SC respondents under this category is 89.[110]

On the basis of discussion and percentage narrated hereinabove, it is concluded that almost respondents, barring few, are in favour of expunction of literary verses of Hindu Scriptures, which are against SCs.

8.12 ISSUANCE OF THE WHIP

Question number 68 of the questionnaire on the subject for Law Makers and Opinion Makers,[111] elicited opinion from M.Ps, Legislators, Media Persons, Social Activists and members of N.G.Os., *etc.,* whether there should not be any whip in the legislatures if the matter under discussions or consideration or voting is concerning atrocities on the members of SCs ?

Table No. 77 : Law Makers and Opinion Makers on Issuance of Whip

Categories		Responses in							
		Number				*Percentage*			
		Yes	*No*	*Und.*	*Total*	*Yes*	*No*	*Und.*	*Total*
Law Makers & Opinion Makers	SCs	27	6	2	35	77	17	6	100
	STs	1	0	0	1	100	0	0	100
	Others	8	5	1	14	57	36	7	100
	Total	36	11	3	50	72	22	6	100

50 respondents were examined on this question. Their responses are depicted in Graph No. 144 and Table No. 77. Out of these, 36 replied in affirmative, 11 in negative and 3 did not give any specific answer.[112] Thus, 72% Law Makers and Opinion Makers replied in affirmative and 22% in negative. The percentage of SCs who are in agreement with this view is 77 and Non SC & ST is 57.[113]

It is, therefore, concluded that more than two-third Law Makers and Opinion Makers are of the opinion that there should not be any whip in the legislatures, if the matter under discussion or consideration or voting is concerning atrocities on the members of SCs.

Notes and References

1. *See*, annexures 1 and 3. The question is, "Do you suggest that asking of caste by a person to any other person when it was not required for giving any benefit to a member of SCs should be made an offence of atrocity under the Act?"
2. *Ibid.* and annexures 1 and 4.
3. *See*, Table No. 59.
4. *See*, Graph No. 61.
5. *See*, Graph No. 60.
6. *See*, Graph Nos. 62 to 66.
7. *See* Graph No. 60.
8. *See*, annexures 1 and 4. The question is, "Do you suggest that employing any child of SCs below the age of 14 years should be made an offence of atrocity under the Act?"
9. *See*, Table No. 60.
10. *See*, Graph No. 59.
11. *See*, annexures 1 and 4. The question is, "Do you suggest that blockade of service career of a member of SCs on false or fabricated report, *etc.*, should be made an offence of atrocity under the Act?"

12. *See*, Table No. 61
13. *See*, Graph No. 59.
14. *See*, annexures 1 and 4. The question is, "Do you suggest that economic exploitation of a member of SCs should be made an offence of atrocity under the Act?"
15. *See*, Table No. 62.
16. *See*, Graph No. 59.
17. *Ibid.*
18. *See*, annexures 1 and 4. The question is, "Do you suggest that practice of untouchability in any form with a member of SCs should be made an offence of atrocity under the Act?"
19. *See*, Table No. 63.
20. *See*, Graph No. 59.
21. *See*, annexures 1 and 4. The questions are, "Do you suggest that omission on the part of concerned authorities for promptly rehabilitating the victims of atrocities or failure to make payment of compensation amount to them within a month from the due date should also be made an offence under the Act?" And, "Do you suggest that omission on the part of concerned authorities to perform their duties under Rules 3 to 18 of the Rules should also be made an offence under the Act?"
22. *See*, Table No. 64.
23. *See*, Graph No. 60.
24. *See*, annexures 1 and 2. The questions are, "Do you think that invasion on body of a man (human) amounts to atrocity?", "Do you think that invasion of property of a man amounts to atrocity?" and, "Do you think that invasion of reputation of a man amounts to atrocity?"
25. *See*, Table Nos. 65, 65A and 65B.
26. *See*, Graph No. 1.
27. *Ibid.*
28. *See*, annexures 1 and 4. The question is, "Do you suggest that invasion on the body or reputation or property of a member of SCs should be made an offence of atrocity under the Act?"
29. *See*, Table No. 65F.
30. *See*, Graph No. 59.
31. *See*, annexures 1 and 2. The question is, "Do you think that subjecting a man to indignities, humiliations and harassment amounts to atrocity?"
32. *See*, Table No. 66.
33. *See*, Graph No. 1.
34. *Ibid.*
35. *See*, annexures 1 and 3. The question is, "Do you think that conducting refresher courses for all those who are in any way connected with giving effect to the provisions of the Act may help in eradication of atrocities on the members of SCs?"
36. *Ibid.* and annexures 1 and 4.
37. *See*, Table No. 67.
38. *See*, Graph No. 61.

39. *See*, Graph No. 60.
40. *See*, Graph Nos. 62 to 66.
41. *See*, Graph No. 60.
42. *See*, annexures 1 and 3. The question is, "Do you think that publicity of the provisions of the Act through *Doordarshan,* Radio and other public media may help in eradication of the atrocities on the members of the SCs?"
43. *Ibid.* and annexures 1 and 4.
44. *See*, Table No. 68.
45. *See*, Graph No. 61.
46. *See*, Graph No. 60.
47. *See*, Graph No. 65.
48. *See*, Graph No. 66.
49. *Supra,* note 46.
50. *See*, annexures 1 and 3. The question is, "Do you suggest for simplification of procedure under the Act?"
51. *Ibid.* and annexures 1 and 4.
52. *See*, Table No. 69.
53. *See*, Graph No. 61.
54. *See*, Graph No. 59.
55. *See*, Graph Nos. 62 to 66.
56. *See*, Graph No. 65.
57. *See*, Graph No. 66.
58. *See*, Graph No. 59.
59. *See*, annexures 1 and 3. The question is, "Do you suggest that the special court under the Act should not be burdened with any other work except the cases under the Act?"
60. *Ibid.* and annexures 1 and 4.
61. *See*, Table No. 70.
62. *See*, Graph No. 61.
63. *See*, Graph No. 59.
64. *See*, Graph No. 66.
65. *See*, Graph Nos. 65 and 66.
66. *See*, Graph No. 59.
67. *See*, annexures 1 and 3. The question is, "Do you suggest prompt rehabilitation of the victim of atrocities by the State?"
68. *See*, Table No. 71.
69. *See*, Graph No. 61.
70. *See*, Graph Nos. 62 to 66.
71. *See*, annexures 1 and 3. The question is, "Do you suggest giving legal Aid to the victim of offence since the time and day of the commission of offence?"
72. *Ibid.* and annexures 1 and 4.
73. *See*, Table No. 72.
74. *See*, Graph No. 61.
75. *See*, Graph No. 59.

76. *See*, Graph Nos. 62 to 66.
77. *See*, Graph No. 59.
78. *See*, annexures 1 and 3. The question is, "Do you suggest providing Legal Aid to SCs' even before commission of atrocity under the Act, in atrocity prone area?"
79. *Ibid.* and annexures 1 and 4.
80. *See*, Table No. 72C.
81. *See*, Graph No. 61.
82. *See*, Graph No. 59.
83. *See*, Graph Nos. 62 to 66.
84. *See*, Graph No. 59.
85. *See*, annexures 1 and 3. The question is, "Do you suggest creation of centralised special enforcement agency for effective implementation of the Act?"
86. *Ibid.* and annexures 1 and 4.
87. *See*, Table No. 73.
88. *See*, Graph No. 61.
89. *See*, Graph No. 59.
90. *See*, Graph Nos. 62 to 66.
91. *See*, Graph No. 59.
92 *See*, annexures 1 and 4. The question is, "Do you think that annihilation of caste system may result into removal of untouchability which in turn may lead to decline in atrocities on the members of the SCs'?"
93. *See*, Table No. 74.
94. *See*, Graph No. 60.
95. *See*, annexures 1 and 3. The question is, "Do you suggest that removal of untouchability may lead to eradication of atrocities on members of the SCs'?"
96. *See*, Table No. 74A.
97. *See*, Graph No. 61.
98. *See*, Graph Nos. 62 to 66.
99. *See*, Graph No. 65.
100. *See*, Graph No. 66.
101. *See*, annexures 1 and 4. The question is, "Do you think that inter-caste marriages at the large scale may destroy the impregnable caste barrier?"
102. *See*, Table No. 75.
103. *See*, Graph No. 60.
104. *See*, annexures 1 and 4. The question is, "Do you think that expunction of literary verses in *Ramayana* or other Literature against SCs on ground of unconstitutionality would be an effective way for the eradication of atrocities on the members of SCs?"
105. *See*, annexures 1 and 3. The question is, "Do you think that expunction of those portions of literature which are contrary to the provisions of constitution of India, may help in eradication of atrocities on the members of SCs?"
106. *See*, Table No. 76.

107 . *See*, Graph No. 61.
108. *See*, Graph No. 60.
109. *See*, Graph Nos. 62 to 66.
110. *See*, Graph No. 60.
111. *See*, annexures 1 and 4. The question is, "Do you suggest that there should not be any whip in the legislatures if the matter under discussion or consideration or voting is concerning atrocities on the members of SCs?"
112. *See*, Table No. 77.
113. *See*, Graph No. 60.

CONCLUSIONS AND SUGGESTIONS

CONCLUSIONS

Atrocities on SCs have assumed the rank of a major social problem in our society

Though atrocities on the SCs have become a regular phenomenon in our society, yet its form and content has been changing and in the contemporary society, atrocities are increasingly assuming violent and aggressive forms such as gang rapes and massacres. The atrocities on the SCs are committed due to caste prejudice or hatred. Initially, castes were formed on the basis of division of labour to facilitate the smooth running of the society which, subsequently, became rigid and repressive. Various Hindu scriptures imposed caste disabilities, which gave birth to practice of untouchability and atrocities on the SCs. The practice of untouchability and caste discrimination were regularly enforced by the Non State Legal Systems and the State Legal System was providing support to it. As the Hindu religious books promoted discriminations on the basis of caste, this led to subjugation of the SCs by all the upper castes. The problem of atrocities on SCs was not taken seriously by the earlier rulers including the British. However, towards the end of their rule in India the British Government changed its approach to caste discriminatory practices by withdrawing support to enforce caste disabilities. Initially support to enforce caste disabilities was withdrawn notionally but subsequently several measures were taken in the form of passing various enactments to remove caste disabilities. Since the time of independence, successive governments have been making efforts to prevent the atrocities on SCs and also enacted certain specific laws, including the Act, to protect the civil rights and to prevent atrocities on SCs. The Constitution of India laid emphasis to provide social, economic and political justice; liberty of thought, expression, belief, faith and worship; equality of status and of opportunity to its citizens, besides, promoting among them all fraternity, assuring the dignity of the individual. So many welfare legislations, such as Abolition of Bonded Labour System Act, Minimum Wages Act, Payment of Wages Act, U.O. Act, PCR Act, *etc.*, were passed and enforced. So many other welfare measures were also taken. All those gave birth to awakening amongst SCs. All those SCs who had been living like animal, started realizing themselves as human being and started asserting their social, economic, religious, educational and political rights. The Non SC & ST did not appreciate this change unreservedly. Rather, they were perturbed by the disturbance it caused to the *status quo*. They thought it right to suppress this change. So more heinous and serious crimes were committed against the SCs. These are before us in the form of massacres, organised gang rapes, burning of houses and crops and arson, *etc.*, of the SCs. All this has given a serious turn to the problem of atrocities on SCs.

Atrocity not only seriously affect the body of the victim but also it affects adversely his feelings. His physical, mental, educational, social, economic and psychological status is adversely affected. It creates a sense of insecurity in the minds of the victims. It also causes empathy amongst all others who are similarly situated.

If there are five brothers in a family and out of them four are wealthy, well educated and cultured and one of them is poor, illiterate and backward due to non-cooperation of his four brothers, none would say that family as advanced, educated and cultured. Likewise, if in a country 24% of population is backward, illiterate and uneducated and living the life of animals, none would say that country is advanced and developed. In this view of the matter, commission of atrocities on SCs has adversely affected advancement and development of our country. There is almost consensus on the point that atrocities on SCs are still being committed and commission and continuation of atrocities on the SCs has not only hampered development and advancement of our country but also it is blot on our society.

It happens in a family that other brothers help and push their brother who has lagged behind so that he could attain his all round development and could come up to their level. But in the matter of SCs, the Non SC & ST do not treat them their brothers and do not make any effort for their advancement and development. Rather, they subjugate them. This attitude has to be changed in the interest of promoting feeling of brotherhood and fraternity amongst our countrymen. This will bring advancement of our country and will save our country from disintegration. Although we find innumerable N.G.Os doing so many works even taking care of animals but we do not find any such N.G.O. in actual working, who could be said to have done commendable job for highlighting the problem of atrocities and trying to prevent or minimize it. It is, therefore, concluded that there is poor social awareness about the problem of atrocities amongst our society in general and Target Group in particular.

Consensus about the Causes of Atrocities

There cannot be different opinions on the point that commission and continuation of atrocities on the SCs is a social evil. This problem has, therefore, to be cured as the doctor cures the diseases. He applies his mind to diagnose the disease and then prescribes the medicine. In the same way, if we want to cure this social evil of atrocities on the SCs, then we have first to identify the causes of subjugation and perpetuation of atrocities on the SCs. Views of the respondents have been analyzed to find out, whether caste system, endogamy, caste hatred, practice of untouchability, religion, cultural backwardness, illiteracy, poverty, economic dependence or backwardness, ignorance of law, self-assertion by the SCs and lack of political will are the causes or factors for subjugation and perpetuation of atrocities on the SCs. It emerged that there are number of reasons, factors and causes for commission of atrocities on them, yet caste system, endogamy, caste hatred, untouchability, illiteracy, poverty, economic backwardness, ignorance of law, self-assertion by SCs and lack of political will are the prominent causes for commission of atrocities on them. There are no two opinions about these causes and factors that are responsible for commission and continuation of atrocities on SCs.

Although it is the view of majority of the respondents that illiteracy is not a cause for commission of atrocities on the SCs, yet if this cause is analyzed, keeping in view that illiteracy is curse and education is boon and education plays an important role in the overall development of human beings; it infuses awakening and social consciousness; help in removing quagmire of ignorance; promotes social mobility and provide chance of placement in government and semi-government services and thereby it is instrumental in shaping the qualities of man, then it can be said that illiteracy not only of Target Group but also of Non SC & ST has contributed a lot in subjugation of atrocities on the SCs. Thus, illiteracy in my view is also a prominent cause for commission and continuation of atrocities on the SCs.

Awareness about the Act and its Implementation

One of the objectives of the present study is to find out the extent of awareness of the anti-atrocities law in the Indian society, particularly the awareness of the key provisions of the Act, the enforcement machinery, the rehabilitative, monetary and other relief provided under the Act and Rules framed thereunder for the victims of the atrocities. It was found that 23% officials forming part of Different Units of the Legal System, *i.e.*, Police Personnel, Prosecutors, Lawyers, Doctors, Judges, Magistrates and other Officials involved under the Act are not aware even about the existence of the Act. It was also found that less than half of the Law Makers and Opinion Makers, *i.e.*, MPs., Legislators, Academicians, Media Persons, Social Activists and members of N.G.Os., are only aware about the existence of the Act. Two-third population of the SCs are not aware about the existence of the Act. It was also revealed that 70% population of Target Group, 62% Law Makers and Opinion Makers and 42% Officials forming Different Units of Legal System are not aware that the Act was enforced *w.e.f.* 30th January, 1990. 72% Law Makers and Opinion Makers did not know about the existence of the Rules.

It also revealed that one-third respondents were not aware about the special features of the Act, *e.g.*, that under the provisions of the Act only Non SC & ST persons can be offenders. The level of awareness of the Officials of Legal System Functionaries is the similar. Percentage of ignorance of Target Group and Law Makers and Opinion Makers was more than that. It was also found that 54% people of SCs and 24% officials forming Different Units of Legal System and 46% Law Makers and Opinion Makers did not know that the Act has categorised several behaviours as atrocities and included them in the definition of the atrocities. It was also found that 57% of the SCs did not know that offenders of atrocities are not entitled to get anticipatory bail and convicts of atrocities, except juveniles, are not entitled to get benefit of probation.

The position of SC persons having post graduates degree was also not found satisfactory. Amongst them 46% did not know about said provisions of the Act. 94% illiterates of SC population were found ignorant about it. About half of the persons of SCs and amongst them more than two-third illiterates and businessmen, were found not knowing that fouling of water amounts to atrocities on them. More than one-third persons of SCs and more than half Under Graduates, Illiterates, Businessmen of Target Group are not aware that causing injury, *etc.*, by dumping obnoxious substance amounts to atrocities on them.

One-third population of SCs and amongst them two-third illiterates are not aware that forcing them to eat or drink inedible substances; stripping or parading them naked; outrage of modesty and sexual exploitation and forcing them to leave their place of residence amounts to commission of atrocities on them.

38% members of SCs and amongst them 52% Under Graduates, 50% Businessmen and 81% illiterates are not aware that giving false information to public servants about them and thereby causing such public servant to use his lawful power to the injury or annoyance to them amounts to atrocities on them.

54% members of SCs and amongst them 60% Post Graduates, 65% Matric Pass, 66% persons engaged in different occupations and 87% Illiterates are not aware that giving false evidence against them or destroying evidence of atrocities amounts to atrocitics on them.

57% members of SCs and amongst them 53% Post Graduates, 56% Under Graduates, 74% Matric Pass and two-third Businessmen and engaged in different occupations and 81% Illiterates are not aware that properties of offenders of atrocities can be attached and properties of convicts can be forfeited.

62% members of SCs and amongst them 67% Businessmen, 68% Under Graduates, 74% Matric Pass, 75% engaged in different occupations and 94% Illiterates are not aware that accused of atrocity offences can neither be given anticipatory bail nor convict can be released on probation.

Minority of the Illiterates and Businessmen of the Target Group did know that in case they are not satisfied with the work of Special Public Prosecutor, they should bring it to the knowledge either of the Director of Prosecution or the District Magistrate. Like is the position regarding making complaints of the investigation officer about his unsatisfactory investigation to the senior officers of the police. It was also found that majority of them are not aware that in case of unsatisfactory investigation by the police, they may file a complaint to the Court.

Large percentage of Illiterates and Matric Pass of the Target Group did not know that F.I.R. could be lodged by registered post, in case of refusal of its registration in the Police Station. The position of Illiterates of the Target Group regarding awareness of the provisions of the Act is much below than the average level of awareness of Target Group. As per latest census conducted in the year 1991 the literacy rate of Target Group was 37.14%. Thus 62.86% population of SC is Illiterate. It was found that 70% population of Target Group, which comes to about 11.31 crores, is not aware about the Act and its provisions.

On the basis of above analysis of the data, it can be concluded that there is little awareness about the provisions of the Act and its implications amongst the population of SCs for whose benefit and welfare the Act was enacted and rules were framed.

The analysis of result also reveals that one-third officials of Different Units of the Legal System who are entrusted to enforce the provisions of the Act are not aware that the Act is applicable only against Non SCs & STs. One-third of them is not aware that forcing a member of SCs or STs to eat or drink inedible or obnoxious substance amounts to atrocities on them.

More than one-fourth of them is not aware that causing injury or annoyance to a member of SCs or STs by dumping obnoxious substance in his premises or neighbourhood amounts to atrocities on them. Like is the awareness amongst them about commission of atrocities on SCs by wrongfully occupying their land or dispossessing them from their properties. One-fifth of them is not aware that stripping of a member of SCs or parading him naked amounts to atrocities on SCs. Like is the awareness amongst them about commission of atrocities on SCs by fouling of water or by denial of access to public place or by humiliation. One-fourth of them are not aware that atrocities on SCs can be committed by compelling or enticing them to do *begar* or bonded labour. 30% of them do not know that interference in the casting of vote by SCs amounts to atrocities. One-third of them do not know that sexual exploitation of a SC woman or outrage of her modesty amounts to atrocity. 40% of them do not know that instituting false, malicious or vexatious suit or criminal or other legal proceedings against them amounts to atrocity. One-third of them are not aware that giving false evidence against a person of SC or removal of evidence of atrocities amounts to atrocities. 30% of them do not know that causing damage or destruction to the properties of SC persons amounts to atrocities on them.

One-fourth of Lawyers and Police Officials and One-third of I.A.S., P.C.S., Doctors and other Officers do not have the knowledge of the Act. 56% Public Prosecutors do not know that forcing a person to eat or drink inedible or obnoxious substances is an offence of atrocities. 50% Police Officials are not aware that Act is applicable only against Non SC & ST persons. 60% of the Judicial Officers are not aware that instituting false or malicious suit, criminal or other legal proceedings against the members of SCs is an offence of atrocities. 50% of them do not know that false information to public servant about the SCs and thereby causing such public servant to use his lawful power to the injury or annoyance of a member of a SC is an offence of atrocities. 46% of them do not know that sexual exploitation of a woman of SC is an offence of atrocities. Public Prosecutors do not stand on a better footing on these aspects.

On careful perusal of the results shown in Graph Nos. 24 to 41, it can be concluded that substantial percentage of officials forming Different Units of Legal System are not aware about the new law, *i.e.,* the provisions of the Act and its implications.

It can be concluded in respect of Law Makers and Opinion Makers that 56% of them even do not know about the salient features of the Act and more than 70% of them are not aware about the existence of the Rules and 50% of them are not aware about categorization of offences of atrocities in the Act. The level of their awareness about the provisions of the Act cannot be said as satisfactory.

It can, therefore, be concluded that a large percentage of Indian society is not aware about existence of the Act, the Rules, the inclusion of several behaviours as offences of atrocities, the enforcement machineries, rehabilitative, monetary and other relief provided under the Act.

Adequacy of Legal and Administrative Infrastructure

The Act and the Rules framed thereunder envisaged the establishment of Special Courts, appointment of Special Public Prosecutors, Investigating Officers, Nodal and Special Officers, creation of SCs & STs Protection Cells and constitution of State and District Level Vigilance and Monitoring Committees. The adequacy of these machineries and infrastructure provided under the Act and the Rules framed thereunder is to be seen from two angles, firstly, it has to be seen if the people for whose benefit the legal and administrative infrastructures has been created have its knowledge? Are the Legal System functionaries, whose duty is to enforce the provisions of the Act, aware about it and discharging their duties accordingly? Have the Law Makers and Opinion Makers who are under a duty to create awareness in the society and to provide congenial receptive environment in the society, discharged their duties to achieve the goal for which the Act was made and the Rules were framed?

The analysis of data shows that 48% population is ignorant about appointment of Special Public Prosecutors. 54% population of Target Group and 43% officials forming Different Units of Legal System do not know that Special Courts have been established for trial of offences of atrocities and Special Public Prosecutors have been appointed to conduct the cases of atrocities.

64% M.Ps., Legislators, Media Persons, Social Activists and members of N.G.Os. do not know about setting up of SCs & STs Protection Cells, nomination of Nodal Officers and appointment of Special Officers for effective implementation of the provisions of the Act. 71% population of SCs under these categories is ignorant about these machineries envisaged under the Act for their welfare. 65% population of Target Group do not know that they may get medical and financial help and compensation from SCs & STs Protection Cells and Special Courts, *etc.*

The data depicted through Table No. 26 and Graph Nos. 23 and 92 shows that 76% Law Makers and Opinion Makers do not know that the Rules framed under the Act envisaged for constitution of State and District Level Vigilance and Monitoring Committees for implementation of the provisions of the Act and reviewing the implementation of the provisions of the Act, respectively.

On the basis of above discussion and result of this study, it is concluded that there is little awareness amongst Target Group and Law Makers and Opinion Makers and inadequate awareness amongst officials forming Different Units of Legal System about machineries and fora provided under the Act and the Rules framed thereunder.

58% of the population of Target Group do not know that they can get services of Senior Advocate for conducting cases of atrocities at government expenses. Amongst them 87% Illiterates are ignorant about this special provision for their benefit. As regards implementation of this provision is concerned. 92% Law Makers and Opinion Makers and 87% officials of Different Units of Legal System admitted that they have neither given nor caused to be given or seen giving the victim of atrocities services of senior advocate of his choice for conducting his case at government expenses under the Act or Rules framed thereunder. 86% Law Makers and Opinion Makers admitted that they never helped the victims of atrocities to obtain compensation from the State.

80% Law Makers and Opinion Makers directly and 16% indirectly opined that SCs & STs Protection Cells have not been functioning effectively in combating atrocities on the members of SCs. There is consensus of Law Makers and Opinion Makers that there is no co-ordination amongst Nodal Officers, District Magistrate, Superintendent of Police and Investigating Officers, *etc.*, for real implementation of the provisions of the Act.

Majority of the Judges, Public Prosecutors, Lawyers, I.A.S., P.C.S., Doctors, M.Ps., Legislators, Academicians, Media Persons, Social Activists and members of N.G.Os. are of the opinion that there is no sufficient infrastructure with the Investigating Agencies to meet the requirement under the Act.

80% Judges are of the opinion that Special Courts have no sufficient infrastructure to discharge their duties promptly, smoothly and efficaciously. Majority of the officials forming Different Units of Legal System is of the same opinion. 62% Law Makers and Opinion Makers are also in conformity of this view.

55% Legal System functionaries and 60% Law Makers and Opinion Makers also opined that the Special Courts constituted under the Act are overburdened with other work which impede them to devote sufficient time for disposal of cases under the Act.

A perusal of data depicted through Table Nos. 58 and 58A and Graph Nos. 44 and 112 show that Legal System functionaries and Law Makers and Opinion Makers have opined that Special Courts, machineries and fora provided under the Act are not adequate.

It is, therefore, concluded that the machineries and infrastructure provided under the Act though seem to be adequate in theory but in practice it is not so as the machineries envisaged under the Act and Rules framed thereunder have not been working satisfactorily.

Attitudes and Motivations of the Functionaries

The functionaries who are entrusted to implement the provisions of the Act or to do other connected duties are the Police Officials, Investigating Officers, Special Public Prosecutors, Special Courts, SCs & STs Protection Cells, Nodal Officers, Special Officers, State and District Level Vigilance and Monitoring Committees.

The result of the study depicted through Table Nos. 49 and 49A and Graph Nos. 42 and 119 shows that only 85% persons of Target Group, amongst them 12% Post Graduates, 13% Graduates, 10% Service Personnel and 0% Illiterates opined that Police Officials lodge their reports and supply them copy of F.I.R. free of cost. Thus 85% population of Target Group and amongst them 100% Illiterates are of the view that those Police Officials neither lodge their report nor supply them copy of F.I.R. free of cost.

It is the duty of the Police Officials to take preventive actions for saving the SCs from atrocities and for keeping the peace and good behaviour and maintenance of public order and tranquillity in the atrocity prone area. The study of Graph Nos. 46, 47 and 102 and Table Nos. 33, 33A and 33B shows that only 17% officials of Different Units of Legal System have performed their duties in this respect. Thus 83% of them never took any preventive measures to save SCs from atrocities.

The Rules framed under the Act cast a duty upon the functionaries to grant arm licences to victims of atrocities and members of SCs and cancel arm licences of offenders of atrocities, *etc.* The study of Graph Nos. 103 and 105 and Table Nos. 34 and 35 shows that only 9% Legal System Functionaries discharged their duties in this respect.

The Act provides that properties of offenders may be attached and properties of convicts may be forfeited. The result shown *vide* Graph No. 99 and Table No. 31B reveals that only 4% Legal System Functionaries enforced this provision.

The Act provides for making available services of Senior Advocate to the victims of atrocities. The Graph No.101 and Table No. 32B show that only 8% officials of Different Units of Legal System implemented this provision.

In respect of role of concerned officials to implement the provisions of the Act, it reveals that the 67% officials of the Different Units of Legal System and Law Makers and Opinion Makers are of the view that concerned officials are lacking in interest to implement the provisions of the Act in letter and spirit 76% Law Makers and Opinion Makers are of the opinion that Investigating Officers and Special Police Officers have not been discharging their duties for implementing provisions of this Act. 86% of them opined that Special Public Prosecutors have not been conducting cases of atrocities vigorously. 74% of them opined that Special Courts have not been deciding cases of atrocities commensurate with the objects of the Act and 90% of them opined that Special Courts have not been awarding adequate sentences to the convicts of atrocity offences. 96% of them opined that SCs & STs Protection Cells are not functioning effectively in combating atrocities on SCs. 100% of them opined that there is no co-ordination amongst Nodal Officers, District Magistrate, Superintendent of Police and Investigating Officers.

It also revealed that minority of Law Makers and Opinion Makers organized workshop and awareness centres to educate the members of SCs about the rights and protections, available to them.

Only minority of officials forming Different Units of Legal System have dealt with atrocity cases, that goes to suggest that very minimum number of atrocities were reported to the police and resultantly very few officials forming Different Units of Legal System had occasion to deal with atrocity cases.

On the basis of above analysis, it may be concluded that the special provisions of the Act and the Rules framed thereunder were seldom used. The officials entrusted with the task of giving effect to the provision of the Act were not doing their duties to the best of their capacities and abilities. The role and attitude of functionaries was thus found negative. Lack of will in Legal System Functionaries and in all those who are in anyway connected with giving effect to the provision of the Act was found. Resultantly, the Act remained on papers for inaction of concerned functionaries.

Responses of the Judiciary

It has been emerged from this study that Law Makers and Opinion Makers are of the view that attitude of the court is not positive in deciding cases of atrocities. They have opined that Special Courts have not been deciding cases of atrocities in a manner commensurate with the objects of the Act and have not been awarding adequate sentences to the convicts of atrocities offences.

On examination of appellate court decisions, it also revealed that its policy responses on the Act, are not in consonance with the philosophy of the Act in the beginning but subsequently its policy response was changed. The Madhya Pradesh High Court in case of *Ram Krishan Balothia* Vs. *Union of India and others*[1] held that Sec. 18 of the Act is violative of Arts. 14 and 21 of the Constitution on the ground that provisions of this section did not conform to the norms of justice and fair play, besides prescribing unfair and unreasonable procedure. In appeal the Supreme Court in case of *State of M.P.* and *another* Vs. *Ram Krishan Balothia*[2] overruled this decision and held that Sec. 18 cannot be considered in any manner as violative of Arts. 14 and 21 of the Constitution.

In case of *Abdul Rasheed Siddiqui and another* Vs. *State of Madhya Pradesh and others,*[3] the Madhya Pradesh High Court even without going into the *vires* of the provisions of the Act, dismissed the writ petition challenging the validity of the Act. It again reiterated its policy decision in case *of Raju Gounder and others* Vs. *Union of India and others*[4] and dismissed writ petition challenging the validity of the Act. It was also held that offences under the Act and other penal laws fall under different categories. The Punjab and Haryana High Court followed the decision of Supreme Court in case of *State of M.P.* Vs. *Ram Krishan Balothia*[5] and held that in view of the clear and unambiguous finding of the Supreme Court further discussion has become unnecessary.

The Kerala High Court dismissed the writ petition challenging the validity of the provision of the Act, on the grounds that these are valid under Arts. 15 and 21 of the Constitution of India, observing that the provisions of the Act, guarantee social justice and dignity of life, which were denied, to vast section of the society for centuries and in this way there is no legal infirmity in Sec. 3(1)(x) of the Act.

In case of *Vasnatha* Vs. *Sivanthi & Ors.,*[6] it was observed that existing social inequalities or imbalances are required to be removed and the existing social order is required to be removed and readjusted through rule of law.

On the basis of these decisions, it can be concluded that appellate courts policy responses on the Act, are in consonance with the philosophy of the Act.

So far as the implementation realities of the provisions of the Act are concerned, it revealed that only few victims could get the compensation from the state. Most of the Law Makers and Opinion Makers and Officials forming Different Units of Legal System are of the view that most of the atrocity trials ended in acquittals. It also revealed that witnesses of atrocities do not appear easily to give their statements before the court. This has contributed in high rate of acquittals and low rate of convictions in trials of cases under the atrocity offences. 13% of officials forming Different Units of Legal System and 8% of Law Makers and Opinion Makers only have knowledge about identification of the atrocities prone area of their district.

On analysis of the empirical study regarding reasons for failure of the Act, it was opined by majority of the Law Makers and Opinion Makers that the Act did not cover all the possible forms of atrocities. They opined that Act is not complete in itself.

It was found that 26% Post Graduates, 32% Under Graduates,

59% Matric Pass, 63% Illiterates, 33% Service Persons, 42% Businessmen and 45% persons of Target Group engaged in different occupations suffered the atrocities. But, only 12% Post Graduates, 16% Graduates, 24% Under Graduates, 21% Matric Pass, 13% Illiterates and Service Persons, 25% Businessmen and 20% persons of Target Group engaged in different occupations, reported commission of the atrocities to the police. Thus, very low percentage of victims of the atrocities reported the matter to the police. This has happened because if somebody realizes again and again that negative consequences cannot be averted even by the determined action, he/she will become passive. Such a person will then not even try to take promising counteraction against an impending disaster or danger. Persons of that sort tend to give up their resistance.

Officials forming part of Different Units of Legal System, Law Makers and Opinion Makers also opined that there is procedural drawback in the Act regarding filing of complaint or producing the accused in the court and for all other connected matters at pre-trial stages. According to them, the procedure provided under the Act for imparting justice is cumbersome. Law Makers and Opinion Makers also opined that low rate of conviction is also responsible for increase in the incidence of the atrocities on the SCs.

So far as reporting of number of atrocity cases is concerned, 15799 cases of atrocities were reported against SCs in the year 1989. This number rose to 16857 in the year 1990, 17646 in the year 1991[7] and 24922 in the year 1992[8]. This has established that since the year 1989 the number of atrocity cases against SCs, instead of decreasing, in fact have increased.

On the basis of above discussion, it may be summarized that there is poor social awareness of the problem of atrocities. Awareness about the provisions of the Act and implications is little amongst the SCs and inadequate amongst the functionaries. The infrastructures and machineries are inadequate to prevent the atrocities on SCs. The functionaries are not doing their duties to the best of their abilities and capacities to enforce the provisions of the Act, as their attitude towards the Act is not positive. Resultantly, it may be concluded that the Act has left little impact on the SCs.

SUGGESTIONS

On the basis of the present study and in order to overcome the inhibiting factors that work against the law discussed in the preceding Chapters and with a view to achieve the objective of eradication and prevention of the incidence of atrocities on the SCs, following suggestions are submitted :

Effective Preventive Measures and Prompt Investigation

One of the reasons of ineffectiveness of the law under study is that the enforcement of the law is in the hands of those who have little faith of commitment to the underlying values of the law. Resultantly, most of these officials, instead of having empathy with the victims, have sympathy with the perpetrators of atrocities. This prevents them to enforce provisions of Law vigorously. It is, therefore, suggested that public at large including all officials must be made aware of the evils of atrocities, its effect on society at large and ultimately on nation and also made aware of the stakes involved in not only combating it sporadically but also of eradicating it from its roots. There is necessity of starting public movement against this evil. To start with those officials, who understand this problem and are aware about the importance of removing it, be those SCs or STs or Non ST & SC should be entrusted with the task to enforce and implement the provisions of the Act.

A perusal of Table Nos. 33, 33A and 33B and Graph Nos. 46, 47 and 102 shows that 83% legal system functionaries did not take any preventive measure to prevent the atrocities on the SCs and for keeping peace and good behaviour and maintenance of public order and tranquillity in the atrocity prone areas. A study of Table Nos. 35B and 35C and Graph No. 105 reveal that 91% officials of Different Units of Legal System have not taken any action for cancellation of arm licences of offenders of atrocities, *etc.* and for grant of arm licences to the victims of atrocities or members of SC. A look at the Table No. 42 and Graph No.113 also depicts that only 13% of the Legal System Functionaries are aware about the atrocity prone areas. Table Nos. 48, 48C and 49 and Graph Nos. 118 and 119 tell us that 50% of the victims of atrocities do not lodge their report and in 85% cases of atrocities Police do not record the F.I.R. of the victims and do not supply them copy of F.I.R. as per rules. Therefore, there is a need to streamline the system of taking preventive measures for saving the SCs from atrocities and also for taking prompt investigation of the atrocity cases to impart justice to the victims. It was suggested, as can be seen on perusal of Table No. 73 and Graph No. 141, by 80% of the officials of Different Units of Legal System and Law Makers and Opinion Makers that a special centralised enforcement agency should be created for prevention of atrocities and effective implementation of the Act. It was also opined that investigating agencies should be provided the required and necessary infrastructure, so that investigation of the atrocity cases may be conducted expeditiously. Some investigating staff consisting of constables, head-constables, sub-inspectors and an inspector should be entrusted in every police station especially to take measures to prevent the commission of atrocities and to render prompt assistance to the Investigating Officer to investigate the atrocity cases.

Fair and Effective Trial

A look at the Table No. 57 and Graph No. 127 shows that 18% of the Legal System Functionaries and Law Makers and Opinion Makers have knowledge about convictions in the trials of atrocity cases. This study also reveals that large number of atrocity trials end up in acquittals. Therefore, there is a need for fair and effective trial of atrocity cases. A perusal of Table No. 55 and Graph No. 125 reveals that 55% Officials of Different Units of Legal System and 60% Law Makers and Opinion Makers are of the view that Special Courts established under the Act are overburdened with other work which inhibit them from devoting sufficient time for disposal of cases of atrocities. It was also opined by them, as can be seen on a perusal of Table No. 53 and Graph No. 123, that Special Courts do not have sufficient infrastructure to discharge their duties promptly, smoothly and efficaciously. They are also of the view that the procedure provided under the Act for imparting justice is cumbersome. They suggested for simplification of procedure. The case of *Meera Bai* Vs. *Bhujbal Singh*[9] and *Sukhlal Jatav* Vs. *State of MP and others*[10] have also established that even the Judges are not in conformity about the procedure to be followed by the Special Court for producing the accused at pre trial stage, filing of Chargesheet by Police and complaint by the victim, *etc.* In the first case the a complaint was filed u/s 323 and 347 of I.P.C and Sec. 3(iv) and (v) of the Act before the Special Judge. The Special Judge dismissed the complaint holding that he had no jurisdiction to take cognisance in view of Sec.193 of the Code. Justice K.M. Pandey, Judge of the Madhya Pradesh High Court in *Sukhlal Jatav* case held that the designated Special Court under the Act was empowered to try the offences under the Act, without its committal by the Court of Magistrate u/s 193 of the Code. Justice Mr. Dwivedi, who was the other Judge of the Bench was having the different opinion. The reference was made. The three Judges in their consensus view observed that Special Courts constituted under the Act has no jurisdiction to try it directly without the case being committed to it u/s 193 of the Code. It emerges from the above discussion that even the Justices of High Courts have different views on the procedure to be followed by the Special Judge. We may imagine the problem at the lower courts level. It is, therefore, suggested that clear and simple procedure should be laid down for trial of atrocity cases. As the ordinary Courts of Judicial Magistrates are overburdened and well experienced Judges should try the atrocity cases, therefore, it is suggested that the Special Courts should have jurisdiction at every stage to hear the cases of atrocities. The exclusive Special Courts should be established. The exclusive Special Courts should be provided necessary infrastructure, so that cases under the Act could be disposed of as expeditiously as possible. This infrastructure should include necessary manpower as well as modern facility like Computers, connected material in the form of Legal Journals, Books, Reports, *etc.* The procedural drawback in the Act, regarding filing complaints or producing of accused in the court and for all other connected matter at pretrial stage should be rectified.

Sec. 14 of the Act should be amended on the following lines:

> "14. *Special Courts*: For the purpose of providing for speedy trial, the State Government shall, with the concurrence of the Chief Justice of the High Court, by notification in the Official Gazette, specify for each district a court of Sessions to be a Exclusive Special Court to try the offences under the Act.
>
> *Explanation* : The Exclusive Special Court shall also be having jurisdiction to hear atrocity cases at pre trial stage and no other court shall hear the atrocities cases at any stage."

Effective Prosecution

76% Law Makers and Opinion Makers, as revealed by Table No. 40 and Graph No. 111 have opined that Special Public Prosecutors have not been conducting cases under the Act vigorously. A look of Table No. 32B and Graph No. 101 shows that 82% Officials of Different Units of Legal System and 88% Law Makers and Opinion Makers have opined that neither they have given nor caused to be given nor seen giving the victims of atrocities, services of Senior Advocate of their choice for conducting their case at Government Expenses. The study also shows, as reveals at looking on at Table No. 31B and Graph No. 99 that 89% of them have neither attached nor caused to be attached the properties of an offender or forfeited or caused to be forfeited the properties of a convict of an offence of atrocity. The discussion in above chapters has also established that attitude of the officials in conducting the atrocity cases is not positive. Therefore, there is need for effective prosecution of the atrocity cases. This will put a check on large numbers of acquittals in atrocity trials and promote the expeditious disposal of cases. Resultantly, the majority of cases of atrocities will end in convictions and this will leave deterrent impact on the potential offenders of atrocities.

Legal Aid

It has been opined by 96% of Law Makers and Opinion Makers and 93% Officials forming Different Units of Legal System, as can be seen on perusal of Table No. 72 and Graph No. 139 that legal aids should be given to the victims of the atrocities, since the time and day of commission of offences of atrocities. 88% Law Makers and Opinion Makers and 80% Officials forming Different Units of Legal System have also opined, as may be seen on perusal of Table No. 72C and Graph No. 140, that legal aid should be provided to the victims and potential victims of atrocities not only since the time and date of commission of atrocities on them but also even before the commission of atrocities in the atrocities prone area or in cases where there are apprehensions of commission of atrocities on them.

Therefore, it is suggested that provisions should be incorporated in the Act by inserting a new section for providing of legal aid to the victims of atrocities and potential victims of atrocities.

Appropriate Sentencing

58% Law Makers and Opinion Makers opined, as can be seen on perusal of Table No. 55 and Graph No. 124 that the Courts have not been deciding cases of atrocities commensurate with the object of the Act. 64% of them are of the view, as can be seen on a perusal of Table No. 54A and Graph No. 124 that Courts have not been awarding adequate sentences to the convicts of the offences under the Act. There are number of decisions of atrocity cases and cases under the PCR Act where inadequate sentences were awarded on the convicts by the Courts.

It is, therefore, suggested that it should be made obligatory for the State Government to file an appeal against the sentence in all such cases in which atrocity has not been sentenced adequately by the Special Court.

Creation of New Offences and Substantive Law Regime

80% Law Makers and Opinion Makers and 56% Officials of Different Units of Legal System have opined, as may be seen on perusal of Table No. 59 and Graph No. 129, that effort to know the caste of a person by another person, when it is not required for giving any benefit to a member of SCs should be made a new offence of atrocity.

84% Law Makers and Opinion Makers and amongst them 91% of SC categories, are of the view, as may be seen on perusal of Table No. 60 and Graph No. 130, that employing any child of the SCs below the age of 14 years should be made an offence of atrocity.

80% Law Makers and Opinion Makers and amongst them 97% of SC categories, are of the view, as may be seen on perusal of Table No. 61 and Graph No. 130, that blockade of services career of a member of SCs on false and fabricated report, *etc.*, should be made an offence of atrocity.

94% Law Makers and Opinion Makers and amongst them 97% of SC categories, are of the view, as may be seen on a perusal of Table No. 62 and Graph No. 130, that economic exploitation of member of SCs in any form and by any mode should be made an offence of atrocity.

92% Law Makers and Opinion Makers and amongst them 97% of SC categories, are of the view, as may be seen on perusal of

Table No. 63 and Graph No. 130, that practice of untouchability with a member of SCs in any form and by any mode should be made an offence of atrocity.

95% persons of Target Group are of the view, as may be seen on perusal of Table Nos. 65, 65A and 65B and Graph No. 132, that the invasion on their bodies or properties or reputation amounts to atrocities on them. 82% Law Makers and Opinion Makers and amongst them 94% of SC categories are of the view, as may be seen on perusal of Table No. 65F, that invasion on body or reputation or property of a member of SCs should be made an offence of atrocity.

98% persons of Target Group are of the view, as may be seen on perusal of Table No. 66 and Graph No. 133, that subjecting a man to indignities, humiliation and harassment amounts to atrocity. It is suggested that indignities, humiliation and harassment of a member of SCs in any form and by any mode and at any place should be made an offence of atrocity.

The decisions of *M.C. Prasannan* Vs. *State,*[11] and *Panibhusan Behera and others* Vs. *State of Orissa*[12] have established that accused of atrocity offences for sexually exploiting a woman of SCs are acquitted on the ground that there was free and voluntary consent of the victims to have sexual intercourse with accused.

It is the view of many noted and eminent jurist that sexual exploitation of a woman of SC by their high caste masters appears to have been so common as to have been habitual,[13] therefore, there is no significance of giving consent by victim for having sexual intercourse with her. Therefore, it is suggested that having sexual intercourse with a woman of SCs with or without her consent should be made an offence of atrocity.

No body can deny the fact that member of SCs are implicated in false cases in order to harass them for so many other reasons.[14] Therefore, it is suggested that false implication of a member of SCs should be made an offence of atrocity.

As discussed above, it has been seen that the functionaries, who are entrusted with the duties to implement the Act, are not discharging their duties to the best of their abilities and capacities. 86% Law Makers and Opinion Makers and amongst them 91% belonging to SCs are of the view, as may be seen on perusal of Table No. 64

and Graph No. 131, that neglect of duties by the public servant for not awarding compensation to the victims should be made an offence of atrocity. 76% Law Makers and Opinion Makers and amongst them 89% belonging to SCs are of the view that neglect of duties by the public servant for not performing their duties under Rules 3 to 18 of the Rules should be an offence of atrocity. It is, therefore, suggested that omissions on the part of concerned authorities for promptly rehabilitating the victims of atrocities or their failure to make payment of compensation amount to victims of atrocities within a month from due date or their omissions to perform their duties under Rules 3 to 18 of the rules should also be made an offence of atrocity.

One of the reasons for ineffectiveness of the Act is that it seeks to prohibit such behaviour of the dominant section of society, which they had been indulging in for a fairly long period. Such behaviours have the explicit or implicit support of the custom. Since the dawn of independence and particularly since coming into the force of the Constitution of India, such behaviours were considered opposed to public policy being contradictory to the objects sought to be achieved by our Constitution. So, in order to make this law effective we have to weaken those customs. This study has shown as to how caste system has given birth to endogamy and prohibition of inter-dining and how this has resulted into caste disabilities and practices of untouchability which are ultimately before us in the form of atrocities on the SCs. Therefore, it is suggested that practice of untouchability should be made an offence of atrocity.

It is suggested that the term 'atrocity', which has not been defined in the Act or in any other legislation or in any case laws, should be defined. We must keep in mind that atrocity is committed due to hatred based on caste. Therefore, while defining the term atrocity we must lay emphasis to protect the autonomy of man belonging to SCs.

Sec. 2 (a) of the Act may be amended on the following lines:

> "2 (a). *Atrocities.* –Whoever, not being a member of Scheduled Castes or a Scheduled Tribes, invade on body or reputation or property of a member of SC or humiliate or harass or indignify a member of SC or exploit a member

of SC sexually or economically or causes wrongful loss to a member of SC, is said to commit atrocities.

Illustrations

(a) A forces a member of Scheduled Castes or Scheduled Tribes to eat or drink any inedible or obnoxious substance. A has committed offence of atrocities.

(b) A dumps excreta, waste matter, carcasses or any other obnoxious substance in the premises or neighbourhood of a member of Scheduled Castes or Scheduled Tribes. A has committed offence of atrocities.

(c) A forcibly removes clothes from the person of a member of Scheduled Castes or Scheduled Tribes or parades him naked or with painted face or body or commits any similar act which is derogatory to human dignity. A has committed offence of atrocities.

(d) A wrongfully occupies or cultivates any land owned by, or allotted to, or notified by any competent authority to be allotted to a member of Scheduled Castes or Scheduled Tribes or get the land allotted to him transferred. A has committed offence of atrocities.

(e) A wrongfully dispossesses a member of Scheduled Castes or Scheduled tribes from his land or premises or interferes with the enjoyment of his rights over any land, premises or water. A has committed offence of atrocities.

(f) A compels or entices a member of Scheduled Castes or Scheduled Tribes to do *'begar'* or other similar forms of forced or bonded labour. A has committed offence of atrocities.

(g) A forces or intimidates a member of Scheduled Castes or Scheduled Tribes not to vote or to vote for a particular candidate or to vote in a manner other than that provided by law. A has committed offence of atrocities.

(h) A institutes false, malicious or vexatious suit or criminal or other legal proceedings against a member of Scheduled Castes or Scheduled Tribes. A has committed offence of atrocities.

(i) A gives any false or frivolous information to any public servant and thereby causes such public servant to use his lawful power to the injury or annoyance of a member of Scheduled Castes or Scheduled Tribes. A has committed offence of atrocities.

(j) A intentionally insults or intimidates with intent to humiliate a member of Scheduled Castes or Scheduled Tribes. A has committed offence of atrocities.

(k) A assaults or uses force to any woman belonging to Scheduled Castes or Scheduled Tribes with intent to dishonour or outrage her modesty. A has committed offence of atrocities.

(l) A exploits a woman belonging to Scheduled Castes or Scheduled Tribes. A has committed offence of atrocities.

(m) A corrupts or fouls the water of any spring, reservoir or any other source ordinarily used by members of the Scheduled Castes or the Scheduled Tribes so as to render it less fit for the purpose for which it is ordinarily used. A has committed offence of atrocities.

(n) A denies a member of Scheduled Castes or Scheduled Tribes any customary right of passage to a place of public resort or obstructs such member so as to prevent him from using or having access to place of public resort to which other members of public or any section thereof have a right to use or access to. A has committed offence of atrocities.

(o) A forces or causes a member of Scheduled Castes or Scheduled Tribes to leave his house, village or other place of residence. A has committed offence of atrocities

(p) A asks to a person belonging to Scheduled Castes or Scheduled Tribes his caste though it was not required for giving benefit to a member of Scheduled Castes or Scheduled Tribes. A has committed offence of atrocities.

(q) A employs a child of Scheduled Castes or Scheduled Tribes below the age of 14 years and thereby exploit him. A has committed offence of atrocities.

(r) A blocks service career of a member of Scheduled Castes

or Scheduled Tribes on false or fabricated reports. A has committed offence of atrocities.

(s) A economically exploits a member of Scheduled Castes or Scheduled Tribes. A has committed offence of atrocities.

(t) A practices untouchability with a member of Scheduled Castes or Scheduled Tribes. A has committed offence of atrocities."

Sec.3 (I) of the Act may be substituted as follows:

> "3. *Punishment for offences of atrocities.*— Whoever commits atrocities shall be punished with imprisonment of either description for a term which shall not be less than six months but which may extend to five years and with fine."

Education and Training

We have seen that there is poor awareness about provisions of the Act and its implications amongst SCs and inadequate amongst the functionaries. 94% Law Makers and Opinion Makers and 88% Officials forming Different Units of Legal System are of the view, as may be seen on perusal of Table No. 67 and Graph No. 134 that refresher courses for all those who are in anyway connected in giving effect to the provisions of the Act, including Judges of the Special Courts, Special Public Prosecutors, Investigating Officers, *etc.*, should be conducted periodically to make them aware about latest development in the laws, case laws and other executive measures being taken or proposed to be taken for combating atrocities on SCs.

It is, therefore, suggested that provisions should be made for conducting of refresher courses. Education to the children up to the age of 14 years should be made compulsory so that the public at large and majority of SCs could be made aware of the provisions of the Act, the Rules and other executive measures for prevention and eradication of atrocities.

It is further suggested that the provisions of the Act should not only be included in school, college and university level curriculum but also these should be included in the syllabus of LL.B., LL.M.,

Indian Civil Services and Provincial Civil Services Examinations, *etc.*

Creation of General Awareness

94% of the Law Makers and the Opinion Makers and 91% Officials forming Different Units of Legal System have opined, as may be seen on perusal of Table No. 68 and Graph No. 135, that publicity of the provisions of the Act through *Doordarshan,* Radio and other Public Media may help in eradication of the atrocities on the members of SCs.

It is, therefore, suggested that provisions of the Act and the Rules and all other relevant matters should be given wide publicity through *Doordarshan*, Radio and all other public media such as Newspapers, Magazines and Cinema Halls, *etc.,* for making the masses aware about atrocities and measures being taken to eradicate it.

Other Measures

This study has also established as to how various literatures have imposed various caste disabilities on the SCs. 80% Law Makers and Opinion Makers and 71% Officials forming Different Units of Legal System are of the view, as may be seen on perusal of Table No. 76 and Graph No. 145, that expunction of literary verses in *Ramayana* or other literature against SCs on the ground of repugnancy with constitutional ethos would be an effective way for eradication of atrocities on the members of SCs.

It is, therefore, suggested that provisions should be made for deletion or expunction of anti SCs & STs literature.

The other suggestions that may be helpful for prevention of atrocities on the SCs are that Inter-caste marriages at large scale should be encouraged. Provisions should be made for preventing political parties to issue whip in the legislatures, if the matter under discussion or voting is concerning atrocities on the members of SCs.

The provisions should be made in the Act for not requiring SCs to prove that atrocities on them were committed on the basis of caste hatred, caste prejudices or practice of untouchability. Instead burden of proof to prove that atrocities were not committed for above reasons should be shifted on the offenders.

A new sub-section after section 8(b) of the Act may be inserted on following lines:

> "(c) If an offence of atrocities is committed then it shall be presumed that it was committed due to hatred based on caste prejudice."

The reason for non-reporting of cases under the Act is not that atrocities are not being committed upon SCs but due to the fact that victims do not know that they have to lodge report under the Act. Therefore, duty should be cast on the Duty Officer to inquire from victim as to whether the dispute is between SCs or Non SC and ST. If the dispute is between them, he must apply his mind if the offence falls under any provisions of the Act. In case, he is of the view that offence does not fall under the Act,. he should mention it in the F.I.R. for judging its correctness by the Court.

If the Court finds that Duty Officer has negligently acted in this regard, provisions should be made for taking appropriate action against him.

Notes and References

1. AIR 1993 Raj. 177 : 1993 CRI.L.J. 2705.
2. AIR 1995 SC 1198 : 1995 CRI.L.J. 2076.
3. AIR 1995 M.P. 138.
4. 1995 CRI.L.J. 3390.
5. *Supra,* note 2.
6. 1999 (1) Crimes 499.
7. *See* Report of NC SC & ST, 1991 at 101 and 121.
8. 2nd Annual Report, 1991-92 at 4.
9. 1995, CRI.L.J. 2376
10. *Ibid.* and Criminal Revision No.149/92 Dt.14.7.93.
11. 1999 CRI.L.J. 998.
12. 1995 CRI.L.J.1561.
13. *See*, Oliver Mendelsohn & Upendra Baxi, *The Rights of Subordinated Peoples,* Oxford University Press, 1994 at 86.
14. *See*, The Forty Sixth Report, 1994-95 at 22.

ANNEXURES

ANNEXURE – 1

A STUDY OF THE IMPACT OF THE SCHEDULED CASTES AND THE SCHEDULED TRIBES (PREVENTION OF ATROCITIES) ACT: WITH A SPECIAL REFERENCE TO THE PROBLEM OF ATROCITIES ON THE SCHEDULED CASTES AND JUDICIAL RESPONSE IN NORTHERN INDIA

Dear Sir,

Everyone of us knows and realises that atrocities on the members of the Scheduled Castes (hereinafter referred to as SCs) have been committed from times immemorial due to various reasons. As commission and continuation of atrocities on them is a blot on the society and is creating inequalities in political, social, economic, educational, religious, cultural and all other conceivable spheres of human activities amongst the inhabitants of our country, so the founding fathers of our Constitution enshrined in preamble; fraternity, dignity of person and equality of status, etc., to remove these inequalities and to abolish the practice of untouchability; to prevent the atrocities on them; and to protect their human rights. But the desired object could not be achieved even after 45 years, since coming into force of our Constitution and international conventions. Despite this and various other measures taken to improve the socio-economic conditions of the SCs, they remained vulnerable. They are denied number of civil rights and are subjected to various indignities, humiliations and harassment, etc. Therefore, using law as an instrument of social change and to prevent commission of atrocities on the SCs and Scheduled Tribes, a special legislation, namely The Scheduled Castes and the Scheduled Tribes (Prevention of Atrocities) Act (hereinafter referred to as "The Act") was enacted by the Parliament.

Sir, as the atrocities are still being committed/reported in daily newspapers, journals, reports, magazines, etc., so a necessity was felt to conduct an impact study of the Act. This study being socio-legal cannot be completed without your active and constructive co-operation since you are also a part of our socio and legal fabric.

So, you are requested to fill in your reply the following questions on a separate Answer Sheet enclosed. The total exercise is research oriented and your reply will be kept confidential.

Thank You,

ANNEXURE – II

QUESTIONNAIRE/INTERVIEW SCHEDULE ON THE SUBJECT FOR TARGET GROUP

1. Are you aware that atrocities still being committed on the members of the SCs?
2. Do you think that invasion on body of a man (human) amounts to atrocity?
3. Do you think that invasion of property of a man amounts to atrocity?
4. Do you think that invasion of reputation of a man amounts to atrocity?
5. Do you think that subjecting a man to indignities, humiliations and harassment amounts to atrocity?
6. Are you aware that various factors are responsible for commission and continuation of atrocities on the members of the SCs?
7. Is practice of untouchability on the members of the SCs, a factor for commission of atrocities on them?
8. Is caste hatred a cause for commission of atrocities on the members of the SCs?
9. Is having no separate religion by the members of the SCs, a reason for commission of atrocities on them?
10. Is illiteracy, a factor for commission of atrocities on the members of the SCs?
11. Is ignorance of law, a factor for commission and continuation of atrocities on the members of the SCs?
12. Is lack of political will, a factor for continuation of atrocities on the members of SCs?
13. Is poverty, a factor for commission and continuation of atrocities on the members of SCs?

14. Is economic dependence/backwardness, a factor for commission of atrocities on the members of SCs?
15. Is cultural backwardness of the members of SCs, a factor for commission and continuation of atrocities on them?
16. Do you have knowledge about the Scheduled Castes and the Scheduled Tribes (Prevention of Atrocities) Act, 1989?
17. Are you aware that the Act has come into force w.e.f. 30th January, 1990?
18. Do you know that the Act has designated several categories of atrocities as offence?
19. Do you know that an offence under the Act can only be committed by Non-Scheduled Castes and Scheduled Tribes on the SCs and the Scheduled Tribes?
20. Do you know that denial of social right, i.e., right of access to public place or denial of use of customary passage to the members of the SCs is an offence under the Act?
21. Do you know that fouling of water ordinarily used by the members of the SCs is an offence under the Act?
22. Are you aware that causing injury, insult or annoyance to the members of the SCs by polluting his premises or neighbourhood is an offence under the Act?
23. Are you aware that forcing a member of the SCs to eat or drink inedible substance is an offence under the Act?
24. Do you know that subjecting a member of the SCs to indignities by stripping, parading naked or with painted face or body, *etc*., is an offence under the Act?
25. Do you know that invading body of a woman of the SCs by outraging her modesty or sexually exploiting her or dishonouring her is an offence under the Act?
26. Are you aware that intentionally insulting or intimidating a member of the SCs to humiliate him within public view is an offence under the Act?
27. Do you know that invading the properties of a member of the SCs by wrongful occupation or his dispossession or its destruction by mischief, etc., is an offence under the Act?
28. Do you know that interfering with the enjoyment of a member

of the SCs over his properties, etc., or getting the land allotted to him transferred is an offence under the Act?

29. Do you know that exploitation of a member of the SCs by compelling him to do *begar* or bonded labour is an offence under the Act?
30. Do you know that prohibiting a member of the SCs for voluntarily casting vote is an offence under the Act?
31. Do you know that instituting false, malicious or vexatious suit or criminal or other legal proceedings against a member of the SCs is an offence under the Act?
32. Are you aware that giving false or frivolous information against a member of the SCs to a public servant causing him injury or annoyance by such public servant is an offence under the Act?
33. Do you know that forcing or causing a member of the SCs to leave his village, house or other place of residence is an offence under the Act?
34. Do you know that giving false evidence against a member of the SCs or destroying evidence of atrocity or giving financial support to offender of atrocity is an offence under the Act?
35. Do you aware that under the Act special provisions relating to investigations, prosecutions, trial of such offence and rehabilitation of victims have been envisaged?
36. Do you know that the special courts have been created and special Public Prosecutors have been appointed for trial of offence of atrocities?
37. Do you know that victim of atrocity may get services of senior advocate for conducting his case at government expenses?
38. Do you know that under the Act, properties of offender may be attached and properties of convict may be forfeited?
39. Do you know that accused of and convict of atrocity can neither be released on anticipatory bail nor on probation?
40. Do you know that arm licence of accused of atrocity, etc., may be cancelled and arm licence to victim of atrocity and members of SCs may be given?
41. Have you ever faced atrocities of above kind or any other kind?

42. Did you lodge F.I.R. about the commission of atrocity?
43. Did the police lodge your report and supplied you a copy of F.I.R. free of cost?
44. Do you know that if your report is not recorded by the police then you should send it to S.P./D.C.P. by Registered Post?
45. Do you know that if you are not satisfied with the work of police, then you may file a complaint to Court?
46. Do you know that if you are not satisfied with the investigation by the police, you should bring it to the knowledge of higher police officers?
47. Do you know that if you are not satisfied with the work of Special Public Prosecutor, you should bring it to the knowledge of the Director of Prosecution or the District Magistrate?
48. Do you know that you should get medical and financial help as well as security from police D.M./SCST Protection Cell/ Nodal Officer, *etc.*?
49. Do you know that you should get compensation and you and your witnesses should get TA/DA/MA/Transport facilities for attending court?
50. Do you know that a Non SC & ST public servant is liable for punishment of 6 to 12 months jail, if he wilfully neglects his duties required to be performed under the Act?

ANNEXURE – III

QUESTIONNAIRE/INTERVIEW SCHEDULE ON THE SUBJECT FOR DIFFERENT UNITS OF THE LEGAL SYSTEM

(Police Personnel, Prosecutors, Lawyers, Doctors, Judges, Magistrates and other Agencies involved under the Act.)

1. Are you aware that atrocities still being committed on the members of the SCs?
2. Do you think that commission and continuation of atrocities on the SCs is a blot on our society?
3. Do you think that commission and continuation of atrocities on the SCs is an impediment in the advancement and development of our country?
4. Are you aware that various factors are responsible for commission and continuation of atrocities on the members of the SCs?
5. Is practice of untouchability on the members of the SCs, a factor for commission of atrocities on them?
6. Is caste hatred, a cause for commission of atrocities on the members of the SCs?
7. Is having no separate religion by the members of the SCs, a reason for commission of atrocities on them?
8. Is illiteracy, a factor for commission of atrocities on the members of the SCs?
9. Is poverty, a factor for commission and continuation of atrocities on the members of the SCs?
10. Is economic dependence/backwardness, a factor for commission of atrocities on the members of SCs?
11. Is cultural backwardness of the members of SCs, a factor for commission and continuation of atrocities on them?

12. Is lack of political will, a factor for continuation of atrocities on the members of SCs?
13. Is ignorance of law, a factor for commission and continuation of atrocities on the members of the SCs?
14. Do you have knowledge about the Scheduled Castes and the Scheduled Tribes (Prevention of Atrocities) Act, 1989?
15. Are you aware that the Act has come into force w.e.f. 30th January, 1990.
16. Do you know that the Act has designated several categories of atrocities as offence?
17. Do you know that an offence under the Act can only be committed by Non-Scheduled Caste and Scheduled Tribe on the SCs and the Scheduled Tribes?
18. Do you know that forcing a member of the SCs to drink or eat any inedible or obnoxious substance is an offence under the Act?
19. Do you know that an act with intent to cause injury, insult or annoyance to any member of SCs by dumping excreta, waste matter, carcasses, or any other obnoxious substance in his premises or neighbourhood is an offence under the Act?
20. Do you know that forcibly removing clothes from the person of a member of SCs or parading him naked or with painted face or body or committing any similar act which is derogatory to human dignity is an offence under the Act?
21. Do you know that wrongfully occupying or cultivating any land owned by, or allotted to, or notified by any competent authority to be allotted to him getting transferred amounts to an offence under the Act?
22. Do you know that wrongfully dispossessing a member of SCs from his land or premises or interfering with the enjoyment of his rights over any land, premises or water amounts to an offence under the Act?
23. Do you know that compelling or enticing a member of the SCs to do *"begar"* or other similar forms of forced or bonded labour other than any compulsory service for public purposes imposed by Government amounts to an offence under the Act?

24. Do you know that forcing or intimidating a member of SCs not to vote or to vote to a particular candidate or to vote in a manner other than that provided by law amounts to an offence under the Act?
25. Do you know that instituting false, malicious or vexatious suit or criminal or other legal proceedings against members of the SCs amounts to an offence under the Act?
26. Do you know that giving any false or frivolous information to any public servant and thereby causing such public servant to use his lawful power to the injury or annoyance of a member of the SCs amounts to an offence under the Act?
27. Do you know that intentionally insulting or intimidating with intent to humiliate a member of the SCs in any place within public view amounts to an offence under the Act?
28. Do you know that assaulting or using force to any woman belonging to SCs with intent to dishonour or outrage her modesty amounts to an offence under the Act?
29. Do you know that being in a position to dominate the will of a woman belonging to SCs and using that position to exploit her sexually to which she would have not otherwise agreed amounts to an offence under the Act?
30. Do you know that corrupting or fouling the water of any spring, reservoir or any other source so as to render it less fit for the purpose for which it is ordinarily used by members of the SCs amounts to an offence under the Act?
31. Do you know that denying a member of the SCs any customary right of passage to a place of public resort or obstruct such member so as to prevent him from using or having access to a place of public resort to which other members of public or any section thereof have a right to use or access to, amounts to an offence under the Act?
32. Do you know that forcing or causing a member of the SCs to leave his village, house or other place of residence is an offence under the Act?
33. Do you know that to give or fabricate false evidence against a member of the SCs is a heinous offence under the Act?
34. Do you know that causing damage by fire or explosive

substance to any property of a member of the SCs is a serious offence under the Act?

35. Do you know that causing destruction by fire and explosive substance of any building which is ordinarily used as a place of worship or as a place for human dwelling or as a place for custody of property of a member of the SCs is a heinous offence under the Act?

36. Do you know that causing disappearance of any evidence of the commission of an offence under the Act, with the intention of screening the offender from legal punishment is an offence under the Act?

37. Do you know that if an offence under the Act is committed by a public servant, then he is liable for more punishment than which would be inflicted upon an ordinary accused person?

38. Do you know that there is enhanced punishment for subsequent convictions under the Act?

39. Are you aware that under the Act special provisions relating to investigation, prosecution, trial of such offences and rehabilitation of victims have been envisaged?

40. Do you know that the special courts have been created and Special Public Prosecutors have been appointed for trial of offences of atrocities under the Act?

41. Whether any part of your District is identified as atrocities prone area?

42. Have you ever dealt with any case of atrocities under the Act in the capacity of police personnel or prosecutor or lawyer or doctor or judge or Magistrate or in any other capacity?

43. Have you taken or caused to be taken or seen taking preventive action for keeping the peace and good behaviour and maintenance of public order and tranquillity in the atrocity prone area?

44. Have you ever attached or caused to be attached the properties of an offender and forfeited and caused to be forfeited the properties of a convict of offence of atrocity?

45. Have you ever cancelled or caused to be cancelled or seen cancellation of the arm licence of an accused or any other person under the Act or Rules framed thereunder?

46. Have you ever granted or helped in grant or seen grant of an arm licence to members of the SCs under the Act or Rules framed thereunder?
47. Have you given or caused to be given or seen giving the victim of atrocity, services of senior Advocate of his choice for conducting his case at Government expenses under the Act or Rules framed thereunder?
48. Do you know any case of atrocity trial which ended in conviction?
49. Do you know any case of atrocity trial, which ended in acquittal?
50. Do you think that the special court, machineries and fora provided under the Act are adequate?
51. Do you think that said Courts machineries and fora are working satisfactorily?
52. Do you think that the procedure for imparting justice under the Act is simple?
53. Do you think that there is procedural drawback in the Act?
54. Do you think that there is lack of interest of concerned officials to implement the Act in letter and spirit?
55. Do you think that there is sufficient infrastructure with the Investigating Agencies to meet the requirements under the Act?
56. Do the police personnel have sufficient time to perform their duties entrusted under the Act *vis-a-vis* their other duties under various laws?
57. Do you think the courts constituted under the Act are overburdened with other work, which impede them to devote sufficient time for disposal of cases under the Act?
58. Do you think that the special court has sufficient infrastructure to discharge its duties promptly, smoothly and efficaciously?
59. Do you think that witnesses of the offence under the Act easily appear and depose before the special court?
60. Do you suggest for simplification of procedure under the Act?
61. Do you suggest creation of centralised special enforcement agency for effective implementation of the Act?

62. Do you suggest that the special court under the Act should not be burdened with any other work except the cases under the Act?
63. Do you suggest giving legal aid to the victim of offence since the time and day of the commission of offence?
64. Do you suggest providing Legal Aid to SCs even before commission of atrocity under the Act in atrocity prone area?
65. Do you suggest prompt rehabilitation of the victims of atrocities by the State?
66. Do you suggest that asking of caste by a person to any other person when it was not required for giving any benefit to a member of SCs should be made an offence of atrocity under the Act?
67. Do you suggest that removal of untouchability may lead to eradication of atrocities on members of the SCs?
68. Do you think that expunction of those portions of literature which are contrary to the provisions of the Constitution of India, may help in eradication of atrocities on the members of SCs?
69. Do you think that conducting refresher courses for all those who are in anyway connected with giving effect to the provisions of the Act may help in eradication of atrocities on the members of SCs?
70. Do you think that publicity of the provisions of the Act through *Doordarshan*, Radio and other public media may help in eradication of the atrocities on the members of the SCs?

ANNEXURE – IV

QUESTIONNAIRE/INTERVIEW SCHEDULE ON THE SUBJECT FOR LAW MAKERS AND OPINION MAKERS

(MPs, Legislators, Academicians, Media Persons, Social Activists and Members of N.G.Os. etc.)

1. Are you aware that atrocities still being committed on the Members of the SCs?
2. Do you think that commission and continuation of atrocities on the SCs is a blot on our society?
3. Do you think that commission and continuation of atrocities on the SCs is an impediment in the advancement and development of our country?
4. Are you aware that various factors are responsible for commission and continuation of atrocities on the members of the SCs?
5. Is caste system, a factor for commission and continuation of practice of untouchability on the member of SCs?
6. Is practice of untouchability on the members of the SCs, a factor for commission of atrocities on them?
7. Is endogamy, a reason for continuation of caste system?
8. Is caste hatred, a cause for commission of atrocities on the members of the SCs?
9. Is having no separate religion by the members of the SCs, a reason for commission of atrocities on them?
10. Is illiteracy, a factor for commission of atrocities on them?
11. Is poverty, a factor for commission and continuation of atrocities on the members of the SCs?

12. Is economic dependence/backwardness, a factor for commission of atrocities of the SCs?
13. Is cultural backwardness of the SCs, a factor for commission and continuation of atrocities on them?
14. Is lack of political will, a factor for continuation of atrocities on the members of the SCs?
15. Is awakening of members of the SCs and resultant demand for their statutory rights and denial thereof by others has accelerated the commission of atrocities on them?
16. Do you have knowledge of the Scheduled Castes and the Scheduled Tribes (Prevention of Atrocities) Act, 1989?
17. Are you aware that the Act has come into force w.e.f. 30th January, 1990?
18. Is ignorance of law, a factor for commission and continuation of atrocities on the members of the SCs?
19. Do you know that this Act has designated several categories of atrocities as offence?
20. Do you know that offences under the Act can only be committed by Non-Scheduled Caste and Non-Scheduled Tribe on the SCs and the Scheduled Tribes?
21. Are you aware about the salient features of the Act?
22. Do you think that the Act has covered all the possible forms of atrocities?
23. Do you have knowledge of the Scheduled Castes and the Scheduled Tribes (Prevention of Atrocities) Rules, 1995?
24. Do you know that these Rules envisaged setting up of the SCs and Scheduled Tribes Protection Cells, nomination of nodal officers and appointment of special officers for effective implementation of the provisions of the Act?
25. Do you know that these Rules also provide for constitution of State and District level Vigilance and Monitoring Committees?
26. Have you ever been member of the State level Vigilance and Monitoring Committee for implementation of the provisions of the Act?
27. Have you ever been a member of the District level Vigilance

and Monitoring Committee for reviewing the implementation of the provisions of the Act?

28. Whether any part of your District has been identified as atrocities prone area?
29. Do you know any case of atrocity trial, which ended in conviction?
30. Do you know any case of atrocity trial, which ended in acquittal?
31. Do you think that the special courts machineries and fora provided under the Act are adequate?
32. Do you think that the investigating officers and special officers have been discharging their duties for giving effect to the provisions of the Act in letter and spirit?
33. Do you think that the SCs and the Scheduled Tribes Protection Cells have been functioning effectively in combating atrocities on the members of SCs?
34. Do you think that the Nodal officers have been effectively coordinating the functioning of the DMs, SPs and investigating officers, *etc.*, for real implementation of the provisions of the Act?
35. Do you think that the special public prosecutors have been conducting cases under the Act vigorously?
36. Do you think that Courts have been deciding cases of atrocities in commensurate with the objects of the Act?
37. Do you think that the courts have been awarding adequate sentences to the convicts of offences under the Act?
38. Do you think that the procedure for justice under the Act is simple?
39. Do you think that there is procedural drawbacks in the Act regarding filing of complaints, or producing accused in court and for all other connected matters at pre-trial stages?
40. Do you think that there is lack of interest in concerned officials to implement the Act in letter and spirit?
41. Do you think that there is sufficient infrastructure with the investigating agencies to meet the requirements under the Act?
42. Do the police personnel have sufficient time to perform their

duties entrusted under the Act *vis-a-vis* their other duties under various laws?

43. Do you think that the courts constituted under the Act are overburdened with other work, which impede them to devote sufficient time for disposal of cases under the Act?
44. Do you think that the special courts have sufficient infrastructure to discharge its duties promptly, smoothly and efficaciously?
45. Have you ever set up Awareness Centres and organised workshops to educate members of SCs about the rights and protections available to them?
46. Have you taken or caused to be taken or seen taking preventive action for keeping the peace and good behaviour and maintenance of public order and tranquillity in the atrocity prone area?
47. Have you ever attached or caused to be attached the properties of an offender and forfeited and caused to be forfeited the properties of a convict of offence of atrocity?
48. Have you ever cancelled or caused to be cancelled or seen cancellation of the arm licence of an accused or any other person under the Act or Rules framed thereunder?
49. Have you ever granted or helped in grant or seen grant of arm licence to a member of SCs under the Act or Rules framed thereunder?
50. Have you given or caused to be given or seen giving the victim of atrocity, services of senior Advocate of his choice for conducting his case at Government expenses under the Act or Rules framed thereunder?
51. Have you ever helped the victim of atrocities to obtain compensation from the State?
52. Do you suggest that invasion on the body or reputation or property of a member of SCs should be made an offence of atrocity under the Act?
53. Do you suggest that practice of untouchability in any form with a member of SCs should be made an offence of atrocity under the Act?
54. Do you suggest that economic exploitation of a member of

SCs should be made an offence of atrocity under the Act?

55. Do you suggest that blockade of service career of a member of SCs on false or fabricated report, *etc.*, should be made an offence of atrocity under the Act?

56. Do you suggest that employing any child of SCs below the age of 14 years should be made an offence of atrocity under the Act?

57. Do you suggest for simplification of procedure under the Act?

58. Do you suggest creation of centralised special enforcement Agency for effective implementation of the Act?

59. Do you suggest that the special court under the Act should not be burdened with any other work except the cases under the Act?

60. Do you suggest giving legal aid to the victims of atrocity since the time and day of the commission of offence?

61. Do you suggest providing legal aid to the SCs even before commission of atrocity under the Act in atrocity prone area?

62. Do you suggest that omission on the part of concerned authorities for promptly rehabilitating the victims of atrocities or failure to make payment of compensation amount to them within a month from the due date should also be made an offence under the Act?

63. Do you suggest that omission on the part of concerned authorities to perform their duties under Rules 3 to 18 of the Rules should also be made an offence under the Act?

64. Do you suggest that asking of caste by a person to any other person, when it was not required for giving any benefit to a member of SCs, should be made an offence of atrocity under the Act?

65. Do you think that inter-caste marriages at large scale may destroy the impregnable caste barrier?

66. Do you think that annihilation of caste system may result into removal of untouchability, which in turn may lead to decline in atrocities on the members of the SCs?

67. Do you think that expunction of literary verses in *Ramayana*

or other Literature against SCs on ground of unconstitutionality would be an effective way for the eradication of atrocities on the members of SCs?

68. Do you suggest that there should not be any whip in the legislatures, if the matter under discussions or considering or voting is concerning atrocities on the members of SCs?

69. Do you think that conducting refresher courses for all those who are in anyway connected in giving effect to the provisions of the Act may help in eradication of atrocities on the members of SCs?

70. Do you think that publicity of the provision of the Act through *Doordarshan,* Radio and all other public media may help in eradication of the atrocities on the member of the SCs?

ANNEXURE–V

THE SCHEDULED CASTES AND THE SCHEDULED TRIBES (PREVENTION OF ATROCITIES) ACT, 1989

No. 33 of 1989

[11th September, 1989.]

An Act to prevent the commissions of offences of atrocities against the members of the Scheduled Castes and .the Scheduled Tribes, to provide for Special Courts for the trial of such offences and for the relief and rahabilitation of the victims of such offences and for matters connected therewith or incidental thereto.

BE it enacted by Parliament in the Fortieth Year of the Republic of India as follows :—

CHAPTER 1

PRELIMINARY

1. Short title, extent and commencement.—(1) This Act may be called the Scheduled Castes and the Scheduled Tribes (Prevention of Atrocities) Act, 1989.

(2) It extends to the whole of India except the State of Jammu and Kashmir.

(3) It shall come into force on such date as the Central Government may, by notification in the Official Gazette, appoint.

2. Definitions.—(1) In this Act, unless the context otherwise requires,—

(a) "atrocity" means an offence punishable under section 3;

(b) "Code" means the Code of Criminal Procedure, 1973 (2 of 1974);

(c) "Scheduled Castes and Scheduled Tribes" shall have the meanings assigned to them respectively under clause (24) and clause (25) of article 366 of the Constitution;

(d) "Special Court" means a Court of Sessions specified as a Special Court in section 14;

(e) "Special Public Prosecutor" means a Public Prosecutor specified as a Special Public Prosecutor or an advocate referred to in section 15;

(f) words and expressions used but not defined in this Act and defined in the Code or the Indian Penal Code (45 of 1860) shall have the meanings assigned to them respectively in the Code, or as the case may be, in the Indian Penal Code.

(2) Any reference in this Act to any enactment or any provision thereof shall, in relation to an area in which such enactment or such provision is not in force, be construed as a reference to the corresponding law, if any, in force in that area.

CHAPTER II

OFFENCES OF ATROCITIES

3. Punishment for offences of atrocities.—(1) Whoever, not being a member of a Scheduled Caste or a Scheduled Tribe,—

(i) forces a member of a Scheduled Caste or a Scheduled Tribe to drink or eat any inedible or obnoxious substance;

(ii) acts with intent to cause injury, insult or annoyance to any member of a Scheduled Caste or a Scheduled Tribe by dumping excreta, waste matter, carcasses or any other obnoxious substance in his premises or neighbourhood;

(iii) forcibly removes clothes from the person of a member of a Scheduled Caste or a Scheduled Tribe or parades him naked or with painted face or body or commits any similar act which is derogatory to human dignity;

(iv) wrongfully occupies or cultivates any land owned by, or allotted to, or notified by any competent authority to be allotted to, a member of a Scheduled Caste or a Scheduled Tribe or gets the land allotted to him transferred;

(v) wrongfully dispossesses a member of a Scheduled Caste or a Scheduled Tribe from his land or premises or interferes with the enjoyment of his rights over any land, premises or water;

(vi) compels or entices a member of a Scheduled Caste or a Scheduled Tribe to do *'begar'* or other similar forms of forced or bonded labour other than any compulsory service for public purposes imposed by Government; .

(vii) forces or intimidates a member of a Scheduled Caste or a Scheduled Tribe not to vote or to vote to a particular candidate or to vote in a manner other than that provided by law;

(viii) institutes false, malicious or vexatious suit or criminal or other legal proceedings against a member of a Scheduled Caste or a Scheduled Tribe;

(ix) gives any false or frivolous information to any public servant and thereby causes such public servant to use his lawful power to the injury or annoyance of a member of a Scheduled Caste or a Scheduled Tribe;

(x) intentionally insults or intimidates with intent to humiliate a member of a Scheduled Caste or a Scheduled Tribe in any place within public view;

(xi) assaults or uses force to any woman belonging to a Scheduled Caste or a Scheduled Tribe with intent to dishonour or outrage her modesty;

(xii) being in a position to dominate the will of a woman belonging to a Scheduled Caste or a Scheduled Tribe and uses that position to exploit her sexually to which she would not have otherwise agreed;

(xiii) corrupts or fouls the water of any spring, reservoir or any other source ordinarily used by members of the Scheduled Castes or the Scheduled Tribes so as to render it less fit for the purpose for which it is ordinarily used;

(xiv) denies a member of a Scheduled Caste or a Scheduled Tribe any customary right of passage to a place of public resort or obstructs such member so as to prevent him from using or having access to a place of public resort to which other members of public or any section thereof have a right to use or access to;

(xv) forces or causes a member of a Scheduled Caste or a Scheduled Tribe to leave his house, village or other place of residence,

shall be punishable with imprisonment for a term which shall not be less than six months but which may extend to five years and with fine.

(2) Whoever, not being a member of a Scheduled Caste or a Scheduled Tribe,

(i) gives or fabricates false evidence intending thereby to cause, or knowing it to be likely that he will thereby cause, any member of a Scheduled Caste or a Scheduled Tribe to be convicted of an offence which is capital by the law for the time being in force shall be punished with imprisonment for life and with fine; and if an innocent member of a Scheduled Caste or a Scheduled Tribe be convicted and executed in consequence of such false or fabricated evidence, the person who gives or fabricates such false evidence, shall be punished with death;

(ii) gives or fabricates false evidence intending thereby to cause, or knowing it to be likely that he will thereby cause, any member of a Scheduled Caste or a Scheduled Tribe to be convicted of an offence which is not capital but punishable with imprisonment for a term of seven years or upwards, shall be punishable with imprisonment for a term which shall not be less than six months but which may extend to seven years or upwards and with fine;

(iii) commits mischief by fire or any explosive substance intending to cause or knowing it to be likely that he will thereby cause damage to any property belonging to a member of a Scheduled Caste or a Scheduled Tribe, shall be punishable with imprisonment for a term which shall not be less than six months but which may extend to seven years and with fine;

(iv) commits mischief by fire or any explosive substance intending to cause or knowing it to be likely that he will thereby cause destruction of any building which is ordinarily used as a place of worship .or as a place for human dwelling or as a place for custody of the property by a member of a Scheduled Caste or a Scheduled Tribe, shall be punishable with imprisonment for life and with fine;

(v) commits any offence under the Indian Penal Code (45 of 1860) punishable with imprisonment for a term of ten years or more against a person or property on the ground that such person is a member of a Scheduled Caste or a Scheduled Tribe or such property belongs to such member, shall be punishable with imprisonment for life and with fine;

(vi) knowingly or having reason to believe that an offence has been committed under this Chapter, causes any evidence of the commission of that offence to disappear with the intention of screening the offender from legal punishment, or with that intention gives any information respecting the offence which he knows or believes to be false, shall be punishable with the punishment provided for that offence; or

(vii) being a public servant, commits any offence under this section, shall be punishable with imprisonment for a term which shall. not be less than one year but which may extend to the punishment provided for that offence.

4. Punishment for neglect of duties.—Whoever, being a public servant but not being a member of a Scheduled Caste or a Scheduled Tribe, wilfully neglects his duties required to be performed by him under this Act, shall be punishable with imprisonment for a term which shall not be less than six months but which may extend to one year.

5. Enhanced punishment for subsequent conviction.—Whoever, having already been convicted of an offence under this Chapter is convicted for the second offence or any offence subsequent to the second offence, shall be punishable with imprisonment for a term which shall not be less than one year but which may extend to the punishment provided for that offence.

6. Application of certain provisions of the Indian Penal Code.—Subject to the other provisions of this Act, the provisions of section 34, Chapter III, Chapter IV, Chapter V, Chapter VA, section 149 and Chapter XXIII of the Indian Penal Code (45 of 1860), shall, so far as may be, apply for the purposes of this Act as they apply for the purposes of the Indian Penal Code.

7. Forfeiture of property of certain persons.—(1) Where a person has been convicted of any offence punishable under this Chapter, the Special Court may, in addition to awarding any punishment, by order in writing, declare that any property, movable or immovable or both, belonging to the person, which has been used for the commission of that offence, shall stand forfeited to Government.

(2) Where any person is accused of any offence under this Chapter, it shall be open to the Special Court trying him to pass an order that all or any of the properties, movable or immovable or both, belonging to him, shall, during the period of such trial, be attached, and where such trial ends in conviction, the property so attached shall be liable to forfeiture to the extent it is required for the purpose of realisation of any fine imposed under this Chapter.

8. Presumption as to offences.—In a prosecution for an offence under this Chapter, if it is proved that—

(a) the accused rendered any financial assistance to a person accused of, or reasonably suspected of committing, an offence under this Chapter, the Special Court shall presume, unless the contrary is proved, that such person had abetted the offence;

(b) a group of persons committed an offence under this Chapter and if it is proved that the offence committed was a sequel to any existing dispute regarding land or any other matter, it shall be presumed that the offence was committed in furtherance of the common intention or in prosecution of the common object.

9. Conferment of powers.—(1) Notwithstanding anything contained in the Code or in any other provision of this Act, the State Government may, if it considers it necessary or expedient so to do,—

(a) for the prevention of and for coping with any offence under this Act, or

(b) for any case or class or group of cases under this Act,

in any district or part thereof, confer, by notification in the Official Gazette, on any officer of the State Government, the powers exercisable by a police officer under the Code in such district or part thereof or, as the case may be, for such case or class or group of cases, and in particular, the powers of arrest, investigation and prosecution of persons before any Special Court.

(2) All officers of police and all other officers of Government shall assist the officer referred to in sub-section (1) in the execution of the provisions of this Act or any rule, scheme or order made thereunder.

(3) The provisions of the Code shall, so far as may be, apply to the exercise of the powers by an officer under sub-section (1).

CHAPTER III

EXTERNMENT

10. Removal of person likely to commit offence.—(1) Where the Special Court is satisfied, upon a complaint or a police report that a person is likely to commit an offence under Chapter II of this Act in any area included in 'Scheduled Areas' or 'tribal areas', as referred to in article 244 of the Constitution, it may, by order in writing, direct such person to remove himself beyond the limits of such area, by such route and within such time as may be specified in the order, and not to return to that area from which he was directed to remove himself for such period, not exceeding two years, as may be specified in the order.

(2) The Special Court shall, along with the order under sub-section (1), communicate to the person directed under that sub-section the grounds on which such order has been made.

(3) The Special Court may revoke or modify the order made under sub-section (1), for the reasons to be recorded in writing, on the representation made by the person against whom such order has been made or by any other person on his behalf within thirty days from the date of the order.

11. Procedure on failure of person to remove himself from area and enter thereon after removal.—(1) If a person to whom a direction has been issued under section 10 to remove himself from any area—

(a) fails to remove himself as directed; or

(b) having so removed himself enters such area within the period specified in the order,

otherwise than with the permission in writing of the Special Court under sub-section (2), the Special Court may cause him to be arrested and removed in police custody to such place outside such area as the Special Court may specify.

(2) The Special Court may, by order in writing, permit any person in respect of whom an order under section 10 has been made, to return to the area from which he was directed to remove himself for such temporary period and subject to such conditions as may be specified in such order and may require him to execute a bond with or without surety for the due observation of the conditions imposed.

(3) The Special Court may at any time revoke any such permission.

(4) Any person who, with such permission, returns to the area from which he was directed to remove himself shall observe the conditions imposed, and at the expiry of the temporary period for which he was permitted to return, or on the revocation of such permission before the expiry of such temporary period, shall remove himself outside such area and shall not return thereto within the unexpired portion specified under section 10 without a fresh permission.

(5) If a person fails to observe any of the conditions imposed or to remove himself accordingly or having so removed himself enters or returns to such area without fresh permission the Special Court may cause him to be arrested and removed in police custody to such place outside such area as the Special Court may specify.

12. Taking measurements and photographs, etc., of persons against whom order under section 10 is made.—(1) Every person against whom an order has been made under section 10 shall, if so required by the Special Court, allow his measurements and photographs to be taken by a police officer.

(2) If any person referred to in sub-section (1), when required to allow his measurements or photographs to be taken resists or refuses to allow his taking of such measurements or photographs, it shall be lawful to use all necessary means to secure the taking

thereof.

(3) Resistance to or refusal to allow the taking of measurements or photographs under sub-section (2) shall be deemed to be an offence under section 186 of the Indian Penal Code (45 of 1860).

(4) Where an order under section 10 is revoked, all measurements and photographs (including negatives) taken under sub-section (2) shall be destroyed or made over to the person against whom such order is made.

13. Penalty for non-compliance of order under section 10.—Any person contravening an order of the Special Court made under section 10 shall be punishable with imprisonment for a term which may extend to one year and with fine.

CHAPTER IV

SPECIAL COURTS

14. Special Court.—For the purpose of providing for speedy trial, the State Government shall, with the concurrence of the Chief Justice of the High Court, by notification in the Official Gazette, specify for each district a Court of Sessions to be a Special Court to try the offences under this Act.

15. Special Public Prosecutor.— For every Special Court, the State Government shall, by notification in the Offcial Gazette, specify a Public Prosecutor or appoint an advocate who has been in practice as an advocate for not less than seven years, as a Special Public Prosecutor for the purpose of conducting cases in that Court.

CHAPTER V

MISCELLANEOUS

16. Power of State Government to impose collective fine.—The provisions of section 10A of the Protection of Civil Rights Act, 1955 (22 of 1955), shall, so far as may be, apply for the purposes of imposition and realisation of collective fine and for all other matters connected therewith under this Act.

17. Preventive action to be taken by the law and order machinery.—(1) A District Magistrate or a Sub-divisional Magistrate or any other Executive Magistrate or any police officer not below the rank of a Deputy Superintendent of Police may, on receiving information and after such inquiry as he may think necessary, has reason to believe that a person or a group of persons not belonging to the Scheduled Castes or the Scheduled Tribes, residing in or frequenting any place within the local limits of his jurisdiction is likely to commit an offence or has threatened to commit any offence under this Act and is of the opinion that there is sufficient ground for proceeding, declare such an area to be an area prone to atrocities and take necessary action for keeping the peace and good behaviour and maintenance of public order and tranquillity and may take preventive action.

(2) The provisions of Chapters VIII, X and XI of the Code shall, so far as may be, apply for the purposes of sub-section (1).

(3) The State Government may, by notification in the Official Gazette, make one or more schemes specifying the manner in which the officers referred to in sub-section (1) shall take appropriate action specified in such scheme or schemes to prevent atrocities and to restore the feeling of security amongst the members of the Scheduled Castes and the Scheduled Tribes.

18. Section 438 of the Code not to apply to persons committing an offence under the Act.—Nothing in section 438 of the Code shall apply in relation to any case involving the arrest of any person on an accusation of having committed an offence under this Act.

19. Section 360 of the Code or the provisions of the Probation of Offenders Act not to apply to persons guilty of an offence under the Act.—The provisions of section 360 of the Code and the provisions of the Probation of Offenders Act, 1958 (20 of 1958) shall not apply to any person above the age of eighteen years who is found guilty of having committed an offence under this Act.

20. Act to override other laws.—Save as otherwise provided in this Act, the provisions of this Act shall have effect notwithstanding anything inconsistent therewith contained in any other law for the time being in force or any custom or usage or any instrument having effect by virtue of any such law.

21. Duty of Government to ensure effective implementation of the Act.—(1) Subject to such rules as the Central Government may make in this behalf, the State Government shall take such measures as may be necessary for the effective implementation of this Act.

(2) In particular, and without prejudice to the generality of the foregoing provisions, such measures may include,—

(i) the provision for adequate facilities, including legal aid, to the persons subjected to atrocities to enable them to avail themselves of justice;

(ii) the provision for travelling and maintenance expenses to witnesses, including the victims of atrocities, during investigation and trial of offences under this Act;

(iii) the provision for the economic and social rehabilitation of the victims of the atrocities;

(iv) the appointment of officers for initiating or exercising supervision over prosecutions for the contravention of the provisions of this Act;

(v) the setting up of committees at such appropriate levels as the State Government may think fit to assist that Government in formulation or implementation of such measures;

(vi) provisions for a periodic survey of the working of the provisions of this Act with a view to suggesting measures for the better implementation of the provisions of this Act;

(vii) the identification of the areas where the members of the Scheduled Castes and the Scheduled Tribes are likely to be subjected to atrocities and adoption of such measures so as to ensure safety for such members.

(3) The Central Government shall take steps as may be necessary to co-ordinate the measures taken by the State Governments under sub-section (1).

(4) The Central Government shall, every year, place on the table of each House of Parliament a report on the measures taken by itself and by the State Governments in pursuance of the provisions of this section.

22. Protection of action taken in good faith.—No suit, prosecution or other legal proceedings shall lie against the Central Government or against the State Government or any officer or authority of Government or any other person for anything which is in good faith done or intended to be done under this Act.

23. Power to make rules.—(1) The Central Government may, by notification in the Official Gazette, make rules for carrying out the purposes of this Act.

(2) Every rule made under this Act shall be laid, as soon as may be after it is made, before each House of Parliament, while it is in session for a total period of thirty days which may be comprised in one session or in two or more successive sessions, and if, before the expiry of the session immediately following the session or the successive sessions aforesaid, both Houses agree in making any modification in the rule or both Houses agree that the rule should not be made, the rule shall thereafter have effect only in such modified form or be of no effect, as the case may be; so, however, that any such modification or annulment shall be without prejudice to the validity of anything previously done under that rule.

ANNEXURE–VI

THE SCHEDULED CASTES AND THE SCHEDULED TRIBES (PREVENTION OF ATROCITIES) RULES, 1995[1]

NOTIFICATION

New Delhi, 31st March, 1995

G.S.R. No. 316(E).—In exercise of the powers conferred by sub-section (1) of section 23 of the Scheduled Castes and the Scheduled Tribes (Prevention of Atrocities) Act, 1989 (33 of 1989), the Central Government hereby makes the following rules, namely:—

1. Short title and commencement.—(1) These rules may be called the Scheduled Castes and the Scheduled Tribes (Prevention of Atrocities) Rules, 1995.

(2) They shall come into force on the date of their publication in the Official Gazette.

2. Definitions.—In these rules, unless the context otherwise requires,—

(a) "Act" means the Scheduled Castes and the Scheduled Tribes (Prevention of Atrocities) Act, 1989 (33 of 1989);

(b) "Dependent", with its grammatical variations and cognate expressions includes wife, children, whether married or unmarried, dependent parents, widowed sister, widow and children of pre-deceased son of a victim of atrocity;

(c) "identified area" means such area where State Government has reason to believe that atrocity may take place or there

1. Vide G.S.R. 316(E), dated 31st March, 1995, published in the Gazette of India, Extraordinary, Part II, Sec. 3(i), dated 31st March, 1995.

is an apprehension of reoccurrence of an offence under the Act or an area prone to atrocities;

(d) "Non-Government Organisation" means a voluntary organisation engaged in the welfare activities relating to the Scheduled Castes and the Scheduled Tribes and registered under the Societies Registration Act, 1860 (21 of 1860) or under any law for the registration of documents or such organisation for the time being in force; .

(e) "schedule" means the Schedule annexed to these rules;

(f) "section" means section of the Act;

(g) "State Government", in relation to a Union territory, means the Administrator of that Union territory appointed by the President under article 239 of the Constitution;

(h) words and expressions used herein and not defined but defined in the Act shall have the meanings respectively assigned to them in the Act.

3. Precautionary and preventive measures.—(1) With a view to prevent atrocities on the Scheduled Castes and the Scheduled Tribes, the State Government shall,

(i) identify the area where it has reason to believe that atrocity may take place or there is an apprehension of reoccurrence of an offence under the Act;

(ii) order the District Magistrate and Superintendent of Police or any other officer to visit the identified area and review the law and order situation;

(iii) if deem necessary, in the identified area cancel the arms licences of the persons, not being member of the Scheduled Castes or Scheduled Tribes, their near relations, servants or employees and family friends and get such arms deposited in the Government Armoury;

(iv) seize all illegal fire arms and prohibit any illegal manufacture of fire arms;

(v) with a view to ensure the safety of person and property, if deem necessary, provide arms licences to the members of the Scheduled Castes and the Scheduled Tribes;

(vi) constitute a high power State-level committee, district and divisional level committees or such number of other committees as deem proper and necessary for assisting the Government in implementation of the provisions of the Act;

(vii) set up a vigilance and monitoring committee to suggest effective measures to implement the provisions of the Act;

(viii) set up Awareness Centres and organise Workshops in the identified area or at some other place to educate the persons belonging to the Scheduled Castes and the Scheduled Tribes about their rights and the protection available to them under the provisions of various Central and State enactments or rules, regulations and schemes framed thereunder;

(ix) encourage non-Government Organisations for establishing and maintaining Awareness Centres and organising Workshops and provide them necessary financial and other sort of assistance;

(x) deploy special police force in the identified area;

(xi) by the end of every quarter, review the law and order situation, functioning of different committees, performance of Special Public Prosecutors, Investigating Officers and other officers responsible for implementing the provisions of the Act and the cases registered under the Act.

4. Supervision of prosecution and submission of report.— (l) The State Government on the recommendation of the District Magistrate shall prepare for each District a panel of such number of eminent Senior Advocates who have been in practice for not less than seven years, as it may deem necessary for conducting cases in the Special Courts. Similarly, in consultation with the Director of Prosecution/in-charge of the prosecution, a panel of such number of Public Prosecutors as it may deem necessary for conducting cases in the Special Courts, shall also be specified. Both these panels shall be notified in the Official Gazette of the State and shall remain in force for a period of three years.

(2) The District Magistrate and the Director of Prosecution/in-charge of the prosecution shall review at least twice in a calendar year, in the months of January and July, the performance of Special

Public Prosecutors so specified or appointed and submit a report to the State Government.

(3) If the State Government is satisfied or has reason to believe that a Special Public Prosecutor so appointed or specified has not conducted the case to the best of his ability and with due care and caution, his name may be, for reasons to be recorded in writing, de-notified.

(4) The District Magistrate and the officer in-charge of the prosecution at the District level, shall review the position of cases registered under the Act and submit a monthly report on or before 20th day of each subsequent month to the Director of Prosecution and the State Government. This report shall specify the actions taken/proposed to be taken in respect of investigation and prosecution of each case.

(5) Notwithstanding anything contained in sub-rule (1), the District Magistrate or the Sub-Divisional Magistrate may, if deem necessary or if so desired by the victims of atrocity, engage an eminent Senior Advocate for conducting cases in the Special Courts on such payment of fee as he may consider appropriate.

(6) Payment of fee to the Special Public Prosecutor shall be fixed by the State Government on a scale higher than the other penal advocates in the State.

5. Information to police officer in-charge of a police station.— (1) Every information relating to the commission of an offence under the Act, if given orally to an officer in-charge of a police station shall be reduced to writing by him or under his direction, and be read over to the informant, and every such information, whether given in writing or reduced to writing as aforesaid, shall be signed by the person giving it, and the substance thereof shall be entered in a book to be maintained by that police station.

(2) A copy of the information as so recorded under sub-rule (1) above shall be given forth with, free of cost, to the informant.

(3) Any person aggrieved by a refusal on the part of an officer in-charge of a police station to record the information referred to in sub-rule (1) may send the substance of such information, in writing and by post, to the Superintendent of Police concerned who,

after investigation either by himself or by a police officer not below the rank of Deputy Superintendent of Police, shall make an order in writing to the officer in-charge of the concerned police station to enter the substance of that information to be entered in the book to be maintained by that police station.

6. Spot inspection by officers.—(1) Whenever the District Magistrate or the Sub-Divisional Magistrate or any other Executive Magistrate or any police officer not below the rank of Deputy Superintendent of Police receives an information from any person or upon his own knowledge that an atrocity has been committed on the members of the Scheduled Castes or the Scheduled Tribes within his jurisdiction, he shall immediately himself visit the place of occurrence to assess the extent of atrocity, loss of life, loss and damage to the property and submit a report forthwith to the State Government.

(2) The District Magistrate or the Sub-Divisional Magistrate or any other Executive Magistrate and the Superintendent of Police/ Deputy Superintendent of Police after inspecting the place or area shall, on the spot,—

(i) draw a list of victims, their family members and dependents entitled for relief;

(ii) prepare a detailed report of the extent of atrocity, loss and damage to the property of the victims;

(iii) order for intensive police patrolling in the area;

(iv) take effective and necessary steps to provide protection to the witnesses and other sympathisers of the victims;

(v) provide immediate relief to the victims.

7. Investigating Officer.—(1) An offence committed under the Act shall be investigated by a police officer not below the rank of a Deputy Superintendent of Police. The investigating officer shall be appointed by the State Government/Director-General of Police/ Superintendent of Police after taking into account his past experience, sense of ability and justice to perceive the implications of the case and investigate it along with right lines within the shortest possible time.

(2) The investigating officer so appointed under sub-rule (1),

shall complete the investigation on top priority basis within thirty days and submit the report to the Superintendent of Police who in turn will immediately forward the report to the Director-General of Police of the State Government.

(3) The Home Secretary and the Social Welfare Secretary to the State Government, Director of Prosecution/the officer in-charge of prosecution and the Director-General of Police shall review by the end of the every quarter the position of all investigations done by the investigating officer.

8. Setting up of the Scheduled Castes and the Scheduled Tribes Protection Cell.—(l) The State Government shall set up a Scheduled Castes and the Scheduled Tribes Protection Cell at the State headquarters under the charge of Director-General of Police/ Inspector General of Police. This Cell shall be responsible for—

(i) conducting survey of the identified area;

(ii) maintaining public order and tranquillity in the identified area;

(iii) recommending to the State Government for deployment of special police force or establishment of special police post in the identified area;

(iv) making investigations about the probable causes leading to an offence under the Act;

(v) restoring the feeling of security amongst the members of the Scheduled Castes and the Scheduled Tribes;

(vi) informing the nodal officer and special officer about the law and order situation in the identified area;

(vii) making enquiries about the investigation and spot inspections conducted by various officers;

(viii) making enquiries about the action taken by the Superintendent of Police in the cases where an officer in-charge of the police station has refused to enter an information in a book to be maintained by that police station under sub-rule (3) of rule 5;

(ix) making enquiries about the wilful negligence by a public servant;

(x) reviewing the position of cases registered under the Act; and

(xi) submitting a monthly report on or before 20th day of each subsequent month to the State Government/nodal officer about the action taken/proposed to be taken in respect of the above.

9. Nomination of Nodal Officer.—(1) The State Government shall nominate a nodal officer of the level of a Secretary to the State Government, preferably belonging to the Scheduled Castes or the Scheduled Tribes, for coordinating the functioning of the District Magistrates and Superintendent of Police or other officers authorised by them, investigating officers and other officers responsible for implementing the provisions of the Act. By the end of every quarter, the nodal officer shall review—

(i) the reports received by the State Government under sub-rules (2) and (4) of rule 4, rule 6, clause (xi) of rule 8;

(ii) the position of cases registered under the Act;

(iii) law and order situation in the identified area;

(iv) various kinds of measures adopted for providing immediate relief in cash or kind or both to the victims of atrocity or his or her dependant;

(v) adequacy of immediate facilities like rationing, clothing, shelter, legal aid, travelling allowance, daily allowance and transport facilities provided to the victims of atrocity or his/her dependants;

(vi) performance of non-Governmental organisations, the Scheduled Castes and the Scheduled Tribes Protection Cell, various committees and the public servants responsible for implementing the provisions of the Act.

10. Appointment of a Special Officer.—In the identified area a Special Officer not below the rank of an Additional District Magistrate shall be appointed to coordinate with the District Magistrate, Superintendent of Police or other officers responsible for implementing the provisions of the Act, various committees and the Scheduled Castes and the Scheduled Tribes Protection Cell. The Special Officer shall be responsible for—

(i) providing immediate relief and other facilities to the victims of atrocity and initiate necessary measures to prevent or avoid re-occurrence of atrocity;

(ii) setting up an awareness centre and organising workshop in the identified area or at the district headquarters to educate the persons belonging to the Scheduled Castes and the Scheduled Tribes about their rights and the protection available to them under the provisions of various Central and State enactments or rules and schemes, etc., framed there- in;

(iii) co-ordinating with the non-Governmental Organisation and providing necessary facilities and financial and other type of assistance to non-Governmental organisation for maintaining centres or organising workshops.

11. Travelling allowance, daily allowance, maintenance expenses and transport facilities to the victim of atrocity, his or her dependant and witnesses.—(1) Every victim of atrocity or his/her dependant and witnesses shall be paid to and fro rail fare by second class in express/mail/passenger train or actual bus or taxi fare from his/her place of residence or place of stay to the place of investigation or hearing of trial of an offence under the Act.

(2) The District Magistrate or the Sub-Divisional Magistrate or any other Executive Magistrate shall make necessary arrangements for providing transport facilities or reimbursement of full payment thereof to the victims of atrocity and witnesses for visiting the investigating offcer, Superintendent of Police/Deputy Superintendent of Police, District Magistrate or any other Executive Magistrate.

(3) Every woman witness, the victim of atrocity of her dependant being a woman or a minor, a person more than sixty years of age, and a person having 40 per cent or more disability shall be entitled to be accompanied by an attendant of her/his choice. The attendant shall also be paid travelling and maintenance expenses as applicable to the witness or the victim of atrocity when called upon during hearing, investigation and trial of an offence under the Act.

(4) The witness, the victim of atrocity or his/her dependant and the attendant shall be paid daily maintenance expenses, for the days he/she is away from the place of his/her residence or stay during

investigation, hearing and trial of an offence, at such rates but not less than the minimum wages, as may be fixed by the State Government for the agricultural labourers.

(5) In addition to daily maintenance expenses the witness the victim of atrocity (or his/her dependant) and the attendant shall also be paid diet expenses at such rates as may be fixed by the State Government from time to time.

(6) The payment of travelling allowance; daily allowance, maintenance expenses and reimbursement of transport facilities shall be made immediately or not later than three days by the District Magistrate or the Sub-Divisional Magistrate or any other Executive Magistrate to the victims, their dependants/attendants and witnesses for the days they visit the investigating officer or in-charge of police station or hospital authorities or Superintendent of Police/Deputy Superintendent of Police or District Magistrate or any other officer concerned or the Special Court.

(7) When an offence has been committed under section 3 of the Act, the District Magistrate or the Sub-Divisional Magistrate or any other Executive Magistrate shall reimburse the payment of medicines, special medical consultation, blood transfusion, replacement of essential clothing, meals and fruits provided to the victim(s) of atrocity

12. Measures to be taken by the District Administration.—(1) The District Magistrate and the Superintendent of Police shall visit the place or area where the atrocity has been committed to assess the loss of life and damage to the property and draw a list of victims, their family members and dependants entitled for relief.

(2) Superintendent of Police shall ensure that the First Information Report is registered in the book of the concerned police station and effective measure for apprehending the accused are taken.

(3) The Superintendent of Police, after spot inspection. shall immediately, appoint an investigating officer and deploy such police force in the area and take such other preventive measures as he may deem proper and necessary.

(4) The District Magistrate or the Sub-Divisional Magistrate or any other Executive Magistrate shall make arrangements for providing immediate relief in cash or in kind or both to the victims

of atrocity, their family members and dependants according to the scale as in the Schedule annexed to these Rules (Annexure-I read with Annexure-II). Such immediate relief shall also include food, water, clothing, shelter, medical aid, transport facilities and other essential items necessary for human beings.

(5) The relief provided to the victim of the atrocity or his/her dependant under sub-rule (4) in respect of death, or injury to, or damage to, property shall be in addition to any other rights to claim compensation in respect thereof under any other law for the time being in force.

(6) The relief and rehabilitation facilities mentioned in sub-rule (4) above shall be provided by the District Magistrate or the Sub-Divisional Magistrate or any other Executive Magistrate in accordance with the scales provided in the Schedule annexed to these Rules.

(7) A report of the relief and rehabilitation facilities provided to the victims shall also be forwarded to the Special Court by the District Magistrate or the Sub-Divisional Magistrate or the Executive Magistrate or Superintendent of Police. In case the Special Court is satisfied that the payment of relief was not made to the victim or his/her dependant in time or the amount of relief or compensation was not sufficient or only a part of payment of relief or compensation was made, it may order for making in full or part the payment of relief or any other kind of assistance.

13. Selection of officers and other staff members for completing the work relating to atrocity.—(1) The State Government shall ensure that the administrative officers and other staff members to be appointed in an area prone to atrocity shall have the right aptitude and understanding of the problems of the Scheduled Castes and the Scheduled Tribes.

(2) It shall also be ensured by the State Government that persons from the Scheduled Castes and the Scheduled Tribes are adequately represented in the administration and in the police force at all levels, particularly at the level of police posts and police station.

14. Specific responsibility of the State Government.—(1) The State Government shall make necessary provisions in its annual budget for providing relief and rehabilitation facilities to the victims of atrocity. It shall review at least twice in a calendar year, in the months of January and July the performance of the Special Public Prosecutor specified or appointed under section 15 of the Act, various reports received, investigation made and preventive steps taken by the District Magistrate, Sub-Divisional Magistrate and Superintendent of Police, relief and rehabilitation facilities provided to the victims and the reports in respect of lapses on behalf of the concerned officers.

15. Contingency plan by the State Government.—(1) The State Government shall prepare a model contingency plan for implementing the provisions of the Act and notify the same in the Official Gazette of the State Government. It should specify the role and responsibility of various departments and their officers at different levels, the role and responsibility of Rural/Urban Local Bodies and non-Government Organisations, *inter alia* this plan shall contain a package of relief measures including the following:—

(a) scheme to provide immediate relief in cash or in kind or both;

(b) allotment of agricultural land and house sites;

(c) the rehabilitation packages;

(d) scheme for employment in Government or Government undertaking to the dependant or one of the family members of the victim;

(e) pension scheme for widows, dependant children of the deceased, handicapped or old age victims of atrocity;

(f) mandatory compensation for the victims;

(g) scheme for strengthening the socio-economic conditions of the victim;

(h) provisions for providing brick/stone masonry houses to the victims;

(i) such other elements as health care, supply of essential commodities, electrification, adequate drinking water facility, burial/cremation ground and link roads to the Scheduled Castes and the Scheduled Tribes habitats.

(2) The State Government shall forward a copy of the contingency plan or a summary thereof and a copy of the scheme,

as soon as may be, to the Central Government in the Ministry of Welfare and to all the District Magistrates, Sub-Divisional Magistrates, Inspectors General of Police and Superintendents of Police.

16. Constitution of State-level vigilance and monitoring committee.—(1) The State Government shall constitute a high-power vigilance and monitoring commission of not more than 25 members consisting of the following:—

(i) Chief Minister, Administrator—Chairman (in case of a State under President's Rule Governor—Chairman);

(ii) Home Minister, Finance Minister and Welfare Minister—Members (in case of State under the President's Rule Advisors—Members);

(iii) some of the Members of the elected Members of Parliament and State Legislative Assembly and Legislative Council from the State belonging to the Scheduled Castes and the Scheduled Tribes—Members (not more than 16);

(iv) Chief Secretary, the Home Secretary, the Director-General of Police, Director/Deputy Director National Commission for the Scheduled Castes and the Scheduled Tribes—Members;

(v) the Secretary in-charge of the welfare and development of the Scheduled Castes and the Scheduled Tribes—Convenor.

(2) The high-power vigilance and monitoring committee shall meet at least twice in a calendar year, in the months of January and July to review the implementation of the provision of the Act, relief and rehabilitation facilities provided to the victims and other matters connected therewith, prosecution of cases under the Act, role of different officers/agencies responsible for implementing the provisions of the Act and various reports received by the State Government.

17. Constitution of District-level vigilance and monitoring committees.—(1) In each district within the State, the District Magistrate shall set up a vigilance and monitoring committee in his district to review the implementation of the provisions of the Act, relief and rehabilitation facilities provided to the victims and other matters connected therewith, prosecution of cases under the Act, role of different officers/agencies responsible for implementing the provisions of the Act and various reports received by District Administration.

(2) The district-level vigilance and monitoring committee shall consist of the elected Members of Parliament and State Legislative Assembly and Legislative Council, Superintendent of Police, three Group 'A' officers/Gazetted officers of the State Government belonging to the Scheduled Castes and the Scheduled Tribes, not more than 5 non-official members belonging to the Scheduled Castes and the Scheduled Tribes and not more than 3 members from the categories other than the Scheduled Castes and the Scheduled Tribes having association with non-Government Organisations.

(3) The district-level committee shall meet at least once in three months.

18. Material for annual report.—The State Government shall, every year before the 1st July, forward the report to the Central Government about the measures taken for implementing the provisions of the Act and various schemes/plans framed by it during the previous calendar year.

THE SCHEDULED CASTES AND THE SCHEDULED TRIBES (Prevention of Atrocities) Rules, 1995

ANNEXURE I

SCHEDULE

[See rule 12(4)]

NORMS for Relief Amount

Sl No.	*Name of Offence*	*Minimum amount of Relief*
1	2	3
1.	Drink or eat inedible or obnoxious substance [Section 3(1)(i)]	Rs. 25,000 or more depending upon the nature and gravity of the offence to each victim and also commensurate with the indignity, insult, injury and defamation suffered by the victim. Payment to be made as follows:-- I. 25% when the chargesheet is sent to the court, II. 75% when accused are convicted by the lower court.
2.	Causing injury, insult or annoyance [Section 3(1)(ii)]	
3.	Derogatory act [Section 3(1)(iii)]	
4.	Wrongful occupation or cultivation of land, etc. [Section 3(1)(iv)]	At least Rs. 25,000 or more depending upon the nature and gravity of the offence. The land/premises/water supply shall be restored where necessary at Government cost. Full payment to be made when chargesheet is sent to the Court.
5.	Relating to land, premises and water [Section 3(1)(v)]	

1	2	3
6.	**Begar** or forced or bonded labour [Section 3(1)(vi)]	At least Rs. 25,000 to each victim. Payment of 25% at FIR stage and 75% on conviction in the lower court.
7.	Relating to right to franchise [Section 3(1)(vii)]	Up to Rs. 20,000 to each victim depending upon the nature and gravity of the offence.
8.	False, malicious or vexatious legal proceedings. [Section 3(1)(viii)]	Rs. 25,000 or reimbursement of actual legal expenses and damages or whichever is less after conclusion of the trial of the accused.
9.	False and frivolous information [Section 3(1)(ix)]	
10.	Insult, intimidation and humiliation [Section 3(1)(x)]	Upto Rs. 25,000 to each victim depending upon the nature of the offence. Payment of 25% when chargesheet is sent to the court and rest on conviction.
11.	Outraging the modesty of a woman [Section 3(1)(xi)]	Rs. 50,000 to each victim of the offence. 50% of the amount may be paid after medical examination and remaining 50%. at the conclusion of the trial.
12.	Sexual exploitation of women [Section 3(1)(xii)]	
13.	Fouling of water [Section 3(1)(xiii)]	Up to Rs. 1,00,000 or full cost of restoration of normal facility, including cleaning when the water is fouled. Payment may be made at the stage as deemed fit by District Administration.

1	2	3
14.	Denial of customary rights of passage [Section 3(1)(xiv)]	Up to Rs. 1,00,000 or full cost of restoration of right of passage and full compensation of the loss suffered, if any. Payment of 50% when charge-sheet is sent to the court and 50% on conviction in lower Court.
15.	Making one desert place of residence [Section 3(1)(xv)]	Restoration of the site right to stay and compensation of Rs. 25,000 to each victim and reconstruction of the house at Government cost, if destroyed. To be paid in full when chargesheet is sent to the lower Court.
16.	Giving false evidence [Section 3(2)(i) and (ii)]	At least Rs. 1,00,000 or full compensation of the loss or harm sustained. 50% to be paid when charge-sheet is sent to Court and 50% on conviction by the lower Court.
17.	Committing offences under the Indian Penal Code punishable with imprisonment for a term of 10 years or more [Section 3(2)]	At least Rs. 50,000 depending upon the nature and gravity of the offence to each victim and/or his dependants. The amount would vary if specifically otherwise provided in the Schedule.
18.	Victimization at the hands of a public servant [Section 3(2)(vii)]	Full compensation on account of damages or loss or harm sustained. 50% to be paid when charge-sheet is sent to the Court and 50% on conviction by lower Court.
19.	Disability. The definitions of physical and mental disabilities are contained in the Ministry of Welfare, G.O.I. Notification	

1	2	3
	No. 4-2/83-HW.III dt. 6-8-1986 as amended from time to time. A copy of the notification is at Annexure-II.	
	(a) 100% incapacitation—	
	(i) Non-earning Member of a family	At least Rs. 1,00,000 to each victim of offence. 50% on FIR and 25% at charge-sheet and 25% on conviction by the lower Court.
	(ii) Earning Member of a family	At least Rs. 2,00,000 to each victim of offence, 50% to be paid on FIR/Medical examination stage, 25% when charge-sheet sent to Court and 25% at conviction in lower Court.
	(b) Where incapacitation is less than 100%	The rates as laid down in a (i) and (ii) above shall be reduced in the same proportion, the stages of payments also being the same. However, not less than Rs. 25,000 to non-earning member and not less than Rs. 30,000 to an existing member of a family.
20.	Murder/Death	
	(a) Non-earning Member of a family	At least Rs. 1,00,000 to each case. Payment of 75% after post-mortem and 25% on conviction by the lower Court.
	(b) Earning Member of a family	At least Rs. 2,00,000 to each case. Payment of 75% after post-mortem and 25% on conviction by the lower Court.

1	2	3
21.	Victim of murder, death, massacre, rape, mass rape and gang rape, permanent incapacitation and dacoity	In addition to relief amounts paid under above items, relief may be arranged within three months of date of atrocity as follows:— (i) Pension to each widow and/or other dependants of deceased, SC and ST @ Rs. 1,000 per month, or Employment to one member of the family of the deceased, or provision of agricultural land, and house, if necessary by outright purchase. (ii) Full cost of the education and maintenance of the children of the victims. Children may be admitted to Ashram, schools/residential schools. (iii) Provisions of utensils, rice, wheat, dals, pulses, etc. for a period of three months.
22.	Complete destruction/burnt houses	Brick/stone masonry house to be constructed or provided at Government cost where it has been burnt or destroyed.

BIBLIOGRAPHY

ARTICLES

Abraham, Abramovsky, "Bias Crime: A Call for Alternative Responses", *Fordham Urban Law Journal,* 19:875.

Abraham, Amrita, "Agenda for the backward classes", *The Indian Express,* September 27th, 1990.

Abraham, A.S., "Promoting Equal Opportunity Positive Discrimination Becomes a Force", *The Times of India,* December 7th, 1979.

Acharya, B.K., "A Caste War", *Mainstream,* 19 (29), March 21st, 1981, II-26.

Aslam, Mohammad, "Scheduled Castes: Some unresolved problem", 32, *J.I.L.I.* 111.

Baxi, Upendra, "Caste, Class and Reservation" (In Memoriam : I.P. Desai) *E.P.W.,* March 9th, 1985. 428.

Beschi, Kathija, "Share the Reservations: Scrap the Varnas", *Caravan* 41 (676) July, 1980, 33-38.

Beteille, Andre, "Caste and Class", *The Hindustan Times,* October 4th, 1990.

Beteille, Andre, "Caste and Politics", Subversion of Public Institutions, *The Times of India,* New Delhi, Tuesday, September 11th, 1990.

Beteille, Andre, "Tackling Inequality", *The Hindustan Times,* November 22nd, 1990.

Buchanan, G. Sidnay, "Hate Speech Case: A pyrrhic Victory for Freedom of Speech?" 21, *Hofstra L:Rev.* 285 (1992).

Buch, M.N., "The will to govern – II", *The Hindustan Times,* August 9th, 1990.

Conrad, D., "The Human Right to Basic Necessities of Life", 10 and 11 *Del.L.Rev.* (1981-82) 1.

Dandavate, Madhu, "Ambedkar's national heritage", *The Hindustan Times,* April 14th, 1993.

Dar, A.N., "What about the poor?" Liberalization, *The Hindustan Times*, June 23rd, 1994.

Deshpande, V.S., "What does SC mean?" *The Hindustan Times,* May 23rd, 1990.

Dhavan, Rajeev, "Scheduled Castes: Anti-atrocity Law", *The Hindustan Times*, March 1st, 1990.

Dhavan, Rajeev, Ambedkar's Prophecy: Poverty of Human Rights in India, 36, *J.I.L.I.* (1994) 8.

Dube, S.C., "Reservations: A retrograde fetish", *The Hindustan Times*, September 3rd, 1990.

Duray, A.P. & Bay, R.I., "Human Rights & the Role of Criminal Courts", 1996 *CRI. L.J.* 39.

Errabbi, B., "Protective Discrimination: Constitutional Prescription and Judicial Perception", 10 and 11 *Del. L. Rev.* (1981-82) 66.

Freeman, Stevenm, "Hate Crime Laws : Punishment which Fits The Crime", *Annual Survey of American Law*, 1992/1993 : 581.

Gaur, K.D., "Poor Victim of Uses and Abuses of Criminal Law and Process in India", 35, *J.I.L.I.* (1993) 183.

Gellman, Susan, "Hate Crime Laws are thought Crime Laws," *Annual Survey of American Law*, 1992/1993 : 509.

Ghose, Sanjay, "Animals and Untouchables: Not Allowed", *The Indian Express*, August 12th, 1990.

Ghosh, S.K., "Gangsterism – I, A national menace", *The Hindustan Times*, July 31st., 1990.

Ghosh, S.K., "Gangsterism-II, Dealing with crime", *The Hindustan Times*, August 1st, 1990.

Jacob, James B., "The War against Hate Crimes : A New York City Perspective", *Criminal Justice Ethics*, Summer/Fall 1992 : 11:55.

Jacob, James B. and Eisler, Barry, "The Hate Crime Statistics Act of 1990", *Criminal Law Bulletin*, February 1993 : 29:99.

Jacob, James B. and Henry, Jessica S., "The Social Construction of a Hate Crime Epidemic", *Journal of Criminal Law and Criminology*, Winter 1996: 86:366.

Jacob, James B., "Should Hate be a Crime?" *The Public Interest*, Fall 1993 : 113:3-14.

Jacob, James B., "The Emergence and Implications of American Hate Crime Jurisprudence", *Israel Yearbook on Human Rights*, 1993 : 22:113-139.

Jain, Meenakshi, "Pre-British India: The myth of caste tyranny", *The Indian Express*, September 26th, 1990.

Jain, Shanti Mal, "Scheduled Castes and Scheduled Tribes (Prevention of atrocities) Act 1989—offences under-treading grey Area for pre-arrest bail", 1992, *CRI. L.J.* Journal, 111.

Jenness, Valerie and Grattet, Ryken, "The Criminalization of Hate : A Comparison of Structural and Policy Influences on the Passage of 'Bias Crime' Legislation in the United States," *Sociological Perspectives*, 1996 : 39:129.

John Garry, "Why Me": Application and Misapplication of 3A1.1, The "Vulnerable Victim" Enhancement of the Federal Sentencing Guidelines, *Cornell Law Review* 79 (1993) 143.

Leo, John, The Politics of Hate. *U.S. News and World Report*, October 1989, 24.

Levin, Brian, "Bias Crimes : A Theoretical and Practical Overview." *Stanford Law and Policy Rev.*, 1992/1993 : 4:165.

Lowrence, Crocker, Hate Crime Statutes: Just? Constitutional? Wise? 1992-1993 *Ann. Surv. AM.L.* 485.

Lowrence, Frederick M., "The Punishment of Hate: Toward a Normative Theory of Bias – Motivated Crimes", *Michigan Law Review*, 93 (1994) 320.

Maldonado, Migdalia, "Practical Problems with Enforcing Hate Crimes Legislation in New York," *Annual Survey of American Law*, 1992/1993 : 3:555.

Marovitz, William A., "Hate or Bias Crime Legislation." In Kelly, Robert J., ed. Bias Crime : *American Law Enforcement and Legal Responses.* Chicago : Office of International Criminal Justice, 1993 : 48-53.

Martin, Max, "Dr. Ambedkar – The Legacy", *Yojana*, May 31st, 1994.

Maurya, B.P., "Ambedkar centenary: Crusader for social justice", *The Hindustan Times*, October 24th, 1991.

Murphy, Jeffrie G., "Bias Crimes : What Do Haters Deserve?" *Criminal Justice Ethics*, Fall 1992 : 11:23.

Muthamma, C.B., "Change the system", *The Hindustan Times*, September 21, 1990.

Nemisarai, Mohandas, "Agra Kand se Ubharate Kuchh Sawal," *Nav Bharat Times*, July 25, 1990.

Olmstead-Rose, Lester, "Hate violence : Symptom of Prejudice," *William Mitchell L. Rev.*, 1991 : 17:439.

Pur, R.K., "The Literacy Hurdles", *The Hindustan Times*, March 21st, 1990.

Pur, R.K., "Whither India's Population?" *The Hindustan Times*, August 19th, 1991.

Rahman, Azizur, "Scheduled Castes and Scheduled Tribes (Prevention of Atrocities) Act, 1989—A Critical study", 1991 *CRI.L.J.* 20.

Sahay, S., "A question of constitutional morality", *The Hindustan Times*, August 10, 1990.

Sahay, S., "Reservation Label", *The Hindustan Times*, May 18, 1990.

Sankhdher, M.M., "Right to work", *The Hindustan Times*, June 8, 1990.

Sardar, M.B., "The Scheduled Castes and Scheduled Tribes (Prevention of Atrocities) Act, 1989—Enforceability", 1993, *CRI.L.J.* Journal 24.

Singh, M.P., "Jurisprudential Foundations of Affirmative Action:

Some Aspects of Equality and Social Justice", 10 and 11 *Del. L. Rev.* (1981-82) 39.

Sinha, B.S., "Untouchability and the Courts" 61 *CRI.L.J.* (1964)1.

Singhvi, Abhishek Manu, "Right to work: Where are the jobs?" *The Hindustan Times*, September 30, 1990.

Sharma, K.L., "A backward step", *The Hindustan Times*, September 19, 1990.

Srivastava, Y.K., "The Scheduled Castes and the Scheduled Tribes (Prevention of Atrocities) Act, 1989—Procedure and Problems", 1991 *CRI.L.J.* Journal 141.

Suraiya, Jug, "Caste in a New Light: Frictional Co-efficient of Mandal", *The Times of India*, September 7, 1990.

Seshadri, Prof. P., "Social Justice and Media: Problems and Perspectives: A Critical Evaluation", *A.I.R.* 1996 Journal 49.

Tripathy, Prabhat Chandra, "Criminal Victimization of Weaker Sex and Failure of Protective Measures : An Analysis", 1996. *CRI.L.J.* 33.

BOOKS

Abbasayulu, Y.B., *Scheduled Caste Elite*, 1978.

Aggarwal, P.C. and Asraf, S., *Equality Through Privileges: A Study of Special Privileges of Scheduled Castes in Haryana*, 1976.

Allport, Gordon, *The Nature of Prejudice*, Cambridge, MA : Addison-Wesley, 1954.

Basu, Dalip K. and Richard Sision. *Social and Economic Development in India*, Sage Publication, New Delhi, 1986.

Baxi, Upendra, *Law and Poverty*, 1973.

Baxi, Upendra. (Ed.), *Mathew: Democracy, Equality and Freedom*, 1978.

Beteille, Andre, *Caste, Class and Power*, 1965.

Beteille, Andre, *Caste: Old and New*, 1969.

Beteille, Andre, *Equality and Inequality*, 1983.

Beteille, Andre, *Inequality among Man*, 1977.

Beteille, Andre, *Inequality and Social Change*, 1972.

Bhardwaj, A.N., *The Problems of Scheduled Castes and Scheduled Tribes in India*, 1979.

Bishwa B. Chatterjee, Sheo Swarath Singh and Dharam Raj Yadav, *Impact of Social Legislation on Social Change*, The Minerva, Associates Publication, 1971.

Centre for Social Studies, Surat, *Caste, Caste Conflict and Reservation*, Ajanta Publications, 1985.

Das, Bhakta, *A Glimpse of the Scheduled Castes and their Socioeconomic Development in Assam*, Om Sons Publications, 1986.

Desai, I.P., *Untouchability in Rural Gujarat*, 1976.

Dhananjaya Keer, *Dr. Ambedkar : Life and Mission*, 1971.

Evic Rakawski, *Equal Justice*, Oxford University Press, 1991.

Emile, Senart, *Caste in India*, Ess Ess Publications, Delhi, 1975.

Gail, Omvedt, *Dalit and the Democratic Revolution: Dr. Ambedkar and the Dalit Movement in Colonial India*, Sage Publications, 1994.

Ghosh, S.K., *Protection of Minorities and Scheduled Castes*, Ashish Publishing House, New Delhi, 1984.

Glanter, Mark, *Competing Equalities, Law and The Backward Classes in India*, 1984.

Government of Maharashtra Publication, *Dr. Babasaheb Ambedkar Writings and Speeches*, Vols. 1 to 15.

Government of Maharashtra Publication, *Source, Material on Dr. Babashaheb Ambedkar and Movement of Untouchables*, 1982.

Government of India Publication, *Ambedkar and Social Justice*, Publication Division, Ministry of Information and Broadcasting, Vols. 1 and 2.

Goyal, B.R., *Educating Harijans*, 1981.

Gupta, G.R. and Khosla, Dr. Dinesh, *Main Currents in Indian Society and Cohesion and Conflicts in Modern India*.

Gupta, G.R. and Khosla, Dr. Dinesh, *Myth and Reality of the Protection of Civil Rights Law*, Hindustan Publication Corporation (India), Delhi, 1987.

Haris, J., *Inequality and Progress*, 1897.

Jag Jivan Ram, *Caste Challenge in India*, 1980.

Jain, M.P., *Indian Constitutional Law*, 1987.

Jogdamd, P.G., *Dalit Women in India: Issues and Perspectives*, Gyan Publishing House, 1995.

Kagzi, Dr. M.C.J., *Segregation and Untouchability Abolition*, 1976.

Kakade, S.R., *Scheduled Castes and National Integration*, 1990.

Kamble, J.R., *Rise and Awakening of Depressed Classes in India*, 1979.

Kamle, N.D., *Atrocities on Scheduled Castes*, 1981.

Kamle, N.D., *Deprived Castes and their Struggle for Equality*.

Khan, Mumtaz Ali, *Scheduled Castes and their Status in India*, 1980.

Khan, Mumtaz Ali, *Social Legislation and the Rural Poor*, 1981.

Kane, P.V., *History of Dharmashastra*, 1974.

Lakshmanna, C. and Inniah, N., *Depressed Group Students*, 1977.

Laurence, Ross H. (Ed.), *Law and Deviance*, Sage Publications, 1981.

Lela Dushbin. *The Policy of the Indian National Congress towards the Depressed Classes and Historical Study*, 1967.

Mahatma Gandhi, *My Philosophy of Life,* Edited by A.T. Hingorani, 1961.

Malik, Suneila, *Social Integration of Scheduled Caste,* Abhinav Publication, New Delhi, 1980.

Majumdar, *Social Anthropology*.

Mathew, K.K., *The Right to Equality and Property under the Indian Constitution*, 1980.

Mayhew, Leon H., *Law and Equal Opportunity : A Study of the*

Massachusetts Commission against Discrimination, Harvard University Press (1968).

Mishra, Vidhyarthi, *Harijan Today*, 1977.

Murthy, B.S., *Depressed and Oppressed*, 1971.

Nancy Taylor (Ed.), *Bias Crime : The Law Enforcement Response*, 1991.

Nandu Ram, *Beyond Ambedkar : Essays on Dalits in India*, Har Anand Publications, 1995.

Narayana, P.S., *The Scheduled Castes and The Scheduled Tribes (Prevention of Atrocities) Act, 1989*, Asia Law House, 1991.

Oliver Mendelsohn and Baxi Upendra, *The Rights of Subordinated Peoples*, Oxford University Press, 1996.

Om Prakash, *Untouchables*, 1970.

Prasad, Anirudh, *Social Engineering of Constitutional Protection of Weaker Section in India*, 1980.

Rao, B. Shiva, *The Framing of India's Constitution*, I.I.P.A. 1968.

Rawls, John, *A Theory of Justice*, 1973.

Rescher, Nicholas, *Distributive Justice*, 1966.

Singh, Dr. Parmanand, *Equality, Reservation and Discrimination in India*, 1982.

Singh, Tarlok, *Poverty and Social Change*, 1969.

Singh, Yogendra, *Social Stratification and Change in India*, 1977.

Singer and Cohn., (Eds.), *Structure and Change in Indian Society*, 1968.

Sivaramayya, B., *Inequalities and the Law*, 1984.

Stone, Julius, *Human Law and Human Justice*, 1966.

Stone, Julius, *Social Dimensions of Law and Justice*, 1966.

Surender Kumar, *Hindu Dharam and Sudra*.

Tiwari, Chitra, *Sudra in Manu*, 1963.

Tripathi, P.K., *Some Insights into Fundamental Rights*, 1972.

Trivedi, H.R., *Scheduled Caste Women*, 1977.

Tumin, Meluin M., *Social Stratification : The Forms and Functions of Inequality*, 1967.

Vakil, A.K., *Reservation Policy and Scheduled Castes in India*, 1985.

Verma, G.P., *Caste Reservation in India*, 1980.

William Glauville, *Salmond on Jurisprudence*.

DICTIONARIES AND ENCYCLOPAEDIA

1. Bhargawa, Standard Illustrated Dictionary of the English Language (Anglo Hindi).
2. Encyclopaedia Britannica, 1911.
3. Illustrated Encyclopaedia of Mankind, Vol. 13.
4. The Chambers Dictionary, New Edition, 1993.
5. The New Shorter Oxford English Dictionary, Volumes 1 and 2, Clarendon Press, Oxford, 1993.

JOURNALS

All India Reporter

Allahabad Criminal

Allahabad Criminal Reports

Allahabad Law Times (Criminal)

Allahabad Weekly Reports (High Court)

Andhra Law Journal

Annual Survey of American Law

Bombay High Court Reports

Bombay Law Reports

Bombay Law Review

British Year Book of International Law, 1988

Calcutta Weekly Notes

California Law Review

Cornell Law Review
Criminal Law Journal
Cuttack Law Times
Fordham Urban Law Journal
Indian Appeal
Indian Appeal Cases
Indian Cases
Indian Cases Journal
Indian Law Reports
Jabalpur Law Journal
Journal of Criminal Law and Criminology
Journal of Indian Institute of Public Administration
Judgment Today
Kerala Law Journal
Kerala Law Reports
Kerala Law Times
Machigan Law Review
Madras Law Journal
Madras Law Judgment (Criminal)
Madras Law Weekly
Madhya Pradesh Cases
Madhya Pradesh Law Journal
Maharashtra Law Journal
Punjab Law Reporter
Rajasthan Law Weekly
Stanford Law and Policy Review
Supreme Court Cases
Supreme Court Judgments
Supreme Court Reports
Supreme Court Weekly Reports
The Administrator
Weekly Reports
William Mitchell Law Review

MAGAZINES AND NEWSPAPERS

1. Front Line
2. The Indian Express
3. India Today
4. The Nav Bharat Times (Hindi)
5. The Hindustan Times
6. The Times of India

REPORTS

- Annual Report of Government of India, Ministry of Welfare, New Delhi, 1996-97.
- Annual Report of Government of India, Ministry of Social Welfare and Empowerment, New Delhi, 1998-99.
- Backward Class Commission Reports.
- Census of India.
- Constituent Assembly Debates.
- India, 1993.
- Reports of the Commissioner for Scheduled Castes and Scheduled Tribes.
- Reports of the Parliamentary Committees on the Welfare of Scheduled Castes and Scheduled Tribes.
- Reports of the National Commission for Scheduled Castes and Scheduled Tribes.
- Report of National Convention on Socio-Economic and Political Status of the SCs and STs in Contemporary India. 16-17 June, 1992 by Parliamentary Forum of Scheduled Castes and Scheduled Tribes.

STATUTES

Code of Criminal Procedure, 1973.

Constitution of India.

Constitution (Sixty-Fifth Amendment) Act, 1990.

Crime in India, 1994.

European Convention of Human Rights, 1948.

Indian Penal Code, 1860.

Protection of Civil Rights Act, 1955.

The Scheduled Castes and the Scheduled Tribes (Prevention of Atrocities) Act, 1989 (No. 33 of 1989).

The Scheduled Castes and the Scheduled Tribes (Prevention of Atrocities) Rules, 1995.

Untouchability (Offences) Act, 1955.

INDEX